THE BONDS OF THE JAPAN-US ALLIANCE

THE BONDS OF THE JAPAN-US ALLIANCE

THE JAPAN-US SECURITY TREATY AND THE SEARCH FOR MUTUALITY

SAKAMOTO Kazuya

Japan Publishing Industry Foundation for Culture

Publisher's Note
This book follows the Hepburn system of romanization, with long vowels indicated by macrons. The tradition of placing the family name first has been followed for Japanese, Chinese, and Korean names.

This English edition includes additional revisions to the 2020 revised Japanese edition for purposes of readability. These include, but are not confined to, the incorporation of the original supplementary notes into chapter endnotes and the conversion of the original Addendum into a new Chapter 6.

The Bonds of the Japan-US Alliance: The Japan-US Security Treaty and the Search for Mutuality
Sakamoto Kazuya. Translated by the Japan Institute of International Affairs (JIIA).

Published by
Japan Publishing Industry Foundation for Culture (JPIC)
2-2-30 Kanda-Jinbocho, Chiyoda-ku, Tokyo 101-0051, Japan

First English edition: March 2022

Published in Japanese under the title *Nichi-Bei dōmei no kizuna: Anpo jōyaku to sōgosei no mosaku zōhoban* by Yuhikaku Publishing Co., Ltd. in 2020. First Japanese edition published in 2000.
English publishing rights arranged with the author.

This publication is the result of a collaborative effort between the Japan Institute of International Affairs (JIIA) and Japan Publishing Industry Foundation for Culture (JPIC).

Book design: alema Co., Ltd.
Jacket and cover artwork: Yakushiji Akio

Printed in Japan
ISBN 978-4-86658-233-7
https://www.jpic.or.jp/

Table of Contents

Preface to the English Edition

This book is an expanded translation of the Japanese edition, first published in 2000 and updated in April 2021, based on diplomatic materials released by Japan and the US governments in the intervening two decades. The book depicts the history of the establishment and revision of the Japan-US Security Treaty, which forms the backbone of the Japan-US alliance.

The bilateral security treaty was first concluded on September 8, 1951. It was, essentially, a provisional treaty for the United States to temporarily maintain a military presence in Japan, for the sake of Japan's own security. Japan had made peace with the Allies of World War II through the San Francisco Peace Treaty, and had emerged from occupation as an independent nation amid the ongoing Korean War.

The essence of an alliance is to cooperate "for and with each other." However, though this treaty is in the form of cooperation between Japan and the United States for the security of Japan exclusively, that cooperation was not made obligatory. Although Japan provided the United States with bases in Japan, the American obligation to defend Japan was not made clear, and thus the treaty could not be called an alliance between two sovereign nations.

It was the revision of the Security Treaty in 1960 that changed it into a mutual treaty, one of "mutual cooperation for mutual benefit." In other words, the Security Treaty was revised to make both countries obligated to cooperate with each other as independent nations with equal sovereignty for the maintenance of peace and security in the Far East, an area of mutual concern for Japan and the United States. The revision also made it Japan's duty to cooperate in counterattacks in the event of an attack on US forces stationed in Japan.

The history of the Japan-US alliance after the treaty revision can be said to be the history of the efforts of both governments to bring about mutuality through supplementary arrangements such as the return of the administration of Okinawa, the enhancement of financial support for US forces ("sympathy budget"), and the Japan-U.S. Guidelines for Defense Cooperation, based on the form of mutuality obtained through the treaty revision.

The first edition of this book was published as a highly specialized book. It received the Suntory Prize for Social Sciences and Humanities, and I am happy that the English edition should be able to attract an even larger readership. I would like to take this opportunity to express my gratitude again to all involved for their hard work.

Sakamoto Kazuya
Kyoto
December 2021

Introduction

The Japanese-US security treaty exhibits a mutuality of a kind unseen among other big-power defense pacts. Japan hosts US military bases in exchange for US assurance of the former's national security. The United States, in other words, ensures Japanese security in exchange for the right to use bases in Japan.

Underlying the Japanese-US security treaty since it first took effect in 1952 has been the mutual perception of compelling benefits. Thus did the Japanese and US negotiators see fit to retain the treaty's basic format in adopting a revised, updated version in 1960. And thus have the Japanese and US governments opted to retain that format over the ensuing decades.

The quid pro quo of exchanging access to bases for military protection is, to be sure, an inherently asymmetrical mutuality. That asymmetry has occasioned continuing dissatisfaction with the treaty in both Japan and the United States. Americans take umbrage at treaty terms that place US troops in harm's way to protect Japan but not vice versa. Japanese bristle at American callousness about the economic cost and sociopolitical friction entailed in hosting the bases.

During the Cold War, Japanese and Americans perceived the US bases in Japan as crucial to military preparedness against the Eastern bloc. That perception has faded as the end of the Cold War has transformed the geopolitical map and as domestic circumstances changed in Japan and in the United States. I offer this book in the spirit of contributing to informed discourse about the role and positioning of the Japanese-US security treaty. Revisiting the treaty's origins and development up to the 1960 revision will fortify our foundation for adapting the treaty to twenty-first century needs.

The revision of 1960 invested the treaty with a formal mutuality, and the two nations have strengthened that mutuality as a real and genuine quality over the past six decades. They have done so in response to the changing international environment and to the changing power balance in their bilateral relationship.

Japan and the United States have strengthened the mutuality of their treaty relationship most visibly through revisions of the Guidelines for

Japan-U.S. Defense Cooperation. The Japanese and US governments established those guidelines in 1978. Their intent was to define the framework for bilateral military cooperation in the event of an attack on Japan. They updated the guidelines in 1997 and again in 2015.

In 2015, US president Barack Obama and Japanese prime minister Abe Shinzo unveiled the revised guidelines at a press conference in the White House Rose Garden. The revision lent an expanded globalism and heightened mutuality to Japanese-US defense cooperation. Obama emphasized this mutuality in his remarks, voicing both the Japanese *otagai no tame ni* and its English equivalent, "with and for each other."

The 2015 revision of the Guidelines for Japan-U.S. Defense Cooperation broadened greatly the scope for activity by the Japanese navy beyond Japanese territory. Specifically, it authorized the Japan Maritime Self-Defense Force (MSDF) to provide the US navy with rear area support, such as refueling, in international waters. It also authorized the Japan MSDF to defend US vessels in the event of attack.

Mutuality unfolds convincingly throughout the Japanese-US alliance in ways that transcend the security treaty. It arises not only from the security treaty but also from the diverse agreements that the Japanese and US governments have concluded to buttress their security cooperation—their alliance. This raises the question, however, as to why the drafters of the underlying security treaty framed its scope so narrowly. Grasping the answer to that question is essential to understanding why the Japanese-US alliance has evolved as it has.

We discover that the ostensibly narrow framing of the security treaty has proved a foundation for continually broadening cooperation. Japan has provided the United States with military bases essential to US global strategy. It has funded the maintenance of US forces stationed in Japan. The Japanese military, meanwhile, has cooperated with the US military in maintaining peace and security in the Far East. And that cooperation has served as a pillar of broader efforts for maintaining security worldwide.

Japan's constitution bars it from exercising military force in the territory of any other nation. That constraint shaped the formal outlines of the Japanese constitution definitively, but proactive cooperation has engendered a robust alliance. Japan has become a US partner second to no other in furthering shared strategic goals. This book describes how the original

Japanese-US security treaty and the revised treaty furnished a solid foundation for the nations' bilateral alliance.

Chapter 1 sketches the origins of the first-generation security treaty in the early Cold War years. In Chapter 2, I examine how US policy makers gradually accommodated the Yoshida government's "go-slow" approach to rearmament even as they prepared for a post-Yoshida government. Chapter 3 centers on a quixotic proposal from the Hatoyama government's foreign minister, Shigemitsu Mamoru, for revising the security treaty. I describe in Chapter 4 how the 1960 revision provided the treaty with at least the appearance of increased mutuality. Chapter 5 covers the principal issues that arose in implementing the revised treaty and secret agreements for addressing some of those issues. Finally, Chapter 6 further discusses the secret agreements, assessing their significance with regard to prior consultation.

Chapter 1

The Birth of the Japan-US Security Treaty

"Better than nothing but inadequate"

John Foster Dulles, consultant to the secretary of state, and Yoshida Shigeru, prime minister of Japan. January 31, 1951. Photo by Mainichi Shimbunsha

1 The Cold War and Japanese National Security

MacArthur's eagerness to get a peace treaty signed

General Douglas MacArthur issued a stunning call on March 17, 1947, for concluding a peace treaty between the United States and Japan. MacArthur commanded the Allied Forces that had occupied Japan since the nation's surrender in August 1945. He bore the title Supreme Commander for the Allied Powers (SCAP) and essentially ruled Japan like an emperor. His every utterance carried immense weight in gauging the Allies' stance vis-à-vis Japan.

MacArthur called for concluding a peace treaty soon—within a year if at all possible—and thereupon dissolving the military hierarchy that he commanded, generally known as the General Headquarters (GHQ), and ending the occupation. He noted that the occupation had long since become a demilitarized undertaking and that the democratization of Japan was largely complete.

The next challenge in the rehabilitation of Japan that MacArthur continued was that of economic revitalization. Revitalizing the Japanese economy would mean rekindling trade, which lay beyond the scope of GHQ's oversight, and concluding a peace treaty, the general emphasized, was crucial to restoring Japan's position as a trading nation. MacArthur's remarks reverberated worldwide and set in motion the process of concluding a peace treaty.[1]

Just five days had passed since US president Harry S. Truman announced his eponymous doctrine, ushering in the Cold War era. The United States and the Soviet Union had fought in World War II as allies and had emerged together as victors. But they had fallen out over how to accommodate their mutual interests in Germany and throughout postwar Europe.

The potential for harmonious accommodation in the postwar world had all but evaporated. Accommodation gave way to confrontation, and the rivalry assumed a character that transcended by far the traditional jockeying for advantage among world powers. The focus of competition shifted to an ideological battle to assert the superiority of one nation-state model—authoritarian communist or liberal democratic—over any other. That ideological battle and the understanding that it would persist for the foreseeable future were the underlying assumptions of the Truman Doctrine.

Truman enunciated his doctrine before a joint session of Congress on March 12, 1947. "I believe," declared the president, "that it must be the policy of the United States to support free peoples who are resisting attempted subjugation by armed minorities or by outside pressures."[2] He requested aid for Greece, which bordered the Soviet satellites Albania, Bulgaria, and Yugoslavia, and for Turkey, which bordered the Soviet Union and Bulgaria.

The president reminded Congress that the retreating German forces had wrought unspeakable devastation in Greece. He explained that

> as a result of these tragic conditions, a militant minority, exploiting human want and misery, was able to create political chaos which, until now, has made economic recovery impossible. . . .
>
> The very existence of the Greek state is today threatened by the terrorist activities of several thousand armed men, led by Communists.

"The future of Turkey as an independent and economically sound state," Truman continued, "is clearly no less important to the freedom-loving peoples of the world than the future of Greece." He emphasized that financial assistance was crucial to maintaining Turkey's national integrity, which was "essential to the preservation of order in the Middle East."

Truman concluded his presentation by asking Congress

> to provide authority for assistance to Greece and Turkey in the amount of $400,000,000 . . . [and] to authorize the detail of American civilian and military personnel to Greece and Turkey, at the request of those countries, to assist in the tasks of reconstruction, and for the purpose of supervising the use of such financial and material assistance as may be furnished. I recommend that authority also be provided for the instruction and training of selected Greek and Turkish personnel.

The US-Soviet rivalry was casting a shadow over Asia, as well as Europe, as Truman enunciated his doctrine to Congress. In China, civil war had erupted between Chiang Kai-shek's Kuomintang (Chinese Nationalist Party), which had ruled the nation since 1928, and Mao Zedong's Communist Party of China. The two had put aside their differences during the joint struggle against the Japanese but had resumed their internecine struggle after the Japanese defeat.

Truman had sought unsuccessfully to persuade China's Nationalists and Communists to join hands in a coalition government. He dispatched George Marshall, who had served as chief of staff during World War II, to China in December 1945 to mediate. The differences between the two sides proved intractable, however, and Marshall abandoned the quest and returned to Washington, DC, in January 1947. He became secretary of state on arriving home and famously oversaw the massive US assistance for the rebuilding of Europe under the Marshall Plan.

On the Korean Peninsula, Soviet and US forces retained positions of occupation north and south of the 38th parallel. Soviet, UK, and US foreign ministers had gathered in Moscow in December 1945 to discuss several postwar issues, including the disposition of Korea. They decided that the US and Soviet military commands there should jointly study and propose ways for establishing a unified Korean government. The foreign ministers agreed to temporarily place Korea under the rule of a four-power trusteeship. That trusteeship comprised China, the Soviet Union, the United Kingdom, and the United States, and its planners intended it to last for up to five years.

The drafters of the Truman Doctrine predicated it on the assumption of continuing confrontation between the United States and the Soviet Union. Conversely, MacArthur predicated his call for concluding a peace treaty with Japan on a thaw in US-Soviet relations, and that assumption proved the undoing of his initiative.

An important product of the Moscow gathering of the Soviet, UK, and US foreign ministers was the eleven-nation (later thirteen-nation) Far Eastern Commission. That commission was a platform for formulating and implementing Allied policy vis-à-vis Japan and initially comprised representatives of Australia, Canada, China, France, India, the Netherlands, New Zealand, the Philippines, the Soviet Union, the United Kingdom, and the United States (later joined by Burma and Pakistan).

The US government proposed that the commission members decide the terms of policy by majority vote at a commission gathering in August 1947. The Soviet government, however, insisted that China, the Soviet

Union, the United Kingdom, and the United States should each wield veto power. That delayed the commencement of negotiations with Japan with regard to a peace treaty.

In the meantime, resistance arose in the US government to pressing ahead swiftly with concluding a peace treaty with Japan. The naysayers argued that rushing ahead with a peace treaty without due consideration for the US-Soviet confrontation would be unwise.

The shift in occupation policy

George F. Kennan, a Soviet expert in the State Department and an early architect of US Cold War policy, argued forcefully against haste in concluding a peace treaty with Japan. Kennan had warned of risk in President Franklin D. Roosevelt's wartime policy of cooperation with the Soviet Union. He famously advocated a policy of Soviet containment in his "Long Telegram" of February 22, 1946, to then secretary of state James Byrnes.[3] At the time Kennan was serving as the deputy chief of mission at the US embassy in Moscow. The input received a positive reception in the Truman administration, which was shifting toward a stance of Soviet containment.

Byrnes's successor, George Marshall, named Kennan the inaugural head of the State Department office now known as the Policy Planning Staff. That office, established in May 1947, is an internal think tank. There, Kennan was an influential force in developing policy proposals for responding to the Cold War.

Kennan, writing under the pseudonym X, placed an article entitled "The Sources of Soviet Conduct" in the July 1947 issue of the US magazine *Foreign Affairs.* He outlined in that article a set of principles for containing Soviet influence, as summarized in the following excerpt:

> The political personality of Soviet power as we know it today is the product of ideology and circumstances: ideology inherited by the present Soviet leaders from the movement in which they had their political origin, and circumstances of the power which they now have exercised for nearly three decades in Russia. . . .
>
> There is ample evidence that the stress laid in Moscow on the menace confronting Soviet society from the world outside its borders is founded not in the realities of foreign antagonism but in the necessity of

> explaining away the maintenance of dictatorial authority at home. . . . The main element of any United States policy toward the Soviet Union must be that of long-term, patient but firm and vigilant containment of Russian expansive tendencies. . . . The United States . . . must continue to expect that Soviet policies will reflect no abstract love of peace and stability, no real faith in the possibility of a permanent happy coexistence of the Socialist and capitalist worlds. . . . Balanced against this are the facts that Russia, as opposed to the western world in general, is still by far the weaker party, that Soviet policy is highly flexible, and that Soviet society may well contain deficiencies which will eventually weaken its own total potential. This would of itself warrant the United States entering with reasonable confidence upon a policy of firm containment, designed to confront the Russians with unalterable counter-force at every point where they show signs of encroaching upon the interests of a peaceful and stable world.[4]

Although Kennan advocated the containment of Soviet influence, he later came to lament what he regarded as the overly military character that US containment policy later assumed. He shared the spirit evoked in the following passage from Truman's enunciation of the Truman Doctrine to Congress:

> The seeds of totalitarian regimes are nurtured by misery and want. They spread and grow in the evil soil of poverty and strife. They reach their full growth when the hope of a people for a better life has died. We must keep that hope alive.

A commitment to engendering hope can be seen in the Marshall Plan, of which Kennan was a prime architect. That plan led to Western Europe's recovery through successful measures for buttressing political and economic stability.

Kennan also took issue with those who sought to contain Soviet influence on a blanket, global basis. He described in his memoir the geographical perspective that he sought to bring to the logic of containment.

> Repeatedly, at that time [1947] and in ensuing years, I expressed in talks and lectures the view that there were only five regions of the world—the

> United States, the United Kingdom, the Rhine valley with adjacent industrial areas, the Soviet Union, and Japan—where the sinews of modern military strength could be produced in quantity; I pointed out that only one of these was under Communist control; and I defined the main task of containment, accordingly, as one of seeing to it that none of the remaining ones fell under such control.[5]

We see here that Kennan regarded Japan as a geographical node of pressing concern in exercising the policy of containment. His State Department think tank shifted its focus to Japan once the formulation of the Marshall Plan was complete. He and his staff felt that MacArthur was overestimating Soviet good faith, and they therefore opposed his proposal for moving ahead swiftly with concluding a peace treaty with Japan.

Hugh Borton, the chief of the State Department's Division of Northeast Asian Affairs, had overseen the drafting of a proposal for a peace treaty. His team predicated the proposed treaty text on the assumption of continuing US-Soviet cooperation and long-term monitoring by the Allied powers of demilitarization and democratization in Japan. A member of Kennan's staff, John P. Davies, Jr., criticized the proposal in an August 11, 1947, memorandum to Kennan.

> It would seem that a peace settlement for Japan proposed by the American Government should further American aims in Japan and the Pacific area. The central American objective in this respect is taken to be a stable Japan, integrated into the Pacific economy, friendly to the US and, in case of need, a ready and dependable Ally of the US.
>
> Rather than assuring a furtherance of our central objective, the Draft Treaty of Peace for Japan appears to be preoccupied with drastic disarmament and democratization under continuing international supervision, including the USSR. But demilitarization is no longer a serious problem in the case of Japan. Even if it so desired, Japan could not in the foreseeable future resurrect itself as a first-class military power. It can only gravitate into the orbit of one or the other of the super powers. As for democratization, it is questionable whether the presence of the USSR on an international supervisory body would contribute to democratic advances. It is likely that the USSR in this position would be a disruptive

> influence in Japan, placing the onus for continued supervision on the US and conspiring to bring about Sovietized totalitarianism.[6]

Kennan raised his and his staff's concerns about the treaty proposal the next day in a memorandum to Undersecretary of State Robert Lovett and recommended putting the treaty proposal on hold.

> It is my view that we should try to delay the opening of these discussions until this matter can be systematically thrashed out, United States objectives agreed upon at a high level, and our peace treaty draft related strictly to those objectives.[7]

Japan was poised to become the first world-class platform in the Far East for military power and industrial output. In Kennan's eyes, that underlined the importance of positioning Japan solidly as a member of the free world. He believed that assimilating Japan into the ranks of free world nations warranted higher priority than concluding a peace treaty, and he feared that undertaking peace treaty negotiations while Japan remained politically and economically unstable would interfere with achieving that goal.

Cold War strategy, Kennan believed, mandated a shift in emphases for the United States in its policy for Japan as well. The primary emphasis, he argued, should shift toward restoring political and economic stability and away from promoting demilitarization and democratization. Peace treaty negotiations could wait until Japan was operating on a steadier footing. Kennan visited Japan in late February and much of March 1948 to observe things firsthand. He met with MacArthur and delivered his appeal for a shift in occupation policy. Kennan's proposals underwent some minor revisions in the State Department, in the Department of the Army, and in MacArthur's General Headquarters, but they survived largely intact and became the gist of National Security Council (NSC) policy paper NSC 13/2.

The shift in Japan policy was a source of profound pride for Kennan. "I consider my part in bringing about this change," he wrote in his memoir, "to have been, after the Marshall Plan, the most significant constructive contribution I was ever able to make in government."

A shift from security against Japan to security for Japan

New US priorities in Japan policy entailed a new perspective on national security. US security concerns with regard to postwar Japan had centered initially on neutering the nation as a military threat. That is explicit in the document "US Initial Post-Surrender Policy for Japan," approved by Truman on September 6, 1945.[8]

The "Post-Surrender Policy" document begins with an explication of the "ultimate objectives of the United States with respect to Japan." And it states that the first of those ultimate objectives is to "insure that Japan will not again become a menace to the United States or to the peace and security of the world." Demilitarization and democratization, later enshrined in the Japanese constitution adopted in May 1947, were essential means of achieving that objective.

As another means of neutering Japan as a military threat, the US government was planning a framework for Allied monitoring. Secretary of State Byrnes announced a proposal in June 1946 for a four-power pact to oversee Japanese disarmament. The pact would comprise the United States, China, the Soviet Union, and the United Kingdom and would operate for twenty-five years.[9]

Byrnes's proposal figured in Borton's peace treaty draft that emerged a year later in the State Department and that received a critical reception from Kennan and his staff. The State Department's peace treaty draft provided for establishing a two-tiered mechanism for monitoring Japan's disarmament and demilitarization for twenty-five years: an oversight council of the ambassadors to Japan from the member nations of the Far Eastern Commission and a working group to conduct on-site surveillance.[10]

US Cold War strategy had already moved beyond the focus of Byrnes and Borton on keeping Japan in check. Assimilating Japan into the ranks of the free world nations had become a strategy priority. Kennan describes in his memoirs his incredulity at the failure of the occupation authorities to absorb that development. He notes that Soviet forces in southern Sakhalin, on the Kurile Islands, and in North Korea half surrounded Japan. Yet the occupation authorities, Kennan observes with disgust, had not prepared any sort of plan for defending Japan.

> If one was to regard the protection of Japan against Communist pressures as a legitimate concern of the United States government, then it was madness to think of abandoning Japan to her own devices in the situation then prevailing.[11]

Japan's national security was vital, in Kennan's geopolitical perspective, to US national security. Kennan perceived in Soviet ideology and strategy a clear and present danger to Japan. The Japanese and their occupation overseers needed to be alert to the threat of Soviet intrigue. And the best defense against Soviet mischief, Kennan had learned in Europe with the Marshall Plan, was robust domestic stability. Thus, he favored extending the occupation long enough to restore Japan's economic and political sustainability.

The Allies would conclude a peace treaty with Japan one day, of course, and end the occupation. Anyone engaged in administering the US government's Japan policy needed to consider those inevitabilities and contemplate how to ensure Japan's national security afterward. Kennan had given careful thought to the issue of Japan's long-term national security.

First of all, Kennan cautioned against proceeding arbitrarily with any schedule for concluding a peace treaty and ending the occupation. The Allies and Japan would settle on a date for that purpose sooner or later, but they should remain vigilant as the date approached. They should be prepared to postpone things if the Soviet Union was exhibiting suspicious behavior or if Japanese domestic politics were in flux. Kennan suggested, too, that gradual Japanese rearmament under US supervision was an option worthy of consideration. He expressed, on the other hand, the hope that the United States and the Soviet Union could reach some sort of accommodation in the Far East.

Kennan summarized his views on a suitable approach to a peace treaty with Japan in a Policy Planning Staff report (PPS 28) dated March 25, 1948 and entitled "Recommendations with Respect to US Policy toward Japan." Especially notable is Kennan's emphasis on the need to retain a lasting military presence in Okinawa.

> The United States Government should make up its mind at this point that it intends to retain permanently the facilities at Okinawa, and the

> base there should be developed accordingly. The problem of obtaining international sanction for our permanent strategic control of the islands should be studied at once in the Department of State.[12]

The report relies heavily on input gleaned from MacArthur during Kennan's visit to Japan earlier that month. Kennan cites at length the general's comments on the strategic importance of US bases in Okinawa.

> General MacArthur here pointed out that if we wish to defend Japanese territory from external aggression we must depend primarily upon Air power rather than upon an Army and Navy. He said that with adequate Air power based upon Okinawa, we could protect Japan from outside attack. He dwelt further upon the strategic importance of Okinawa; pointing out that the California coast is now no longer our outer line of defense. This line now passes through the Marianas, the Ryukyus and the Aleutians, with Okinawa as its key bastion. The line has advanced outposts on its southern flank in the Philippines, Australia and the British and Dutch islands adjacent thereto. Its northern outpost is Japan. He said that all of the nations except Russia fully recognize the military importance of Okinawa to the United States, and desire that we retain it as a military stronghold. He said that Australia and New Zealand, particularly, wish to see us powerfully ensconced therein, feeling that such a position assures their own defense far more efficiently than they themselves could ever hope to do. He pointed out that Okinawa has adequate space to provide for the operation of a powerful and effective Air Force, which could assure the destruction of enemy forces or harbor facilities along the Asiatic coast from Vladivostok to Singapore. He said, therefore, that by properly developing and garrisoning *Okinawa* [all italics in original] we can assure the safety of Japan against external aggression without the need for maintaining forces on Japanese soil. He emphasized again, that we should retain these occupation forces until the *peace treaty* only, as a means of insuring internal order, and in order to impress upon the Japanese people the fact that we are not deserting them. General MacArthur strongly urged that in the light of these considerations, the US reach a decision *now* to remain in Okinawa and that we devote adequate funds at once to the necessary construction for a permanent garrison.[13]

A year after his talks with Kennan, MacArthur elaborated on US strategic expectations of Japan. He expressed those expectations in a March 2, 1949, interview with a reporter for the UK newspaper *Daily Mail.*

> Japan's role is to be the Switzerland of the Pacific. [If Japan were attacked] we should certainly defend her. . . . But I do not believe Russia will attack Japan. Even if the Soviet government had aggressive intentions toward Japan, Russia would be incapable of carrying them out unless she could secure mastery of the air and either had a far eastern fleet of her own or possessed the means of neutralizing any action by our fleet. Russia could not obtain air predominance. On Okinawa I had constructed at the end of the war 25 air fields with the capacity to dispatch B-29s, then our largest bombers, on 3,500 missions a day. The whole of eastern Asia from Singapore to Vladivostok would lie within range of those machines.

The phrase "Switzerland of the Pacific" resonated with the Japanese and became a popular bon mot to drop in conversation. What is questionable, however, is whether the happy conversers realized what MacArthur envisioned for their Pacific Switzerland: an archipelago that would host US airbases at its southern tip in perpetuity.

The Ashida letter and notions of ensuring Japanese security with a US troop presence

Japan, as noted, figured in US strategic planning in the early postwar years as a threat to be neutralized. The advent of the Cold War, however, prompted a policy shift, and US strategic planners began to regard Japan's national security as essential to US national security. A shift occurred at the same time in the perspective on national security in the Japanese government.

The Japanese Foreign Ministry began convening internal study sessions early after the surrender with regard to peace treaty issues. An initial assumption was that all of the Allied powers, including the Soviet Union, would be cosignatories of the treaty. Another assumption was the likely Allied insistence, as per the Potsdam Declaration, on "convincing proof that Japan's war-making power is destroyed." The Foreign Ministry officials were concerned with how to respond to any Allied demands and how to secure renewed sovereignty for Japan in the world. They realized, meanwhile, that questions of national security would be central to any peace treaty negotiations.

The early results of the study sessions weighed in favor of securing Japan's national security by pledging permanent Japanese neutrality to the eleven member nations of the Far Eastern Commission. Subsequent results of the study sessions suggested that Japan should pursue national security by acceding to membership in the United Nations and thus becoming part of the UN collective security regimen. Some in the Foreign Ministry argued, however, that simply joining the United Nations would be insufficient to ensure Japan's national security. They noted that the UN charter permitted regional mutual defense pacts and suggested that Japan would need to supplement its UN affiliation with participation in such an arrangement.[14]

Come autumn 1947, a new line of thinking took hold in the Foreign Ministry that addressed the reality of Soviet-US confrontation. It acknowledged the value of a lasting US military presence to ensure Japan's national security. Influential figures in the US military also voiced support for a sustained presence in Japan. One was Lieutenant General Robert L. Eichelberger. He headed the US 8th Army, which was part of the Japanese occupation and maintained its command headquarters in Yokohama.

Eichelberger was vocally dubious about MacArthur's call for the early conclusion of a peace treaty. He opined that US airbases in Okinawa alone would be wholly inadequate to safeguard Japan and that a US military withdrawal would allow Communists to have their way with the nation. Eichelberger shared his concerns about Japanese national security in the wake of a US withdrawal with the career diplomat Suzuki Tadakatsu.

Suzuki headed the Yokohama branch of Japan's Central Liaison Office, which handled interchange with the occupation forces. He recounted a comment by Eichelberger in a chapter that he contributed to a book published in 1986.

> After a withdrawal by the Allied forces, [domestic] Communist elements will wax and Soviet influences will infiltrate Japan. You could soon see an invasion from southern Sakhalin and the Kuriles. I'm thinking about how to prevent that from happening. You could strengthen Japan's constabulary to deal with the threat posed by domestic Communist elements. In the event of a Soviet invasion, [the US military] could monitor

> things from Okinawa and Guam and, if necessary, could drop atomic bombs on Vladivostok and other [Soviet military] strongpoints. [On the other hand, the Soviets] could occupy Hokkaido cities overnight, and we couldn't bomb them on account of the presence of Japanese residents.[15]

Eichelberger sought the views of the Japanese government on the possible course of events that he was describing. Suzuki relayed his request to the Foreign Ministry. The foreign minister, Ashida Hitoshi, and ministry officials discussed Eichelberger's scenario and sketched a potential stance on national security for the Japanese government after the conclusion of a peace treaty. Suzuki passed a summary of their conclusions, the so-called Ashida letter, to Eichelberger on September 13, 1947.

The Ashida letter discussed Japanese national security after the conclusion of a peace treaty with respect to two scenarios: (1) improved US-Soviet relations and a well-functioning United Nations and (2) deteriorating US-Soviet relations and a dysfunctional United Nations. In the first scenario, Japan would entrust its national security to the United Nations. In the second, it would entrust its national security to the United States.

Fundamental to the first scenario was the assumption "that American-Soviet relations will improve to such an extent as to warrant elimination of all apprehensions about world peace." In that event,

> it may be expected that the United Nations will soon function properly as the guarantee for peace. Then Japan, demilitarized but provided with police forces adequate to maintain internal peace and order, can afford to wait for the United Nations to provide her with security without the fear of any danger.[16]

The drafters of the Ashida letter viewed a dramatic improvement in US-Soviet relations as implausible and their second scenario as the more likely. Underlying that scenario was the assumption that "unfortunately American-Soviet relations do not improve, causing world-wide unrest." The letter was thus essentially a request for the US occupation forces to ensure Japanese national security. It marked the first time in the Cold War that the Japanese government had made such a request.

Ashida's letter cited two possibilities for US assurance of Japanese national security after the conclusion of a peace treaty. One possibility was for the United States to station troops in Japan to monitor the fulfillment of the treaty. In this approach, preventing an invasion of Japan would be a fringe benefit of the presence of the US troops.

The other possibility was that of providing for the deployment of US troops to Japan under a separate security pact. Readily evident from the text is the drafters' preference for that option.

> In the case of the worsening of the world situation the best measures of guaranteeing Japan's security is for her to conclude with the United States a specific agreement against aggression by third Powers, and at the same time to reinforce her police forces on land and water. . . . At all events . . . the United States will maintain sufficient military strength on certain strategic points in areas outside of but adjacent to Japan. Such specific agreement . . . would have provisions that if and when Japan's independence and security is threatened (that is, peace of the Pacific is menaced), the United States may, after consultation with the Japanese Government, send her armed forces into Japan and use military bases there. Of course, the necessary stipulations will have to be made, under which the military bases can be constructed and maintained in Japan as satisfactorily as possible to the American requirements.

Eichelberger appears at least to have shown the Ashida letter to several influential figures in the US government and military. Among them was General Frank McCoy, the chairman of the Far Eastern Commission.[17] The letter seems to have exercised no influence, however, on US policy and became, in that sense, nothing more than a historical footnote. Yet the concerns and hopes expressed in the letter offer a telling foretaste of the security treaty subsequently concluded between Japan and the United States.

Yoshida Shigeru, the Japanese prime minister who set the stage for postwar Japanese-US relations, acknowledged the Ashida letter in his memoir. That output, he noted, was perfectly consistent with the subsequent direction of Japanese-US relations with regard to Japan's national security.[18] The Ashida letter was a transitional relic, however, in the sense that it retained the conceptual dichotomy of security against Japan and security for Japan: station US troops in Japan to monitor the fulfillment of the peace treaty, an implicit reference to securing against Japan, or provide for deploying US troops to Japan under a separate security pact, a reference to security for Japan.

Japanese government thinking was shifting, Yoshida wrote in his memoir, from the former to the latter.

> If Allied troops were to remain in Japan after the signing of a peace treaty, that would be like the occupation of Germany after the signing of the Treaty of Versailles. Most people in the Japanese government assumed that [any such presence of Allied troops] would be for the purpose of ensuring the fulfillment of the peace treaty. However, mounting US-Soviet tensions rendered Japanese security increasingly difficult for the United States to ignore. We perceived a gradual shift in the US attitude toward the view of Japanese security as integral to international security. Japanese thinking, meanwhile, shifted toward acceptance of the need for relying for some time after the signing of the peace treaty on US support for national security. That seemed preferable than counting on the United Nations, which appeared at the time to be unreliable in that regard.[19]

Another transitional aspect of the Ashida letter was in regard to the duration of a US troop presence. The letter expressed the assumption that a troop presence under a security pact would be temporary. That differed fundamentally from the permanent presence enshrined in the security pact ultimately concluded between Japan and the United States.

The drafters of the Ashida letter assumed that the United States would deploy troops to Japan only in times of emergency. Ordinarily, the United States would station the troops "on certain strategic points in areas outside of but adjacent to Japan." It would deploy them in Japan only "if and when Japan's independence and security is threatened" and only "after consultation with the Japanese Government." Japan, meanwhile, would maintain domestic bases to accommodate the US troops when and as necessary. The letter does not specify the sites meant by "areas outside of but adjacent to Japan," but scholars have confirmed that the letter's drafters had in mind Okinawa and Iwo Jima (Iwo Tō) and other islands of the Ogasawara Archipelago.[20]

Also unspecified in the Ashida letter is the reason for assuming that the United States would station troops in Japan only in times of emergency. We can surmise the reason, however, from the following passage in the letter: "Such an agreement, without compromising Japan's independence in peace time, will permit the United States to make full use of the bases in Japan in times of emergency."[21] Clearly, Ashida and the Foreign Ministry officials feared that a permanent US military presence in Japan would impinge on Japanese independence.[22]

2 The US Government's Stance

Disagreement between the State Department and the military establishment

Hope for the early conclusion of a peace treaty and the end of the occupation glimmered briefly in spring 1947 with MacArthur's dramatic proposal. Opposition by Kennan and others in the US government, however, put any such moves on hold for the time being, and Japan remained an occupied nation. Not until September 1949 did progress toward concluding a peace treaty gain visible momentum.

Dean Acheson, who succeeded George Marshall as secretary of state in January 1949, met on September 13 in Washington, DC, with UK foreign minister Ernest Bevin. Moving ahead with concluding a peace treaty with Japan was among the matters that they discussed.

The occupation had continued for four years. US control over Japan had loosened considerably, and such figures of speech as "peace without a treaty" and "de facto peace" had become common in discussions of Japan's status. The Japanese people yearned, however, for genuine sovereignty and would not settle indefinitely for the status of a subjugated nation. On the other hand, Japanese politics remained unstable under the occupation, and economic recovery had yet to gain traction. The United Kingdom and the Soviet Union, meanwhile, each sought a peace treaty with Japan in conjunction with their different circumstances.

Developments elsewhere in East Asia obliged the US government to rethink its posture in the region. In China, the Communists were on the cusp of a sweeping victory over the Nationalists and would establish the People's Republic of China on October 1, 1949. The partitioning of the Korean Peninsula had become formal in the previous year with the establishment of the Republic of Korea in the south and the Democratic People's Republic of Korea in the north.

The Acheson-Bevin talks occasioned a shift in US government policy and the beginning of the process of concluding a peace treaty with Japan. Underlying that process was the assumption of continuing tensions between the United States and the Soviet Union. Impeding the progress of the process were differences between the State Department and the military establishment—the Defense Department and the armed forces—about how to proceed.

Concern in the State Department focused on strengthening political solidarity with Japan and, conversely, avoiding the rise of anti-US sentiment that prolonging the occupation would entail. In the military establishment, concern focused on retaining bases in Japan and the right to use those bases freely in connection with containing Soviet influence. The State Department was thus eager to move ahead swiftly with concluding a peace treaty, while the military establishment abided by a more guarded stance in that regard.

We find a clear exposition of the military establishment's position in a report prepared by the Joint Chiefs of Staff (JCS) and submitted to the National Security Council on June 9, 1949. That report, "Strategic Evaluation of United States Security Needs in Japan," became National Securities Council document NSC 49. It begins with an appraisal of the strategic value that accrued from Japan's geographical position.

> The Japanese Islands are of high strategic importance to United States security interests in the Far East, primarily because of their geographic location with respect to the trade routes of the North Pacific, the exits and entrances of the Sea of Japan, the East China and Yellow Seas, and, to a lesser degree, the ports of Asia north of the Shanghai-Woosung area, inclusive. Japan, also because of her geographic location, could under USSR control be used as a base for aggressive action directly against United States bases in the Western Pacific, in anticipation of step-by-step advances

> eastward and to the Southeast Asia region. Conversely, United States control of Japan, either directly or indirectly, will not only deny to the USSR an extremely important strategic base for aggressive or defensive action but also, in the event of war, will make available to us strategic outposts for early denial to the USSR, and eventually for control or neutralization by us, of the Sea of Japan and the Yellow and East China Seas. In addition, it would provide us with staging areas from which to project our military power to the Asiatic mainland and to USSR islands adjacent thereto.[23]

Next, the report explains that Japan's strategic value was destined to increase further on account of the nation's manpower and industrial potential. And it calls for making use of Japanese capacity for waging war.

> Japan's strategic importance is increased by her manpower and her industrial potentials. These several potentials could, under readily foreseeable circumstances, and, despite the logistic demand that would need to be met in making her support useful, have great influence either for or against the interests of the United States in the event of global war.
>
> The ability of the Japanese to wage both aggressive and defensive war was proven in the last world conflict. It is almost inconceivable that the Japanese manpower potential would be permitted to continue in peaceful pursuits in the event of another global conflict. Under USSR control, Japan probably would provide both the arsenal personnel and the manpower for aggressive military campaigns in the Pacific and to the southwest. If United States influence predominates, Japan can be expected, with planned initial United States assistance, at least to protect herself and, provided logistic necessities can be made available to her, to contribute importantly to military operations against the Soviets in Asia, thus forcing the USSR to fight on the Asiatic front as well as elsewhere.

The report continues with a description of Japan's positioning in "the Asian offshore island chain." That island chain, the report notes, was a bulwark of the "United States position in the Far East vis-à-vis the USSR."

> From the military point of view, the ultimate minimum United States position in the Far East vis-à-vis the USSR, one to which we are rapidly

> being forced, requires at least our present degree of control of the Asian offshore island chain. In the event of war, this island chain should constitute in effect a system of strong outposts for our strategic position. It would have only limited offensive value, however, and might well be untenable, if any major portion of the chain, such as Japan, were unavailable at the outset of the struggle.

Especially notable in the report is a description of strategic considerations that figured decisively in the peace treaty ultimately concluded.

> a. The . . . Navy Department has examined the possibilities of Okinawa for development as a naval base and has determined that it is not suitable as a year-around naval base because of unfavorable meteorological and hydrographic features. The Joint Chiefs of Staff, therefore, consider that arrangements for the continued use of Yokosuka as a base are of major importance. To provide against future contingencies, the peace treaty should not be such as to preclude bilateral negotiations for base rights in the Japanese main islands;
> b. If it should prove impracticable or impossible to obtain bases on the Japanese main islands, bases on Okinawa or other islands of the Ryukyus along with other US bases in or near the Pacific would not meet our essential needs.

Caution, as the report shows, was the order of the day for the Joint Chiefs of Staff. They were determined to ensure the fulfillment of their conditions before negotiating a peace treaty.

> With these points in mind, the Joint Chiefs of Staff are of the opinion, from the military point of view, that a peace treaty would, at the present time, be premature since the continuing Soviet policy of aggressive communist expansion makes it essential that Japan's democracy and western orientation first be established beyond all question, and since global developments are still in such a state of flux that measures leading to the risk of loss of control of any area might seriously affect our national security.

The State Department parried with a forceful rebuttal of the position evoked by the JCS. That rebuttal, submitted on September 30, 1949, became National Security Council document NSC 49/1.

> With respect to . . . the [JCS] paper, the Department of State would add that, from the political, as well as the military point of view, our essential objectives with respect to Japan are its denial to the Soviet Union and the maintenance of Japan's orientation toward the Western powers. . . .
>
> The Department of State does not doubt that, in the event of an overt Soviet attack on Japan in the foreseeable future—the contingency which must necessarily be foremost in the thinking of the JCS—the military effort of the US would be the decisive factor. The Department of State believes that the JCS would agree, however, that the degree of effort required of the US would be radically conditioned by the orientation of the Japanese.
>
> In the event that the present world situation continues much as at present, the denial of Japan to the USSR constitutes a problem of combatting, not overt attack and invasion, but concealed aggression. The threat to Japan in these circumstances comes from agitation, subversion and *coup d'état*. The threat is that of a conspiracy inspired by the Kremlin, but conducted by Japanese. It is essentially a conspiracy from within—and whether it succeeds depends primarily on the political, economic and social health of Japan itself. . . .
>
> The orientation of any people toward a foreign country is a subjective political-psychological condition. It is the product of domestic political, economic, and social factors, together with the nature and quality of a nation's relations with foreign countries. This being the case, the US can neither impose nor enforce a pro-western orientation on any foreign people, including the Japanese. We can contribute to such an orientation only through (*a*) fostering in Japan, so far as we are able, conditions conducive to a pro-western orientation and (*b*) conducting our relations with Japan in such a way that, in the developing scene within Japan, we continue to be respected and, if possible, regarded with favor. . . .
>
> The only hope for the preservation and advancement of such democracy and western orientation as now exist in Japan lies in the early conclusion of a peace settlement with that country. From the political point of view, the achievement of our objectives with respect to Japan are now less likely to be thwarted by proceeding promptly to a peace treaty than

by continuance of the occupation regime, provided that essential US military needs in Japan are assured in the treaty or other concurrent arrangements.[24]

MacArthur's justification for a continued US military presence

Truman resolved to break the deadlock between the State Department and the military establishment and to clear the way for negotiating a peace treaty between Japan and the Allied nations. For that purpose, he put John Foster Dulles in charge of orchestrating the treaty in May 1950.

Dulles, a lawyer by training, had recently assumed the title of consultant to the secretary of state. He brought to the post an impressive pedigree and résumé. His maternal grandfather and a maternal uncle had each served as secretary of state. President Woodrow Wilson had appointed the thirty-year-old Dulles to serve as legal counsel to the US delegation to the Versailles Peace Conference in 1918. Dulles had worked for a time between the wars in brokering international finance. He had even served briefly as a Republican senator from New York, replacing an incumbent forced into retirement by ill health.

Truman, a Democrat, needed to marshal bipartisan support for a peace treaty. Dulles, possessed of immense international experience and Republican affiliation, was an ideal lieutenant for tackling that quest. Truman's China policy had come under sharp criticism from Republican lawmakers. The Republicans accused the president of "losing China" after the Communist victory over the Nationalists there. And Truman wanted to prevent plans for a peace treaty with Japan from falling victim to the mounting anti-Communist hysteria.

MacArthur was a valuable ally for Dulles in mobilizing support for the treaty in the government. He made the case for an early signing to Louis Johnson, the secretary of defense, and to Omar Bradley, the chairman of the JCS. That was while they were in Japan in early June 1950. Concerns about ensuring Japanese national security were the thorniest issue in garnering support for a peace treaty. MacArthur explained his perspective on that matter to Johnson and Bradley and to Dulles, who visited Japan later in June. Fatefully, both visits occurred just before the outbreak of the Korean War in late June.[25]

The State Department and the defense establishment—the Defense

Department and the Joint Chiefs of Staff—had each floated a proposal for a peace treaty. Each proposal reflected the stance of its source, and each contained features designed to mollify opposition in the other camp. MacArthur held that neither proposal would satisfy the Japanese.

Sentiment had coalesced in the State Department in favor of forming a Pacific pact—a regional collective defense arrangement that would comprise Australia, Canada, Japan, New Zealand, the Philippines, and the United States. Proponents of that arrangement reasoned that it would prevent a revival of militarism in Japan while protecting the nation from external aggression. They envisioned the United States concluding a separate treaty with Japan that would allow it to maintain bases there.[26] MacArthur argued, however, that the Japanese would regard the State Department proposal as a means of ensuring US security rather than Japanese security and that the proposal would kindle a nationalistic response.

The proposal hatched in the defense establishment posited a peace treaty that would occasion a partial return of Japanese sovereignty. Even after the signing of the treaty, the US military occupation would continue, though Japan would regain sovereignty in all other respects. MacArthur rejected that proposal as being worse from the Japanese standpoint than the then current arrangement. The Japanese, he reiterated, longed for genuine sovereignty and would view anything less as betrayal.

MacArthur offered an alternative. His proposal rested on deft sleight of hand in reinterpreting the Potsdam Declaration of July 26, 1945.

The Potsdam Declaration stated that

> a new order of peace, security and justice will be impossible until irresponsible militarism is driven from the world. Until such a new order is established and until there is convincing proof that Japan's war-making power is destroyed, points in Japanese territory to be designated by the Allies shall be occupied to secure the achievement of the basic objectives we are here setting forth.[27]

By "irresponsible militarism," the framers of the Potsdam Declaration were unquestionably referring to Japan's prewar and wartime militarism. MacArthur deftly redirected that reference, however, to Soviet Communism. The Soviet Union and its ideology, he reasoned, would remain a threat after the conclusion of the peace treaty. So US troops would remain in Japan to protect the nation from that threat.

Thus would MacArthur justify a US military presence in a fully sovereign Japan after the conclusion of the peace treaty. That presence, in his reinterpretation of the Potsdam Declaration, would be for the express purpose of protecting Japan. And the potential geographical scope of that presence would span the entirety of Japanese territory. Technological advances, MacArthur noted, had rendered obsolete the traditional practice of confining a military presence to fixed positions.

MacArthur had retreated from his earlier insistence that a US military presence on Okinawa would be sufficient to protect Japan. That was presumably a concession to the views expressed in the proposals from the Defense Department and the Joint Chiefs of Staff. It was likely a compromise, intended to smooth the way for the early conclusion of a peace treaty.[28]

Curiously, MacArthur betrayed no sign of sensing any contradiction between his new proposal and his espousal of Japanese neutrality. He was apparently sincere in his reinterpretation of the Potsdam Declaration. In other words, the US military presence would truly be a consequence of complying with a multilateral international covenant and not of drawing Japan into military alignment with the United States. MacArthur seems to have honestly believed that "from every standpoint, it is more essential that Japan be denied to the Soviet than that she be an active military ally of the United States."[29] Underlying this judgment, of course, was the assumption that Okinawa would remain under US control.

The MacArthur proposal's logic proved useful in stimulating momentum in the US government toward concluding a peace treaty with Japan. For one thing, it catalyzed agreement between the State Department and the military establishment. The two camps came to terms with regard to concluding a peace treaty predicated on a lasting US military presence. And on September 8, 1950, Truman agreed to commence formal treaty negotiations with Japan. A condition for the commencement of negotiations was that "the Treaty must give the United States the right to maintain armed forces in Japan, wherever, for so long, and to such extent as it deems necessary."[30]

Meanwhile,

> questions regarding the relationship of the armed forces to the Japanese

> Government, the extent to which Japan will be required to contribute to the cost of maintaining those forces, and similar questions regarding the detailed implementation of the security arrangements will be the subject of a supplementary bilateral agreement between the United States and Japan to come into effect simultaneously with the coming into effect of the Treaty.[31]

MacArthur's rationalization for a lasting US military presence was especially welcome to Dulles. Both men realized that any proposal for retaining US troops in Japan would require the agreement of the US Congress and of the United States' allies and Japan. MacArthur's reinterpretation of the Potsdam Declaration reinforced their case with the weight of an international agreement.

Dulles and MacArthur's discussions in Japan began on the morning of June 22, 1950. At that time, Dulles described an idea for translating MacArthur's Potsdam logic into UN logic for maintaining international peace and security.[32] MacArthur agreed that the Japanese would find such an approach acceptable. Dulles described the meeting in a memorandum of June 30.

> In further discussing this concept of security with General MacArthur I mentioned that any arrangements about security with Japan should be cast in the mold of overall international peace and security rather than in terms of any special advantage to the United States at the expense of Japan. In this connection I prepared and handed to General MacArthur a memorandum of which a copy is attached indicating what would be the "normal" procedure if the United Nations were operating one-hundred percent and suggesting that arrangements with Japan could be assimilated and put into the mold of the United Nations concept so that [facilities] made available by Japan would be considered as part of the structure of international peace and security. General MacArthur at that time and at a subsequent conference said that he fully agreed with such a presentation as being the way to make the arrangement acceptable to the Japanese people. . . .
>
> It is suggested that pending Japan's admission to the United Nations and the coming into force of Article 43 agreements, that Japan would make

> comparable agreements for military facilities with the United States acting under the Potsdam Declaration as representative of the signatories, these facilities to be merged into the international security system of the United Nations when it is finally established.[33]

Dulles's ideas, revised somewhat, appeared in the September 11, 1950, peace treaty draft prepared by the State Department.[34] That draft provided that Japan, before acceding to UN membership, would undertake the obligations cited in Article 2 of the UN Charter. Namely, it would pledge to

> settle [its] international disputes by peaceful means in such a manner that international peace and security, and justice, are not endangered . . . refrain in [its] international relations from the threat or use of force against the territorial integrity or political independence of any state, or in any other manner inconsistent with the Purposes of the United Nations . . . [and] give the United Nations every assistance in any action it takes in accordance with the present Charter.[35]

The Japanese and US governments shared concern that the "irresponsible militarism" cited in the Potsdam Declaration had yet to be "driven from the world." In that spirit, they would conclude an agreement aimed at ensuring peace and security in Japanese territory, Japan would request military assistance of the United States, the United States would provide that assistance, and Japan would grant the US military the right to maintain bases in Japan and the right of passage through Japanese territory. These basic elements of the State Department draft remained intact in the final version of the peace treaty.

The effect of the Korean War on the progress of the peace treaty

North Korea invaded its southern neighbor on June 25, 1950, while Dulles was in Japan. The United Nations promptly authorized UN military assistance for South Korea and authorized the US government to appoint the commander of the UN force. On the unanimous recommendation of the JCS, MacArthur became the commander in chief of the United Nations Command while retaining his position as the Supreme Commander for the Allied Powers in Japan.

The war presented a new obstacle for Dulles, MacArthur, and others who sought to conclude a peace treaty with Japan. Logistical support based in Japan would be crucial to US military operations on the Korean Peninsula. The Defense Department and the Joint Chiefs of Staff were loath to lose free access to Japan as a staging platform. They feared that concluding a peace treaty with Japan could impinge on that access and were therefore resistant to beginning treaty negotiations while hostilities continued on the Korean Peninsula.[36]

Defense establishment pressure to delay treaty negotiations with Japan mounted after the Chinese entered the war on behalf of North Korea. That occurred in late October 1950, forcing MacArthur to acknowledge that he faced "an entirely new war."[37] The JCS stated in a December 28 memorandum to the secretary of defense that they urged "most strongly that the United States refrain from proceeding now with any negotiations with Japan leading to a peace treaty" and called for "any such negotiations [to] await a resolution of the situation in Korea.[38]

Dulles believed, in contrast to the defense establishment's stance, that the Korean War would heighten Japanese awareness of the Communist threat and viewed it as a further reason for proceeding with treaty negotiations. He and his State Department colleagues regarded the peace treaty as indispensable for drawing Japan into the Western fold, and their position became US government policy.

The eruption of the Korean War greatly heightened Japan's strategic value for the United States. Most of all, it underlined the geographical value described, as we have seen, by the Joint Chiefs of Staff in NSC 49. The United States–led UN force could not have undertaken its Korean operations without the staging platform that Japan provided.

Also heightening Japan's strategic value was the emergence of China as an implacable enemy of the United States. Until early 1950, the US government retained hope that Mao Zedong's China would maintain a distance from Stalin's Eastern bloc. Josip Tito's Yugoslavia, which had broken with the Eastern bloc in 1948, offered a model in that respect. China dashed that hope in February 1950, however, by concluding the Sino-Soviet Treaty of Friendship, Alliance and Mutual Assistance. Its anti-US orientation became conspicuous when Chinese troops engaged in open war with the US-led UN forces in October. Japan's importance as a counterweight to China in East Asia then became abundantly clear to all in the US government.

Although the Korean War bolstered the case for a peace treaty with Japan overall, it also complicated the treaty process. That is because it prompted the US military establishment to press for Japanese rearmament. The US military wanted more than just the right to maintain and operate bases in Japan; it wanted the Japanese to deploy substantive military power on their own.

MacArthur, following the June 1950 outbreak of the Korean War, ordered the Japanese government in July 1950 to establish the National Police Reserve. That organization, established in August, was a lightly armed paramilitary force about 75,000 strong. MacArthur ordered the government at the same time to expand the staffing of the Maritime Safety Agency, established in 1948, to 8,000. Shifting occupation troops from Japan to the Korean Peninsula would leave the US forces in Japan undermanned, and the newly established and expanded Japanese forces were to take over their duties for ensuring domestic security.

Prime Minister Yoshida Shigeru was eager to strengthen domestic security and complied happily with the order to establish the National Police Reserve. The US military establishment, however, wanted Japan to pick up the pace in rebuilding its military. That reflected concerns that the US military's broadening global commitments were stretching it too thin. Even while mobilizing for the Korean War, the United States was dispatching four divisions to Western Europe. Those divisions would serve under the North Atlantic Treaty Organization (NATO), newly activated to allay concerns about the potential threat from the Eastern bloc.

The Joint Chiefs of Staff wanted a bolstering of the West's conventional military forces, and Japan was part of their calculations. They submitted their Japanese calculations to the secretary of defense in a later memorandum.[39] Among the assumptions that underlay those calculations was that "world conditions during the period of the next several years will continue to be extremely critical and any attack on Japan by the Communist forces will occur with little warning." The JCS concluded, among other things, that the US forces would require support from a Japanese army 10 divisions strong. (See Chapter 2 of this work for a detailed discussion of their conclusions.)

Rearmament in the context of a Pacific pact

Truman had determined by January 1950 that the United States should be prepared for full-scale war with the Eastern bloc. On January 31, he directed the Defense Department and the State Department to draft what became National Security Council document NSC 68: "United States Objectives and Programs for National Security." Truman received NSC 68 on April 14 and signed it into policy on September 30. On December 16, he declared a national state of emergency in response to China's wholesale entry into the Korean War.[40]

A December 28 report by the Joint Strategic Survey Committee to the JCS described an alarming state of affairs.

> During the past two and a half months the military position of the United States in the world in general and in the Far East in particular has radically altered for the worse. The United States has suffered especially serious reverses in Asia. The success of future United States military operations in Korea is now open to serious question.[41]

Japan, continued the report, was a troubling weak point in the US military position in the Far East.

> There are no United States combat forces in Japan available either for the enforcement of occupation controls or for opposing any possible military encroachment by the USSR into any part of Japan, nor does it appear probable that such forces will become available prior to resolution of the situation in Korea. Further, all major United States Navy and Air Force forces in the Far East are fully occupied in the military effort in Korea. In this connection, General MacArthur has made an urgent request that he receive substantial reinforcements of Army forces at once in order to provide reasonable safeguards against any sudden Soviet thrust at Japan while our forces are committed in Korea. Japanese internal security forces, although presently maintaining law and order, are wholly inadequate to resist any possible military aggression by the USSR and may not even be sufficient effectively to provide for the internal security of Japan in the face of internal communist activities. Thus, Japan is, in effect, a military vacuum.

The report argues against moving ahead at that time with peace treaty negotiations with Japan.

> The Joint Chiefs of Staff consider that the military interests of the United States would now best be served by steps which would lead to the increased capability of Japan to provide for its own security and defense at the earliest practicable date. They believe that such an effort on the part of Japan, in order to be effective, will require changes in the Japanese constitution. The Joint Chiefs of Staff feel it essential, therefore, that no negotiations for a peace treaty with Japan should be undertaken until such changes have been made.

The State Department accepted the need for Japan to rearm, but it faced a diplomatic conundrum. Rearming Japan would meet resistance from US allies in the region that had suffered from Japanese aggression. The United States would need to assuage their concerns. Equally daunting was the task of persuading the Japanese, who had just been disarmed by the Allies, to reverse course and embark on rearmament.

As a solution to the conundrum, the State Department returned to the concept of a Pacific pact, which MacArthur had criticized. The idea was for the United States to forge a pact with Australia, Japan, New Zealand, the Philippines, and, if possible, with Indonesia. Those nations could undertake collective defense in accordance with Article 51 of the UN Charter. Each participant would regard an attack on any other participant as an attack on itself and would respond accordingly.[42]

Dulles envisioned two primary objectives for the Pacific pact. One, the arrangement would provide for a joint response to an attack by any aggressor, even an attack by Japan. That would reassure the other pact members as to their safety from potential Japanese aggression. The security assurance would be operative regardless of whether the impending peace treaty with Japan imposed limits on Japanese rearmament.

Two, the arrangement would position Japan's new military might as part of an international security-assurance organization rather than as an autonomous national force. "This would be responsive," Dulles suggested, "to what seems to be the preponderant wish of the Japanese people and their leaders and might make it possible for Japan to rearm without a head-on collision with the present Japanese Constitution."[43]

Dulles returned to Japan in late January 1951 and commenced peace treaty negotiations with the Japanese government. He proposed a three-fold approach that reflected the logic described above: (1) a peace treaty equipped with a security clause based on the UN Charter; (2) a bilateral agreement that granted the United States the right to maintain military bases in Japan; (3) a Pacific pact that would be a framework for Japanese rearmament.[44]

3 The Japanese Government's Stance

Positioning Japan as a free world nation

Japan's government learned in autumn 1949 that possible approaches to a peace treaty were under study in the US government. That triggered vigorous debate about what sort of treaty was desirable and possible and about how to approach the negotiations. The central question was whether to pursue a comprehensive treaty with all the Allied Powers, including China and the Soviet Union, or whether to pursue a treaty just with the United States and other free world counterparts.

In the event, the government adopted the stance of favoring a peace treaty with just the United States and other free world nations. Backing a comprehensive treaty were the Socialist Party and the Communist Party. Also expressing support for a comprehensive treaty was the Peace Study Group. That group, which comprised several dozen Japanese scholars, issued a statement on January 15, 1950, that called for a comprehensive treaty.[45]

The peace treaty, insisted the Peace Issues Discussion Group in its statement, needed to be comprehensive in content and in the scope of signatories. Otherwise, it would be a peace treaty in name only and would have the opposite effect to that of making and maintaining peace. Signing a treaty with just Western nations would aggravate East-West tensions and increase the risk of another war.

A comprehensive approach to the peace treaty, the statement asserted, was especially important in atoning for Japan's wartime aggression. Japan needed to "tackle the daunting task of bridge building between [East and West]." The statement characterized the United Nations as "the present-day crystallization of humankind's striving since antiquity for peace" and called for Japan to attain UN membership and abide rigorously by the UN principle of neutral nonintervention. It noted, additionally, that "providing military bases for use by an individual nation" violated Japan's constitution. The statement also suggested that failing to conclude a comprehensive peace treaty would sever Japan's trade relations with China and complicate the task of achieving economic self-sufficiency.

Yoshida had no patience for such arguments. The prime minister, a diplomacy realist, found the Peace Issues Discussion Group's argument divorced from reality and unworthy of serious consideration. Yoshida had enunciated his view on the proper scope of the treaty signatories on November 12, 1949, in response to a question on the floor of the upper house of the Diet.

> The question of whether we should have a peace treaty with a limited range of counterparties or with a comprehensive range of counterparties is not at issue for us here today. It's a matter determined by circumstances beyond our borders; that is, by international relations. We don't have any choice in the matter.[46]

What Yoshida was expressing was his frank perception of Japan's clout as a nation and position in the world. From his perspective, concluding a peace treaty simultaneously with both Eastern and Western counterparties was out of the question. That approach might appeal to some as an ideal, but it was, in his eyes, utterly unpracticable. Yoshida later ridiculed the calls for a comprehensive peace treaty as akin to grasping for a blossom seen in a mirror. Heeding those calls, he reflected later amid the heightening of Cold War tensions, would have simply extended the occupation and delayed the signing of the peace treaty.[47]

Yoshida's assertion about the scope of the peace treaty being in the hands of Japan's counterparties was just part of the story. He had another, more proactive reason for opting for a treaty with a limited range of signatories. The prime minister had what he perceived to be Japan's best interests at heart. In his view, narrowing the scope of counterparties to the United States and other free world nations positioned Japan squarely in the Western camp. He was confident that alignment with the United States was the best footing for Japan's postwar foreign relations.

Yoshida was alert to the historical record with respect to Japanese relations with the United States and the United Kingdom. Robust political and economic ties with those nations, starting after the Meiji Restoration of 1868, had engendered prosperity for Japan. The Japanese became drunk, however, on economic growth and on military victories over the waning imperial might of Qing dynasty China and czarist Russia. They acquired a grossly exaggerated sense of national power and embarked foolishly on an expansionary war in China and, worse, on war in the Pacific with the United States and the United Kingdom. The inevitable, total defeat erased Japan's economic and industrial attainment.

Making enemies of the United States and the United Kingdom had proved a fatal deviation from Japan's formerly successful foreign policy. Japan was a maritime nation. Its national vitality hinged on trade across the ocean. The United States held sway over Pacific. It possessed the world's largest economy and boasted a democratic tradition. Japan's practical national interest took precedence over ideological or philosophical considerations for Yoshida, and US alignment was the natural choice in that respect.[48]

Bases for the US military

Yoshida went to work on promoting a peace treaty. His finance minister, Ikeda Hayato, traveled to the United States in April 1950, ostensibly to observe US fiscal and economic practices firsthand. Ikeda was also traveling as an emissary charged with conveying Yoshida's thoughts on Japanese national security to the US government. Ikeda later served as Japan's prime minister in the early 1960s, when he instituted the famously successful Income Doubling Plan.

On May 3, Ikeda met with Joseph Dodge, then the fiscal advisor to the undersecretary of the army. Dodge had served previously in Japan as MacArthur's economic advisor, and Ikeda had worked with him in implementing the rigorous fiscal guidelines known as the Dodge Line. The American sent a detailed report of his discussion with Ikeda to the assistant secretary of state, William Butterworth. In his report, Dodge conveyed the message from Yoshida as follows:

> [T]he Government desires the earliest possible treaty. As such a treaty probably would require the maintenance of US forces to secure the treaty terms and for other purposes, if the US Government hesitates to make these conditions, the Japanese Government will try to find a way to offer them.[49]

Butterworth forwarded Dodge's report to Dulles, accompanying it with a note that characterized Yoshida's message as worthy of attention. "It is the first expression we have had at an official level," Butterworth commented, "of the attitude of the Japanese Government on the peace treaty and related questions."[50]

Japanese generally assumed that confining the scope of treaty counterparties to the United States and other free world nations would mean retaining US bases. Opposition to the bases was the reason cited by numerous Japanese for preferring a treaty with all the Allied powers.

For Yoshida, hosting US bases was a foregone conclusion. The only issues were when to propose the retention of the bases in Japan and whether the proposal should emanate from the Japanese government or the US government. Yoshida apparently decided that a Japanese offer to host US bases would stimulate US government progress on the peace treaty.

Hosting the US bases was, of course, a means of ensuring Japanese national security. Yoshida had concluded that after concluding the peace treaty Japan needed to depend on US military protection. As the Joint Chiefs of Staff had concluded, "Japanese internal security forces . . . [were] wholly inadequate to resist any possible military aggression by the USSR and may not even [have been] sufficient effectively to provide for the internal security of Japan in the face of internal communist activities."[51]

Relying on the United Nations for national security might have seemed the ideal course for ensuring Japanese security. Yoshida had determined, however, that the United Nations was less than functional in that regard and that concluding a security pact with an individual nation or group of nations was, realistically, the only option for Japan. The United States, meanwhile, was the only nation that possessed sufficient military might to protect Japan and that was suited to the task in respect to ongoing bilateral relations.[52]

No rearmament for the time being

Hosting US bases thus became a quid pro quo for Yoshida in securing a peace treaty with the United States and other Western powers. It entailed a delicate balancing act for the prime minister, however, in connection with rearmament. Yoshida detailed his views on that issue in a memorandum presented to the Dulles mission on January 30, 1951. The memorandum, titled "Suggested Agenda," carried a typewritten note in the margin: "I am setting forth below my private views, on which the cabinet is yet to be consulted. They do not, therefore, represent necessarily the official and final opinion of the government.–S[higeru] Y[oshida]."[53] In the memorandum, the prime minister explained that Japan was not in a position to undertake rearmament and offered the following three reasons:

> There are Japanese who advocate rearmament. But their arguments do not appear to be founded on a thorough study of the problem, nor do they necessarily represent the sentiment of the masses. . . .
>
> Japan lacks basic resources required for modern armament. The burden of rearmament would immediately crush our national economy and impoverish our people, breeding social unrest, which is exactly what the Communists want. Rearmament, intended to serve the purposes of security, would on the contrary endanger the nation's security from within. Today Japan's security depends far more on the stabilization of people's livelihood than on armament. . . .
>
> It is a solemn fact that our neighbor nations fear the recurrence of Japanese aggression. Internally, we have reasons for exercising caution against the possibility of the reappearance of old militarism. For the immediate purpose we should seek other means than rearmament for maintaining the country's security.

Yoshida expressed another concern about rearmament in conversation with Frank Kowalski, Jr., the chief of staff of the US Military Advisory Assistance Group. Kowalski had served as the chief military governor of Kyoto, of Osaka, and of the Chugoku region (western Honshu). As the head of the Military Advisory Assistance Group, he was overseeing the creation of Japan's National Police Reserve. Yoshida emphasized to Kowalski that dispatching members of the police reserve to serve in Korea was absolutely not an option. That apparently reflected his awareness of sensitivity in Australia and elsewhere to the threat of resurgent Japanese militarism and his concern about the potential adverse impact on the peace treaty.[54]

Nishimura Kumao headed the Japanese Foreign Ministry's Treaties Bureau and had a firsthand grasp of Yoshida's anti-rearmament stance in advance of the peace treaty negotiations. He summarized Yoshida's position in notes dated January 13, 1950.

> The prime minister is adamantly opposed to rearmament. The objective reality [of East-West relations] is that the two sides will not plunge into all-out war. The present confrontation, though subject to fluctuations in intensity, will continue indefinitely. In the meantime, we need to avoid succumbing to a war of nerves and the occasional shouts of "War!" "War!" The Soviet Union is not about to invade Japan. From that perspective, the prime minister's opposition to rearmament and his determination to ensure [Japan's] national security by other means made sense.[55]

The ideal proposal that wasn't

Yoshida instructed the Japanese peace treaty negotiators to draft a treaty proposal centered on the ideas of demilitarizing Japan and the Korean Peninsula, designating a swath of territory to be free of military air bases, and reducing the great powers' naval presence in the Western Pacific. He wanted the proposal as a bargaining chip in the upcoming negotiations.[56] The prime minister had consulted occasionally with trusted former officers in the Japanese military on an informal basis. And he issued a request to them on October 24, 1950, to help with drafting the treaty.

> In regard to rearming Japan, I want to abide by the stance of eschewing rearmament until the peace treaty is in place. That will mean exposing us to the question of how we intend to provide for Japan's national security. I want to be ready with a proposal invested with the ideal of a demilitarized zone and a warship exclusionary periphery. I want you to lend assistance in preparing a draft that expresses that ideal.[57]

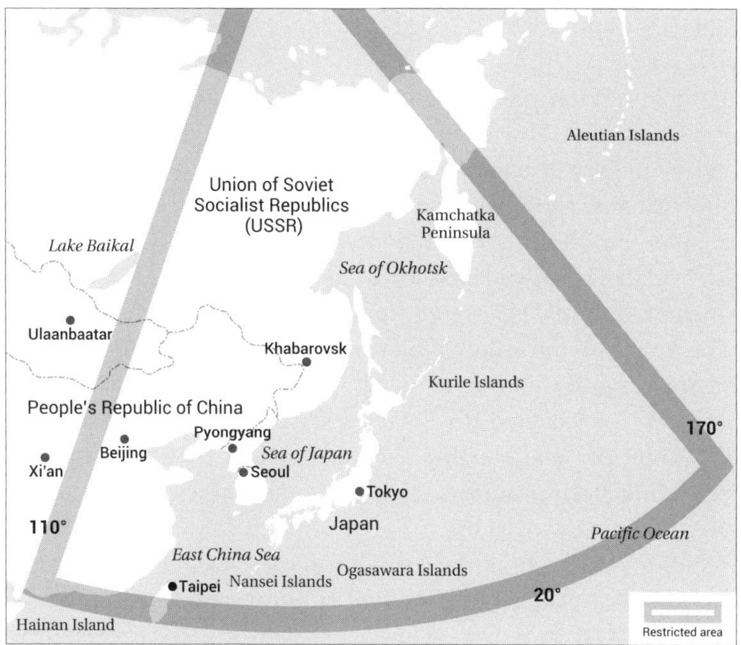

Map of the restricted area according to Yoshida's idealistic proposal. Adapted from information in Japan Ministry of Foreign Affairs, *Heiwa jōyaku no teiketsu*, 3:209–212, and Ōtake, *Sengo Nihon*, 2:26–27.

The treaty draft prepared with the assistance of Yoshida's military advisors emerged two months later as the "Proposal for Promoting Peace and Security in the Northern Pacific." It called for demilitarizing Japan and the Korean Peninsula and for China, the Soviet Union, the United Kingdom, and the United States to observe limits on their military capacity under monitoring by the United Nations. The proposed limits on military capacity included: (1) demilitarizing the Korean border zone and other regions agreed by the four powers; (2) imposing a freeze on land and sea military installations in the area east of 110 degrees east longitude, west of 170 degrees east longitude, and north of 20 degrees north latitude; and (3) restricting the functionality of land and sea military forces in that area to national self-defense. Under the proposal, the four powers would refrain from deploying aircraft carriers, submarines, or other strategically potent warships in the restricted area. Activity by UN members in accordance with the UN Charter would be exempt, however, from the treaty restrictions.[58]

Yoshida did not produce the idealistic proposal described above in his talks with Dulles. The restrictions in the proposal, had they been implemented, would not necessarily have been strategically disadvantageous to the United States. They would have prohibited an increase in US troop levels in Japan, but the treaty would have permitted the US bases there to remain in place. Meanwhile, US forces deployed under the UN flag to fight the Korean War would be exempt from the treaty restrictions.

The treaty, on the other hand, would have limited military expansion by the Soviets and Chinese. Its geographical freeze on military installations would have covered the Soviet east, from Lake Baikal to the Kamchatka Peninsula, and roughly the eastern half of China. Even if the Americans had been receptive, the Soviets and Chinese would never have accepted the treaty provisions.

Issues unaddressed in the treaty proposal included how to reconcile the contradictory claims by China's victorious Communists and defeated but unvanquished Nationalists and what sort of political system would prevail on the demilitarized Korean Peninsula. The proposal, in other words, amounted to little more than idealistic musing and never had a chance of taking hold. Sure enough, Yoshida decided to delete the reference to that proposal from the talking points for his negotiations with Dulles.[59]

Some scholars have suggested that Yoshida was remiss in withholding the idealistic proposal. Producing that proposal,[60] however, would surely have proved counterproductive with regard to resisting US pressure to rearm. The US military establishment was opposed to negotiating a peace treaty with Japan while war raged on the Korean Peninsula. Dulles and his kindred spirits in the State Department were contending with that opposition in struggling to bring a peace treaty about. They would have regarded the idealistic proposal, which had no chance of taking shape, as a lack of good faith.

The Foreign Ministry's perspective

Yoshida decided that hosting US bases was the least bad way to ensure Japanese national security under the peace treaty. That presented Japan's Foreign Ministry with the task of working out the details of how to accommodate the bases. The ministry had been studying the implications of different peace treaty arrangements for Japan since autumn 1949. It had generated several documents that detailed the advantages of restricting the range of counterparties to the United States and other Western nations. The ministry had not worked out a stance, however, on how Japan should approach the issue of national security.

That restricting the peace treaty signatories to Western nations and Japan would mean relying on the United States for protection was clear. What was anything but clear was how Japan would manage security assurance in the context of its constitution, how it would assert the stature of a sovereign nation, or how it would reassure the citizenry of not getting drawn into a foreign war. Nor had the Foreign Ministry developed a coherent position on the specifics of hosting bases. Most in the ministry were of the same attitude as that expressed in the earlier Ashida letter. That is, they would have preferred, if possible, to avoid having an enduring US military presence on Japanese soil.[61]

The alternatives became moot on September 14, 1950. That was when Truman announced at a press conference that the US and Japanese governments would commence negotiations on a peace treaty. Press coverage of the announcement conveyed the broad outlines of the peace treaty envisioned by the US government. Japan would conclude the treaty with the United States and its principal Western allies, and the United States would maintain military bases in Japan on a continuing basis.

Implementing the peace treaty would require an administrative agreement. Japan's Foreign Ministry hastily began work on a proposal for that agreement. That meant developing guidelines for accommodating the US bases in conformance with Yoshida's intentions and with the ministry's study findings. The ministry predicated its work on three emphases:

1. The administrative agreement should be a separate instrument from the peace treaty;
2. The express rationale for the US military presence should differ definitively from that of the occupation;
3. The bilateral administrative agreement between Japan and the United States should mesh with the principles of the United Nations.

Here is what the Foreign Ministry had to say about each of those points:

1. That the administrative agreement should be a separate instrument from the peace treaty:

> Enshrining directly in the peace treaty the principle of stationing [US] troops [in Japan] would portray the presence of the troops as something imposed [on Japan]. For us [in government], explaining the stationing of troops as something imposed on us might be the easier way to proceed in regard to domestic relations, but it is hardly the appropriate way to proceed in regard to the larger scheme of Japanese-US relations.
>
> First of all, enshrining the stationing of troops in the peace treaty, which is possessed of the character of permanence, would impart psychologically the impression of semipermanence, even if, for example, the treaty specified that the troop presence was to be of limited duration. In addition, various aspects of the [US] military presence could become the subject of future negotiations. That could mean [if the stationing of US troops was prescribed in the peace treaty] making changes in the peace treaty. The peace treaty ought properly to be sacrosanct, and any such changes could discomfit the United Nations.
>
> Secondly, the quartering of troops is an emotional issue for the Japanese, and the citizenry will inevitably perceive and criticize [the US military presence] as something imposed unilaterally by the victor on the vanquished. The Communists will take advantage of negative perceptions of the US military presence to fan anti-US sentiment.[62]

2. That the express rationale for the US military presence should differ definitively from that of the occupation:

> The peace treaty needs to occasion the restoration of Japanese sovereignty and across-the-board renewal that will allow for tackling national rebuilding with a fresh spirit. . . . Concluding a separate treaty with the United States that resulted in leaving the present occupation forces in place, both in form and in substance, would simply betray our expectations and elicit the antipathy of the people. If [US] troops are to be stationed [in Japan], we need to prescribe their locations, the cost of their upkeep, their

privileges, and the duration of their presence with a treaty and ensure that they are not, in name or in reality, a continuation of the occupation.[63]

3. That the bilateral administrative agreement between Japan and the United States should mesh with the principles of the United Nations:

> A clear linkage with the United Nations is absolutely necessary. As renewed sovereignty dawns, one thing about which all Japanese will agree is the need for UN assurance of our national security. . . . We understand, of course, that we will essentially be asking the United States to defend our nation and that we will need to furnish the United States with all necessary cooperation and assistance in that regard. To openly conclude outright a defense pact with the United States would reveal overly a brazen focus on a third-party nation or third-party nations. Even if that were to be the case in reality, we need to craft the treaty formally in a manner that fulfills our obligations and that will admit of criticism from no one. Then and only then will we be able to avoid constitutional debate over whether or not the provisions of the treaty violate Article 9 of our constitution (which renounces war and pledges nonmilitarization) and address the sentiment of the Japanese people. We can conclude an agreement with the United States in regard to stationing [US] troops [in Japan] only if the treaty includes a provision that states clearly that we believe that the United States is acting on behalf of the United Nations, a global security-assurance organization, in accordance with a UN resolution and that doing so enables both Japan and the United States to fulfill their obligations.[64]

At the heart of the Foreign Ministry's plan for ensuring Japan's national security was the third of the three points emphasized cited: "a clear linkage with the United Nations." As noted, the United Nations had emerged as an influential consideration early in the ministry's study of peace treaty issues: "Pursue national security by acceding to membership in the United Nations and thus becoming part of the UN collective security regimen." That choice would satisfy three crucial conditions: philosophical consistency with Japan's peace constitution, the reality of Japan's disarmament, and the Japanese people's desire for sovereign autonomy.[65]

Alas, Japanese recognized amid the Cold War that the United Nations would not fulfill the role that some had hoped. Relying on the United States for national security became Japan's only realistic choice. The Foreign Ministry sought to express that choice as one based on the UN Charter, the "constitution" of the international community. Its hope was to earn support for that choice among the Japanese people and in the international community while fulfilling the above three conditions.

Emphasis on Article 51 of the UN Charter

The Foreign Ministry, in favoring US protection linked to the UN security regimen, needed a mechanism for that linkage. It outlined a proposed linkage in a policy paper submitted to Yoshida on October 5, 1950.[66] The proposal was not well-received by the prime minister.

Titled "Policy Requests for Responding to the Conceptual Framework of the US Proposal for a Peace Treaty with Japan," the paper recommended basing the US military presence in Japan on a resolution by the UN general assembly. Its authors argued that such conceptual positioning was the ideal way of framing the security arrangement. It would avoid presenting the arrangement as a special relationship for Japan with a single counterparty. Instead, it would position the arrangement in the framework of an international security-assurance organization, the United Nations.

Yoshida rejected the paper out of hand, writing on its cover,

> Right out of the mouths of the opposition parties. Meaningless argument, absolutely worthless. Needs a lot more work to qualify as a statesmanlike study. SY[67]

Heading the working team in the Foreign Ministry that prepared the paper was the aforementioned Nishimura Kumao. He interpreted Yoshida's rejection as criticism of

> our inability to fully abandon our earlier fixation with thinking and conclusions predicated on a peace treaty with a comprehensive range of counterparties.[68]

Exactly which portion or portions of the text Yoshida found most similar to the opposition's rhetoric and most unstatesmanlike is unclear.

What we do know is that Yoshida's criticism provoked intense debate in the Foreign Ministry and that the working team then changed tack. It elected to cite Article 51 of the UN Charter in linking the Japanese-US agreement to UN principles.[69] The group's new approach took shape in a policy paper titled "About a Japanese-US Treaty for National Security."

> As a practical matter and as became clear in the Korean unrest, the United Nations requires a certain amount of time to decide on a response in the wake of a military attack. That is the case even if the United Nations begins its deliberations promptly. The United Nations has acknowledged that problem in its charter and has addressed the problem with the inclusion of Article 51. Thus would the treaty envisioned between Japan and the United States meet with UN approval. In practice, [the provisions of Article 51] denote a crucially important function [emphasis added].[70]

Article 51 of the UN Charter reads as follows:

> Nothing in the present Charter shall impair the inherent right of individual or collective self-defence if an armed attack occurs against a Member of the United Nations, until the Security Council has taken measures necessary to maintain international peace and security. Measures taken by Members in the exercise of this right of self-defence shall be immediately reported to the Security Council and shall not in any way affect the authority and responsibility of the Security Council under the present Charter to take at any time such action as it deems necessary in order to maintain or restore international peace and security.

In invoking Article 51, the Foreign Ministry was implicitly suggesting a NATO-like solution for stationing troops in Japan. The authors of the aforementioned "Policy Requests for Responding to the Conceptual Framework of the US Proposal for a Peace Treaty with Japan" had confessed to "an extremely weak connection with the United Nations." Invoking Article 51, however, positioned the US military presence in Japan as the Japanese and US fulfillment of collective defense obligations. It underlined the importance of Japanese and US bilateral ties and asserted an ostensibly equal footing for those ties.

The Foreign Ministry was preoccupied with achieving a security treaty that would go down well domestically. Any agreement for hosting US troops would need to respect Japan's sovereign pride and the feelings of the Japanese people. That preoccupation accounts for all three emphases cited previously: that the administrative agreement should be a separate instrument from the peace treaty; that the express rationale for the US military presence should differ definitively from that of the occupation; and that the bilateral administrative agreement between Japan and the United States should mesh with the principles of the United Nations.

Yoshida was interested primarily in avoiding rearmament and was less concerned than the Foreign Ministry was with the formal rationalization for hosting US troops. That said, he, too, was concerned with managing the US relationship in a manner that would not offend Japanese self-respect, and his government observed the above three emphases. That became its stance in pursuing an agreement under which Japan would rely on the United States for national security, would host US military bases, and would refrain from rearmament for the time being.

4 Japanese-US Negotiations

Low expectations

The treaty talks between Japan and the United States took place intermittently from January to August 1951. Dulles arrived in Japan on January 25 for the first round of talks, which continued until February 11. Working out a security treaty was part of the work on the peace treaty, and the Japanese and US negotiators hammered out the basic outlines of a security treaty during Dulles's stay. The description of the purpose of the US military presence in Japan became a sticking point, however, and underwent extensive revision before the signing of the treaty. Even after the signing, negotiating the details of the stationing of US troops in Japan proved difficult, and the outcome was less than agreeable for the Japanese.

Dulles and Yoshida's first session got off to an awkward start at 4:30 p.m. on January 29. Yoshida appeared sans retinue and declared at the outset that he had "one or two points he wished to raise." Dulles's deputy and later ambassador to Japan, John Allison, recounted the ensuing discussion in a detailed report. An extensive portion of his report appears below:

> [Yoshida] recalled his statements to Mr. Dulles last June that in dealing with the Japanese people it was necessary to consider their *amour-propre* [italics in original] and in this connection there were certain aspects of ordinances and legislation which had been inspired by the Occupation which, in Mr. Yoshida's opinion, should be altered prior to concluding a peace treaty. He stated that he was having a list of these matters prepared for presentation to SCAP. . . .
>
> The Prime Minister then went on to speak of certain economic problems which were of concern and he mentioned particularly necessity for expansion of fishing areas, increase in ship-building and also the necessity of continuing and increasing investments from the United States in Japanese industrial enterprises. Mr. Yoshida spoke of the long term necessity of trading with China, and while he realized that in view of the present communist domination of that country it would not be possible to expect great results in the near future, nevertheless, he believed that in the long run the Chinese would adopt the attitude that "war is war and trade is trade" and that it would be possible for a reasonable degree of trade to take place between Japan and China. In this connection, Mr. Yoshida advanced the thought that Japanese business men, because of their long acquaintance with and experience in China, will be the best fifth column of democracy against the Chinese communists. . . .
>
> In an effort to elicit from Mr. Yoshida definite opinions on some of the major problems connected with the treaty, Mr. Dulles brought up the question of Japan's security and asked Mr. Yoshida for his views as to how this problem should be dealt with. The Prime Minister said that it was necessary to go very slowly in connection with any possible rearmament of Japan as he foresaw two great obstacles. The first was the danger that any precipitate rearmament would bring back the Japanese militarists who had now gone "underground" and might expose the State to the danger of again being dominated by the military. Mr. Yoshida said that it would be necessary to adopt legislation which would ensure that the military could not take over the Government as in the past and that other

> steps should be taken to avoid the dangers inherent in the recreation of a military class. The other obstacle which confronted Japan in rearmament was the economic one. Japan was a proud country and did not want to receive charity from anyone but the creation of a military force just at the time when Japan was beginning to get on its feet financially would be a severe strain and probably result in a lower standard of living. Here again, time would be necessary in order to lay a sound foundation for the economic support of any rearmament. Mr. Dulles stated that he recognized these problems but that in the present state of the world it was necessary for all nations that wanted to remain free to make sacrifices. He outlined some of the sacrifices which the people of the United States were making and then inquired whether the Premier was taking the position that the dangers mentioned constituted a reason for doing nothing or merely a recognition of obstacles to be overcome. Mr. Dulles pointed out that, at the present time, free nations of the world through the UN were endeavoring to create a system of collective security and that it was necessary for all who expected to benefit by such a system to make contributions in accordance with their own means and abilities. No one would expect the Japanese contribution at present to be large but it was felt that Japan should be willing to make at least a token contribution and a commitment to a general cause of collective security. While Mr. Yoshida did not make a definite answer to Mr. Dulles' question, the idea of some form of collective security arrangement to which Japan could contribute seemed to appeal to him and he did say that Japan would be willing to make some contribution. No indication, however, was given as to what form such a contribution might take, and it appeared that Mr. Yoshida did not wish at this time to be definitely committed in any manner.[71]

In calling for Japan "to make at least a token contribution," Dulles unquestionably had rearmament in mind. He was also emphasizing, however, the importance of Japan's demonstrating the will and the effort to participate in free world collective security.[72] Dulles therefore presumably regarded Yoshida's mention of a readiness "to make some contribution," even if Japan would need to "go very slowly," as something of a concession. He was disappointed, though, at the prime minister's reticence to offer any "indication . . . as to what form such a contribution might take."

Dulles expressed frustration at the difficulty of getting "the conversation around to a point where he could get any reaction at all from Mr. Yoshida." And he described the prime minister's stance as "a puff ball performance."[73]

Ambassador William Sebald, the State Department representative in Japan, attended the Dulles-Yoshida talks and wrote an evaluation of the talks that accompanied Allison's report. His evaluation included the following observation:

> It is my view that the Prime Minister came to yesterday's conference totally unprepared to discuss detailed provisions and that his remarks were more in the nature of feelers rather than any effort to come to grips with the real problems.[74]

Dulles and Yoshida paid a courtesy call on MacArthur after their meeting. Yoshida reported that Dulles had asked him how Japan would contribute to the free world and that he had struggled to provide a satisfactory answer. He had visited MacArthur about ten days earlier to request help, if necessary, with the upcoming talks with Dulles. The prime minister had been especially concerned about how to deal with the inevitable pressure for Japan to rearm swiftly.[75] To Yoshida's relief, MacArthur delivered exactly the message that he had hoped to hear.

> The free world shouldn't demand military might of Japan at this time. That's not something that Japan can provide right now. Japan possesses military production capacity, however, and it possesses a large labor force. We should tap those assets to strengthen the might of the free world.[76]

Dulles and Yoshida's second session took place on January 31 and proceeded in reference to the memorandum "Suggested Agenda," submitted by the Japanese on the previous day.[77] The meeting was, Dulles said afterwards, "more satisfactory than the first one, specific problems of the security arrangements and stationing of troops having been discussed."[78]

Yoshida's "Suggested Agenda" included, as noted, a three-point explanation as to why rearmament was impossible for Japan at the time. The prime minister hedged that explanation with the following expression of interest in contributing to international peace in other ways. He instructed his staff to add these two paragraphs, along with the disclaimer that the memorandum comprised his "private views," after the meeting with Dulles and MacArthur on January 29.[79]

> Nowadays international peace is directly tied up with internal peace and order. In this sense, we must preserve domestic peace, for which0 we are determined to assume full responsibility by ourselves alone. For this purpose, it will be necessary for us to increase forthwith the numbers of our police and maritime security personnel and reinforce their equipment.
>
> We desire consultation on the question of Japan's specific contribution to the common defense of the free world, in which we are eager to play a positive role.[80]

Dulles commented that he understood the economic issues cited in Yoshida's "Suggested Agenda." He argued, however, that those issues were a poor excuse for not participating in defending the free world, and he called on Japan to overcome the issues and fulfill its responsibility. Dulles added that strengthening the police should be a first step. He said that he wanted the Japanese to determine what sort of steps they should take next and to put their determination gradually into action. Dulles insisted in passing that he harbored only modest expectations.[81]

Yoshida replied that

> the cooperation Japan can provide in strengthening the defense of the free world includes, apart from military force, the nation's production capacity. We will provide information about Japan's excess production capacity in shipbuilding and in other sectors.[82]

We assume that by "military force" Yoshida meant the police function.

Dulles returned repeatedly during the talks with Yoshida to a core US expectation of Japan: demonstrate the will and the effort to participate in and contribute to the sound development of the free world. Where Dulles and Yoshida differed was with regard to whether rearmament was essential to demonstrating that will and effort.

Yoshida wanted the Americans to recognize that Japan could not undertake true rearmament at that time and wanted them to accept the strengthening of the police function and the provision of military production capacity as a sufficient demonstration of the will and effort in question. Dulles, on the other hand, acknowledged the economic difficulty inherent in Japanese rearmament but wanted the Japanese to overcome that difficulty. He was prepared to moderate his expectations and to countenance rearmament at a gradual pace.

The emphasis on Japan's becoming a member of the free world and contributing to free world vitality was true to Dulles's well-established orientation. Dulles had inherited the internationalist perspective of Woodrow Wilson. He regarded strengthening the free world and nurturing solidarity among free world nations as a quest of universal and unwavering importance. Perhaps on account of his training as a lawyer, Dulles dwelled on fundamental principles in his work in international negotiations in the private and public sectors.[83]

War was raging on the Korean Peninsula as Dulles was holding talks in Japan with Yoshida. The US military was scrambling to reverse the momentum of the unexpectedly ferocious onslaught from the North Korean and Chinese forces. A sense of urgency permeated Dulles's philosophical preoccupation with free world solidarity and his calls for Japan to contribute to that solidarity.

The urgency was possessed of a concrete dimension for his counterparts in the Defense Department and in the military. For them, securing an increase in Japan's self-defense capability would free up US troops to redeploy on the Korean Peninsula. The strengthening of Japan's self-defense capacity was crucial, conversely, to maintaining the presence that the US military needed and demanded in Japan. In the absence of a visible Japanese commitment to self-defense, a continued US military presence would simply be an extension of the occupation.

No rearmament to secure a peace treaty

Japan's negotiating team became seriously concerned about the progress of the Dulles-Yoshida talks after the first two sessions. On February 1, the Japanese team presented its US counterpart at a working-level session with a document titled "Formula Concerning Japanese-American Cooperation for Their Mutual Security."[84]

The "formula" included a provision for a continuing US military presence in Japan. It also provided that "Japan shall cooperate by all possible means with the United States to meet the act of aggression against Japan." That elicited a question from the US negotiating team as to exactly what cooperation Japan was prepared to offer. To this question, the Japanese replied as follows:

> We are prepared to cooperate by all conceivable means that are legally and practically possible. That includes, with regard to physical force, policing capacity, industrial production capacity, labor, the provision of sites for [US military] facilities, and transport capacity.[85]

Japan's negotiating team was adhering to its formerly stated stance of confining military cooperation to what was possible without rearmament. The US team, predictably unsatisfied, replied accordingly.

> If Japan is prepared to cooperate with the United States through policing capacity and industrial capacity, we would expect it to at least deploy some degree of ground forces by way of cooperation. We understand that Japan recognizes the need for strengthening its National Police Reserve. However, that is a matter, at this stage, of fortifying Japan's domestic security capacity. Our concern is with the next stage and what degree of ground forces Japan can muster. Expanding the ground forces, of course, should progress gradually. The United States, meanwhile, will shift forces from Japan to other sites in step with that progress. We need to start, however, by at least gaining a grasp of the size of the ground forces that Japan is prepared to create. We are prepared fiscally and materially to assist Japan with creating the ground forces in question.[86]

Yoshida saw that a compromise would be necessary to achieve meaningful progress in the negotiations. He instructed his negotiating team on February 3 to draw up a proposal that would include two new measures: one, establish a 50,000-man security force apart from the National Police Reserve and the Maritime Safety Agency (coast guard), and two, establish a Security Planning Headquarters as the precursor of a future military command headquarters.[87] Yoshida describes this second initiative in his memoir, though he omits direct mention of the new security force that he proposed.

> Something that had become clear from the negotiations was that we would never secure a treaty without indicating to Dulles some sort of readiness to devote genuine effort to self-defense. The Americans were insistent about us showing a plan for ground forces as the first stage in self-defense efforts after the conclusion of the peace treaty. After considering various options, I proposed strengthening the National Police Reserve and the Maritime Safety Agency and coordinating things with a Ministry of National Security. The idea for a national security ministry had been around for a while, and it was somewhat satisfactory for Dulles.[88]

Here is the proposal that Yoshida actually submitted to Dulles.

> Initial Steps for Rearmament Program
> Simultaneously with the coming into force of the Peace Treaty and the Japanese-American Security Cooperation Agreement it will be necessary for Japan to embark upon a program of rearmament. The following are the principal features of this program contemplated by the Japanese government.
>
> a) Security forces, land and sea, totaling 50,000, will be created apart from the existing police forces and the National Police Reserve. These security forces will be specially trained and more powerfully equipped, and placed under the proposed Ministry of National Security. The 50,000 men will mark the start of Japan's new democratic armed forces.
> b) What might be termed a "Security Planning Headquarters" will be set up in the National Security Ministry. Experts, conversant with American and British military affairs, will be assigned to this Headquarters; they will participate in the activities of the Joint Committee to be established under the Japanese-American Security Cooperation Agreement, and they will constitute the nucleus for the future General Staff of Japan's democratic armed forces. The government will seek the advice of American military experts (soldiers).
>
> February 3, 1951[89]

The origins of Yoshida's proposal and the basis for his "50,000" figure are unclear. Tanaka Akihiko, an authority on international relations, has suggested that it emerged just before Dulles arrived in Japan. Tanaka notes that Yoshida received a report from a group of military experts on January 19, 1951, about domestic security needs. That report suggested that Japan would need 50,000 additional police personnel, including supervisory staff and officers on the street, to maintain public order. Tanaka speculates that Yoshida latched onto that figure in a spur-of-the-moment sleight of hand.[90]

Japan, in any event, would require an additional 50,000 security personnel. Yoshida apparently used that figure to placate the Americans by representing it as the beginning of a military force. That interpretation meshes with the explanation by the Japanese Foreign Ministry to the US negotiators on February 2 about rearmament and the Japanese constitution. The Foreign Ministry's explanation emphasized that amending Article 9 of the constitution would be necessary for rearmament but that amending the constitution was an extremely delicate matter and essentially impossible.

> To assume that the peace treaty will be concluded in the not distant future and to build a ground force in the name of military preparedness quickly and simultaneously with concluding the peace treaty would be extremely complex for Japan and would entail difficult problems. From the government's perspective, the only feasible way to achieve the objective of rearmament is, until the peace treaty has been concluded, Japan has reentered the international community, and the Japanese people have come to regard armament as something Japan should rightly possess, through building a physical force within the conceptual framework of strengthening police capacity for ensuring domestic order.[91]

The 50,000-person increase was a best-effort offer by Yoshida to fulfill the billing for "initial steps for rearmament program." It was something he could pitch to his domestic audience as an increase in police capacity for maintaining domestic order and to the Americans as "the start of Japan's new democratic armed forces."

We find no mention of how the Americans received Yoshida's offer in the official Japanese and US documentation of the negotiations. Michael M. Yoshitsu, however, interviewed US diplomats who participated in the negotiations for his 1983 book *Japan and the San Francisco Peace Settlement.* He quotes "a senior US official" as characterizing the Yoshida offer as "better than nothing but inadequate."[92]

Lukewarm regard for Yoshida's "initial steps" notwithstanding, the Americans accepted the proposal. They seem to have recognized that it truly was the best that Yoshida could do for the time being, and they held him to his word in the text ultimately adopted for the security treaty. Witness this passage from the preamble to the treaty:

> The United States of America, in the interest of peace and security, is presently willing to maintain certain of its armed forces in and about Japan, in the expectation, however, that Japan will itself increasingly assume responsibility for its own defense against direct and indirect aggression, always avoiding any armament which could be an offensive threat or serve other than to promote peace and security in accordance with the purposes and principles of the United Nations Charter.[93]

We suspect that the reference to Japan taking more responsibility for self-defense reflected a healthy dose of American optimism. It surely also reflected, however, substantive assurances from Yoshida during the talks with Dulles. That input was inevitable, given the weak hand that the prime minister was playing. Yet we marvel at how he made the most of the hand he'd been dealt.

Yoshida persevered, to the point of exasperating the Americans, in insisting on the need for proceeding "very slowly" with rearmament. He offered the concession of "initial steps for a rearmament program," but the substance of the offer fell far short of real rearmament, and the prime minister managed to avoid committing Japan to any concrete deadlines. Indeed, Japan made no formal commitment to rearmament in any public documents except the reference in the treaty preamble.

A three-document solution

The Japanese achieved a peace treaty on terms that were, considering their weak bargaining position, impressive. Yoshida attained his goal of concluding a peace treaty without committing to rearming Japan. He and the Foreign Ministry succeeded in avoiding any mention of a US military presence in Japan in the peace treaty. The Foreign Ministry had been concerned with avoiding treaty provisions that positioned Japan as a potential enemy of the Western powers, and the treaty addressed that concern completely by positioning Japan as a partner with Western nations in ensuring mutual security.[94] Japan secured affirmation in the treaty of its right under the UN Charter to conclude a security pact with another nation or with other nations, and it concluded a bilateral security treaty with the United States under that provision.[95]

We note that Dulles declined throughout the negotiations to propose a multilateral security arrangement on the order of NATO.[96] That was apparently due in part to UK resistance.[97] It also seems to have been partly due to Dulles's reading of the negotiations. He apparently determined that such an arrangement would not serve as a framework for Japanese rearmament.[98]

The Japanese surely would have resisted a proposal for a Pacific Treaty Organization, and the proposal would have impeded the progress of the Dulles-Yoshida talks. A proposal for a multilateral pact would have carried strong connotations of providing for security against Japan. The Japanese would hardly have felt comfortable about entering into such an arrangement.[99] Equally unreceptive were two natural partners for Japan and the United States in a Pacific security pact, Australia and New Zealand.

Dulles broached the idea of a multilateral pact with Australian and New Zealand government representatives after his first negotiating session with Yoshida. Both expressed strong resistance to joining hands with Japan in a security arrangement. The United States, abandoning the idea of a Pacific NATO, instead established a bilateral security treaty with the Philippines in August 1951 and the Australia, New Zealand, United States Security Treaty (ANZUS) the next month.[100] Those treaties complemented the Japanese-US treaty with regard to ensuring regional security while assuaging Australian, New Zealand, and Philippine concerns about Japan.

Another emphasis for the Foreign Ministry in the security treaty was making the US military presence palatable for the Japanese people. Thus were the Japanese nonplussed when the Americans submitted the draft proposal, Agreement Concerning Japanese-American Cooperation for Their Mutual Security, on February 2. That proposal drew heavily on the base-siting agreement that the United States concluded with the Philippines in 1947. It contained a plethora of provisions that detailed the rights and privileges of the resident US forces.[101]

All in all, the draft gave full and unvarnished voice to the aforementioned demands of the US military establishment: "The Treaty must give the United States the right to maintain armed forces in Japan, wherever, for so long, and to such extent as it deems necessary" (see endnote 30). Nishimura recalls that "a perusal [of the text] imparted a sense of discomfort" to the Japanese.[102]

The Japanese negotiators expressed their reservations about the draft's focus on rights and considerations to be granted the resident US forces. They suggested setting up a joint committee to consider such issues as the locations of the bases, the facilities required, the financial responsibility for base upkeep, and the legal standing of the bases and of the base personnel. Their idea was that joint work would produce a treaty that would be acceptable to the Japanese people.[103]

In response, the Americans suggested adopting a concise format for the basic bilateral treaty. The details of the US bases, they urged, could appear in a two-government agreement not subject to congressional scrutiny. Japan's negotiators welcomed this proposal, and Japan and the United States ended up cementing a mutual security arrangement that spanned three documents:

1. The Treaty of Peace with Japan (The Treaty of San Francisco)
   Avoids any direct reference to the stationing of US troops in Japan but acknowledges the permissibility of such a move:

> The Allied Powers for their part recognize that Japan as a sovereign nation possesses the inherent right of individual or collective self-defense referred to in Article 51 of the Charter of the United Nations and that Japan may voluntarily enter into collective security arrangements.
>
> Article 5

> Nothing in this provision shall, however, prevent the stationing or retention of foreign armed forces in Japanese territory under or in consequence of any bilateral or multilateral agreements which have been or may be

made between one or more of the Allied Powers, on the one hand, and Japan on the other. Article 6

2. The Security Treaty between the United States and Japan
Establishes a broad framework for Japanese-US security cooperation predicated on a US military presence in Japan.

3. An administrative agreement for implementing the security treaty
Provides for such specifics as the legal standing of the bases and of the base personnel, the privileges enjoyed by the US military personnel, the financial responsibility for base upkeep, and the establishment of a Japanese-US committee for administering the US military presence.[104]

Birth pangs for the administrative agreement

Japan and the United States began negotiating the administrative agreement in January 1952. Four months had passed since the conclusion of the peace treaty and the Japanese-US security treaty, and the two treaties would take effect three months later. The administrative agreement negotiations proved a trying ordeal for the Japanese.

Inspiring the Japanese negotiators was the fervent wish of their compatriots for the earliest possible end to the military occupation. The Americans, however, were eager to smooth the transition from occupying a conquered nation to stationing troops in an allied nation under a partnership of equals. Every provision in the draft underwent thorough debate. Nishimura writes of the ordeal that it was "miserable" and that he "hate[d] to recall the experience."[105]

The best intentions of the Japanese negotiators notwithstanding, the administrative agreement fared poorly in the court of Japanese public opinion. Especially galling for the Japanese was the manner of extending the US hold on existing bases. The Japanese sought a format where, at least in principle, the United States would return the base sites to Japan and Japan would extend rights anew to sites as appropriate. In contrast, the United State sought a format where the US armed forces would continue to use existing bases while, as necessary, reducing the footprints of the bases.

In any event, Japan swallowed onerous terms in connection with the administrative agreement. Formalizing the humiliation were the terms agreed in an official exchange of notes. Japan and the United States would, if possible, determine by the time the security treaty took effect the base sites to be provided. If they failed to reach agreement, the joint committee would endeavor to resolve the matter. The US bases would remain intact, however, if no agreement coalesced within 90 days after the security treaty took effect.

Miyazawa Kiichi, a protégé of Finance Minister Ikeda and later prime minister himself, who participated in the negotiations, expresses disappointment in his memoir at "the mistakes made at the time of the signing of the Administrative Agreement." He argues that the Japanese negotiating approach resulted in what the Japanese people regarded as the continuation of the occupation. Miyazawa suggests that what resulted from the negotiations heightened Japanese antipathy toward the US military presence and aggravated the sense of national humiliation.[106]

To assess the Japanese negotiators "mistakes" seems somewhat severe in view of the stubborn US stance they confronted. Nishimura, however, sympathizes with the citizenry in their opposition to the US retention of the bases.[107] Japan also absorbed disagreeable terms in other facets of the administrative agreement. Here are three notable examples.

1. Criminal jurisdiction

   Japan basically ceded its sovereignty with respect to legal jurisdiction over the US troops and civilian personnel and their dependents.

> [T]he United States service courts and authorities shall have the right to exercise within Japan exclusive jurisdiction over all offenses which may be committed in Japan by members of the United States armed forces, the civilian component, and their dependents, excluding their dependents who have only Japanese nationality. Article 17

The agreement, to be sure, continues with the provision that "such jurisdiction may in any case be waived by the United States."

2. Emergency response

   Japan's negotiators were unhappy with an inconsistency in the US negotiating position. The US negotiators refused to include language in the security treaty that would commit the United States to defend Japan. They insisted, however, on including different language in the administrative agreement. The US proposal for that document provided for committing both nations to engage in joint defense. Japan and the United States would respond jointly to defend "the Japan area" in the event of attack.

> In the event of hostilities, or imminently threatened hostilities, in the Japan area, the Governments of the United States and Japan shall immediately consult together with a view to taking necessary joint measures for the defense of that area and to carrying out the purposes of Article 1 of the Security Treaty.* Article 24

*Article 1 of the security treaty:

> Japan grants, and the United States of America accepts, the right, upon the coming into force of the Treaty of Peace and of this Treaty, to dispose United States land, air and sea forces in and about Japan. Such forces may be utilized to contribute to the maintenance of international peace and security in the Far East and to the security of Japan against armed attack from without, including assistance given at the express request of the Japanese Government to put down large-scale internal riots and disturbances in Japan, caused through instigation or intervention by an outside power or powers.

3. Cost allocation

Japan incurred what most Japanese regarded as a disproportionate share of the cost of maintaining the US military presence.

> 2. It is agreed that Japan will:
>
> a) Furnish for the duration of this Agreement without cost to the United States and make compensation where appropriate to the owners and suppliers thereof all facilities, areas and rights of way, including facilities and areas jointly used such as those at airfields and ports, as provided in Articles II and III.
>
> b) Make available without cost to the United States, until the effective date of any new arrangement reached as a result of periodic reexami-

> nation, an amount of Japanese currency equivalent to $155 million per annum for the purpose of procurement by the United States of transportation and other requisite services and supplies in Japan. Article 25

Resistance to a collective self-defense agreement with Japan

Most galling for the Foreign Ministry about the 1951 negotiations was the failure to link the security treaty to the UN Charter. As noted, the Japanese submitted a draft proposal for the security treaty on February 1 titled "Formula Concerning Japanese-American Cooperation for Their Mutual Security" (see endnote 84). They brought forth that document before the Americans had tabled a proposal for the text. Nishimura later summarized the Japanese draft as follows:

> Maintaining Japan's peace and security is fundamental to maintaining peace and security for the Pacific region and for the United States. Accordingly, the United States will defend Japan if Japan comes under armed attack, and Japan will provide all cooperation possible in that cause. The two nations, in other words, will establish a relationship of collective self-defense as stipulated in Article 51 of the UN Charter. In view of that relationship, Japan agrees to host US military forces.[108]

The UN Charter guaranteed "the inherent right of individual or collective self-defense" (Article 51). In addition, it expressly countenanced "the existence of regional arrangements or agencies for dealing with such matters relating to the maintenance of international peace" (Article 52). The Foreign Ministry negotiators believed that Japan and the United States could form a bilateral security agreement in the context of those assurances. Their US counterparts, however, rejected that logic.

On February 6, the Americans submitted a counterproposal for the security treaty.[109] Their proposal carried the title "Agreement Between the United States of America and Japan for Collective Self-defense Made Pursuant to the Treaty of Peace Between Japan and the Allied Powers and the Provisions of Article 51 of the Charter of the United Nations." And it resonated with the Japanese proposal in citing the UN Charter's guarantee of a nation's right to enter into collective self-defense arrangements. It differed fundamentally, however, from the Japanese proposal.

The Japanese emphasized the central importance of Japan to peace and security in the Pacific region and founded their proposal squarely on the UN Charter, specifically citing Article 51 of the charter. In contrast, the US proposal emphasizes Japan's vulnerability and mentions the UN Charter only in passing and in conjunction with the peace treaty. The differences in tone and in substance are immediately apparent in the preamble to the US proposal:

> Japan has this day signed a Treaty of Peace with the Allied Powers. On the coming into force of that Treaty, Japan will not have the means to exercise her inherent right of self-defense because, pursuant to the Surrender Terms, Japan has been disarmed. There is danger to Japan in this situation because irresponsible militarism has not yet been driven from the world. The Treaty of Peace gives Japan the right to enter into collective self-defense arrangements with one or more of the Allied Powers and the Charter of the United Nations recognizes that all nations possess an inherent right of individual and collective self-defense. In exercise of these rights, Japan desires, as a provisional arrangement for her defense, that the United States, which is one of the Allied Powers, should maintain armed forces of its own in and about Japan so as to deter armed attack upon Japan. The United States, in the interest of peace and security, is presently willing to maintain certain of its armed forces in and about Japan, in the expectation, however, that Japan will itself increasingly assume responsibility for the defense of its own homeland against direct and indirect aggression, always avoiding any armament which could be an offensive threat or serve other than to promote peace and security in accordance with the purposes and principles of the United Nations Charter.

Nishimura laments the deviation of the US proposal from the integral linkage to the UN Charter attempted in the Japanese proposal.

> We conceived our proposal in the framework of the UN Charter. We sought to establish a collective self-defense relationship between Japan and the United States based on Article 51 of the UN Charter and to acknowledge the stationing of US forces in Japan as a result of that relationship. The US proposal, on the other hand, did not make a clear con-

> nection with the UN Charter. It posits, instead, a relationship preliminary to collective self-defense and [thus] unrelated to the collective self-defense authorized in Article 51 of the UN Charter. The preamble to the agreement explains emphatically that Japan's circumstances oblige the nation to settle for such a relationship. It essentially says that "the United States will deploy forces in Japan and protect the nation until Japan is able to enter into a relationship of collective self-defense based, as it desires, on the UN Charter."[110]

The US negotiators noted that their government had based its participation in NATO on the self-defense capacity of the other participating nations. Clearing the way for US participation in founding NATO was the Vandenberg Resolution of 1948. That resolution, introduced by Senator Arthur Vandenberg and passed by the Senate, defined criteria for pursuing security-related objectives through the framework of the UN Charter. The resolution provided that the United States should confine any participation in "regional and other collective arrangements" to those "as are based on continuous and effective self-help and mutual aid, and as affect its national security."[111]

Japan, explained the US negotiators, did not fulfill the conditions for "continuous and effective self-help and mutual aid." Dulles felt that the United States could not, for the time being, conclude a NATO-like arrangement for mutual self-defense with Japan. He expressed that view at a mission staff meeting on February 5:

> Until Japan is in a position to undertake corresponding obligations of its own the US would want rights rather than obligations. The US cannot press the Japanese to assume military obligations until they have dealt with their Constitutional problem and are in a position formally and publicly to assume such obligations.[112]

Dulles had received instructions from Truman, he mentioned, to seek base rights from the Japanese in negotiating the peace treaty. Carrying out those instructions took precedence over assuming obligations to defend Japan. To be sure, the US military presence would have the effect of ensuring Japanese security. But formally assuming Japan's defense as a US obligation should wait, Dulles believed, until Japan had demonstrated initiative in self-defense.

The Japanese negotiators retorted that Japan's constitution, drafted under the Allied occupation, limited Japan's ability to extend military cooperation. They pointed out that Japan could make a "continuous and effective" contribution to US security through its production capacity and labor force. Hosting US bases, they added, was in and of itself a big contribution to US security.[113]

Even NATO, the Japanese negotiators observed, had, in Iceland, a militarily defenseless member. But the US negotiators were unyielding. Iceland, they parried, was a small nation, whereas Japan was a nation of large population and potentially immense economic and industrial might.[114]

The gap between the Japanese and US negotiators was larger, in any case, than the issue of capacity for "continuous and effective self-help and mutual aid." Japan's negotiators, at the end of the day, were seeking nothing other than military protection for their nation. They buttressed their case by asserting, correctly, that hosting US military bases in Japan would fortify US security. But that was a far cry from the commitment to mutual self-defense pledged by the NATO members. As such, it was eminently unpersuasive for the Americans.

Of note here is a stratagem employed by the Japanese when Dulles returned for a second round of talks from April 16 to 23, 1951. They submitted a document titled "Concerning the Character of the Proposed Japanese-American Agreement" to the US delegation through Ambassador Sebald on April 20. It contained three strikingly pertinent questions about the then current draft of the administrative agreement:

(a) Is the stationing of American troops in Japan to be considered as being based solely on Japanese request, having no reference to any provision of the U.N. Charter?

(b) In the event of an armed attack against Japan, the American troops in Japan would presumably resort to military action. Is such military action to be viewed as the exercising of Japanese right of self-defense? Or, is it to be regarded partly as invocation of America's inherent right of self-defense?

(c) Supposing an American-controlled territory in the Japanese area

> (e.g. Okinawa) is attacked, and the American forces stationed in Japan resort to military action, Japan as an American base would naturally extend assistance and cooperation. How is such assistance and cooperation by Japan to be explained except in the light of Japan's invocation of her right of collective self-defense?[115]

No record remains of the US response to the Japanese questions. Striking about the queries, however, is the evidence they offer of the debate then under way in the Foreign Ministry. The query about Okinawa is especially interesting.

Okinawa was clearly destined to remain under US control after the conclusion of the peace treaty. Some in the Foreign Ministry believed that assisting with its defense would constitute exercising Japan's right to engage in collective self-defense. They adhered to that belief despite the constraints of Article 9 of the Japanese constitution and despite Japan's limited military capacity, and they tried to get the US negotiators to accept their logic.[116] Their appeal, however, went unheard.

A problematic reference to the Far East

The US proposal tabled in the first round of security treaty negotiations underwent successive revisions in subsequent negotiations. It became, as revised, the basis for the Security Treaty Between the United States and Japan, which took effect along with the Treaty of San Francisco on April 28, 1952. None of the revisions changed the basic content of the proposal. Two revisions figured significantly, though, in defining the purpose of the US military presence in Japan. One pertained to the potential role of the US troops in suppressing domestic unrest, the other to the geographical scope of the US striking power to be based in Japan.

"Japan grants, and the United States accepts the right," stated the original proposal, "to station United States land, air and sea forces in and about Japan. Such dispositions would be designed solely for the defense of Japan against armed attack from without." As for domestic civil order, the draft emphasizes that "any forces contributed pursuant hereto would not have any responsibility or authority to intervene in the internal affairs of Japan." It adds the caveat, however, that "assistance given at the express request of the Japanese Government to put down large-scale internal riots and disturbances in Japan would not be deemed intervention in the internal affairs of Japan."

Yoshida and his government felt that Japan should, as a rule, take responsibility for maintaining civil order and should rely on the US military only for defense from external threats. Japan at the time lacked the capacity, however, to maintain civil order. Thus did the Japanese government accept the US proposal and retain the option of securing US military assistance to put down "large-scale internal riots and disturbances." It qualified that acceptance, however, with a revision to the treaty text.

The revision limited the scope of domestic unrest subject to US military engagement to that "caused through instigation or intervention by an outside power or powers." Nonetheless, the acceptance of a possible role for the US military in maintaining domestic civil order drew criticism. It became a lasting target for the numerous Japanese who protested the security treaty as an affront to national pride and sovereignty.

More impactful than the above revision was one added at the insistence of the US military establishment. The original US proposal, as noted earlier, defined the purpose of the US military presence in Japan as "solely for the defense of Japan against armed attack from without." This definition broadened, however, in the final version of the security treaty.

The corresponding passage in the final version reads, "Such forces may be utilized to contribute to the maintenance of international peace and security *in the Far East* [italics added] and to the security of Japan against armed attack from without. . . ." The sentence continues with the discussion, described above, of the potential for mobilizing US troops to suppress domestic unrest: "including assistance given at the express request of the Japanese Government to put down large-scale internal riots and disturbances in Japan, caused through instigation or intervention by an outside power or powers."

On reviewing the State Department's proposed draft for the security treaty, members of the US Defense Department and military demanded the addition of "the Far East." They wanted the forces stationed in Japan to be available for broader duty than simply defending their host nation. Military emergencies could arise anywhere in the Far East, as had occurred on the Korean Peninsula. And the US military establishment wanted the Japan-based forces to be available for responding to such exigencies.[117]

The Joint Chiefs of Staff conveyed their views on the peace treaty on July 17 to Robert Lovett, then the acting secretary of defense, through the secretaries of the army, navy, and air force, and Lovett relayed their input to Secretary of State Acheson on August 11. With regard to Japan-based forces, the JCS expressed their demand as follows:

> As a matter of overriding importance and in order to meet the demands of the security interests of the United States, the mutual security arrangements with Japan proposed in the basic draft should additionally provide for:
>
> a. Authorization for the United States to use Japan as a base for military operations in the Far East, including, if necessary, operations against the mainland of China (including Manchuria), the USSR, and on the high seas, regardless of whether such use is under United Nations aegis; and
>
> b. Permission by Japan for the United Nations to continue to support United Nations forces in Korea through Japan for as long as this may be necessary.[118]

Acheson, accepting the input from the Joint Chiefs of Staff, issued instructions to Sebald to revise the security treaty draft.

> Change second sentence of Art 1 to read "Such forces may be utilized to contribute to the maintenance of intl peace and security in the Far East and to the security of Jap against armed attack from without, etc."
>
> The purpose is to make clear that the US forces in and about Jap are not earmarked and dedicated so exclusively for Jap that they cld not be used elsewhere to maintain intl peace and security as, for example, US forces in and about Jap were used for the aid of So. Korea when it was attacked. Recognition of this fact is in our common interest. In view of the responsibilities of the US in the area and its commitments to the Phils, NZ and Austr, the US cld not afford to earmark any particular forces exclusively for any particular area. We don't think that this was ever the intent of Art 1 but DepDef now insists on necessity of expressly negativing any such possibility.[119]

The State Department submitted the revised draft on July 30 to the Japanese government, which accepted the changes. Japan's official records of the back-and-forth suggest that the addition of "the Far East" went down easily with the Japanese. That, if true, is incongruous in light of the criticism to which the change exposed the treaty. Broadening the potential scope of mobilization for the Japan-based US forces was doubly problematic for the Japanese. It called into question the priority that defending Japan would receive in US military strategy. At the same time, it suggested that Japan could get drawn into US military action in the Far East. Nishimura writes as follows of the episode:

> The draft proposal had, until then, specified that the US military forces in Japan would be for contributing to Japanese safety from attack from outside, and no doubt had arisen about the Japan-based US forces defending Japan. However, certainty about the defense of Japan by the Japan-based US forces disappeared from the treaty text with the addition of the phrase "the maintenance of international peace and security in the Far East," especially as couched by "may be utilized to contribute to." This point commanded overriding concern for us in the secretariat. We assembled an interpretation of the phrasing [consistent with continued certainty about the US commitment to defending Japan] and concentrated on striving to secure affirmation of our interpretation from Washington, but we didn't succeed. The "Far East" phrasing presented important issues. One was the question of the geographical range that it denoted. Another pertained to the use of facilities and territory provided by Japan if the Japan-based US forces were to be used in contributing to maintaining international peace and security in the Far East. That presented the question as to how much the Japanese government would be involved in approving that usage. We casually rendered the opinion, without considering those issues carefully, that the prime minister ought to agree to the change. I cringe to this day on recalling how we in the secretariat failed to do our duty.[120]

A weakened legal foundation

Broadening the scope of the security treaty with the insertion of "the Far East" might have bolstered the treaty's strategic value, but it weakened its legal standing. Nishimura's reference to assembling an interpretation is in connection with the newly added phrase "may be utilized." He and his colleagues in the Foreign Ministry sought assurance from the State Department that the US commitment to defending Japan from attack remained absolute and that the conditionality implicit in "may be utilized" pertained only to Far Eastern action beyond Japanese territory. They requested confirmation that

> such forces may be utilized to contribute to the maintenance of international peace and security in the Far East and to the security of Japan against armed attack from without, including assistance given at the express request of the Japanese Government to put down large-scale internal riots and disturbances in Japan, caused through instigation or intervention by an outside power or powers,

meant that

> such forces will be utilized to contribute to the security of Japan against armed attack from without, including assistance given at the express request of the Japanese Government to put down large-scale internal riots and disturbances in Japan, caused through instigation or intervention by an outside power or powers, and may be utilized to contribute to the maintenance of international peace and security in the Far East.[121]

The Japanese received a response in the affirmative from the State Department staffer who responded to their query, but no official reassurance was forthcoming.

We note here an interesting rationalization by the Foreign Ministry of an untoward, from its standpoint, development in the treaty text. The treaty was becoming something other than a collective self-defense agreement, as described in Article 51 of the UN Charter and as had been desired by the Japanese. It would not expressly oblige either signatory to defend the other. The Foreign Ministry, however, put a positive spin on things with the following interpretation:

> An attack on Japan would be, simultaneously, an attack on the US forces stationed in Japan, and the US forces would exercise their right to self-defense. That would inherently serve to defend Japan. A cooperative

> relationship for defending Japan, which will use all means at its disposal for self-defense, will arise between Japan and the United States.[122]

This logic is an inversion of the Foreign Ministry's original hope and intention. The Foreign Ministry had abandoned its plan to explain the Japanese-US security relationship in terms of the right to collective self-defense. Originally, the Foreign Ministry envisioned formally establishing a cooperative relationship of collective self-defense between Japan and the United States. Japan would then countenance the stationing of US forces in Japan as a natural part of that relationship.

In the inversion, the United States would maintain bases in Japan in accordance with Japanese wishes, and, as a result, a cooperative defense relationship based on each nation's right to self-defense would arise. The Foreign Ministry would explain that relationship as a regional security arrangement of the sort expressly recognized by the United Nations. It would assure the Japanese people that the US commitment to defend Japan was rock-solid and that the security treaty was based on the UN Charter.

The US government declined to endorse this interpretation officially. Nishimura writes, however, that the US government spokesperson offered reassurance on that point after the signing of the security treaty. The Americans insisted, he writes, that inserting "the Far East" was not intended to dilute US responsibility for defending Japan.[123]

At the end of the day, the reference to "the Far East" occasioned hardly any of the trouble feared by Nishimura and his colleagues. The Foreign Ministry negotiators might actually have seen the reference as strengthening Japan's position. That would explain, despite Nishimura's professed regrets, why they urged Yoshida to sign the document. They had asserted repeatedly during the negotiations that hosting US bases was a contribution to security for the free world. Affirming the potential for Japan-based US forces to strike on behalf of peace and security in the Far East reinforced that assertion. The Japanese did indeed want the United States to station troops in Japan, and the US government did indeed want to station troops there. Providing bases served, in that sense, the interests of both parties in equal measure.[124]

Stating in the security treaty that Japan-based US forces could act to maintain Far Eastern peace and security entailed a legal issue. It called into question Japan's legal basis for countenancing such action, which was hardly explainable in terms of self-defense. Nishimura and his colleagues had been unsuccessful in promoting the establishment of a collective self-defense relationship for Japanese-US security cooperation. They apparently had no appetite for tackling the legal justification for the action in question.

Nishimura and his colleagues had made a case for a joint response by Japan and the United States to an attack on Japan. They had built their case on each nation's right to self-defense. That begged the question, however, as to how Japan would respond to an attack on the United States. Nishimura's response was that the United States would presumably counterattack from its positions in Japan but that such action (by the United States or by Japan) lay outside the purview of the Japanese-US security cooperation agreement.[125]

If a Japanese response to an attack on the United States lay outside the purview of the Japanese-US security cooperation agreement, a joint Japanese-US response to an attack on a third nation—say, on the Philippines—was surely out of the question. Nishimura and his colleagues proffered a passive interpretation, meanwhile, of the problematic "Far East" addition to the security treaty text. It simply meant, they insisted, that "Japan would have no objection to the United States using its armed forces in Japan for the purpose of contributing to the maintenance of international peace and security in the Far East."[126]

Quid pro quo

Japanese and US government representatives signed the Treaty of Peace with Japan (the Treaty of San Francisco) in San Francisco's War Memorial Opera House on September 8, 1951. They then moved to the 6th Army headquarters at the Presidio of San Francisco to sign the Security Treaty Between the United States and Japan. More than eight months had passed since Dulles arrived in Japan in late January to begin negotiating the security treaty. Japan and the United States would conclude the administrative agreement for implementing the security treaty on February 28, 1952.

The security treaty and its administrative agreement constituted what a Foreign Ministry negotiator called a "base-siting agreement."[127] History has generally categorized the terms of the treaty and agreement as humiliating for Japan, and scholars and others have attributed those terms to inadequate negotiating prowess on the part of the Foreign Ministry.[128]

Clearly, maintaining bases in Japan was crucial to US military strategy. That lends credence to the argument that Japan could have struck a harder bargain in extending rights to the bases. Japan, meanwhile, ended up ceding more than originally intended in the way of rights and privileges in connection with the bases. Nishimura and other former members of the Foreign Ministry who participated in the negotiations have expressed regret on that count.

Shortcomings in Japanese diplomacy might well have figured in the outcome of the treaty negotiations, but to blame the Japanese negotiators for the heavy weighting of base concessions in the final agreement is unfair. That outcome was more a reflection of the power balance between Japan and the United States than of Japanese negotiating ineptitude. The bases, as noted, were partly a quid pro quo for concluding the peace treaty, and the terms were apparently satisfactory to the Japanese who had taken part in the negotiations.

> The United States, having confirmed that it would be able to station forces in Japan after the conclusion of the peace treaty and the restoration of Japanese independence, revealed the terms of the peace treaty that it was taking up with the other Allied nations. Those terms greatly impressed the Japanese who had participated in the treaty negotiations with their fairness and generosity.[129]

Refusing to grant the rights and privileges that the US government was seeking would have had unacceptable consequences for Japan. It most certainly would have extended the occupation and delayed Japan's entry into the ranks of free world nations. Yoshida and his government, meanwhile, viewed aligning with the US as valuable in seeking optimal treaty terms in negotiations with the Allied nations.[130] They were eager, therefore, to avoid serious frictions with the United States.

Multiple factors had ruled out a truly mutual treaty between Japan and the United States. Japan, for one thing, was essentially unarmed, and its government was planning to pledge to forgo rearmament in concluding the peace treaty. For another, the Japanese-US security relationship envisioned by the Foreign Ministry was anything but mutual. It was a one-sided relationship focused on defending Japan.

The terms of the security treaty were ultimately an unvarnished tit for tat. Japan provided the United States with rights to bases, and the United States provided Japan with national security. Actual bases, rather than any conceptual notion of collective self-defense, became the basis for a Japanese-US alliance. Even characterizing the resultant relationship as an "alliance" is questionable. The US commitment to defending Japan was less than unequivocal.

We should perhaps regard the Japanese-US agreement less as a treaty than as a stopgap, base-siting arrangement. It would tide things over until a truly mutual agreement became possible. That is what Dulles and the US government wanted, and that is what the Japanese government accepted.

The security treaty, to be fair, fulfilled a huge role for nine years in ensuring Japanese national security. It occasioned immense dissatisfaction, however, in the Japanese government and in the Japanese populace. Thus did pressure begin building for revising the security treaty before the ink on the peace treaty had even begun to dry.

Chapter Notes

1 For background to MacArthur's call for a peace treaty, see Ōtake Hideo, ed., *Sengo Nihon bōei mondai shiryōshū* [Archives of Postwar Japanese Defense Issues], vol. 1, *Higunjika kara saigunbi e* [From Demilitarization to Rearmament] (Tokyo: San-Ichi Shobo, 1991), 203–205; Hosoya Chihiro, *San Furanshisuko kōwa e no michi* [The Path to the San Francisco Peace Treaty] (Tokyo: Chuokoronsha, 1984), 9–13; and Igarashi Takeshi, *Sengo Nichi-Bei kankei no keisei: Kōwa, Anpo to Reisengo no shiten ni tatte* [The Formation of Postwar Japanese-US Relations: From the Perspective of the Peace Treaty, the Security Treaty, and the Post–Cold War Era] (Tokyo: Kodansha, 1995), 14–19.

2 "President Harry S. Truman's Address before a Joint Session of Congress, March 12, 1947," Avalon Project (New Haven: Lillian Goldman Law Library, Yale Law School), https://avalon.law.yale.edu/20th_century/trudoc.asp.

3 US Department of State, *Foreign Relations of the United States* (*FRUS*), 1946 (Washington, DC: Government Printing Office, 1969), Document 475.

4 *Foreign Affairs*, https://www.foreignaffairs.com/articles/russian-federation/1947-07-01/sources-soviet-conduct. For a discussion of Kennan's role in shaping Cold War policy in the Truman administration, see Wilson D. Miscamble, *George F. Kennan and the Making of American Foreign Policy, 1947–1950* (Princeton: Princeton University Press, 1992).

5 George F. Kennan, *Memoirs: 1925–1950,* vol. 1 (Boston: Little, Brown, 1967), 359. For a discussion of how US containment policy evolved during the Cold War, see John L. Gaddis, *Strategies of Containment: A Critical Appraisal of Postwar American National Security Policy* (Oxford: Oxford University Press, 1982). Gaddis's *The United States and the Origins of the Cold War, 1941–1947* (New York: Columbia University Press, 1972) is a classic of Cold War scholarship.

6 US Department of State, *FRUS,* 1947 (Washington, DC: Government Printing Office, 1972), Document 393.

7 US Department of State, *FRUS,* 1947, Document 394.

8 "United States Initial Post-Surrender Policy for Japan (SWNCC150/4)," https://www.ndl.go.jp/constitution/shiryo/01/022/022tx.html.

9 US Department of State, *Department of State Bulletin* (June 30, 1946), 1113.

10 US Department of State, *FRUS,* 1948 (Washington, DC: Government Printing Office, 1974), Document 497.

11 Kennan, *Memoirs,* 375–376; Tanaka Akihiko, *Anzen hoshō: Sengo 50-nen no mosaku* [Military Security: Fifty Postwar Years of Searching] (Tokyo: Yomiuri Shimbunsha, 1997), 36.

12 US Department of State, *FRUS,* 1948, Document 519. For recent research findings on Kennan and Okinawa, see Robert D. Eldridge, "Jōji F Kenan, PPS to Okinawa: Beikoku no Okinawa seisaku kettei katei, 1947–1949" [George F. Kennan, the Policy Planning Staff, and Okinawa: The Process of US Policymaking toward Okinawa], *Kokusai seiji* [International Relations] 120 (February 1999).

13 US Department of State, *FRUS,* 1948, Document 519.

14 For a discussion of Foreign Ministry deliberations on security issues anticipated after concluding the peace treaty, see Watanabe Akio, "Kōwa mondai to Nihon no sentaku" [Peace Treaty Issues and Japan's Choice], in *San Furanshisuko kōwa* [The San Francisco Peace Treaty], ed. Watanabe and Miyazato Seigen (Tokyo: University of Tokyo Press, 1986). For more recent research findings, see Kusunoki Ayako, "Senryōka Nihon no anzen hoshō kōsō: Gaimushō ni okeru Yoshida Dokutorin no keisei katei: 1945–1949" [Occupied Japan's Approach to National Security: The Process of Developing the Yoshida Doctrine in the Foreign Ministry], *Rokkōdai ronshū hōgaku seijigaku-hen* [The Rokkodai Ronshu, Law and Political Science] 45, no. 3 (March 1999).

15 Suzuki Tadakatsu, "Heiwa jōyaku seiritsugo no waga kokubō mondai: Daihachigun shireikan tono kaidan" [Defense Issues for Japan after the Conclusion of the Peace Treaty: Talks with the Commander of the Eighth Army] (September 13, 1947), Diplomatic Archives of the Japan Ministry of Foreign Affairs, *Tai-Nichi heiwa jōyaku kankei* [Japan Peace Treaty], *Junbi ken kankei* [Preliminary Research], Document 61; and Shindō Eiichi and Shimokōbe Motoharu, eds., *Ashida Hitoshi nikki* [Ashida Hitoshi's Diary] (Tokyo: Iwanami Shoten, 1986), 7:398–403. For background to Eichelberger and the subsequently mentioned Ashida letter, see Michael M. Yoshitsu, *Japan and the San Francisco Peace Settlement* (New York: Columbia University Press, 1983), 16–23.

16 Japan Ministry of Foreign Affairs, *Tai-Nichi heiwa jōyaku, Junbi ken kankei,* vol. 3, microfilm reel B'.4.0.0.1, B' 0008, 84.

17 Suzuki's diary entry for July 21, 1948, quotes Eichelberger to that effect. The July 19, 2015, issue of the *Sankei Shimbun* features an article discussing one of Suzuki Tadakatsu's journal entries, dated July 21, 1948 (written in English and in the possession of the Suzuki family). According to the entry, Eichelberger spoke with Suzuki about the "Ashida letter" that he had received in September 1947, saying that he had "made considerable use of the document, which dealt with the security of Japan's future," and that "many prominent figures, including Far Eastern Commission Chairman General Frank McCoy, had read it."
18 Yoshida Shigeru, *Kaisō jūnen* [A 10-Year Memoir] (Tokyo: Chuokoronsha, 1998), 3:141; and Nishimura Kumao, *San Furanshisuko heiwa jōyaku: Nichi-Bei Anpo jōyaku* [The San Francisco Peace Treaty: The Japanese-US Security Treaty] (Tokyo: Chuokoron Shinsha, 1999), 206–207.
19 Yoshida, *Kaisō jūnen*, 3:139.
20 Nishimura writes that the Japanese abandoned the idea of an "emergency-only" US military presence because of Yoshida's opposition. According to Nishimura, Yoshida wanted to ensure the return of Okinawa and the Ogasawara Islands to Japanese sovereignty and feared that the emergency-only scheme threatened their return. His concern was that using them as platforms for US emergency-response forces could result in their becoming permanent US possessions. For more about this issue, see Kusunoki, "Senryōka Nihon no anzen hoshō kōsō," 31.
21 A Japanese translation of the Ashida letter appears in Shindō and Shimokōbe, *Ashida Hitoshi nikki*. It renders the passage "without compromising Japan's independence in peace time" as "as a means of preserving Japan's independence in ordinary times."
22 For commentary on the difference in nuance and on the issue in question, see Miura Yōichi, *Yoshida Shigeru to San Furanshisuko kōwa* [Yoshida Shigeru and the San Francisco Peace Treaty] (Tokyo: Ōtsuki Shoten, 1996), 1:82–84.
23 US Department of State, *FRUS*, 1949 (Washington, DC: Government Printing Office, 1976), Document 97.
24 US Department of State, *FRUS*, 1949, Document 145.
25 US Department of State, *FRUS*, 1950 (Washington, DC: Government Printing Office, 1976), Document 721; and Nakanishi Hiroshi, "Yoshida-Daresu kaidan saikō: Mikan no anzen hoshō taiwa" [A Reappraisal of the Yoshida-Dulles Talks: An Unfinished Security Dialogue], *Hōgaku ronsō* [Kyoto Law Review] 140, no. 1/2 (November 1996): 221.
26 US Department of State, *FRUS*, 1950, Document 695.
27 "Potsdam Declaration," https://www.ndl.go.jp/constitution/e/etc/c06.html.
28 US Department of State, *FRUS*, 1950, Document 725.
29 US Department of State, *FRUS*, 1950, Document 721.
30 US Department of State, *FRUS*, 1950, Document 756.
31 US Department of State, *FRUS*, 1950, Document 756.
32 For commentary on Dulles's thinking, see Nakanishi, "Yoshida-Daresu kaidan saikō," 226.
33 US Department of State, *FRUS*, 1950, Document 727.
34 US Department of State, *FRUS*, 1950, Document 758.

35 "United Nations Charter," https://www.un.org/en/about-us/un-charter/full-text.
36 US Department of State, *FRUS*, 1950, Document 797.
37 US Department of State, *FRUS*, 1950, Document 888.
38 US Department of State, *FRUS*, 1950, Document 797.
39 US Department of State, *FRUS*, 1951 (Washington, DC: Government Printing Office, 1977), Document 789.
40 For a discussion of the shock of China's entry into the Korean War and of its effect on Japanese rearmament, see Igarashi, *Sengo Nichi-Bei kankei no keisei*, 265–273.
41 US Department of State, *FRUS*, 1950, Document 797.
42 US Department of State, *FRUS*, 1951, Document 32.
43 US Department of State, *FRUS*, 1951, Document 33. For a discussion of Japanese rearmament in connection with a Pacific treaty agreement, see Chapter 5 in Kan Hideki, *Bei-So Reisen to Amerika no Ajia seisaku* [The US-Soviet Cold War and American Asia Policy] (Kyoto: Minerva Shobo, 1992).
44 Nakanishi, "Yoshida-Daresu kaidan saikō," 233.
45 Ōtake, *Sengo Nihon*, 1:362–364.
46 Inoki Masamichi, *Hyōden Yoshida Shigeru* [A Critical Biography of Yoshida Shigeru] (Tokyo: Chikuma Shobo, 1995), 4:332.
47 Yoshida Shigeru, *Sekai to Nihon* [The World and Japan] (Tokyo: Chuokoronsha, 1992), 154.
48 For an overview of Yoshida's basic thinking on cooperation with the United States, see Yoshida, *Kaisō jūnen*, ch. 1, vol. 1, and ch. 28, vol. 4.
49 US Department of State, *FRUS*, 1950, Document 714. Interestingly, what the Dodge report records as "to secure the treaty terms and for other purposes" appears in the original Japanese as "to ensure security for Japan and for the Asian region."
50 US Department of State, *FRUS*, 1950, Document 714. For a discussion of the outcome of Yoshida's initiative, see Robert D. Eldridge and Kusunoki Ayako, "To Base or Not to Base? Yoshida Shigeru, the 1950 Ikeda Mission, and Post-Treaty Japanese Security Conceptions," *Kobe University Law Review*, no. 33 (1999).

Newsweek magazine carried an article in its January 9, 1950, issue about the US military's designs on Okinawa and the Ogasawara Islands. It reported that the military wanted to retain some troops and bases there but was encountering resistance from the State Department. The State Department reportedly argued that the United States would appear to be imposing a military presence on a vanquished nation, and both factions needed to seek a way to achieve the military's objectives without incurring criticism. *Newsweek*'s article appeared about four months before Ikeda's US visit, and the *Asahi Shimbun* newspaper reported the article in its morning edition of January 6, 1950 (the *Newsweek* issue having appeared several days before its nominal date). The *Asahi Shimbun* ran its article under a heading that suggested that the intragovernmental squabbling could impede progress on the peace treaty.
51 US Department of State, *FRUS*, 1950, Document 797.
52 Yoshida, *Kaisō jūnen*, 3:143.
53 US Department of State, *FRUS*, 1951, Document 489; Japan Ministry of Foreign Affairs, *Heiwa jōyaku no teiketsu ni kansuru chōsho* [Documents Related to the

Conclusion of the Peace Treaty], 4:135–144, Dōba Hajime Papers, in the collection of Aoyama Gakuin University's School of International Politics, Economics and Communication (see References for details on volume and page references); Hosoya Chihiro, Aruga Tadashi, Ishii Osamu, and Sasaki Takuya, eds., *Nichi-Bei kankei shiryōshū, 1945–1947* [Collected Works on Japanese-US Relations, 1945–1997] (Tokyo: University of Tokyo Press, 1999), 84–88; and Ōtake, *Sengo Nihon*, 2:40–41. For a discussion of the preparation and submission of the "Suggested Agenda," see Japan Ministry of Foreign Affairs, *Heiwa jōyaku no teiketsu*, 4:13–26.

54 Frank Kowalski, *An Inoffensive Rearmament: The Making of the Postwar Japanese Army*, ed. Robert D. Eldridge (Maryland: Naval Institute Press, 2013), 52.

55 Japan Ministry of Foreign Affairs, *Heiwa jōyaku no teiketsu*, 3:78; and Inoki, *Hyōden Yoshida Shigeru*, 4:388.

56 Nishimura, *San Furanshisuko heiwa jōyaku*, 82.

57 Japan Ministry of Foreign Affairs, *Heiwa jōyaku no teiketsu*, 3:23–29; and Nishimura, *San Furanshisuko heiwa jōyaku*, 82.

58 Japan Ministry of Foreign Affairs, *Heiwa jōyaku no teiketsu*, 3:209–211; and Ōtake, *Sengo Nihon*, 2:26–27. For background to this idealistic proposal, see Nakanishi Hiroshi, "Kōwa ni muketa Yoshida Shigeru no anzen hoshō kōsō" [Yoshida Shigeru's Security Concept in Approaching the Peace Treaty], in *Kantaiheiyō no kokusai chitsujo no mosaku to Nihon: Daiichiji Sekai Taisengo kara 55-nen taisei seiritsu* [Japan and the Pursuit of International Order in the Pacific Basin: From the End of World War I to the Formation of the 1955 Framework], ed. Itō Yukio and Kawada Minoru (Tokyo: Yamakawa Shuppansha, 1999).

59 Japan Ministry of Foreign Affairs, *Heiwa jōyaku no teiketsu*, 4:10–11.

60 Toyoshita Narahiko, *Anpo jōyaku no seiritsu: Yoshida gaikō to tennō gaikō* [The Birth of the Security Treaty: Yoshida Diplomacy and Imperial Diplomacy] (Tokyo: Iwanami Shoten, 1996).

61 Kusunoki, "Senryōka Nihon no anzen hoshō kōsō," 50.

62 Japan Ministry of Foreign Affairs, *Heiwa jōyaku no teiketsu*, 3:128.

63 Japan Ministry of Foreign Affairs, *Heiwa jōyaku no teiketsu*, 3:129.

64 Japan Ministry of Foreign Affairs, *Heiwa jōyaku no teiketsu*, 3:129.

65 Watanabe, "Kōwa mondai to Nihon no sentaku," 34.

66 Japan Ministry of Foreign Affairs, *Heiwa jōyaku no teiketsu*, 3:89–94.

67 Japan Ministry of Foreign Affairs, *Heiwa jōyaku no teiketsu*, 3:17–18; and Nishimura, *San Furanshisuko heiwa jōyaku*, 81.

68 Nishimura, *San Furanshisuko heiwa jōyaku*, 81.

69 Japan Ministry of Foreign Affairs, *Heiwa jōyaku no teiketsu*, 3:20.

70 Japan Ministry of Foreign Affairs, *Heiwa jōyaku no teiketsu*, 3:130.

71 US Department of State, *FRUS*, 1951, Document 487. For a discussion of the first round of Dulles-Yoshida talks, see Miura, *Yoshida Shigeru to San Furanshisuko kōwa*, vol. 2. Also see Nakanishi, "Yoshida-Daresu kaidan saikō."

According to Yoshida's comments to Vice Minister for Foreign Affairs Iguchi Haruo and Treaties Bureau Director Nishimura about the meeting, Yoshida had asked Dulles to "incorporate Japan into the US sphere in the broadest sense as the global community separated into two divergent worlds." See "1951-nen, 1-gatsu

29-nichi gogo no Sōri, Daresu daiichiji kaidan memo" [Notes on the First Meeting between the Prime Minister and Dulles on the Afternoon of January 29, 1951], Japan Ministry of Foreign Affairs, *Heiwa jōyaku no teiketsu ni kansuru chōsho* [Documents Related to the Conclusion of the Peace Treaty], 2:143–144.

Yoshida likely informed Dulles that he wanted Japan to be a member of the free world after the peace agreement had been reached, but no comments to that effect appear in records of the meeting in official US diplomatic documents (*FRUS*, 1951, 827–30).

72 Nakanishi, "Yoshida-Daresu kaidan saikō," 247.
73 US Department of State, *FRUS*, 1951, Document 488.
74 US Department of State, *FRUS*, 1951, Document 487.
75 Yoshida, *Sekai to Nihon*, 105–107; Miura, *Yoshida Shigeru to San Furanshisuko kōwa*, 2:147–151.
76 Japanese government record as related in Ōtake, *Sengo Nihon*, 2:42.
77 US Department of State, *FRUS*, 1951, Document 489. Also see Hosoya, Aruga, Ishii, and Sasaki, *Nichi-Bei kankei shiryōshū*, 84–88; and Ōtake, *Sengo Nihon*, 2:40–41.
78 US Department of State, *FRUS*, 1951, Document 491.
79 Japan Ministry of Foreign Affairs, *Heiwa jōyaku no teiketsu*, 4:14.
80 US Department of State, *FRUS*, 1951, Document 489.
81 Japan Ministry of Foreign Affairs, *Heiwa jōyaku no teiketsu*, 4:27–28.
82 Japan Ministry of Foreign Affairs, *Heiwa jōyaku no teiketsu*, 4:30.
83 Among the numerous research works available on Dulles's diplomacy, especially insightful on an issue-by-issue basis is Richard H. Immerman, ed., *John Foster Dulles and the Diplomacy of the Cold War* (Princeton: Princeton University Press, 1990). A good biography is Ronald W. Prussen, *John Foster Dulles: The Road to Power* (New York: The Free Press, 1982), though it covers only the years to 1952. For discussions of Dulles's philosophy and diplomacy, see Iguchi Haruo, "Jon Fosutā Daresu no gaikō shisō: Senzen-sengo no renzokusei" [John Foster Dulles's Diplomatic Philosophy: Prewar-Postwar Continuity], *Dōshisha Amerika kenkyū* [Doshisha US Studies] 34 (March 1998); and Takamatsu Motoyuki, "Gaikōkan no shōzō: Jon F Daresu" [John F. Dulles: Portrait of a Diplomat], *Gaikō Forum* 2 (November 1988) and 3 (December 1988).
84 Japan Ministry of Foreign Affairs, *Heiwa jōyaku no teiketsu*, 4:151–153.
85 Japan Ministry of Foreign Affairs, *Heiwa jōyaku no teiketsu*, 4:154.
86 Japan Ministry of Foreign Affairs, *Heiwa jōyaku no teiketsu*, 4:155.
87 Japan Ministry of Foreign Affairs, *Heiwa jōyaku no teiketsu*, 4:45.
88 Yoshida, *Kaisō jūnen*, 3:146.
89 Japan Ministry of Foreign Affairs, *Heiwa jōyaku no teiketsu*, 4:182.
90 Tanaka, *Anzen hoshō*, 61–63.
91 Japan Ministry of Foreign Affairs, *Heiwa jōyaku no teiketsu*, 4:164. Contemporary source material confirms that Yoshida approved the explanation. Japan Ministry of Foreign Affairs, *Heiwa jōyaku no teiketsu*, 4:39.
92 Yoshitsu, *Japan and the San Francisco Peace Settlement*, 65. Anonymity was apparently a condition for Yoshitsu's interviews, but he provides an overall list of his interviewees. Two individuals on the list who would have been familiar with

the events in question are John Allison, Dulles's deputy at the time and later US ambassador to Japan, and Dean Rusk, the assistant secretary of state for Far Eastern affairs at the time and later secretary of state.

93 "Security Treaty Between the United States and Japan; September 8, 1951," Avalon Project, https://avalon.law.yale.edu/20th_century/japan001.asp.

94 Nishimura, *San Furanshisuko heiwa jōyaku*, 19.

95 Concluding a bilateral security treaty separate from the peace treaty might to some extent reflect UK influence. The UK chiefs of staff opposed incorporating security provisions in the peace treaty. Sir Alvary Gascoigne, the chief of the UK liaison mission in Tokyo, conveyed their views to Dulles at a meeting on February 2, 1951. A US State Department memorandum summarizes Gascoigne's comments as follows:

> United Kingdom Chiefs of Staff have reaffirmed their preference for having defense pact separate from peace treaty. They consider that the United States proposal to include security provisions in the peace treaty would be likely to give the impression that such provisions have been imposed and this might imply that any subsequent defense pact had not been freely entered into. Chiefs of Staff welcome the intention to include a supplementary bi-lateral agreement between the United States and Japan, but they consider that this agreement should be the appropriate instrument for providing for all main aspects of Japanese security and rearmament and that it should not be restricted to matters of detail. (US Department of State, *FRUS*, 1951, Document 493)

For a discussion of the role played by the UK government in shaping the security treaty, see Hosoya Yūichi, "Igirisu gaikō to Nichi-Bei dōmei no kigen, 1948–50: Sengo Ajia Taiheiyō no anzen hoshō wakugumi no keisei katei" [UK Diplomacy and the Origins of the Japanese-US Alliance, 1948–1950: The Process of the Formation of a Security Framework in Postwar Asia-Pacific], *Kokusai seiji* [International Relations] 117 (March 1998).

96 The only time that Dulles is known to have veered from this stance is when he offered informal remarks to Japanese guests at a party. According to a State Department memorandum, "He said that he had informed certain Japanese at one of Ambassador Sebald's receptions that the military agreement would initially be just between the United States and Japan but that it might later be broadened out." *FRUS*, 1951, Document 498.

Allison, however, expressed a more positive stance in working-level negotiations on February 1, 1951. "The US government hopes that regional collective security on the NATO model can take shape in the Pacific region and that Japan will take part, though that might take some time. I would like to know what sort of contribution Japan is prepared to make to such a regional collective security arrangement." The Japanese replied that they could not offer a response beyond what they had pledged in connection with the Japanese-US [security] cooperation agreement. Japan Ministry of Foreign Affairs, *Heiwa jōyaku no teiketsu*, 4:34.

97 Hosoya, *San Furanshisuko kōwa e no michi*, 187–192.

98 Miyazato, "Amerika Gasshūkoku seifu to tai-Nichi kōwa" [The US Government

and the Peace Treaty with Japan], in *San Furanshisuko kōwa* [The San Francisco Peace Treaty], ed. Watanabe and Miyazato (Tokyo: University of Tokyo Press, 1986), 131–132.

99 A Foreign Ministry memorandum of January 24, 1951, entitled *Anzen hoshō ni tsuite no mondaiten* (Difficulties in Ensuring Security), cites a difficulty with the mooted Pacific pact: "A concept has arisen for establishing a Pacific pact among democratic powers to assert collective security against the communist bloc. . . . The concept provides for the other pact participants to join hands against Japan if Japan were to engage in aggression. That provision is unacceptable. For [the United States] to station troops in Japan to defend our nation from invasion is one thing. For those troops to anticipate the possibility of Japanese belligerence and fulfill the additional function of monitoring Japanese behavior is something else again." Japan Ministry of Foreign Affairs, *Heiwa jōyaku no teiketsu*, 3:79–80.

100 For a discussion of the flurry of treaty-making by the United States, see Frederick S. Dunn, *Peacemaking and the Settlement with Japan* (Princeton: Princeton University Press, 1963).

101 US Department of State, *FRUS*, 1951, Document 494.

102 Japan Ministry of Foreign Affairs, *Heiwa jōyaku no teiketsu*, 4:40; and Nishimura, *San Furanshisuko heiwa jōyaku*, 91. The draft the Americans submitted on February 2 differed greatly from one they had prepared in advance of the Dulles-Yoshida talks. US Department of State, *FRUS*, 1950, Document 794; and 1951, Documents 475 and 494.

Apparently, the Americans honored the Japanese desire to provide for a US military presence in the bilateral security treaty, rather than in the peace treaty. They appear to have combined elements of the proposal submitted on the previous day by the Japanese with the US draft that demanded a litany of rights and privileges. The US negotiators welcomed the Japanese proposal as "extremely helpful," and their hybrid version of the two proposals, though awkward, served as the basis for advancing the negotiations. Japan Ministry of Foreign Affairs, *Heiwa jōyaku no teiketsu*, 4:32.

103 Japan Ministry of Foreign Affairs, *Heiwa jōyaku no teiketsu*, 4:175–182. Interestingly, the joint committee also acquired a secret mandate to develop plans for Japanese rearmament and to work out procedures for responding to a military emergency. Japan Ministry of Foreign Affairs, *Heiwa jōyaku no teiketsu*, 4:44.

104 Japan Ministry of Foreign Affairs, *Heiwa jōyaku no teiketsu*, 4:61–64.

105 Nishimura, *San Furanshisuko heiwa jōyaku*, 100–108. For further commentary on the administrative agreement, see Aketagawa Tōru, *Nichi-Bei gyōsei kyōtei no seijishi: Nichi-Bei chii kyōtei kenkyū josetsu* [A Political History of the Japanese- US Administrative Agreement: An Introduction to Research into the Japan-US Status of Forces Agreement] (Tokyo: Hosei University Press, 1999).

106 Miyazawa Kiichi, *Secret Talks between Tokyo and Washington: The Memoirs of Miyazawa Kiichi, 1949–1954*, trans. Robert D. Eldridge (New York: Lexington Books, 2007), 60.

107 Nishimura, *San Furanshisuko heiwa jōyaku*, 102.

108 Nishimura, *San Furanshisuko heiwa jōyaku*, 21–22.

109 US Department of State, *FRUS*, 1951, Document 497. The *FRUS* document bears the date February 5, presumably because of the time difference between Tokyo and Washington, DC.
110 Nishimura, *San Furanshisuko heiwa jōyaku*, 36–37.
111 "U.S. Senate Resolution 239: 80th Congress, 2nd Session ('The Vandenberg Resolution')," NATO, e-Library, https://www.nato.int/cps/en/natohq/official_texts_17054.htm.
112 US Department of State, *FRUS*, 1951, Document 498.
113 Nishimura, *San Furanshisuko heiwa jōyaku*, 37–38.
114 Japan Ministry of Foreign Affairs, *Heiwa jōyaku no teiketsu*, 6:785–787.
115 Japan Ministry of Foreign Affairs, *Heiwa jōyaku no teiketsu*, 5:265–266; and 6:785–787.
116 Nishimura, *San Furanshisuko heiwa jōyaku*, 69–70.
117 For a discussion of the insertion of the reference to "Far East," see Toyoshita, *Anpo jōyaku no seiritsu*, 99–108.
118 US Department of State, *FRUS*, 1951, Document 685.
119 US Department of State, *FRUS*, 1951, Document 661.
120 Japan Ministry of Foreign Affairs, *Heiwa jōyaku no teiketsu*, 6:223.
121 Japan Ministry of Foreign Affairs, *Heiwa jōyaku no teiketsu*, 6:193–194, 711–712; and Nishimura, *San Furanshisuko heiwa jōyaku*, 50–51.
122 Japan Ministry of Foreign Affairs, *Heiwa jōyaku no teiketsu*, 6:192–193.
123 Nishimura, *San Furanshisuko heiwa jōyaku*, 50–51.
124 Japan Ministry of Foreign Affairs, *Heiwa jōyaku no teiketsu*, 4:41.
125 Japan Ministry of Foreign Affairs, *Heiwa jōyaku no teiketsu*, 6:193.
126 Japan Ministry of Foreign Affairs, *Heiwa jōyaku no teiketsu*, 6:711–712.
127 Nishimura, *San Furanshisuko heiwa jōyaku*, 46.
128 Toyoshita, *Anpo jōyaku no seiritsu*. Also see Toyoshita, "Anpo jōyaku no ronri" [The Logic of the Security Treaty], in *Anpo jōyaku no ronri: Sono seisei to tenkai* [The Logic of the Security Treaty: Its Formation and Application] (Tokyo: Kashiwa Shobo, 1999).
129 Japan Ministry of Foreign Affairs, *Heiwa jōyaku no teiketsu*, 4:103.
130 Yoshida, *Kaisō jūnen*, 3:24–26..

Chapter 2

Incremental Rearmament

Yoshida's go-slow approach and US urging to pick up the pace

US ambassador to Japan John Allison. June 12, 1953.
Photo from Kyodo News

1 Pressure for Strengthened Self-Defense

The Security Treaty Between the United States and Japan, which took effect along with the Treaty of San Francisco on April 28, 1952, was a provisional arrangement. "Japan," as noted in the introduction to the security treaty, "will not have the effective means to exercise its inherent right of self-defense because it has been disarmed." The Japanese were thus vulnerable to "irresponsible militarism" (that is, the Communist threat), which had "not yet been driven from the world." They therefore desired "as a provisional arrangement for [their] defense, that the United States of America should maintain armed forces of its own in and about Japan so as to deter armed attack upon Japan."

On the other hand, the Americans were counting on the Japanese to take responsibility for a gradually larger share of their national defense. The security treaty predicates the foregoing provisional arrangement on "the expectation . . . that Japan will itself increasingly assume responsibility for its own defense against direct and indirect aggression." This implies that Japan and the United States would encounter, sooner or later, the political issue of abrogating or revising the security treaty. That issue would arise inevitably if and as Japan assumed growing responsibility for its national defense in accordance with US expectations; that is, if and as Japan acquired "effective means to exercise its inherent right of self-defense."

Japan, as noted in the previous chapter, had established the National Police Reserve in August 1950. But that constabulary force, lightly armed and about 75,000 strong, hardly qualified as the "effective means" in question.

US expectations were indeed the initial source of pressure for revising the security treaty with an eye to rearming Japan. Japanese prime minister Yoshida Shigeru had assured US secretary of state John Foster Dulles that Japan would rearm. Yoshida had given that assurance, as noted in the previous chapter, in the course of negotiating the Treaty of San Francisco. And the prime minister's pledge was the basis for enshrining US expectations for Japanese rearmament in the security treaty.

The US expectations attained a concrete, numerical dimension in 1952, the year after the signing of the security treaty. Tatsumi Eiichi, a former lieutenant general in the Japanese army and a trusted military advisor to Yoshida, recounted the numerical development in an interview with Ōtake Hideo, a specialist on postwar security policy.

> The escalating hostilities in Korea occasioned audacious pressure from the United States for Japan to rearm. A debate over the suitable size for the Japanese land defense force unfolded through several exchanges between the Japanese government and [the US military command for Japan] in January 1952. The US demand was for Japan to expand its army's troop count to 325,000 within a few years.[1]

Yoshida writes in his memoirs of dispatching Tatsumi to the headquarters of the Supreme Commander for the Allied Powers as his envoy. Tatsumi received, Yoshida writes, "a thoroughgoing explanation" of the need for Japan to fortify its military.[2] The explanation detailed why Japan's national defense required an army of 325,000 troops arrayed in 10 frontline divisions, artillery battalions, and support units, along with ancillary naval and air force capabilities. Its basis was a memorandum that the US Joint Chiefs of Staff had submitted to the secretary of defense on December 12, 1951.[3]

The joint chiefs' memorandum presented recommendations for the mission and size of the US and Japanese military forces, respectively, in connection with defending Japan. It preceded those recommendations with a list of "planning assumptions," the first five of which were as follows:

> a. That world conditions during the period of the next several years will continue to be extremely critical and any attack on Japan by the Communist forces will occur with little warning.
> b. That alignment of Japan with the free world is of vital importance to the United States and the United States will continue to participate in the defense of Japan.
> c. That the Peace Treaty with Japan, the Security Treaty Between the United States and Japan, and a satisfactory Administrative Agreement for implementation of the Security Treaty will go into effect simultaneously.
> d. That the Japanese Constitution will be amended to authorize armed forces for the protection of Japan.

e. That, for the next several years, there will be United States and Japanese military forces in the Far East, the one assisting the other in the preservation of peace and security in the Japan area.

As for Japan's military strength, the joint chiefs called for transforming the Japanese National Police Reserve into a potent defensive force. They grouped their recommendations under the headings "first phase" and "later phases." Their principal recommendations were as follows:

First phase	**Later phases**
Army	*Army*
10 divisions, aggregate personnel strength of 300,000	No major increase
Navy	*Navy*
10 patrol frigates	Indeterminate
50 large landing ships for operational support	
Air force	*Air force*
1 fighter-bomber squadron	6 fighter-interceptor squadrons
1 tactical reconnaissance squadron	12 fighter-bomber squadrons
	3 tactical reconnaissance squadrons
	6 transport squadrons

The army was the primary emphasis in the US military's expectations for Japanese rearmament, as research by Uemura Hideki has verified, and the navy and air force secondary emphases.[4] And the core US demand for the Japanese army was as specified in the December 12, 1951, memorandum: 10 divisions and 300,000 troops. That demand, albeit subject to tweaking with regard to size (that is, increased from 300,000 to 325,000) and composition, became the central plank in subsequent negotiations.

Tatsumi, as a military expert, perceived a persuasive logic in the US military command's "thoroughgoing explanation." He agreed that Japan would need something like the specified force to defend its territory, from Hokkaido in the north to Kyushu in the south.[5] Yoshida, however, would have nothing to do with the US demands conveyed by Tatsumi.

"Japan's circumstances," Yoshida declared, "don't allow for deciding the size of our forces solely on the basis of military considerations. The most pressing need that we face right now is that of restoring the nation's economic strength and stabilizing the foundation for people's livelihoods. The war enervated our national vitality, and our nation is like an emaciated horse. Place an excessive load on this staggering nag, and the horse will simply collapse. Make that clear [to the US military command]."[6]

Tatsumi found himself between a rock and a hard place. He had precious little wiggle room between the US military command's "insistent demands" and Yoshida's "hardline stance in refusing to even consider complying with the demands."[7]

Yoshida had no intention of reneging, of course, on the assurance of rearmament that he had given Dulles. He had followed up his negotiations with the secretary of state with concrete measures for initiating the rearmament process.[8]

The measures for initiating Japan's rearmament began with two personnel reactivations undertaken at Tatsumi's urging. Japan opened its National Police Reserve in autumn 1951 to former career soldiers from the middle-echelon officer corps. Six months later, Japan fortified the National Police Reserve further by opening it to colonel-class veterans.

Another step toward rearmament was the establishment of an officer training school. Yoshida issued a directive in May 1951 to set up the school, and it opened in April 1953 as the National Safety Academy. That name reflected the October 1952 reorganization of the National Police Reserve as the National Safety Forces. The reorganization included increasing the forces' personnel complement to 110,000 and placing them under the newly established National Safety Agency. Similarly, the July 1954 reorganization of the National Safety Forces as the Japan Self-Defense Forces would occasion the school's renaming as the National Defense Academy.

Yoshida took a strong interest in the curriculum and in the quality of teaching at the National Safety Academy. He was determined for the academy to provide a more liberal educational environment than the prewar officer training schools had. And he oversaw its development closely.

The National Safety Agency was responsible for Japan's coast guard, as well as for the National Safety Forces. Its mandate under the National Safety Agency Law of July 1952 was as follows: "Act as required by special exigencies to maintain peace and order in our nation and to safeguard

[the] life and property [of Japanese citizens].” That mandate placed the National Safety Forces a step further from the traditional police function than the previous position of the National Police Reserve. It implied a purpose that transcended simply maintaining domestic public order.

Japan maintained the stance in its official pronouncements that the National Safety Forces were not military in nature, but the distinction was becoming increasingly weak. Yoshida served briefly as the director general of the National Safety Agency in 1952 during his premiership, and he acknowledged the military character of the National Safety Forces in official remarks made in that capacity. The National Safety Agency, Yoshida stated unequivocally, “[is] the bedrock for rearmament, the foundation for a new national military.”[9]

Yoshida’s honesty about the role of the National Safety Forces notwithstanding, he argued as prime minister that rearmament should proceed slowly and resisted the US pressure with regard to the scale and pace of rearmament. That pressure continued under Matthew Ridgway, who succeeded Douglas MacArthur as the military governor of Japan in April 1951. Ridgway assumed that post when President Harry Truman relieved MacArthur of command for insubordination. He called for Japan to expand the National Safety Forces to a troop strength of 150,000 in the fiscal year to March 1953, but Yoshida insisted on capping the forces for the time being at 110,000.[10]

US expectations of Japanese rearmament are evident in a US National Security Council policy paper adopted on August 7, 1952, as NSC 125/2. That paper carried the title “United States Objectives and Courses of Action with Respect to Japan.” The courses of action cited in the title spanned 26 items under the three headings “Political,” “Military,” and “Economic.” An item under the military heading called for assisting Japan, “as a first stage” in rearmament, “to develop a balanced ten-division ground force and appropriate air and naval arms.”

The document calls additionally for assisting Japan, “upon completion of the [first stage of rearmament] and in the light of circumstances then prevailing, to develop military capabilities for participating in the defense of the free nations of the Pacific area, keeping under constant review the nature and timing of assistance which will best serve the security interests of the United States.” NSC 125/2, which received authorization from President Truman, confirms an important aspect of US strategic policy: engaging Japan in collective security arrangements in the Pacific region was a US objective in the first stage of Japanese rearmament.[11] In 1953, President Dwight D. Eisenhower and the Republican Party evicted the Democrats from the White House for the first time in 20 years, but the Republican president abided by his predecessor's authorization of NSC 125/2.

2 The Ikeda-Robertson Talks

Acceptance of military assistance under the Mutual Security Act

A notable event in US-Japanese diplomacy in the aftermath of the signing of the Treaty of San Francisco occurred in October 1953. That event was a four-week set of talks in Washington, DC, between a delegation led by Ikeda Hayato and a team of US government representatives headed by Walter Robertson. Ikeda, later prime minister, chaired the Liberal Party's Policy Research Council and was a trusted protégé of Yoshida. Robertson was the US assistant secretary of state for the Far East.

Historians once credited the Ikeda-Robertson talks with laying a definitive framework for gradually fortifying Japan's military, but recent research findings suggest that the earlier appraisal exaggerated the importance of the talks.[12] The talks, we now know, failed to yield targets for the scale and pace of Japan's defense buildup. They also failed to quell the US pressure on Japan to press ahead with strengthening its national defense.

Whatever the failings of the Ikeda-Robertson talks, the confab was a step of undeniable importance in asserting Yoshida's core policy: devote top priority to economic reconstruction while undertaking minimal rearmament under US military protection. The talks, if nothing else, underlined the differences between the Japanese and US stances with regard to Japan's rearmament.

A lot of information about the Ikeda-Robertson talks has come to light in Japan and in the United States in recent years. Here is a new appraisal of the talks on the basis of that information.

Dulles took office as secretary of state in the new Eisenhower administration. In May 1953, he gave testimony to the Senate Appropriations Committee about the administration's approach to foreign aid. Dulles testified that the mutual-security budget for fiscal 1954* included funding for weaponry for ensuring Japan's domestic security and national defense. His testimony was the first indication that the new administration would furnish Japan with military assistance based on the Mutual Security Act of 1951. That text of the act includes a clear statement of purpose.

> The Congress declares it to be the purpose of this Act to maintain the security and to promote the foreign policy of the United States by authorizing military, economic, and technical assistance to friendly countries to strengthen the mutual security and individual and collective defenses of the free world, to develop their resources in the interest of their security and independence and the national interest of the United States and to facilitate the effective participation of those countries in the United Nations system for collective security.[13]

Thus did the Mutual Security Act provide for furnishing nations friendly to the United States with military, economic, and technical assistance. Congress had streamlined US foreign aid by integrating in a single piece of legislation the provisions of formerly separate laws. As for Japan, the United States had been able to fund military assistance during the occupation under the defense budget. The end of the occupation in April 1952 obliged the US government to find other avenues for funding that assistance, and the Mutual Security Act had apparently become the avenue of choice for that purpose.[14]

Dulles's testimony riveted attention in Japan on the US Mutual Security Act. The opposition factions, led by the Socialist Party, criticized the acceptance of assistance under that act. They argued that accepting the assistance would undermine Japan's constitution and set the stage for shouldering an onerous burden in connection with rearmament. The Japanese government hoped, conversely, that the assistance would encompass more than support for strengthening Japan's national defense and include support for achieving economic self-reliance.

---

* Year to June. The beginning of the US fiscal year changed from June to September in 1976.

Japan's business establishment worried, meanwhile, about the end of the economic stimulus from the Korean War. That stimulus had kick-started Japan's postwar economic recovery, and it would fade with the signing of the truce in July 1953 that occasioned the suspension of hostilities. Support under the Mutual Security Act for ordnance production offered the prospect of a new source of economic stimulus.[15]

The Japanese government was moving toward accepting assistance under the Mutual Security Act. That would entail presenting the US government with a long-term plan for Japan's national defense. The Mutual Security Act predicated military assistance on self-help initiative by the recipient nations, as specified in the following passage (section 511):

> No military, economic, or technical assistance authorized pursuant to this Act . . . shall be supplied to any nation in order to further military effort . . . unless the recipient country has agreed to . . . fulfill the military obligations which it has assumed under multilateral or bilateral agreements or treaties to which the United States is a party [and to] take all reasonable measures which may be needed to develop its defense capacities.

Dulles stated in his testimony to the Senate Appropriations Committee that the administration eyed a target of 10 divisions and 350,000 troops for Japan's National Safety Forces and that US financial assistance would be necessary to attain that target.[16] The secretary of state's remarks set off a wave of debate over rearmament planning in the Japanese government and private sector. Several proposals arose, the principal ones being three government proposals, from the National Safety Agency, the Economic Deliberation Agency, and the Ministry of Finance, respectively, and a private-sector proposal from the Japan Federation of Employers' Associations (Keidanren, now the Japan Business Federation). The different proposals spanned a broad range of visions for rearmament. They ranged, for example, from 100,000 to 300,000 troops for the army, from 100,000 to 387,000 tons for the navy, and from 1,000 to 3,750 aircraft for the air force.[17]

Yoshida was playing a weak hand as he set about solidifying his government's position in regard to rearmament. After Japan emerged from the occupation, he faced calls from both sides of the political spectrum to resign the premiership. The calls emanated from familiar sources in the leftist and reformist factions and from new sources on the right. Conservative politicians, led by Miki Bukichi and Kōno Ichirō, urged Yoshida to cede the premiership to Hatoyama Ichirō. The latter had returned to politics in 1951, after a five-year purge from all political activities imposed by the occupation authorities.

Political disarray obliged Yoshida to dissolve the lower house of the Diet and call elections twice in the year after the occupation ended. The elections took place in October 1952 and in April 1953, and Yoshida's Liberal Party lost its majority in the lower house in the second of those elections. Seeking to shore up his minority government, Yoshida reached out to the Reform Party, the largest opposition party. Headed by Shigemitsu Mamoru, the Reform Party was the closest of the opposition parties to the Liberal Party with regard to policy. Yoshida and Shigemitsu met on September 27, 1953, and their discussions set in motion a broad accommodation between their parties.

The biggest policy difference between the Liberal Party and Reform Party had been rearmament. Yoshida and Shigemitsu reached a basic agreement for overcoming that difference. They agreed that the Japanese government should work out a long-term plan for strengthening national defense and that it should reorganize the National Safety Forces as the Self-Defense Forces. The reorganization would include strengthening the forces to equip them to be able to counter a direct attack on Japan.[18]

Yoshida and Shigemitsu's agreement skirted the question of the constitutionality of Japan's armed forces, and it hewed to the Yoshida approach of undertaking rearmament gradually. The prime minister had thus succeeded in drawing the Reform Party into his policy orbit, at least in that respect.[19] Interestingly, calling for a vigorous approach to rearmament had lost seats for the Reform Party and for the Hatoyama-led conservative faction of the Liberal Party in the lower house election of April 1953, and opposition to rearmament had won seats for the Socialist Party and the Social Democratic Party. Shigemitsu presumably recognized that rearmament, if it was to proceed at all, would need to proceed gradually, as advocated by Yoshida.

Differing strategic perspectives

Fortified by the agreement with Shigemitsu, Yoshida resolved to travel to the United States and engage in talks directly with the US government. He dispatched the Ikeda mission to Washington, DC, in October 1953 to lay the groundwork for a visit. The delegation consisted largely of Finance Ministry officials. On hand for talks with the delegation were Robertson and other State Department officials, along with representatives of the defense and treasury departments and of the Bureau of the Budget and the Foreign Operations Administration.

The Ikeda-Robertson talks were the first instance of formal and wide-ranging Japanese-US negotiations under the Eisenhower administration. They began on October 2 and concluded with the issuance of a joint statement on October 30. During that four-week span, the participants held twelve sessions, including a preparatory session, and the talks were, by all accounts, robust and thoroughgoing. The Japanese and US officials discussed bilateral issues that had remained unresolved since the signing of the peace treaty. Chief among those issues were the rearmament of Japan and the strengthening of Japan's defense; Japan's trade with Southeast Asian nations and its reparation obligations to those nations; Japanese trade with China; Japanese debt to the United States incurred during the occupation as credits received for food, fertilizer, petroleum, and medical supplies under the Government and Relief in Occupied Areas (GARIOA) program; and Japanese access to international lending and other sources of foreign currency.[20]

Discussion of the US demands for Japan to strengthen its national defense began in earnest at the second round of talks, which took place on October 8. Frank Nash, the US assistant secretary of defense for international security affairs, kicked things off with a summary of the defense department's stance. He described the department's perspective on strategic concerns in the world at large and, especially, in the Far East.

Nash began with a summary of his impressions of a recent observation tour of Europe. He described the capacity of the North Atlantic Treaty Organization to repel potential Communist aggression in Europe, and he reported that the NATO members had strengthened that capacity greatly over the past four years. The Communist threat was thus becoming a thing of the past in Europe, he explained, but remained a clear and present danger in the Far East. Nash observed that the Soviet Union was a nation that would move to fill a power vacuum and that the Far East matched that description.

The Soviet Union, according to Nash, had approximately 500,000 troops and 5,000 to 6,000 military aircraft in eastern Siberia. He noted that the Soviets could supplement their forces with some of China's five million men and women in uniform and surmised that they could easily muster 500,000 troops for lightning strikes on Japan simultaneously from the north and south. The US military would move to assist Japan with a "mobile striking force," but Japan would need to take primary responsibility, he emphasized, for defending its territory.

Nash warned his Japanese listeners that the US military could not maintain a large presence in their nation indefinitely. Having outlined the strategic challenge for Japan, he repeated the US demands for strengthening Japan's national defense. He reminded the Japanese that their archipelago presented extensive needs for coastal defense. And he reiterated the US assertion that Japan would require at least 10 divisions and 325,000 army troops to protect its territory. Nash did not offer quantitative targets for bolstering Japan's navy and air force but offered to provide detailed figures on request.[21]

Miyazawa Kiichi, later prime minister, attended the Ikeda-Robertson talks as a member of the upper house of the Diet and as Ikeda's personal interpreter. He included a discussion of the gathering in his memoir, *Tōkyō-Washinton no mitsudan* (Secret Talks between Tokyo and Washington). Miyazawa laments that the Japanese delegation possessed no military expertise and was therefore unable to hold its own in debate with the US military experts. Nash's arguments, recalls Miyazawa, simply went in one Japanese ear and out the other.[22]

Contrary to Miyazawa's recollection, the Japanese delegation's minutes of the meetings record Ikeda as asking questions that were probing, albeit nontechnical. "How," he asked, "can you imagine the Soviets landing 500,000 troops in Japan, considering the presence of the US navy and air force as a protective umbrella? Something especially noteworthy is the Soviet shortage of ships. Surely the Soviets could never transport such a huge number of troops."[23]

Ikeda regarded naval and air power as a definitive factor in defending the island nation of Japan. The United States deployed far more naval and air power in East Asia than the Soviet Union did, and that differential, Ikeda was suggesting, negated the need for Japan to maintain a large army for national defense.

Nash acknowledged in response to Ikeda's question and comments the US advantage in naval and air power. The US navy and air force could inflict severe damage, he conceded, on an invading Soviet force. He cautioned the Japanese, however, that the notion of a protective umbrella was naive. A Soviet invasion would begin, he reasoned, with a vicious air assault. The Soviets would then secure beachheads, Nash continued, and could land large numbers of troops easily in the absence of stout resistance.

The rebuttal by Nash was apparently unconvincing to the members of the Japanese delegation. That is evident in a report by Murakami Kotarō, a Finance Ministry official who took the minutes of the October 8 session. Murakami delivered that report to his superior at the ministry. It contains a withering assessment of Nash's comments.

Murakami dismisses Nash's warning of a lightning attack by 500,000 Soviet troops as a "bluff" and expresses agreement with Ikeda's doubts about the Soviet capacity to transport such a volume of personnel. He complains of an overall ambiguity in Nash's presentation, starting with the figure of 500,000 troops in Siberia. Murakami notes that Nash didn't clarify whether that was the total for the Far East overall or for coastal deployments. He is also dubious about Nash's figure of "5,000 to 6,000 military aircraft in Siberia." The US Far East Air Force command, he notes, had placed the number at 4,500. Murakami is equally critical of Nash's imprecision about the operational range of the Soviets' MiG fighter jets. Typifying the tone of Murakami's report is the following passage:

> [Nash's] strategic pronouncements rely on data that differs little from what appears in Japanese magazines. And the US demands that he voices for Japanese rearmament are extreme. He disregards fact in exaggerating threats to fan fear. In conclusion, we come away with the same impression that we get from talks in Tokyo with the National Safety Agency and the [US military] supervisors. [Nash and his colleagues] would seem to be urging haste without thinking.[24]

The Japanese and the Americans thus approached the discussion of strengthening Japan's defense with differing perspectives on strategic requisites. And the differences in perspectives shaped the progress of the discussion mightily.

An Ikeda proposal for a five-year defense plan

Contrasting visions of a strengthened national defense for Japan emerged from the Japanese and the US delegations at the Ikeda-Robertson talks. Neither, however, was especially rich in detail. An exchange in the third session, on October 12, is a case in point. The US delegation put forth the figures of ten divisions and 325,000 troops for the army. Asked by the Japanese delegation about the army's composition, the Americans declined to offer a concrete response. They said simply that such details would be up to the Far East Command.

The Japanese delegation's confidence in the integrity of the US figures suffered further on October 21. On that day, the US delegation briefly upped the ante to 350,000 troops. The new figure matched the number that Dulles had offered in his May 1953 testimony to the Senate Appropriations Committee, but its more immediate source was strategizing under way at the Far East Command. To be precise, the strategists at the Far East Command had decided that Japan should have an army of 15 divisions and 348,000 troops.

While the US demands were escalating, Ikeda submitted a five-year defense proposal for Japan under his name on October 13. He prepared his proposal by tweaking a plan under consideration at Japan's Finance Ministry that devoted priority to budgetary constraints. Ikeda indicated plainly on the proposal that it was "the result of personal study." He indicated, too, that the proposal "reflected the latest thinking in the Japanese government but that it was not, by any means, an official document or a finalized proposal."

The Ikeda proposal in Washington, DC, was among multiple Japanese proposals in play at the time. Japan's National Safety Agency, for example, had broached a proposal for a Japanese army of ten divisions and 200,000 troops with the US Far East Command.[25]

That the Ikeda-Robertson meetings did not produce finalized proposals is understandable in the light of their original purpose. Yoshida had proposed the meetings, after all, largely as a means of testing the waters for a formal state visit.

The Japanese and US negotiators in Washington, DC, differed over the suitable sizes of the Japanese forces for land, sea, and air. But the biggest sticking point, by far, was the number of troops for the army.

Ikeda's proposal of October 13 called for a Japanese army of 10 divisions and 180,000 personnel; a navy of 210 ships, which would total 156,550 tons, and 31,300 personnel; and an air force of 518 aircraft, including 300 trainer aircraft, and 7,600 personnel. The US proposal on the table at the time called for a Japanese army of 10 divisions and 325,000 personnel, a navy of 108 ships and 13,500 personnel, and an air force of 800 aircraft and 30,000 personnel.

Japan's geography underlay basic agreement with regard to the need for 10 army divisions. The Japanese archipelago is extremely long from north to south, and inadequate road infrastructure would impede troop movement in some parts of the nation. Everyone agreed that 10 divisions were the minimum requirement for sound defense and that they should be deployed across the archipelago. Ikeda's proposal posited a deployment of 4 divisions on Hokkaido, 4 on Honshu, and 2 on Kyushu.

Where the Japanese and US proposals diverged greatly was in regard to the number of troops that each division warranted. Ikeda assumed in preparing his proposal that no overseas deployment was in the offing for the Japanese ground forces and that they could make do with a minimum of logistical and other support. Miyazawa explained Ikeda's calculation.

> The biggest difference is the fact that each time the US military goes on one of its missions abroad (of course, they have not fought or had to fight an enemy on its shores), it tends to bring everything with it. In the case of our Safety Force, they are not intended to go abroad. If their vehicles were to break, they could just take them to a local repair shop. It would not be necessary to bring a fully equipped maintenance team. In this sense it would be quite possible to do without military-owned and -managed assets and to get the help of the civilian sector if an enemy were to invade Japan. This is the biggest difference between an expeditionary military and that which fights on the home ground. As a result, it is possible to greatly reduce the rear area support forces.
>
> In order to resolve the problem over the number of personnel for the division (experts supposedly call this a division slice), it is necessary to understand that of the 32,500 making up a US division, 20,000 are combat troops, whereas a division in the Japanese Safety Forces is comprised of 27,500 persons, of which about 17,000 are combat forces. So, if these

> were reduced, the size of a Japan Safety Force division could be about 18,000, including rear area support forces. In the North Atlantic Treaty Organization today, the size of a peacetime division is about 18,000.[26]

Ikeda posited reducing the noncombat personnel in each ground division of Japan's National Safety Forces by one-third to one-half and reducing the number of combat personnel in light-arms units by one-third. That was his formula for getting the average size of a division down to 18,000.

Members of the US Joint Chiefs of Staff took part in the fifth session of the Ikeda-Robertson talks, on October 15, and a series of questions and answers about the Ikeda proposal ensued. Ikeda argued that Japanese ground forces of 10 divisions and 180,000 troops would be sufficient as long as US sea and air support was available.[27]

The US military representatives expressed a degree of agreement with Ikeda's proposed figures for strengthening Japan's naval and air forces but objected that his proposed figure for the ground force was inadequate. Colonel M. N. Houston explained that the figures proposed by the US delegation were purely for the defense of Japan and incorporated no assumptions of dispatching troops abroad. He argued that even wholly domestic deployment would necessitate substantial numbers of personnel for the command organization and for combat-support functions.

Houston asserted, meanwhile, that Japan should group its ground forces in three corps, rather than the single corps proposed by Ikeda, and that each corps should have its own supply, artillery, engineering, chemical, and armored units. He added that Ikeda's proposal was overly reliant on civilian support.[28]

The task of explaining the details of Ikeda's proposal at the October 15 session had fallen to Murakami. He acknowledged that the proposal relied heavily on civilian support for noncombat functions. Murakami then described three underlying assumptions for the Ikeda proposal, admitting that the Japanese should have described the assumptions earlier.

1. Japanese ground forces would repel an attempted invasion at water's edge with the assistance of US naval and air power.

2. The figure of 18,000 troops per army division was for peacetime deploy-

ment, and the size and composition of the divisions would change in the event of hostilities.

3. The Japanese forces would take up geographically optimal positions to repel an attempted invasion.[29]

These three assumptions are fundamental to the thrust of the Ikeda proposal. Ikeda assumes that US naval and air support will enable Japan to avoid a land battle with a prospective invader and that even if the invader gains a beachhead the Japanese forces can compensate for their limited number through superior geographical positioning. He is predicating the entire exercise, meanwhile, on the assumption that an attempted invasion is extremely unlikely.

We can perhaps regard a certain complacency as the defining characteristic of the Ikeda proposal. Clearly, the Japanese and US delegations were possessed of vastly different notions of urgency about preparedness for a possible invasion. The Americans took issue with Murakami's explanation. Insufficient ground forces, they argued, posed a strategic risk, regardless of however satisfactory the naval and air power might be. No one could deny the possibility that an invader could secure beachheads and that the defenders would then need to stage land-based action to repel the enemy.

The Americans noted, meanwhile, that assuming an attempted invasion to be unlikely was a poor basis for framing military strategy and that the notion of increasing troop strength after an invasion was under way was unrealistic. They questioned, too, the assumption that the Japanese defenders would have a strategic advantage with regard to geographical positioning. The Americans cited the vulnerability of rail logistics, for example, to sabotage.

The pace and budget for rearmament

The number of troops to allocate to Japan's ground forces remained a sticking point throughout the Ikeda-Robertson talks. Something that gradually became clear, however, was that the Americans were more interested in the pace of rearmament than in the ultimate size of the Japanese army. Here is how Norman Paul, who attended the Ikeda-Robertson talks as a representative of the Foreign Operations Administration, explained that interest. The Foreign Operations Administration was responsible for administering foreign assistance under the Mutual Security Act. Paul provided this explanation at the second session of the talks, on October 8.

Preliminary deliberations were under way, Paul reported, over the allocation of foreign assistance in fiscal 1955 (July 1954–June 1955). To secure assistance for Japan under the Mutual Security Act, the Foreign Operations Administration needed to convince Congress that Japan was committed to defense. That would mean demonstrating that the Japanese government had agreed to a plan for strengthening Japan's defense and for undertaking a specified share of the cost of that strengthening.

Paul also advanced another budgetary concern. The defense department's budget included sufficient funding to pay for Japan to deploy ground forces of up to 180,000 troops, but it needed to use that funding by June 30, 1954. And that support, too, hinged on a visible commitment by Japan to its own defense.

Paul and his colleagues in the Foreign Operations Administration calculated that Japan could afford to approximately double its defense expenditures, to about ¥200 billion. Japan's annual defense expenditures totaled 2.4 percent of the nation's GNP at the time, and the Americans had concluded that Japan could afford to increase that figure to 4 percent.[30]

The expectations voiced by Paul presented the Japanese with daunting challenges. They would need to revise national policy to allow for strengthened defense, and they would need to secure increased budgetary allocations for that purpose in the fiscal years to March 1955 and 1956.

Paul's remarks on October 8 marked the beginning of earnest debate of military issues at the Ikeda-Robertson talks. That debate continued with the US delegation's presentation of a proposal for strengthening Japan's defense on October 12, with the submission of the Ikeda proposal on the 13th, and with questioning by US military representatives about the Ikeda proposal on the 15th.

The back-and-forth consisted basically of the sides stating and reiterating their respective positions. To summarize the results of the talks, the delegations agreed on the exchange of memorandums. The Japanese delegation submitted a memorandum to the US delegation on October 19, the US delegation submitted a response on the 21st, and the Japanese delegation resubmitted its memorandum, revised to address the US response, on the 27th. According to Miyazawa, the memorandums exchanged were honest and highly forthright expressions of the two sides' positions.[31] The defense debate's focus shifted through the honest exchange to the pace and budget for Japan's rearmament over the next two years.

In the October 19 memorandum, the portion dealing with defense begins with a reconfirmation of what the delegation had stated earlier: "The Japanese representatives explained the four restrictions on Japan's fully possessing defense capabilities."[32] It noted that the delegation had explained those constraints in the foregoing talks in Washington, DC, and that Prime Minister Yoshida and his subordinates had emphasized the constraints in official and unofficial pronouncements.

The constraints, as identified anew in the memorandum, were legal, sociopolitical, economic, and physical. Japan's peace constitution precludes possessing the capacity to make war. Education under the occupation propagated a commitment to peace in the populace. Living standards remain low. Japan lacks the option of instituting military conscription, meanwhile, and would therefore be unable to raise a large force of quality recruits quickly.[33]

Next, the memorandum confirms that the two delegations, having acknowledged Japan's four constraints, have reached three agreements. One, summarized below, acknowledges that Japan will require financial assistance from the United States to fulfill its defense commitment. The other two are that (1) the United States acknowledges that Japanese expenditures on the upkeep of US forces will decline as the nation's defense capabilities increase and that (2) the Japanese government acknowledges its responsibility to heighten popular awareness of the need for patriotism and self-defense.

> The delegations agreed that establishing a defensive force on the order of what is appropriate for Japan and even merely maintaining the force will require military aid for Japan of a substantial sum over the coming several years. In regard to this point, a proposal was made by the Japanese delegation for the size of a force believed to be the largest believed possible to implement under the present circumstances. The US representatives stated that the figures and scale indicated in the proposal were

> insufficient but was of the opinion that the proposal could be improved and acted on without especially great difficulty. The Japanese delegation stated that it wanted to know what kinds and amounts of military assistance were to be assumed under the [US] plan that had been submitted that it would like confirmation as to how the plan could be improved without altering its basic theme.[34]

The phrasing is nebulous and indirect,[35] but the underlying message is clear: The Japanese and US delegations have exchanged proposals for Japan's defense planning. Large differences loom between the proposals. The participants perceive room for overcoming the differences through future discussions.

Miyazawa, who was responsible for drafting the Japanese memorandum, paraphrased the above item.

> They agreed that even to maintain the existing level of Japanese defense, a major level of military aid was necessary. Moreover, regarding this, the Japanese side presented a plan to possess a force of approximately this level. In response to this proposal, the US side pointed out it was still too little, but through continued consultations, a conclusion both sides would be happy with was possible. The Japanese side stated it would like to know what extent and at what point would aid be forthcoming.[36]

The Japanese and US delegations had, in a sense, reached an accord with respect to the troop strength for the Japanese army. To be sure, the Americans clung to their insistence on 325,000 troops, and the Japanese remained adamant that 180,000 was the most they could muster. They had agreed, however, to shelve the issue for the time being. Thus did Miyazawa write that "neither side won or lost" with regard to that issue.[37]

Japan's delegation possessed a degree of latitude for compromise over the issue of troop strength.[38] That was evident in Ikeda's response to a question from Paul at the end of the morning session on October 15. Paul asked if Japan could increase its troop strength without violating the constitution or other laws if the United States provided the required equipment and training and if the economic issues were thereby overcome.

"I'd like to say that it would be possible," Ikeda replied, "though it would depend on the size of the increase. I would say that on the assumption that Japanese attitudes would change during the term [of the plan]. That would depend to a large extent on how much assistance the Japanese could expect from the United States."[39]

On close reading, the memorandum reveals that Ikeda and his cohorts expected a quid pro quo for compromising on the defense issue. They realized that foreign assistance would be useful in nurturing a commitment among the Japanese to self-sufficiency in national defense. The delegation therefore sought assurance (1) that the United States would provide Japan with economic assistance, as well as military aid; (2) about the scale of future US procurement of military materiel in Japan for Japan and for other nations; and (3) that the proceeds that would accrue from selling surplus US agricultural produce to Japan and that the US would recirculate as assistance would total about $50 million and could be used in part for repairing roads, which had military strategic value, and for strengthening military-related industries. The Americans, meanwhile, assumed that offers of economic assistance would prove a persuasive carrot and that the Japanese would agree to consider expanding their army to more than 180,000 troops.[40]

Ikeda and his cohorts had hoped to reach a draw with respect to troop strength with subtle phrasing couched in generalities. And they had hoped to secure assurances of economic assistance with their hints of military bolstering. The US response on October 21 betrayed the Japanese expectations. It was the product of careful coordination among the pertinent government departments and agencies and was stern in content. A Japanese newspaper quoted insiders as suggesting that Japanese news coverage of the US response would shake the Yoshida government. The atmosphere at Japan's embassy in Washington was tense as Ikeda and his team moved to parry the US demands.[41]

Economic constraints as an unconvincing factor

The US delegation, in its memorandum, took note of the four constraints cited in the Japanese memorandum. It refrained from commenting on the legal and sociopolitical constraints on the grounds that they were domestic issues for Japan. The delegation touched on the Japanese claims of economic and physical constraints, but only indirectly and dismissively.

Here is what the US delegation was demanding: Japan should budget ¥200 billion for defense spending in the fiscal year to March 1955 and ¥235 billion in the fiscal year to March 1956, and it should add 24,000 troops to its army in the fiscal year to March 1954 and 46,000 in the fiscal year to March 1955. The increases in troop strength would expand the army to 180,000 troops by March 31, 1955. Whatever Japan's economic and physical constraints, they were not so severe, the Americans reasoned, as to preclude making those budgetary allocations and troop-strength increases.

The US delegation demanded additionally that Japan accept, as a longer-term target, an army troop strength of 325,000 or even 350,000. This was the first time that the figure of 350,000 had arisen in the Ikeda-Robertson talks. The Americans denied any linkage, meanwhile, between Japan's strengthening its defense and securing economic assistance from the United States. They declared that their government had no plans for bestowing economic aid on Japan and that they saw no grounds for considering such aid.[42]

Throughout the talks, the US delegation resisted the notion of Japan's economic circumstances as a constraint on strengthening national defense. The US delegation's stance was, as noted elsewhere, that Japan could and should allocate 4 percent of its GNP—¥200 billion—to national defense. Dulles had raised the example of Italy in his August 1953 meeting with Yoshida in Tokyo. He had pointed out to the prime minister that Italy was far more distant than Japan was from Communist nations but allocated 7 percent of its national income to defense. Japan, he was saying, could certainly do better than the 2 or 3 percent that it was spending on defense.[43]

Ikeda resorted at the October 8 session to per capita GNP as an indicator of Japan's alleged economic frailty and, thus, as justification for limiting defense spending. That was by way of rebutting Paul's call for Japan to double its defense spending. Ikeda's stratagem backfired, however, when the Americans produced the data presented here in tables 1 and 2. The data showed clearly that nations comparable to Japan in per capita GNP were spending far more on defense.[44]

Another theme that the US delegation sounded throughout the talks pertained to economic management by the Japanese government. The Japanese delegation was claiming economic frailty as a constraint on defense spending and was pleading for economic assistance. In response, the US delegation suggested, as discussed below, that Japan's economic malaise reflected government failure to tackle inflation properly.

Table 1. US government calculations of defense spending for FYE June 30, 1953 (March 31, 1953, for Japan)

	Per capita GNP	Per capita defense spending	Defense spending as percentage of GNP
Greece	$298	$25	8.5%
Turkey	$204	$13	6.5%
Japan	$200	$3	1.6%
Yugoslavia	$199	$36	18.2%
Portugal	$166	$8	5.0%

Table 2. US government calculations of defense spending for FYE June 30, 1954 (March 31, 1954, for Japan)

	Per capita GNP	Per capita defense spending	Defense spending as percentage of GNP
Greece	$309	$26	8.4%
Yugoslavia	$228	$36	15.7%
Turkey	$216	$14	6.7%
Japan	$210	$5	2.4%
Portugal	$171	$9	5.0%

Both tables reproduced from Joseph Dodge, "Ways and Means of Strengthening the Japanese Economy" (1949)

A grasping for grounds for compromise

We perceive in the proceedings of the October 23 session a renewed grasping by the Japanese delegation for grounds for compromise. The proceedings were a combination of questioning and objecting. On one hand, the Japanese were at a loss as for how to respond to the US memorandum of October 21. On the other hand, they had come to terms with what they now realized were the Americans' primary concerns: (1) using the US defense department's current budget allocation to fund an increase in the Japanese army's troop strength to 180,000 and (2) being able to assure

Congress that Japan would be allocating 4 percent of its GNP to defense spending and to thereby fulfill a key condition for securing assistance for Japan under the Mutual Security Act. Miyazawa provides a lucid account of the October 23 session in his memoir.

Ikeda was proposing that Japan increase the troop strength of its army to 180,000 by the end of March 1957, and the US delegation was calling for Japan to increase the army's troop strength to that level by the end of March 1955. Miyazawa came up with the idea of using the difference in Japanese and US fiscal years to narrow that two-year gap. The March 31, 1957, deadline in Ikeda's proposal coincided with the US government fiscal year to June 1957. Moving the deadline up to June 30, 1956, would shift up one year on the US fiscal calendar (from the July 1956–June 1957 fiscal year to the July 1955–June 1956 fiscal year) while keeping it in the same Japanese fiscal year (April 1956 to March 1957). Ikeda agreed to the adjustment, and Miyazawa incorporated it in a revised memorandum draft.[45]

Accelerating the troop-strength increase, Ikeda knew, would be difficult, but he was prepared to commit to that measure in the pursuit of compromise. The Japanese presented their revised memorandum to the US delegation on October 27. In it, they sought to finesse the issue of constraints. They thanked their American counterparts for recognizing the legal, sociopolitical, economic, and physical constraints on Japan in strengthening its military. And they argued that realistic defense planning needed to reflect prudent, bilateral consideration of those constraints.[46]

Robertson and his compatriots might not have thought much of the constraints, but the Americans had at least acknowledged their existence. The Japanese were seeking to elicit basic, minimal recognition of that point. Their memorandum went on to basically parrot what the US delegation had demanded with regard to Japanese defense budgeting.

The US delegation's minutes of the October 27 session note that the Japanese delegation accompanied the memorandum with an oral pledge to achieve the figures cited.[47] As for troop strength, the memorandum cites the US demand—325,000 to 350,000 troops—but does not indicate the Japanese position on that demand. Whereas the Japanese delegation's memorandum of October 19 had addressed in detail the figures put forth by the US delegation, the Japanese memorandum of October 27 simply acknowledges the US demands without offering anything in the way of commentary.

No mention of final targets for troop strength appears in the State Department memorandum that summarized the differences between the US memorandum of October 21 and the Japanese memorandum of October 27.[48] That suggests that the State Department had shelved the question of the Japanese-US differences with regard to that matter. What the Japanese pledged in the memorandum of October 27 was as follows: increase the troop strength of Japanese ground forces by 24,000 troops during the fiscal year from April 1954 to March 1955 and follow up with an increase of 46,000 troops to possess ground forces of 180,000 troops by summer 1956.

Note that "summer 1956" is in reference to the June end of the US government fiscal year. Miyazawa records in his memoir the following analysis of the different figures for troop strength:

> We were able to imagine over the past two weeks of meetings . . . that the figures . . . of 325,000 or 350,00 in ground forces used by the US side were not really based on any particular foundation. On the other hand, the number 180,000 put forth by the US side does appear to have had a reason for sticking to this number. Our position from the time we left Japan was that the US would probably push 180,000, so the question was over how many years to make this happen. . . . It would be in the interest of both countries if we could spread the number 325,000 or 350,000 over a lifetime.[49]

Alas, the Japanese attempt at compromise fell short. On hand to submit the revised memorandum was Aichi Kiichi, Japan's parliamentary vice minister of finance. Ikeda, Aichi, Miyazawa, and other key members of the Japanese delegation had traveled to New York for talks with American business leaders. Aichi returned to Washington, DC, a day ahead of Ikeda and Miyazawa in time to submit the revised memorandum at an informal session on October 27.[50]

Accepting the memorandum on behalf of the US delegation was Robert J. G. McClurkin, the deputy director of the State Department's Office of Northeast Asian Affairs. Qualifying his query as a personal perspective, he asked if Japan couldn't strengthen its [ground forces] by 35,000 troops in the fiscal year to March 1955 and by a further 35,000 troops in the fiscal year to March 1956.

Only three months separated the Japanese proposal and McClurkin's suggestion with respect to the timing for attaining the troop strength of 180,000. The potential for bridging that gap receded, however, on account of an ill-advised response by Aichi. He rejected McClurkin's suggestion with the flimsy excuse that the Japanese delegation hadn't cleared the memorandum with Ikeda.[51]

The 10th and essentially final session of the Ikeda-Robertson talks took place on October 28, and it was the scene of continued discussion of defense budgeting. Robertson asked the Japanese how much their government could allocate to defense spending over the coming two years. Ikeda emphasized at the outset that the issue at hand was one of principle rather than numbers. He reminded his host that he had begun his career in the Finance Ministry and had a great deal of experience with preparing budgets. Ikeda noted that a budget is the product of assembling diverse spending items deemed essential and adjusting the different amounts as necessary. No individual item could be sacred, he stressed, in the process of compiling a budget.

Ikeda then launched into a final effort at compromise. He began by revisiting the question of whether pensions for veterans counted as part of the defense budget. The Japanese had raised that question on October 23, when Ikeda and Robertson were both absent, and the Americans had responded that the pensions did not count as a defense-spending item. Ikeda revisited the question in the context of an overall defense budget that he had sketched.

The figures that Ikeda had assembled for the defense budget in the fiscal year to March 1955 totaled ¥258 billion. That total comprised ¥103 billion for the National Safety Agency, including ¥25 billion carried forward from the previous fiscal year; ¥62 billion for the Japanese share of US defense expenses in Japan, including ¥5 billion carried forward from the previous fiscal year; ¥67 billion for veterans' pensions; ¥20 billion for the national government's share of regional police budgets, which Ikeda had included all along in his defense-budget figures; and ¥6 billion for the Maritime Safety Agency. Ikeda's numbers failed to impress Robertson. The American expressed disappointment that the Japanese couldn't come up with a more robust proposal for their national defense and changed the subject.[52]

An agreement abandoned

Representatives of the pertinent departments and agencies in the US government discussed the Japanese memorandum received on October 27. They were unable to reach a consensus, however, on how "to bring the US and Japanese proposals together."[53]

The defense department's Charles Sullivan delivered a damning appraisal of the Japanese proposals at an interdepartmental meeting held on October 30. Sullivan was the chief of the Northeast Asian Section in the Office of Foreign Military Affairs. He prefaced his remarks with the caveat that he hadn't heard back from the Far East Command about the Japanese proposals. Sullivan then noted that the Japanese proposal for strengthening the Japanese army fell far short of the Americans' expectations. He expressed the opinion that the Japanese proposal was so weak as to be "worthless" as a pledge and that it should not appear in any memorandum of agreement. The other participants agreed to leave numerical targets for strengthening the Japanese army out of any agreement that they might be able to cobble together that day.[54]

John Allison, the US ambassador to Japan, also recommended not including figures for strengthening the Japanese army in any memorandum of agreement, though his reason differed from Sullivan's. Allison was forwarded received detailed reports about the progress of the Ikeda-Robertson talks, and he received an urgent request in the afternoon of October 29, Japan time, for his views on the Japanese proposal. The request was in a telegram sent under the name of the secretary of state, John Foster Dulles.

> Urgently request Embassy evaluation political implications GARIOA settlement this year. Also request Embassy and Command comments what timetable on buildup ground forces is worth trying to get in writing in present talks whether in writing in secret memorandum/understanding or public communiqué. Specifically which of following would be acceptable and what would be Embassy and Command judgment re order preference? (1) Omit entirely (2) include US expression of desirable goal of 325 to 350 thousand with Japanese noting and indicating general willingness move that direction (3) 180 thousand goal reached by March 31,

> 1956 through 35 thousand increments Japanese fiscal years 1954 and 1955 (4) Japanese proposal cited above [this final item being in reference to the following in the first paragraph of the telegram: "Re ground forces buildup best Japanese suggestion so far is 24 thousand Japanese fiscal year 1954 and 46 thousand additional by summer 1956"].[55]

Allison replied with a telegram at 9 p.m. on the 29th. His response to the question about the Japanese delegation's proposals for strengthening the Japanese army was as follows:

> On ground-force build-up our order of preference is 1, 4, 3, 2. . . . I believe it should be omitted entirely from any understanding or communiqué. Japanese ready to go ahead and preference 4 or 3 will only commit us to a ceiling and either tie our hands or put on us onus of once again pushing Japanese do what they themselves should do in own interest. There is nothing to be gained by committing ourselves now rather than a month or two months hence to preference 4 or 3. There is nothing to be said in my opinion for preference 2. We may at some point have to agree for time being to 180,000 but if so it would be preferable to have this come up from the Japanese side in the course of the next few weeks or months than as a result of what will be interpreted as American pressure on Ikeda in Washington. Believe actually pressures in Japan to settle problem on nation's future security likely increase and conservative elements who now know what we want and why will become increasingly uneasy at lack of agreement on force goals.[56]

Achieving an internal consensus proved impossible in the American camp, and that precluded a formal agreement between the Japanese and US delegations. The delegations settled instead on a joint statement phrased in noncommittal tones. They issued the statement on October 30, bringing their talks to a close. Their statement explained that "the talks covered various interrelated problems of mutual interest such as Japan's defense build-up, United States assistance, settlement for United States postwar economic aid (GARIOA), foreign investment, and trade with Communist China." With regard to strengthening Japan's defense, the statement characterized the results of the talks as follows:

> The conferees agreed on the necessity of increasing Japan's self-defense forces in order to protect her from possible aggression, and to reduce the United States burden related to the defense of Japan. It was, however, noted that under present circumstances there are constitutional, economic, budgetary and other limitations which will not allow the immediate building of Japan's self-defense forces to a point sufficient for Japan's defense. With due regard to these limitations, continued effort on the part of Japan will be made to expedite the build-up. Subject to necessary Congressional authorization, the United States conferees offered to assist Japan in developing the Japanese forces by supplying major items of military equipment for the land, sea and air forces which Japan raises. Questions relating to Japanese defense forces and United States military assistance will be discussed further in Tokyo in the near future by representatives of the two governments with a view to reaching a definite understanding.[57]

Bend-but-don't-break tactics

Allison urged realism in resuming the negotiations over strengthening Japan's defense. In that spirit, the negotiations in Tokyo focused initially on the most immediate issue: Japan's budgetary allocation for defense spending in the fiscal year to March 1955.[58]

The negotiations in Tokyo paved the way for the signing of the United States and Japan Mutual Defense Assistance Agreement in March 1954. Foremost among the points agreed by the negotiators was that Japan would increase the staffing of its National Safety Agency by 41,000. That increase was to comprise 31,000 uniformed personnel and 10,000 civilian personnel, and the increase in uniformed personnel was to include 20,000 troops in the ground forces.[59]

Japanese and US negotiators agreed in Tokyo that Japan would allocate ¥200 billion to defense in the fiscal year to March 1955 and increase the number of Japanese army divisions, deployed by district, to six, from four. The agreed-upon budgetary allocation comprised ¥78 billion for the National Safety Agency, including ¥20 billion carried forward from the previous fiscal year; ¥58.5 billion for the Japanese share of US defense expenses in Japan; ¥10 billion in unused allocations for miscellaneous defense expenses; ¥8 billion in contractual obligations incurred in connection with defense and not included in other defense-related expenses; ¥4 billion for coastal policing by the Maritime Safety Agency; and ¥20 billion for the rental-equivalence value of government-owned assets provided to the US military to use.[60]

In Tokyo, the question of whether to aim for a Japanese army of 180,000 troops or more than 300,000 became a secondary issue. The US government had clung to strong notions, however, about the level of defense that Japan should possess.

Not for another year or so would the US pressure for a Japanese military buildup relax visibly. The new stance would be in response to the changing geopolitical landscape.

In the meantime, the US political pressure on Japan to strengthen its military remained strong. Vice President Richard Nixon opined in Japan in November, the month after the Ikeda-Robertson talks, that disarming Japan had been a mistake. The next month, the US Joint Chiefs of Staff adopted new targets for the Japanese. Those targets centered on the previously mentioned targets that had been under study in the Far East Command; namely, 15 divisions and 348,000 troops for the Japanese army.[61]

The delegations at the Ikeda-Robertson talks had failed to reach accord with respect to a final target for strengthening Japan's defense. Japan's delegation also argued that their nation's economic privation precluded any more of a defense buildup than they were offering. The US delegation insisted, however, that Japan could afford to double its defense spending, even under the prevailing economic conditions.

Each delegation's stance reflected background circumstances at home, as John Dower has described.[62] Japan's delegation argued throughout that they were offering as much as was possible in view of Japanese sentiment. The US delegation was reflecting Congressional views and expectations, meanwhile, in rejecting the Japanese proposals as insufficient.

Underlying the differences between the two sides were differing perceptions of the threat to Japanese security. The Japanese believed that the protection available from the US military was sufficient to address that threat and that a minimal self-defense capacity was adequate as long as they could depend on that protection. Curiously, the Japanese and Americans refrained from confrontation and sought throughout their negotiations, albeit unsuccessfully, to reach a compromise.

The Japanese ultimately succeeded in maintaining a bend-but-don't-break stance in resisting the US demands for a defense buildup. That is attributable to the positioning of the negotiations in overall strategy for the Americans and for the Japanese. The US negotiators were happy to defer to the judgment of the Far East Command with regard to concrete targets for strengthening Japan's defense. Their Japanese counterparts, meanwhile, were advancing a proposal that Ikeda had put together on his own discretion and that had not received cabinet approval.

In Tokyo, the National Safety Agency, with Yoshida's blessing, exchanged opinions about Japanese defense with the US Far East Command.[63] The Ikeda-Robertson talks had been primarily a round of preparations for a state visit by Yoshida to the United States and had borne no obligation to reach a final agreement. Both sides had thus been free to explore negotiating positions freely.

Criticism of Japanese financial and economic policy

Engaging in the Ikeda-Robertson talks and in the follow-up negotiations in Tokyo had enabled the Americans to pressure the Japanese for a stepped-up defense commitment, but that was just part of the value of the exercise for the Americans. Resolving trade and economic issues had ranked alongside resolving defense issues as the original purpose of the Ikeda-Robertson talks.[64] That is why Finance Ministry officials constituted the core of the Japanese delegation.

Concern at the State Department in the negotiations focused less on achieving any specific target for increasing Japan's self-defense capacity than on moderating the pressure applied for that purpose. Aichi, the parliamentary vice minister of finance, wrote as much in a report filed at the conclusion of the Ikeda-Robertson talks. He reported that State Department officials had exhibited a sensitive understanding of the Japanese position, and that they had worked hard to impart that understanding to the defense department.[65]

Ambassador Allison had recommended applying continuous pressure on Japan in advance of the Ikeda-Robertson talks to strengthen its defense but concentrating once the talks were under way on illuminating "shortcomings in Japanese financial and economic policies." He described his concerns in a September 7 telegram to the State Department.

> In recent months there has been a consumption boom in domestic market; at same time evidence is accumulating of serious deterioration underneath surface of this prosperity. Inflationary pressures are accelerating by reason of past shortcomings in governmental policy, i.e., tax reduction, deficit financing, bank loans in excess of deposits, easy credit facilities, non-essential investment, too high a proportion of increased production going into domestic consumption, etc. . . . In short what I am prescribing is another dose of Dodge's medicine, which enabled Japan to surge forward so remarkably between 1949 and 1951, as a condition of further United States special direct assistance.[66]

"Dodge's medicine" refers to the economic guidelines administered under the occupation by the aforementioned Joseph Dodge as the "Dodge line":

- Balance the national budget to reduce inflation;
- Collect taxes more reliably;
- Dissolve the Reconstruction Finance Bank, which was making uneconomical loans;
- Narrow the scope of government intervention; and
- Fix the exchange rate at ¥360 to the dollar to keep Japanese export prices low.

Two days after Allison's dispatch, the director of the State Department's Office of Northeast Asian Affairs, Kenneth Young, wrote to Robertson in the same vein. He recommended refraining for the time being from pressuring Japan publicly to strengthen its defense. Such pressure, he cautioned, would impart momentum to anti-Yoshida factions. That would cloud the prospects for the governing conservative coalition, the survival of which should be the top priority.

Young suggested that economic revitalization was the key to positioning Japan as a pillar of strength in the Far East. He argued that Japan would serve US interests in the region better by fortifying its economy than by augmenting its military. Young cautioned against allowing Japan to rely on special demand provided by the United States and thus becoming an inflationary, inadequately mobilized, and mistakenly managed economy.[67]

The Americans did in fact press the Japanese when the Ikeda-Robertson talks got under way for corrections in economic policy. Dodge took part in the fourth session, on October 14, and presented the Japanese delegation with a paper entitled "Ways and Means of Strengthening the Japanese Economy." He encouraged Ikeda to reduce imports and increase exports through belt-tightening and other autonomous measures.[68]

Japan's *Mainichi Shimbun* noted the economic focus of the Ikeda-Robertson talks in an editorial. The editorial appeared on October 27, as the talks were about to conclude, and contained the following observation:

> Japan's economic stability has emerged as an important subject of debate at the [Ikeda-Robertson talks] in connection with concrete plans for strengthening Japan's national security. The discussions have gone so far as to touch hyperbolically on adopting a "second Dodge Line." Clearly, the Americans are dissatisfied with Japan's progress in achieving a stable economic foundation for armament and are eager for Japan to rein in inflation.[69]

An economic emphasis stood out in the joint statement issued at the end of the Ikeda-Robertson talks. Witness the Japanese commitment to curtailing inflation articulated in the following passage from the statement:

> The Japanese conferees expressed their belief that vigorous efforts on the part of Japan to resist inflation are most important in order to strengthen Japan's economic position and to promote further economic cooperation between the United States and Japan.[70]

The Yoshida cabinet adopted a belt-tightening economic policy, starting in autumn 1953. That resulted in what became known as the "Yoshida deflation." The *Christian Science Monitor* characterized the policy shift as a diplomatic victory for the United States.[71] And Yoshida acknowledged in his memoir that US pressure from the Ikeda-Robertson talks had figured in the shift to deflationary policy. He insisted that he was already feeling a need for fiscal rigor but that he took note of the US admonishment delivered by Ikeda: "Nations that are stumbling into inflation cannot secure loans."[72]

Japan's balance of international payments had deteriorated as the economic windfall of the Korean War faded, and Japan's dollar reserves would shrink by June 1954 to half of what they had been at 1953 year-end.[73] The deterioration of the international payments balance reflected overheated demand for imports, which resulted from what had been inflationary policy. Deflationary policy plunged Japan initially into a severe economic contraction but ultimately contributed greatly to the nation's economic revival. Global economic recovery occasioned a surge in Japanese exports, and the nation's balance of payments improved.

Allison and the people responsible for Japan at the State Department in Washington, DC, held Japan's policy initiatives in high regard. The nation had, after all, striven to strengthen its defense, albeit not as rapidly as the US government desired, while undertaking economic curtailment. In the eyes of Allison and his colleagues, Japan had compensated through economic policy for any shortcomings in defense policy.[74] The Ikeda-Robertson talks had perhaps come up short in resolving the Japanese-US differences with regard to strengthening Japan's defense, but they had lent momentum to the Yoshida doctrine of favoring economic revitalization over rearmament.

3 A New Perspective on Japan

The year 1954 as a turning point

Dulles, the face of US foreign policy, was familiar with Japan's diplomacy. And he was unhappy with the Japanese stance evidenced at the Ikeda-Robertson talks with regard to national defense. Following the return of the Amami Islands to Japan on Christmas Day, he expressed his dissatisfaction in a December 28, 1953, dispatch to Allison.

> I am frankly disappointed that [the] Japanese [have] fallen far behind Germany in recovery and willingness to contribute to security. . . . Also, the Japanese squandering of windfall from Korean war rather than practice of austerity makes very bad impression. Japanese are constantly asking

> more and more from US without feeling any obligation themselves to do what is necessary to promote security in Asia.[75]

Dulles wrote around the same time to Dean Rusk of his disappointment with Japan's postwar reformation. A former assistant secretary of state for Far Eastern affairs and a future secretary of state, Rusk was serving at the time as the president of the Rockefeller Foundation.

> There has not been any rebirth of moral strength, as in the case of Germany. . . . If the Japanese had developed otherwise, I would have taken a stronger position for the restoration of Japanese administration in the other Ryukyuan islands. However, as it is, I do not want to encourage this.[76]

Allison sought to allay Dulles's frustration with Japan. He received from the secretary of state a missive worded similarly to that sent to Rusk, and he responded in a telegram of December 31, 1953.

> The fact that Japanese are talking back and not immediately saying "yes" to every American request is indicative of a resurgence of the old Japanese spirit—if we can continue to work with that and guide it, in the right direction, which I believe we are now doing—we will have an ally with spirit, and eventually strength, on whom we can rely.[77]

Dulles's exasperation was not to be assuaged. The secretary shared Allison's hope that Japan would one day become a strong ally of the United States, but the two differed in the energy of their expectations. Their different expectations likely reflected the positions they now found themselves in—Allison, the ambassador to Japan, and Dulles, the secretary of state.

Allison, who succeeded Robert Murphy as the US ambassador to Japan in May 1953, had studied in Japan and was an expert in East Asian issues. Familiar with Japan's circumstances, he sympathized with the Japanese government's interest in devoting priority to economic revitalization over rearmament.[78] Dulles, on the other hand, was preoccupied with fortifying the Western alliance. He was aware of Japan's individual circumstances but was prone to view the nation in the larger context of US Cold War policy. The Japanese government's lack of military initiative, especially in contrast with Germany's and Italy's, was hard for him to countenance.

Dulles's attitude toward Japan's approach to strengthening its defense changed in the following year. That change was evident in his remarks at a meeting of the National Security Council in Washington, DC, on December 9, 1954. A memorandum of that meeting includes the following mention of Dulles's remarks:

> Japan was a desperately poor country and it should not be pressed too hard to reestablish a large military force until its economy had grown more healthy. Let us try, therefore, to get the Japanese economy on a sounder base first.[79]

Foreshadowing this comment were comments that Dulles made at meetings of the council in September and in October. The first of the earlier meetings was on September 12, 1954. It took place at Lowry Air Force Base, in Denver, Colorado, as military tensions were mounting in the Taiwan Strait. A memorandum of a meeting records that Dulles "expressed the belief that we may have to lower our sights on Japanese rearmament."[80] Dulles voiced further thoughts in the same vein at the next security council meeting, on October 6. He revealed that he had "detected a feeling among the Japanese that we were pressing Japan a bit too hard on her military contribution" and cautioned that "we might . . . lose the vital political sympathy of Japan in our effort to get the desired military levels."[81]

What we see in Dulles's changing attitude toward Japan is a shift in US government policy. That shift would have been readily apparent to Yoshida and his entourage when they arrived in Washington, DC, in November 1954. They would surely have sensed a change in US expectations of Japan with regard to rearmament and defense buildup. Indeed, the US hosts refrained from even touching on those subjects during Yoshida's state visit.[82] The Japanese government was, to be sure, strengthening the nation's defense capability gradually, but the reasons for the shift in the US government's stance lay elsewhere. And the change in tone evident in Dulles's remarks reflected the Eisenhower administration's response to Japan's changing circumstances, both internal and external.[83]

Cracks in Yoshida's political foundation

As noted elsewhere, Japan suffered an economic downturn in 1954 as the result of deflationary policy adopted in autumn 1953. Although that policy succeeded in curtailing imports and lowering production costs, it resulted, too, in sharp increases in bankruptcies and unemployment. Japan's worsening economic circumstances occasioned a revision of the hitherto optimistic appraisal of the nation's recovery.[84]

Three incidents rocked Yoshida's political foundation even as his cabinet was struggling to manage Japan's economic difficulties. One was the radioactive contamination of a Japanese fishing vessel by a US thermonuclear test on Bikini Atoll. A second was the furor that erupted over the revision of Japan's Police Act. The third was a bribery scandal that occurred as Yoshida was pushing the Police Act revision through the Diet.

Yoshida was already taking flak for his alignment with the United States and for the economic downturn that had seemingly resulted from that alignment. Then, a thermonuclear test by the United States on Bikini Atoll on March 1, 1954, inflamed anti-US sentiment further. The *Daigo Fukuryu-maru* (No. 5 Lucky Dragon), a 100-ton fishing vessel based in Yaizu, Shizuoka, was trawling for tuna near the Marshall Islands. Records of the *Daigo Fukuryu-maru*'s position are ambiguous, but the vessel was apparently operating outside the maritime no-entry zone that the US government had established. The blast was stronger than expected and radioactive coral dust blasted from the atoll rained down on the vessel and its crew.

Japanese were aghast at what ensued. The *Daigo Fukuryu-maru* reached its home port of Yaizu on March 14, and all 23 of its crew members were hospitalized for radiation sickness. Officials ordered the discarding of the *Daigo Fukuryu-maru*'s catch, and fish prices collapsed throughout Japan amid concerns about possible radioactive contamination.

Bad feelings toward the United States fermented through the ham-fisted handling of the aftermath of the incident: official determination and acknowledgement of what had happened and subsequent apologies, disposal of the vessel, and medical treatment and compensation for the crew members. Kuboyama Aikichi, the *Daigo Fukuryu-maru*'s chief radio operator, died of hepatitis C in September 1954 while receiving treatment for acute radiation syndrome. The US embassy reported that the *Daigo Fukuryu-*

maru incident had triggered the worst tension seen in Japanese-US relations in the decade since the war's end.[85]

Diplomats and other members of the US government were concerned that the *Daigo Fukuryu-maru* incident and continued thermonuclear testing would rekindle Japanese horror at nuclear weapons and cast the United States as a warmongering nation. Ambassador Allison reported to Dulles in a telegram of May 20, 1954, that, as a result of the incident, the "position of neutralists, pacifists, feminists, and professional anti-Americans while by no means dominant has been strengthened. Doubts re wisdom and feasibility of Japanese rearmament in nuclear age have increased." He concluded later in the same dispatch that "neutralism in Japan will vary in direct proportion to conclusion Japanese leaders reach as to whether relationship with US can provide, more than any other course of Japanese action, defense and security in period when both US and USSR possess thermonuclear weapons."[86]

Dulles thought enough of Allison's telegram to share it with President Eisenhower. The ambassador's words prompted the president to instruct the State Department to analyze the information available about the *Daigo Fukuryu-maru* incident and to develop measures for resolving the matter as well as possible.[87] Thermonuclear weapons were a central plank in Eisenhower's New Look policy for national security, and the president had become concerned about the negative image that was accruing to those weapons around the world. "Everyone seems to think," he lamented at a meeting of the National Security Council on May 6, 1954, "that we're skunks, saber rattlers and warmongers. We ought not to miss any chance to make clear our peaceful objectives."[88]

Amending the Police Act, meanwhile, was in keeping with Yoshida's long-standing belief in strengthening law and order. The deliberations in the Diet broke down, however, along partisan lines. Chaos erupted as the opposition parties, led by the Socialists, opposed the revision of the act vociferously. Things got so bad that fights broke out on the floor of the lower house on June 3, 1954, during debate about extending the Diet session.

The parliamentary disorder obliged Yoshida to postpone his planned state visit to the United States at the last minute. As he scrambled to salvage the revision of the Police Act, events cast his avowed commitment to law and order in a questionable light. Especially damaging was the exposure of bribery in connection with subsidies for the shipbuilding industry and Yoshida's intervention on April 21 to defer the arrest for bribery of his Liberal Party secretary general, Satō Eisaku. Yoshida retained enough support to survive a no-confidence motion introduced by the opposition, but the furor dogged him throughout his remaining months in office. The center of gravity in Japanese politics was shifting toward the emerging conservative coalition.

Two truces in East Asia

Away from the tumult unfolding in Japan, a pair of truces ended the Korean War in July 1953 and the First Indochina War in July 1954. The Eisenhower administration avoided direct intervention in Indochina, but the world viewed the French defeat there as a reversal for the United States. Ikeda, who had succeeded Satō as the secretary general of the Liberal Party, declared as much at a party gathering on August 10, 1954. Allison summarized the news coverage of Ikeda's remarks in an August 11 telegram to Dulles.

The US ambassador's summary included Ikeda's suggestions that the "United States failed in its 'roll-back policy' when the Indochina truce was signed" and that "this is not time for Japan to choose outright between west and east." Allison mused that "expectations of [economic assistance] are running high [in Japan] and entering into Ikeda's own calculations."

Ikeda met with Allison in the wake of the party gathering. They met at the finance minister's official residence in an unsuccessful effort to avoid the prying eyes of the Japanese press. Ikeda took the opportunity to explain that the news coverage had misrepresented his remarks.[89] Even discounting for possible distortion, Ikeda's remarks at the party gathering were disconcerting to the US government. The remarks, in light of the upsurge in neutralism that was occurring in Japan, were disappointing and alarming for the Americans.

Dulles, at this juncture, was still disappointed with the Japanese government's stance. He bemoaned what he regarded as Japan's continuing lack of commitment to fulfilling its proper role in the Far East. Dulles touched on that matter at a meeting of the National Security Council on August 12, 1954.

> We should not build up Japanese military strength unless we [have] confidence that Japan's future political orientation [will] be toward the West. Japan [is] the heart and soul of the situation in the Far East. If Japan is not on our side our whole Far Eastern position will become untenable.[90]

A changing geopolitical landscape heightened the US sense of urgency about seeking a solid Japanese alignment with the West. The Soviet Union had begun evoking a policy of peaceful coexistence since the death of Josef Stalin in March 1953. In Asia, the principle of non-aligned neutrality espoused by India's prime minister, Jawaharlal Nehru, and other leaders was gaining momentum. Military tensions had receded greatly, meanwhile, with the truces that ended the hostilities on the Korean peninsula and in Indochina, and the changing character of East-West confrontation across the region.

Geopolitical developments were thus strengthening the Yoshida government's hand in seeking to devote higher priority to economic rebuilding than to a defense buildup. The US delegation at the Ikeda-Robertson talks had cited the threat of lightning strikes on Japan by 500,000 Soviet troops, but the notion of such an invasion had become implausible, at least for the time being. East-West competition was shifting away from direct confrontation toward a rivalry to demonstrate a politico-economic model of staying power. Dulles alluded to that shift at the August 12 security council meeting.

> Secretary Dulles said the great danger in the Far East was subversion, which was furthered by economic weakness and social distress. Delay in getting started on a program which would help alleviate such economic weakness and social distress would be dangerous.[91]

Mounting concern in the US government with strengthening Japan economically reinforced Yoshida's position with regard to that policy priority. And the US concern included a growing show of interest by the president. Allison's May telegram about the *Daigo Fukuryu-maru* incident had registered strongly with Eisenhower, and he began exhibiting heightened attention to Japan in summer 1954. The president emphasized the need for helping foster Japanese trade as a means of steadying the nation's economy.[92]

Abandonment of Yoshida and continued acceptance of his doctrine

Yoshida's value to the United States declined as Japan's circumstances changed, at home and abroad. Allison gave high marks to Yoshida for managing to increase defense expenditures while curtailing fiscal expenditures overall. The prime minister's standing took a hit in the eyes of the US government, however, in June 1954. That was when the Yoshida government announced plans for across-the-board budget reductions of 10 percent and included defense spending in the fiscal retrenchment.

Cutting the defense budget amounted to reneging on a pledge that the Japanese government had made only two months earlier, and the announcement of the cuts came with no advance notice to the US government.[93] Allison was dissatisfied, meanwhile, with the handling of the *Daigo Fukuryu-maru* incident by Yoshida and the Japanese government. The Yoshida cabinet had been unable to quell the anti-US sentiment aroused by the incident and, in Allison's view, had provided insufficient cooperation to the US government in resolving the matter.[94]

What most concerned Allison and his staff at the US embassy about Yoshida was overall doubt about his capacity to continue governing. No alternative to Yoshida, to be sure, offered guaranteed prospects of serving US interests better. Yoshida's leadership position had deteriorated severely, however, as was clear in the chaos that afflicted Japan's domestic politics. Encouraging the emergence of strong conservative leadership was the long-term US goal in Japan and maintaining a stance of singular support for Yoshida was no longer desirable with regard to that goal.

Yoshida's rescheduled state visit to the United States took place in November 1954. Allison recommended in advance of the visit that the US government adopt a stance of "studied neutrality" toward Yoshida and that it refrain from offering any "souvenirs" of economic assistance.[95] The trip, as could have been expected, ended up short on substantive results.

Although the US government was disappointed in Yoshida and wrote off his long-term viability, it continued to countenance the Yoshida Doctrine of devoting priority to economic revitalization over rearmament. US acceptance of that policy had become manifest by the time of Yoshida's resignation at the end of 1954. Economic and political instability had taken hold in Japan amid shifting geopolitical dynamics worldwide. A consensus was coalescing in the US government that stabilizing Japan economically and politically was the best policy for the time being. The emerging consensus favored addressing that priority even if it meant settling for a slower pace of rearmament.

A proposal drawn up at the US embassy in Tokyo was instrumental in reshaping the US stance toward Japan. In summer 1954, Allison and his staff took the initiative in reappraising that stance and proposing what they called a "new look" at Japan policy. Dulles visited Japan in September 1954, and Allison spelled out the embassy's proposal for him in a memorandum of September 9, 1954.[96]

Allison emphasizes up front the importance of the ongoing negotiation of Japan's defense spending for the fiscal year to March 1956. That negotiation, he stresses, "will bring to the fore perhaps the most important decision the US has had to make in Japan since the peace treaty went into effect." Allison reiterates that Japan's government decided, without informing the US government, to cut its budget, including defense spending, by 10 percent. And he is adamant about the potency of "Japanese neutralism."

> The force of Japanese neutralism should not be underrated. It is fed by *military considerations* [all italics in original] (participation in war on either side in a thermonuclear age would mean the extinction of the Japanese people); by *economic* (Japan suffered greatly in the last war, while neutrals such as Sweden, Switzerland, and India profited; Japan itself profited hugely from the Korean War); by *political* (a deep racial sentiment that Japan should not fight against Asians on the side of Western powers); and by *social* (the effort to prepare for war is too great; it would bring back a military ascendancy; it would entrain severer domestic consequences than accommodations and compromises with any potential enemy).

The ambassador speculates that, "by a major effort which would shake US-Japan cooperation to its foundations, we could off-set these considerations and obtain the same, or a slightly higher, level of military expenditure by Japan." But he calls for preceding any such effort with "a hard look at the practical gains and losses involved" and "a searching examination of a number of our assumptions about Japan and the Far

East." Allison then enumerates what he counts "among the most important questions to be asked":

> a. Do we expect war with the Soviets or Chinese Communists so soon as to compel the most rapid accumulation of military power at any cost, economic or political? . . . If we think however we are in for a longer pull in which the cold war may continue for decades . . . then our effort should be directed more toward the development of durable relationships within the non-communist world. . . .
>
> b. To what extent have our strategic concepts for Japan been refined by special [that is, nuclear] weapons developments? From the strategic point of view, how useful is Japan as a base for military operations? . . . In the event of war, Japan as a defensive base would be burdensome; as an offensive base it could quickly be nullified.
>
> c. If these conditions [of strategic fragility] obtain for existing plant, what is the justification for our insistence that US economic aid . . . should be directed exclusively toward the expansion of defense industries? . . .
>
> d. How feasible economically and over what period of time, are our force goals for the Japanese? So far as the Embassy is aware, no accurate projections of the ultimate costs of the Japanese defense establishment have ever been compiled. . . . What are the prospects for expanding Japanese exports . . . sufficiently to pay these costs . . . ?
>
> e. How practical is it to continue our support and our advocacy of expanded and modern military forces and an industrial mobilization base in a country where the most rudimentary internal security controls have yet to be established? No legal definitions of treason, espionage, or state secrets exist. The communist party, the communist fronts, and communist labor unions are all legal, flourishing, and unmolested. . . .

"These are not questions," Allison acknowledges, "which can be answered in a day." He offers, however, "to initiate a study of them . . . with a view to submitting a reappraisal of our Japan position prior to Mr. Yoshida's arrival in Washington. . . . The premise would be defense against attack from *within* [all italics in original], not *without* as at present. It would require a shift in the emphasis of our policy over the immediate period ahead from defense to economics and internal security." Allison describes how he envisions using the carrot of economic assistance to steer Japan in the desired direction.

> We would then seek to use economic aid . . . to promote the reintroduction of Japan into the world trading community, to solve the reparations deadlock and foster [Southeast Asian] economic regionalism, and to modernize Japan's industries. We would insist that the Japanese Government deal effectively with the problem of internal security, the communist manipulated press, the leftist-controlled schools. We would seek to assist in creating a stronger Japanese government at home and in increasing the prestige and participation of Japan in Asian and world affairs.

Allison counsels patience as the most realistic approach.

> This would involve, for some years, an acquiescence in the military impotence or neutralization of Japan. But until a stronger Japanese Government comes into being, until there is a recovery of national spirit and purpose, until Japan's international economic position is considerably improved, and until there is an effective internal security system, this acquiescence would be no more than a recognition of the facts of the situation. . . .

In conclusion:

> Out of such a shift in our policies should come a stronger and, very possibly, a more cooperative Japan. Unless there is such a Japan our military assistance program will have no future. We should not of course abandon our military aid program, but we should limit it to what the Japanese decide they wish to have and we should be prepared to proceed with the relocation of the Far East Command and the withdrawal of our forces on whatever schedule the US national interest alone dictates. Paradoxically, for Japan, the absence of US insistence that Japan increase its military forces and the conviction that the US has only a secondary strategic interest in Japan may do more to establish valid and reciprocal defense commitments than any other course of action we might select.

What comes across lucidly through Allison's memorandum is the sense of crisis at the embassy. The ambassador and his staff are seriously concerned about the domestic instability that has beset Japan even as the geopolitical balance in East Asia shifts. They feel a sense of urgency about favoring political and economic stability over rearmament in US policy priorities.

Dulles responded positively and encouraged Allison to continue with the reappraisal of Japan policy.[97] The basic message of the memorandum resonated with sentiment that was taking hold in the Eisenhower administration's military and diplomatic policy.[98] Dissent, however, was also audible. Lieutenant General Carter Magruder, the chief of staff of the US Far East Command, criticized Allison's memorandum in a telegram to the embassy of September 24, 1954.

> No government can be strong which is not prepared to defend itself. . . . [M]aking Japan rich before we make her militarily strong would only weaken the moral fiber of her people and . . . would make her a more desirable prize to the Russians.[99]

Allison responded to Magruder in a letter of September 28. He argues that the embassy's proposal is consistent with Eisenhower's thinking, and he buttresses his rebuttal with a quotation from Eisenhower's May 5, 1953, message to Congress with regard to the Mutual Security Program.

> The United States and our partners throughout the world must stand ready, for many years if necessary, to build and maintain adequate defenses. To accomplish this objective we must avoid so rapid a military buildup that we seriously dislocate our economies. Military strength is most effective—indeed it can be maintained—only if it rests on a solid economic base. We must help the free nations to help themselves in eradicating conditions which corrode and destroy the will for freedom and democracy from within.[100]

The proposal from the US embassy in Tokyo ultimately took shape as part of a National Security Council policy paper. Its basic thrust figures prominently in NSC 5516/1, which the council adopted at a meeting on April 7, 1955. In that paper, the security council affirmed the principle that the US government should not press Japan to undertake a defense buildup to the extent of undermining its political or economic stability and that the size and composition of Japan's military should basically be up to the Japanese government to decide. The paper contained no mention of the "ten-division ground force and appropriate air and naval arms" cited in NSC 125/2, of August 1952, or any other specific figures.[101]

Eisenhower and his administration continued the Truman administration's policy of containment with regard to the Soviet Union. In other words, US government policy toward the Soviet Union remained basically consistent across the transition from Democratic to Republican administration. Eisenhower, however, sought a new strategy on taking office as president in January 1953 for achieving the goal of containment. He was concerned about (1) the burgeoning growth in US military expenditures since the outbreak of the Korean War and (2) the related issue of how to put in place a sustainable format for national defense.[102]

US defense expenditures had surged from about $13 billion in fiscal 1950 (the year to June 1950), immediately before the Korean War, to about $50 billion in fiscal 1953. As a percentage of GNP, defense outlays had increased from 4.8% to 13.8%. Eisenhower possessed a fiscal conservatism and worried about the economic effects of the growth in military spending. A strong military was essential to US national security, but so was economic vitality. Military expenditures would enervate the nation if they became so burdensome as to inhibit private-sector economic growth.

Eisenhower sensed that the Soviet leadership was using a military buildup to steer the United States toward economic ruin. He warned the American people about that threat in a radio address shortly after taking office. "Communist guns," cautioned the president, "have been aiming at an economic target no less than a military target."[103]

As for sustainability in national defense, Eisenhower was critical of the Truman administration's plan for increasing military spending. That plan, adopted after the outbreak of the Korean War, provided for increasing military expenditures sharply up to fiscal 1954. Eisenhower believed that a defense buildup aimed at a year of anticipated maximum crisis was folly. The American people, he feared, would become cynical about national defense if the alleged threats failed to materialize, and vigilance would wane rapidly.

The Communist threat, Eisenhower reasoned, was an enduring challenge and thus called for a US response based on long-term planning. A pattern of sudden increases and reductions in the defense effort, he believed, would be counterproductive. As a career soldier, Eisenhower knew well the military bureaucracy's penchant for specifying deadlines for military expansion and for presenting their armament targets as "absolutely necessary." He was opposed to a rapid buildup targeted at a year of supposedly impending crisis.[104]

Eisenhower shared the perspective articulated by Dulles in a May 17, 1953, letter to the president. In that letter, Dulles wrote that the Communists, unlike Adolf Hitler, had a worldview that transcended any individual lifespan and spanned eras and that no one, therefore, could know when the peril that they posed would manifest.[105] This was also the view held by George Kennan, the architect of the US policy of Communist containment.

The New Look strategy was what emerged from Eisenhower's determination to carry out the containment policy without incurring an excessive economic burden. It provided for reducing military costs by relying heavily on nuclear deterrence and by reducing ground strength while fortifying sea and air strength. The strategy accepted the immense risk inherent in nuclear weaponry in exchange for the benefit of reducing personnel costs.[106] Its economically sustainable approach to Cold War strategy meshed with Yoshida's doctrine of devoting top priority to economic revitalization and undertaking rearmament at a gradual pace.

"What we are striving to develop," Allison wrote in the previously cited memorandum of September 9, 1954, "is the strength of the non-communist world, not the maximum military forces in being that they can build. We do not follow such a course ourselves."

The New Look's emphasis in national security on economic vitality and long-term growth was an emphasis primarily, of course, on US economic vitality and long-term growth. Its extension to Japan occurred only after a geopolitical shift in East Asia occurred. That shift was a function of the truce in Indochina and the advent of a sense of economic competition with Communism.

As we have seen, the Indochinese truce lessened military tensions in East Asia and diluted notions of urgency about military buildups. It and the economic rivalry with the Communists made Yoshida's emphasis on economic revitalization over rearmament more acceptable to the US government. Conversely, the geopolitical transformation under way in East Asia made the Eisenhower administration's basic approach to the Cold War a better fit with Japanese aims. Indeed, the New Look proved a positive factor in reinforcing the momentum of the Yoshida Doctrine.

The New Look was, first and foremost, a strategy for economizing in US national defense. It offered no benefits for Japan or for any other US ally in reducing budgetary needs for national defense. On the contrary, any reduction in US military spending logically implied a need for increased defense spending by US allies. The New Look had the effect in Japan, however, of diminishing the significance of strengthening the army.

Relying on nuclear deterrence left the New Look strategy at a loss for how to deal with small-scale military encounters and with guerilla attacks. Nuclear retaliation was an inconceivable response to such actions, and the threat presumably called for offsetting with commensurate ground forces. That said, tactical considerations and Japan's noncontiguous geography suggested that minimal ground forces would be sufficient to repel an incursion from Russia or from China. Excepting the unlikely event of a large-scale invasion, Japan's defense forces would not need to deal with small-scale engagements or with guerilla actions. Even in the event of an attempted large-scale invasion, land-based retaliation, though necessary, would be less important than a naval and air response.

Strengthened capacity for a nuclear response to threats was part of the New Look strategy for defending Japan with air and sea power. The US delegation at the Ikeda-Robertson talks had cited the danger of an enemy securing a beachhead in Japan and the need for being prepared to repel such an enemy. That argument was out of sync, however, with the views of Eisenhower. And this was the selfsame Eisenhower who had overseen the Normandy landings of June 6, 1944—the largest amphibious assault in history. The disconnect was apparent in the president's comments at a press conference on March 17, 1954. Eisenhower expressed doubt at that time about the contemporary viability of a massive, Normandy-like invasion. Such an action, he noted, would be vulnerable to extinction with nuclear weapons.[107]

The nuclear era and Eisenhower's New Look strategy were rendering ground forces increasingly irrelevant in defending an island nation like

Japan. Allison's memorandum of September 9, 1954, resonant with the Eisenhower administration's foreign strategy, proved a fulcrum for rethinking US Japan policy, the first significant rethink since the Kennan recommendations in 1947–1948 described in the previous chapter. The embassy's revisiting of that policy contributed materially, as noted, to a heightened emphasis on political and economic stability and a lessened preoccupation with a military buildup. Let us bear in mind, however, that the shift in policy emphases was one of degree and that Japan's strengthening of its defense remained a high priority for the US government.

We perceive the subtlety of the shift in emphasis in the wording adopted in security council memorandum NSC 5516/1; for example, "The amount and timing of the build-up of Japanese military forces should be related to the necessity for developing political and economic stability, as well as military strength, in Japan." Meanwhile, the US Far East Command abided by its military assessment that Japan required an army of around 350,000 troops.[108]

Something that warrants attention here is the larger policy shift that Allison's memorandum could have been interpreted as proposing. The memorandum would seem to be proposing, albeit subject to interpretation, a more profound shift than the adjustment that resulted. Note how it calls for a reappraisal of Japan's strategic value in light of the strategic implications of nuclear weaponry. It cites the need for that reappraisal in "b" and "c" of the "most important questions to be asked," quoted earlier.

Allison and his staff had consulted with the Military Assistance Advisory Group-Japan (MAAG-J) in evaluating the military threat posed by the Communists. MAAG-J, established under the United States–Japan Mutual Defense Assistance Agreement of March 1954, administered the Mutual Defense Assistance Program in Japan until mid-1969. Based at least partly on the MAAG-J input, Allison and his staff reached a fundamental conclusion about the Communist threat: "Reduction of [every industrial area in Japan] could be accomplished with nuclear weapons in a matter of minutes, not months. In the event of war, Japan as a defensive base would be burdensome; as an offensive base it could quickly be nullified."[109]

The US Far East Command took exception with the embassy's memorandum. Here is a summary of its rebuttal:

1. The Japanese archipelago is the United States' largest platform for mounting naval and air actions against Communist forces in the Far East. It is therefore a natural target for potential surprise attacks by enemies.
2. If the United States did not have bases in Japan, it would need to deploy its retaliatory capabilities at bases in less-suitable positions. Japan offers, meanwhile, supply facilities across a geographical range that is uniquely extensive in the Pacific Basin. If the United States did not use those facilities, the Communists would surely seize and use the facilities for their purposes.
3. For the United States to abandon its network of forward bases and withdraw into the Western Hemisphere would be to cede the Pacific initiative to the Soviets. The United States would be giving up bases essential to mounting effective counterattacks. The Soviets, meanwhile, could leave unused the weapons of mass destruction deployed to destroy the US bases and seize the bases unopposed. They could then advance their network of forward bases geographically toward the United States.

Japan, in other words, might be vulnerable to enemy attack, but it was a vital link in the chain of US forward bases. Ceding the bases to the Communists without a fight would deal a double blow to US national security. It would strengthen the enemy's military capabilities. And it would allow the enemy to take up military positions closer to the US homeland.[110]

The Far East Command's General John Hull reaffirmed his view of Japan's strategic value in a January 7, 1955, document catalogued in the US National Archives as CINCFE (Commander-in-Chief, Far East) 71040. The original remains classified, but another document that is clearly a copy of the original is among State Department materials that have been declassified: "Message from CINCFE Tokyo to Department of Army, 10 February 1955." A summary of that document circulated among senior government officials engaged in coordinating national security across agencies. Its content emphasized Japan's strategic value as follows:

> Japan is still capable of serving as a strong outpost . . . of defense. . . . Japan is capable of being a formidable ally of the US and of assisting in the development of means by which Communism can be stopped and defeated in Asia.[111]

The views of the Far East Command carried the weight of authority, which the embassy needed to accept. Reconsideration of US Japan policy at the embassy continued after the issuance of Allison's September 9, 1954, memorandum. The resultant report appeared on October 25, 1954, as "A Preliminary Reappraisal of United States Policy With Respect to Japan."[112] It acknowledges that "the potential usefulness of Japan may not be less than had been assumed in our mid-1952 policies" and that Japan's strategic value as a platform for air and naval bases might well outweigh concerns about its nuclear vulnerability. The embassy thus acknowledged Japan's value in US military strategy, and its rethinking of US Japan policy occasioned far less than the sweeping overhaul that the reappraisal's proponents surely envisioned. Nonetheless, the embassy's reappraisal was instrumental in inducing the US government to accept the Japanese government's proposed pace of rearmament and to take a strong interest in Japan's economic issues. The change in the US government's stance was significant for Japan. It reinforced the Yoshida Doctrine's momentum in devoting higher priority to economic revitalization than to rearmament. The US government had accepted the Yoshida Doctrine even as it was writing off Yoshida as a national leader and Yoshida himself lost power.

4 The Yoshida Doctrine and the Security Treaty

Yoshida after the peace treaty

Public opinion had turned against Yoshida decisively by autumn 1954. Japanese had wearied of the authoritarian demeanor that his government had assumed after years in power and of the insider politics that had festered under his watch. Yoshida resigned in December amid political disarray amplified by the exposure of corruption scandals. He had clung to power in the face of a conservative coalition that was taking shape in opposition to his leadership but reluctantly turned loose the reins of power at the urging of his closest confidants.

The end came as a stunning fall from grace. Still fresh in memory was the figure of Yoshida basking in adulation after concluding the peace treaty in San Francisco. His supporters grieved that the man revered for restoring Japan's independence needed to resign under such circumstances.[113]

Yoshida would unquestionably have served his legacy better by retiring in the still-fresh glow of the newly minted peace treaty. Politicians who have attained prominence are rarely able, though, to relinquish that standing gracefully. Some cling to office out of a taste for power, and some out of a sense of responsibility. Yoshida's resistance to resigning seems to have been a genuine result of the latter. The Treaty of San Francisco had launched Japan anew as an independent nation, but the work of regaining trust in the international community and restoring Japan's national vitality had just begun. And Yoshida believed that he was the person best suited to oversee that work.[114]

For two and a half years after the signing of the peace treaty, the Yoshida government had overseen important progress in Japan's rebirth. Japan's postwar recovery owed a great deal to minimizing expenditures on rearmament and thereby allowing for channeling the people's energy into economic revitalization. Yoshida's latter years in power coincided with the establishment of that pattern for national development.

Several factors figured, of course, in Japan's postwar recovery. Yoshida's leadership in resisting US pressure for accelerated rearmament and in tweaking economic policy was surely important. Also important, however, were the changes that occurred in Japan's geopolitical environment and the attendant change in US Japan policy.

Whether Yoshida or any other Japanese leader could have chosen a different course is questionable. Any policy success owes at least something, however, to the thinking that underlay the policy, to the commitment of the politicians who carried out the policy, and to the timing of the policy initiative with regard to external developments. Yoshida deserves credit for persevering with the same stance after the signing of the peace treaty that he had maintained earlier: emphasizing economic revitalization over rearmament.

Japan after the signing of the peace treaty presented Yoshida with challenging political issues. The need to deal with those issues prevented him from focusing fully on his policy priorities.[115] A challenge that was especially demanding of Yoshida's energies was that of cementing the foundation of his political leadership. His leadership under the occupation had accrued from the relationships that he had built with MacArthur and with the other occupation authorities. The end of the occupation and the withdrawal of the Supreme Commander for the Allied Powers obliged Yoshida to look elsewhere for support for his policy initiatives.

Yoshida mustered support while coping with continued attacks from the political left and with new attacks from politicians whose postwar banishments had been lifted. He did not enjoy the work of laying a political foundation by assuaging diverse interests and by addressing the sensitivities of the Japanese people. Yoshida ultimately became an obstacle in the path of the formation of a conservative coalition.

The security treaty and the Japanese spirit of independence

Looming before Yoshida was the dissonance between the Japanese spirit of independence and the Security Treaty Between the United States and Japan. US troops remained in Japan after the signing of the peace treaty, and the US government continued to speak in terms of protecting Japan and supporting the nation's development. Signing the peace treaty had ostensibly meant renewed independence for Japan, but the nation's subservience to the United States appeared to be continuing. That apparent contradiction discomfited a growing number of Japanese.

The presence of foreign troops in any nation is inherently a source of friction. That friction was all the more severe in Japan, where foreign forces had entered by way of conquest and had remained under a treaty that was egregiously unequal. Japan and the United States, to be sure, had become allies, and the Japanese government countenanced the presence of the US troops as being in the nation's interests. That fragile logic was understandably unconvincing to Japanese who had welcomed the long-awaited end of the occupation as signifying independence, and the Security Treaty Between the United States and Japan became a subject of criticism.

Yoshida rejected any suggestion that Japan was subordinating itself to the United States. Such a suggestion struck Yoshida as nurturing a pessimistic sense of persecution. He contrasted criticism of the security treaty with the acceptance of the alliance that Japan concluded with the United Kingdom in 1902.

> The United Kingdom at the time of the conclusion of the Anglo-Japanese

> Alliance was at the height of its imperial power. It ruled the waves across the seven seas, and people spoke of the sun never setting on the British Empire. Japan, on the other hand, was just emerging in world history and was a small, barely significant island nation in the Far East. The discrepancy between the British Empire and Japan then was far greater than that between the United States and Japan of today. Japanese throughout the land . . . nonetheless welcomed enthusiastically the establishment of the Anglo-Japanese Alliance.
>
> No one voiced the pessimistic argument that Japan would become a puppet of British imperialism or that the British would colonize our nation. Rather, Japanese prided themselves on being "the United Kingdom of the East" and exhibited no sense of inferiority whatsoever.
>
> In contrast are the Japanese of recent years who represent themselves as progressive persons of culture or as the possessors of left-leaning reformist philosophy. Whenever the subject of US relations arises, they complain that we are a colony of the United States or that we are becoming the orphan of Asia. Their pathetic lamentations betray thoughts that would never occur to persons of any other nation. On hearing them, I struggle to believe that these are Japanese barely a half century removed from the conclusion of the Anglo-Japanese Alliance.[116]

Yoshida goes on to observe that most Japanese retain the same firm mettle as their predecessors of 50 years earlier and to express the hope that they will turn a deaf ear to the "pathetic lamentations." He reminds his compatriots that Japan never became the least bit subservient to the United Kingdom on account of the Anglo-Japanese Alliance. Yoshida perceived no need for Japan to end its dependence on the United States with regard to national security and recognized that ending that dependence was, in any case, not feasible. He was of the strong belief that the times called for collective, rather than stand-alone, defense. That belief reinforced his resistance to criticism of alleged subservience to the United States, and he spoke forcefully of the importance of joint defense, as in the following passage:

> Numerous are those who regard the Security Treaty [Between the United States and Japan] as humiliation. They continue to dwell on whether the arrangement is equal or otherwise, casting the issue in terms of superior-

> ity and subordinacy. Such individuals know nothing of current world affairs and lack an understanding of the modern significance of national defense. We can but regard them as like a frog at the bottom of a well, ignorant of matters in the world at large. Can any nation of today support its national defense entirely on its own? In the middle of the United Kingdom, the US air force shares the duty of air defense. UK and US forces provide defense along parts of the borders of Italy and France. A French-UK-US trinational force occupies bases under the North Atlantic Treaty in West Germany near its border with Soviet-controlled East Germany, and West Germany welcomes that presence. It has even expressed resistance to a proposal for reducing the UK contingent. [West Germany] is grateful that the presence of foreign forces allows it to avoid the burden of huge military expenditures and to allocate resources to post-defeat reconstruction that contribute greatly to that cause. [The West Germans] impart from [the foreign military presence] no sense of humiliation and no sense of inferiority.

Thus does Yoshida rebut critics of Japan's reliance on US assistance for national security. Japan was hardly alone, he notes, in relying on the United States for security assistance in an era of collective defense. The United States stationed troops in several other nations, where they were a welcome presence. Yoshida challenged his critics to identify how such reliance impinged in any way on Japanese interests. He rejected vehemently the principal criticisms of the security treaty: that it was something that the United States had imposed on Japan and that it was a unilateral arrangement.

The security treaty, Yoshida insisted, was something conceived by Japan and proposed by Japan. It was entirely bilateral in its fundamental mechanism: Japan would furnish facilities, the United States would mobilize military forces, and the two would thereby defend Japan jointly.

Yoshida became impatient with sophistic quibbling over the text of the treaty. Critics objected, for example, that the treaty did not specify the defense of Japan clearly as a US obligation. Yoshida ridiculed that interpretation as a gross misreading of the treaty. He scoffed that US forces in Japan were hardly likely to sit on their heels in the face of an enemy attack.

> Understanding a political agreement, such as the Security Treaty Between the United States and Japan, demands a grasp of the essence of the agreement, as well as a literal reading of the text. No one who lacks that basic understanding is qualified to comment on the treaty.[117]

This position led Yoshida initially to oppose the revision of the security treaty that Prime Minister Kishi Nobusuke signed in January 1960. The negotiations for revising the security treaty began formally in October 1958, and Yoshida offered withering commentary on Kishi's approach in a letter to Ikeda Hayato of November 6.

> Kishi plays up to the mob in regard to the security treaty and displays nothing in the way of a principled stance. We cannot, in this era of joint defense and international interdependency, support hackneyed arguments about such notions as autonomous or bilateral.[118]

Yoshida deplored ostentatious preoccupation with formalities that lacked grounding in a position of strength and therefore unproductive with regard to practical benefit. In his view, the era mandated joint defense, and cooperation with the United States enhanced Japan's national security and supported the nation's economic development; the format of the cooperation was of secondary importance. "Hackneyed arguments about such notions as autonomous or bilateral" were almost beyond his ken. That position, however noble it might have been, proved a weak point in Yoshida's diplomacy.

The Yoshida Doctrine of resisting pressure for rearmament, entrusting Japan's national security to the United States, and concentrating on economic revitalization succeeded for a while. That success hinged, however, on the existence of a strong sense of independence among the Japanese people. An international relations specialist who was close to Yoshida in the 1960s prior to the latter's passing in 1967, Kōsaka Masataka describes the role of that sense of independence in his classic analysis, a biography of Yoshida published in 1968.

As interpreted by Kōsaka, defense cooperation with the United States engendered a growing sense of dependence on that nation and a weakening sense of Japanese independence. That threatened to undermine national self-respect and enervate the spirit of the nation. Ironically, Yoshida's policy of relying on the United States required for its success a strong sense of independence and a strong desire to be free of US domination.[119]

Questions of autonomous or bilateral become in the foregoing analysis more than just a "hackneyed argument." The security treaty, whatever the merits of Yoshida's logic in its defense, was largely about stationing US troops in Japan, and it undeniably offended the Japanese sense of independence. Yoshida erred in failing to take more substantive measures to rekindle the sense of independence that underlay the argument about autonomy and bilateralism. Such measures, even if predicated on cooperating with the United States and engaging in collective defense, presumably would have included renegotiating the security treaty.

Yoshida cites the Anglo-Japanese Alliance as an example of why cooperation needn't entail subservience, but he ignores an important difference between that arrangement and the US-Japanese security treaty. The Anglo-Japanese Alliance was, at least formally, a bilateral undertaking between equals, and that is a big reason that it did not occasion feelings of inferiority in Japan. "The [Anglo-Japanese] alliance," notes Kōsaka, "defined mutual rights and responsibilities clearly, and Japan was by no means utterly dependent on the United Kingdom [under the agreement]."[120]

Equal standing under the Anglo-Japanese Alliance was evident in the second renewal of the alliance, in 1911. The renewal included an amendment in which the two nations recognized each other's territorial holdings and rights in East Asia and on the Indian subcontinent.

Yoshida, his rebuttal of criticism of the US-Japan security treaty notwithstanding, well understood the imperfect circumstances of the treaty's origin and regarded the treaty as a provisional arrangement. He explained that he envisioned from the outset "a shift to a [more] permanent framework." And he defined "a shift to a permanent framework" as meaning "moving beyond a relationship of [Japan] receiving protection to a relationship providing protection jointly."[121]

Clearly, Yoshida envisioned a more reciprocal defense relationship where Japan would not rely unilaterally on the United States. What is unclear is exactly how he envisioned accomplishing that transition and how long he expected the transition to take. The Yoshida Doctrine provided for strengthening Japan's self-defense capability gradually without revising the constitution and while maintaining the official stance that Japan was not rearming. Its architect surely viewed the transition to a truly reciprocal defense relationship as a long-term project, but we can only speculate as to just how long term he had in mind.

Chapter Notes

1 Ōtake Hideo, ed., *Sengo Nihon bōei mondai shiryōshū* [Archives of Postwar Japanese Defense Issues], vol. 1, *Higunjika kara saigunbi e* [From Demilitarization to Rearmament] (Tokyo: San-Ichi Shobo, 1991), 512–513.

2 Yoshida Shigeru, *Kaisō jūnen* [A 10-Year Memoir] (Tokyo: Chuokoronsha, 1998), 2:207–208.

3 US Department of State, *Foreign Relations of the United States* (*FRUS*), 1951 (Washington, DC: Government Printing Office, 1977), Document 789; Ōtake, *Sengo Nihon*, vol. 2, *Kōwa to saigunbi no honkakuka* [Peace and Full-Scale Rearmament] (Tokyo: San-Ichi Shobo, 1992), 299–302.

4 Uemura Hideki, *Saigunbi to 55-nen taisei* [Rearmament and the 1955 Framework] (Tokyo: Bokutakusha, 1995), 56–57.

5 Ōtake Hideo, *Saigunbi to nashonarizumu: Hoshu, riberaru, shakai minshu shugisha no bōeikan* [Rearmament and Nationalism: Conservative, Liberal, and Social Democratic Perspectives on Defense] (Tokyo: Chuokoronsha, 1988), 92; Ōtake, *Sengo Nihon*, 1:512–513.

6 Yoshida, *Kaisō jūnen*, 2:208–209.

7 Ōtake, *Sengo Nihon*, 1:512–513.

8 Ōtake, *Saigunbi to nashonarizumu*, ch. 2; Tanaka Akihiko, *Anzen hoshō: Sengo 50-nen no mosaku* [Military Security: Fifty Postwar Years of Searching] (Tokyo: Yomiuri Shimbunsha, 1997), ch. 3.

9 Ōtake, *Sengo Nihon*, 2:449.

10 Ōtake, *Saigunbi to nashonarizumu*, 90–93.

11 US Department of State, *FRUS*, 1952–1954 (Washington, DC: Government Printing Office, 1985), Document 588.

12 Uemura, *Saigunbi*, 168–187.

13 "Public Law 165," US Government Publishing Office, https://www.govinfo.gov/content/pkg/STATUTE-65/pdf/STATUTE-65-Pg373.pdf.

14 Ōtake, *Sengo Nihon*, vol. 3, *Jieitai no sōsetsu* [Creation of Self-Defense Forces] (Tokyo: San-Ichi Shobo, 1993), 310–316, 354.

15 Yoshitsugu Kōsuke, "MSA kōshō to saigunbi mondai" [The Mutual Security Act and Rearmament Issues], in *Anpo jōyaku no ronri: Sono seisei to tenkai* [The Logic of the Security Treaty: Its Formation and Application], ed. Toyoshita Narahiko (Tokyo: Kashiwa Shobo, 1999), 121–127.

16 Ōtake, *Sengo Nihon*, 3:358–359.

17 *Mainichi Shimbun*, September 24, 1953.

18 Miyazawa, *Secret Talks*, 86.

19 Tanaka, *Anzen hoshō*, 119.

20 "Ikeda Talks," US Department of State, Central Files (CF) 611.94/10-53, National Archives.
21 "Ikeda Talks," minutes of the October 8 session.
22 Miyazawa, *Secret Talks*, 110.
23 "Ikeda Talks," minutes of the October 8 session.
24 The US documentation lists Murakami's title as "Chief, Legal Section, Budget Bureau, Ministry of Finance." Murakami's report covers the exchanges regarding defense issues at the sessions held on October 5, 8, 12, and 15 and is a valuable source of information about those exchanges. It appears as the "Murakami Memo" in Ōtake, *Sengo Nihon*, 3:380–386.
25 Ōtake, *Sengo Nihon*, 3:376–380; Uemura, *Saigunbi*, 171–183.
26 Miyazawa, *Secret Talks*, 114.
27 "Ikeda Talks," minutes of the October 15 morning session.
28 "Ikeda Talks," October 15 morning.
29 "Ikeda Talks," October 15 morning; "Murakami Memo" in Ōtake, *Sengo Nihon*, 3:384.
30 "Ikeda Talks," October 8; Ōtake, *Sengo Nihon*, 3:373–375.
31 Miyazawa, *Secret Talks*, 119–126.
32 Miyazawa, *Secret Talks*, 120.
33 "Ikeda Talks," October 19; Ōtake, *Sengo Nihon*, 3:388–391.
34 "Ikeda Talks," October 19.
35 See Sakamoto Kazuya, "Ikeda-Robātoson kaidan saikō" [Ikeda-Robertson Talks of 1953: A Reconsideration], *Hōkei ronsō* [Journal of Law and Economics] 9, no. 1 (December 1991) for a discussion of the rhetorical obscurity of the US memorandums.
36 Miyazawa, *Secret Talks*, 121.
37 Miyazawa, *Secret Talks*, 119.
38 Ikeda, seeking to secure room for concessions, deleted three anti-aircraft battalions from his initial proposal. "Murakami Memo" in Ōtake, *Sengo Nihon*, 3:383.
39 "Ikeda Talks," October 15 morning; Ōtake, *Sengo Nihon*, 3:385.
40 US Department of State, *FRUS*, 1952–1954, Document 704.
41 "Washinton kōshō no uchimaku 1" [The Inside Story of the Washington, DC, Negotiations, Part 1], *Sangyō Keizai Shimbun*, November 14, 1953.
42 Ōtake, *Sengo Nihon*, 3:391–393.
43 Miyazawa, *Secret Talks*, 92–93.
44 Joseph Dodge took part in the October 14 session of the Ikeda-Robertson talks. Dodge had served as financial advisor in Japan to the occupation authorities in 1949 and was the director of the Bureau of the Budget in the Eisenhower administration at the time of the talks. He presented the Japanese delegation with a paper entitled "Ways and Means of Strengthening the Japanese Economy." The data presented in tables 1 and 2 appeared in that paper.
45 Miyazawa, *Secret Talks*, 128.
46 "Ikeda Talks," October 27.
47 For a US summary of the differences between the Japanese and US memorandums, see US Department of State, CF 794.5 MSP/10-2853.

48 US Department of State, CF, 794.5 MSP/10-2853.
49 Miyazawa, *Secret Talks*, 128.
50 Miyazawa, *Secret Talks*, 128.
51 "Ikeda Talks," October 27.
52 "Ikeda Talks," October 28; Ōtake, *Sengo Nihon*, 3:399–400.
53 Miyazawa, *Secret Talks*, 130.
54 "Ikeda Talks," October 30 interdepartmental meeting.
55 US Department of State, *FRUS*, 1952–1954, Document 708.
56 US Department of State, *FRUS*, 1952–1954, Document 710.
57 US Department of State, *FRUS*, 1952–1954, Document 713.
58 US Department of State, *FRUS*, 1952–1954, Document 719.
59 Uemura, *Saigunbi*, 327; for Robertson's explanation to Dulles that most of the additional civilian employees will do work formerly handled by uniformed employees and that the troop-strength increase will be close to the 24,000 Japanese proposal at the Ikeda-Robertson talks, see US Department of State, CF 611.94/8-3054; CF 794.5 MSP/1-1154 (tel.1709); *FRUS*, 1952–1954, Document 733.
60 US Department of State, *FRUS*, 1952–1954, Document 752. Japan's Diet allocated ¥56 billion in the budget for the fiscal year to March 1953 for future strengthening of the National Police Reserve (renamed the National Safety Force in October 1952), and that allocation ended up funding work on US bases in Japan and on road improvements. The funding took place under the name of national security expenses, and it continued until the allocation was fully depleted in the fiscal year to March 1956, as described in Asahi Shimbun Anzen Hoshō Mondai Chōsakai, ed., *Asahi shimin kyōshitsu: Nihon no anzen hoshō* [Asahi Citizens' Classroom: Japan's National Security], vol. 9, *Nihon no bōei to keizai* [National Defense and the Japanese Economy] (Tokyo: Asahi Shimbunsha, 1967), 58–59.
61 US Department of State, *FRUS*, 1952–1954, Document 720.
62 John Dower, *Empire and Aftermath: Yoshida Shigeru and the Japanese Experience, 1878–1954* (Cambridge: Harvard University Asia Center, 1979).
63 Uemura, *Saigunbi*, 173.
64 See the letter of August 9, 1953, from Yoshida to Dlles, reproduced in Murakawa Ichirō, ed., *Daresu to Yoshida Shigeru: Purinsuton daigaku shozō Daresu bunsho o chūshin toshite* [Dulles and Yoshida Shigeru: As Seen Primarily through Materials in the Collection of Princeton University] (Tokyo: Kokusho Kankōkai, 1991), 72. For an account of the Japanese delegation's unsuccessful attempt to secure economic assistance under the Mutual Security Act, see Yasuhara Yōko, "Keizai enjo o meguru MSA kōshō: Sono kyozō to jitsuzō" [Negotiations for Economic Assistance under the Mutual Security Act: Their Virtual Image and Their Real Image], *Japanese Journal of American Studies* 22 (1989).
65 Aichi Kiichi, "Ikeda special emissary, including the Ikeda-Robertson talks of October 1953," 296, Japan Ministry of Foreign Affairs, diplomatic records disclosure, A'1.5.2.1-1.
66 US Department of State, *FRUS*, 1952–1954, Document 684. For a discussion of the strong interest at the US State Department in rectifying Japanese financial and economic policy, see Hiwatari Yumi, *Sengo seiji to Nichi-Bei kankei* [Postwar Poli-

tics and Japanese-US Relations] (Tokyo: University of Tokyo Press, 1990), 82–83.

67 US Department of State, CF 611.94/9-953.

68 Sakamoto, "Ikeda-Robātoson," 35–41.

69 *Mainichi Shimbun*, October 27, 1953.

70 US Department of State, *FRUS*, 1952–1954, Document 713.

71 *Christian Science Monitor*, January 14, 1954; *Asahi Shimbun*, January 17, 1954, evening edition.

72 Yoshida, *Kaisō jūnen*, 3:303–304.

73 For discussions of Japan's economic circumstances at the time, see Chapter 2 in Uchino Tatsurō, *Japan's Postwar Economy: An Insider's View of Its History and Its Future*, trans. Mark A. Harbison (New York: Kodansha International, 1983) and contemporary newspaper coverage, as compiled in a two-part article in the *Asahi Shimbun* of March 30 and 31, 1954, under the title "Nihon no keizai kiki: Rondon Taimuzu Tōkyō tokuhainki" [Japan's Economic Crisis as Seen by the Tokyo Correspondent for the *London Times*].

74 US Department of State, *FRUS*, 1952–1954, Document 732.

75 US Department of State, *FRUS*, 1952–1954, Document 726.

76 Dulles to Dean Rusk, 29 December 1953, Strictly Confidential Q-S, General Correspondence Series, John Foster Dulles Papers, Mudd Library, Princeton University.

77 US Department of State, *FRUS*, 1952–1954, Document 727.

78 For discussions of Allison's role, see Frederick Dickinson, "Nichi-Bei Anpo taisei no hen'yō: MSA kyōtei ni okeru saigunbi ni kansuru ryōkai" [The Metamorphosis of the Japanese-US Security Arrangement: Acknowledgement of Rearmament under the Mutual Security Act Agreements], 1 and 2, *Hōgaku ronsō* [Kyoto Law Review] 121, no. 4 (July 1987) and 122, no.3 (December 1987); and Ikeda Shintaro, "Jon Arison to Nihon saigunbi: 1952–1953" [John Allison and Japanese Rearmament: 1952–1953], *Gaikō jihō* [Diplomacy Journal], no. 1343 (November–December 1997).

79 US Department of State, *FRUS*, 1952–1954, Document 835.

80 US Department of State, *FRUS*, 1952–1954, Document 801.

81 US Department of State, *FRUS*, 1952–1954, Document 373.

82 US Department of State, *FRUS*, 1952–1954, Document 828.

83 The material presented here appears in Sakamoto Kazuya, "Aizenhauā no gaikō senryaku to Nihon 1953–1954 nen" [Eisenhower's Diplomatic Strategy and Japan 1953–1954], pts. 1 and 2, *Hōgaku ronsō* [Kyoto Law Review] 122, no. 3 (December 1987), and 123, no. 3 (June 1988). See also ch. 6, "Reisen no henka to 1954 nen no kiki" [Change in the Cold War and the Crises of 1954], 123–146, in Ishii Osamu, *Reisen to Nichi-Bei kankei: Pātonāshippu no keisei* [The Cold War and Japanese-US Relations: The Formation of a Partnership] (Tokyo: Japan Times, 1989) for a discussion of how 1954 was a watershed in US-Japanese relations.

84 John M. Allison, *Ambassador from the Prairie; or, Allison Wonderland* (New York: Houghton Mifflin, 1973), 266; US Department of State, CF 794.00/3-2554 (tel. 2300).

85 For an account of the *Daigo Fukuryu-maru* incident and its effect on Japanese-US relations, see Sakamoto Kazuya, "Kakuheiki to Nichi-Bei kankei: Bikini jiken

no gaikō shori" [Nuclear Weapons and Japanese-US Relations: The Diplomatic Handling of the Bikini Incident], in *Nenpō kindai Nihon kenkyū* [Journal of Modern Japanese Studies], vol. 16, *Sengo gaikō no keisei* [Formation of Postwar Diplomacy], ed. Kindai Nihon Kenkyūkai [Society of Modern Japanese Studies] (Tokyo: Yamakawa Shuppansha, 1994).

86 US Department of State, *FRUS*, 1952–1954, Document 303.

87 For a discussion of how Allison's telegram prompted presidential action, see Ishii, *Reisen to Nichi-Bei kankei*, 131.

88 US Department of State, *FRUS*, 1952–1954, Document 209.

89 US Department of State, *FRUS*, 1952–1954, Documents 786 and 790.

90 US Department of State, *FRUS*, 1952–1954, Document 430.

91 US Department of State, *FRUS*, 1952–1954, Document 430.

92 For a discussion of Eisenhower's mounting concern with Japan, see Ishii, *Reisen to Nichi-Bei kankei*, 131–133, and Sakamoto, "Aizenhauā no gaikō senryaku."

93 US Department of State, *FRUS*, 1952–1954, Document 782 and 798.

94 For a discussion of this issue, see Sakamoto, "Kakuheiki to Nichi-Bei kankei."

95 US Department of State, *FRUS*, 1952–1954, Document 814; US Department of State, CF 611.94/6-754.

96 US Department of State, *FRUS*, 1952–1954, Document 798.

97 US Department of State, *FRUS*, 1952–1954, Document 803.

98 Ishii, *Reisen to Nichi-Bei kankei*, 215–219.

99 US Department of State, *FRUS*, 1952–1954, Document 806.

100 Ambassador's letter to General Magruder, 28 September 1954, US Department of State, CF 611.94/10-1354.

101 US Department of State, *FRUS*, 1955–1957 (Washington, DC: Government Printing Office, 1991), Document 28.

102 Sakamoto, "Aizenhauā no gaikō senryaku."

103 Public Papers of the Presidents: Dwight D. Eisenhower, 1953 (Washington, DC: Government Printing Office, 1960), 307.

104 Stephen E. Ambrose, *Eisenhower: The President* (New York: Simon and Schuster, 1984), 88–91; Chester J. Pach, Jr., and Elmo Richardson, *The Presidency of Dwight D. Eisenhower* (Lawrence: The University Press of Kansas, 1991); Richard A. Melanson and David Mayers, eds., *Reevaluating Eisenhower: American Foreign Policy in the 1950s* (Champaign: University of Illinois Press, 1987).

105 Dulles to Eisenhower, 17 May 1953, Dulles, John Foster, May 1954, Dulles-Herter Series, Ann Whitman File, Eisenhower Library (Abilene, Kansas).

106 For a discussion of the development and deployment of Eisenhower's New Look strategy, see Douglas Kinnard, *President Eisenhower and Strategy Management: A Study in Defense Politics* (Lexington: University Press of Kentucky, 1977).

107 Public Papers of the Presidents: Dwight D. Eisenhower, 1954 (Washington, DC: Government Printing Office, 1960), 330.

108 As described in Chapter 3, the chairman of the US Joint Chiefs of Staff expressed dissatisfaction with Japan's defense plan in August 1955. That was when Shigemitsu visited Washington, DC, as foreign minister and presented a six-year plan for strengthening Japan's national defense. That plan called for six army divisions

deployed by region, four armored battalions, and 180,000 army troops. US Department of State, *FRUS*, 1955–1957, Document 45.

Not until spring 1956 did the Joint Chiefs of Staff lower their target for Japan's defense buildup in accommodation of Japan's reality. US Department of State, CF 794.5 MSP/11-2756; *FRUS*, 1955–1957, Document 176.

109 US Department of State, *FRUS*, 1952–1954, Document 798.

110 US Far East Command, "Comments on Embassy Memorandum of 9 September 1954," US Department of State, CF 611.94/10–1354.

111 US Department of State, *FRUS*, 1955–1957, Document 3.

112 US Department of State, *FRUS*, 1952–1954, Document 818.

113 Miyazawa, *Secret Talks*, 149.

114 Yoshida, *Kaisō jūnen*, 3:45, 54–55.

115 Kōsaka Masataka, *Saishō Yoshida Shigeru* [Yoshida Shigeru as Prime Minister] (Tokyo: Chuokoronsha, 1968), in Iokibe Makoto, Sakamoto Kazuya, Nakanishi Hiroshi, Sako Susumu, eds., *Kōsaka Masataka chosakushū* [The Writings of Kōsaka Masataka], vol. 4 (Tokyo: Toshi Shuppan, 2000).

116 Yoshida, *Kaisō jūnen*, 1:26–27; Kōsaka, *Saishō Yoshida Shigeru*, 143.

117 Yoshida, *Kaisō jūnen*, 4:42; Yoshida Shigeru, *Sekai to Nihon* [The World and Japan] (Tokyo: Chuokoronsha, 1992), 162–163.

118 Yoshida Shigeru, *Yoshida Shigeru shokan* [Yoshida Shigeru's Letters] (Tokyo: Chuokoronsha, 1994), 71.

119 Kōsaka, *Saishō Yoshida Shigeru*, 87.

120 Kōsaka, *Saishō Yoshida Shigeru*, 144.

121 Yoshida, *Sekai to Nihon*, 164–165.

Chapter 3

A Stillborn Scheme for Revising the Security Treaty

The Shigemitsu-Dulles talks

Vice President Richard Nixon (*left*), Secretary of State John Foster Dulles (*right*), and Foreign Minister Shigemitsu Mamoru (*center*) in Washington, DC. August 29, 1955. Photo from Mainichi Shimbunsha

A group of conservative politicians led by Hatoyama Ichirō left the Liberal Party and joined forces with the Reform Party, led by Shigemitsu Mamoru, to form the Democratic Party in November 1954. Yoshida's cabinet resigned en masse on December 10, 1954, amid declining support, and Hatoyama won the election held on that day in the Diet to select a successor. His party would merge in November 1955 with the Liberal Party to form the Liberal Democratic Party.

Hatoyama took office on a wave of public support that contrasted with the broad disapproval that drove Yoshida from office. Such was the optimism spawned by the new prime minister that people talked of a "Hatoyama Boom." Japanese welcomed his sunny disposition and admired how he had overcome the adversity of being purged from politics for five years and then suffering a mild stroke shortly before his return to public life. Most of all, they were simply ready for a change. Governments led by Yoshida had held power for six years, dating from before the signing of the Treaty of San Francisco, and the once-popular prime minister had worn out his welcome.

Hatoyama's government promptly adopted a foreign policy that departed sharply from the Yoshida government's. The opportunity for a departure in diplomacy fell into Hatoyama's lap soon after his government took power. That was when the Soviet Union proposed talks aimed at restoring diplomatic relations. Yoshida had earned a reputation for managing Japan's international relations well. The talks with the Soviets led to the restoration of ties in October 1956 and enabled Hatoyama to assert his diplomatic credentials to the Japanese people.

Numerous politicians who had been active since before the war gravitated to the Democratic Party. Yoshida's policies sat poorly with their political principles, however popular those policies might have been initially with the electorate. The Democratic Party members abided by a traditional perspective on the importance of autonomy for a nation-state, and they felt that Yoshida's diplomacy was overly accommodating of the United States.

To be sure, the Democratic Party politicians accepted Yoshida's basic premise in international relations. They regarded maintaining close ties with the United States as fundamental to postwar Japanese diplomacy. The Hatoyama government sought, however, to develop an autonomous foreign policy suitable to an independent state while honoring those ties.

This chapter examines a scheme advanced by Shigemitsu to revise the Security Treaty Between the United States and Japan. That scheme, along with the restoration of relations with the Soviet Union, epitomized the new government's efforts to move away from Yoshida's diplomatic policies while maintaining close relations with the United States.

Revising the security treaty was a policy priority of long standing for Hatoyama and his kindred spirits. It was a priority when they left the Yoshida-led Liberal Party and merged with the Shigemitsu-led Reform Party to form the Democratic Party. And it remained a priority after they formed the Liberal Democratic Party with the Liberal Party a year later.

Shigemitsu, a career diplomat, became a prominent figure in Japanese foreign relations in the prewar and wartime years. He overcame the loss of his right leg in a terrorist bomb attack that occurred in 1932 while he was serving in China. The loss obliged him thereafter to walk with a cane and prosthesis. But he went on to serve as the Japanese ambassador to the Soviet Union and then to the United Kingdom and as Japan's foreign minister from 1943 until shortly after the end of the war. He was a cosignatory of the surrender document aboard the USS *Missouri* on September 2, 1945.

General Douglas MacArthur, as the supreme commander of the Allied powers, had Shigemitsu arrested and charged with Class A war crimes (joint conspiracy to start and wage war) in April 1946. Shigemitsu had opposed the war, and MacArthur apparently moved to arrest him only at the insistence of the Soviet Union. The International Military Tribunal for the Far East (the Tokyo War Crimes Tribunal) found Shigemitsu guilty in November 1948 and sentenced him to seven years in prison. He spent two years in Tokyo's Sugamo Prison before receiving parole in November 1950.

Like Hatoyama, Shigemitsu was among the former government leaders purged from public service by the occupation authorities. The authorities lifted his ban in March 1952, and Shigemitsu accepted a request from a group of politicians who had just formed the Reform Party to head the party. He became the party leader in June and won election to the lower house of the Diet in October. But he never displayed the political acumen of his fellow former diplomat, Yoshida, and was unable to wrest power from the latter.

The Reform Party won only 85 of the 466 seats in the lower house of the Diet in the October 1952 election, whereas Yoshida's Liberal Party won 240. The Reform Party failed to gain traction with the Japanese electorate and lost 9 seats in the next general election, in April 1953. Shigemitsu became the vice president of the newly formed Democratic Party in November 1954, but his political fortunes were on the wane, and he was becoming something of a figurehead.

As the Hatoyama government's foreign minister, Shigemitsu traveled to the United States in 1955 for talks with the US secretary of state John Foster Dulles. The talks unfolded over three days, from August 29 to 31. Shigemitsu's basic stance was that the security treaty concluded by Yoshida was inequitable and that it injured the Japanese sense of independence. He argued that the treaty thus imperiled the conservative forces in Japan that the US government sought to nurture and that it was an impediment to promoting close coordination between the two countries. He called for revising the treaty with an eye to eliminating its failings and accommodating Japanese pride.

Shigemitsu's idea for a treaty revision proved too much too soon for Dulles, who had negotiated the original treaty and thus rejected the proposal. Kishi Nobusuke, later prime minister, accompanied Shigemitsu to Washington, DC, as the secretary general of the Democratic Party at that time. He records in his memoir that Dulles was extremely curt and forceful in his rejection of Shigemitsu's overture.[1] Histories of the security treaty have generally reported this episode only in terms of Shigemitsu's failure to secure Dulles's agreement. That treatment, however, misrepresents the importance of the talks between the foreign minister and the secretary of state. This chapter corrects that misrepresentation and examines the gist of the revision that Shigemitsu was proposing.[2]

Previous accounts of Shigemitsu's scheme for revising the security treaty have suffered from insufficient documentary evidence. Commentators have tended to attribute Dulles's brusque rejection to Shigemitsu's personal inadequacy as a negotiator and to overall failings on the part of the Japanese government. That explanation is valid to an extent, but it fails to recognize that Shigemitsu's proposal contained elements of compelling appeal to the US government. Recognizing those elements is essential to a sound grasp of the historical significance of the Shigemitsu-Dulles talks.

This chapter, drawing largely on US materials, sheds new light on the Shigemitsu proposal. It highlights an important facet of the progress toward the revision of the security treaty that took place in 1960.[3]

1 A Proposal for a Mutual-Defense Treaty

"So much success in only three days"

We have little in the way of personal reflections by Shigemitsu on his US visit and talks with Dulles. He died suddenly of a heart attack on January 26, 1957, following what had been a hugely stressful month. Shigemitsu had addressed the United Nations on December 18, 1956, on the occasion of Japan's accession to that body. Just two days later, he had stepped down from his post as foreign minister when the entire Hatoyama cabinet resigned.

A Shigemitsu memoir appeared in 1988, but it contains almost no mention of the results of his talks with Dulles.[4] We have records of his remarks at press conferences and at official announcements, but they reveal little of Shigemitsu's personal views. True to his professional upbringing as a diplomat, Shigemitsu was guarded in his public utterances. His manner was standoffish, his syntax occasionally cryptic.

The Dulles-Shigemitsu interchange included a follow-up to the 1955 talks in Washington, DC: a pair of August 1956 meetings during the London conference convened to deal with the Suez Crisis. Shigemitsu presented Dulles there with a memorandum entitled "The Present Status of the Negotiations for the Normalization of Relations between Japan and the Soviet Union" and sought understanding of the Japanese position on territorial issues. The State Department accounts of the London exchanges reveal a continuing distance, however, between the two.[5]

Japanese understanding of what went on at the 1955 Shigemitsu-Dulles talks has relied disproportionately on commentary left by Shigemitsu critics: Kishi and Kōno Ichirō, who attended as agriculture minister. Perceptions of Shigemitsu's role in the talks with Dulles have therefore been generally negative.[6] The foreign minister, however, seems to have regarded the talks in a positive light.

Yasukawa Takeshi, of the Foreign Ministry's European and American Affairs Bureau, also accompanied Shigemitsu to Washington, DC. He reported to a US embassy staffer that the foreign minister had been upbeat on the plane back to Japan. According to Yasukawa, his boss had characterized the talks as follows: "Never in Japanese history have diplomatic negotiations generated so much success in only three days."[7]

Shigemitsu's self-evaluation as conveyed by Yasukawa contradicts the standard picture of the foreign minister: a man who traveled to Washington, DC, determined to secure a revision of the security treaty and who came away chastened by Dulles's blunt rejection. Yasukawa's account invites suspicion, of course, that Shigemitsu was simply trying to put on a brave face and rationalize a humiliation. Worse, he could have utterly misinterpreted the US response to his proposal. The episode warrants, however, a more nuanced perspective. Headway toward revising the security treaty is evident in the following passage from the joint statement issued after the Shigemitsu-Dulles talks:

> It was agreed that efforts should be made, whenever practicable on a cooperative basis, to establish conditions such that Japan could, as rapidly as possible, assume primary responsibility for the defense of its homeland and be able to contribute to the preservation of international peace and security in the Western Pacific. It was also agreed that when such conditions are brought about it would be appropriate to replace the present Security Treaty with one of greater mutuality.[8]

Note here the positing of conditions where "it would be appropriate to replace the present Security Treaty with one of greater mutuality." This is the first public acknowledgement by the Japanese and US governments of interest in revising the treaty. The communiqué conditions the revision of the treaty, to be sure, on the eventuality "when such conditions are brought about," and it leaves the conditions undefined.

More problematic in the realm of Japanese public opinion was the communiqué's reference to "conditions such that Japan could . . . be able to contribute to the preservation of international peace and security in the Western Pacific." Japanese naturally regarded this phrase as countenancing the dispatching of troops to theaters abroad, and the communiqué drew intense criticism for that reason.

Shigemitsu's response to the criticism was half-honest.[9] The foreign minister held a press conference in New York right after the talks with Dulles. There, he denied having offered to dispatch troops abroad as a quid pro quo for revising the treaty. And that denial is presumably true as far as it went. The US records of the Shigemitsu-Dulles talks reveal no clear-cut pledge by the Japanese with regard to dispatching troops abroad. And Shigemitsu's weak standing in the government and in his party suggests that he was ill-positioned to make such a pledge.

However, Shigemitsu asserted at the press conference that the question of dispatching troops abroad had never arisen in the talks. That assertion is demonstrably untrue. Records of the talks reveal clearly that Dulles and Shigemitsu debated that issue heatedly. Dulles argued that revising the treaty would hinge on the Japanese agreeing to dispatch troops abroad and on revising their constitution to permit that dispatching. Shigemitsu responded with the suggestion that the constitution could be interpreted, sans revision, as permitting the overseas dispatching of troops.

Dulles asked on the second day of the talks if Japan could provide military assistance if the United States were attacked. Shigemitsu responded in the affirmative, whereupon Dulles expressed incredulity at the foreign minister's constitutional interpretation.[10] This exchange appears in the following excerpt from the US record of the talks.

> The Secretary then inquired whether Japan could send forces outside of Japan to help the United States if it were attacked, adding that this appeared doubtful and that the Japanese Government would have to be stronger before a basis of mutuality existed. The Secretary commented that the situation would be different when Japan had adequate forces, a sufficient legal framework and an amended constitution. He asked specifically whether Japan could go to the defense of the United States if Guam were attacked. The Foreign Minister replied that Japan could do so and that under its present system Japan can organize forces for self-defense. The Secretary said that this would not be a case of the self-defense of Japan but rather of defense of the United States. The Foreign Minister replied that in such a situation Japan would first consult with the United States and would then decide whether or not to use its forces. The Secretary said that he was not clear as to the Foreign Minister's interpretation of the Japanese Constitution and added that he had thought the broadest commitment Japan could make would be to use its forces for the defense of Japan. The Foreign Minister replied that Japan's forces must be used for self-defense and that Japan could consult, in the case of an attack in connection with a treaty, regarding the use of its forces.

> The Secretary commented that consultation would not mean very much if the constitution prevented the sending of forces abroad. The Foreign Minister answered that Japan's interpretation included the use of forces for self-defense and consultation as to whether or not forces should be sent abroad. He commented that Japan would like to have a treaty like the United States-Philippine treaty and that this is possible even under the present constitution. The Secretary said that he had not previously realized that Japan thought it could do this.[11]

In Dulles's view, the Japanese, if they wanted a truly mutual treaty, required the ability to dispatch troops abroad and to help defend the United States. The secretary emphasized that acquiring that ability would mean attaining a suitable level of military strength and that attaining that level would require a revision of the constitution. Dulles's pointed questioning of Shigemitsu and the foreign minister's clumsy response underlay a joint statement that was stunningly provocative. The communiqué called for Japan to contribute to Western Pacific security in terms inconceivable for Japan at that time.

Shigemitsu had explained to Dulles that Japan could dispatch its Self-Defense Forces abroad under the nation's constitution as it stood. That constitutional interpretation elicited the expression of doubt from the secretary, as cited above, and was indeed of questionable standing in constitutional jurisprudence. Several members of the Hatoyama cabinet voiced concern at the press reports that Shigemitsu had pledged to dispatch troops overseas.

For example, Sunada Shigemasa, the director general of the Defense Agency: "Dispatching forces overseas would clearly be in violation of Article 9 of the constitution." And Takasaki Tatsunosuke, the director general of the Economic Planning Agency: "[The notion of dispatching forces overseas and defending the Western Pacific] is inconceivable to anyone acquainted with Japan's present circumstances."[12]

The upper house of the Diet had passed a resolution on June 2, 1954, that expressly forbade dispatching troops abroad. That was in advance of the July 1954 reorganization of the National Safety Forces as the Japan Self-Defense Forces (JSDF or simply, SDF). The Yoshida government, meanwhile, had declared at the time that dispatching forces overseas was not an option.[13] Shigemitsu's constitutional interpretation differed even from that issued by the Hatoyama government on December 22, 1954, just twelve days after taking power.

Hatoyama's newly installed government laid out a case for the constitutionality of the Self-Defense Forces. It stressed that the SDF existed only as a means of repelling a military strike against Japan, that they possessed a capacity only sufficient to fulfill that function, and that they therefore posed no violation of the constitution.[14]

Revising the Japanese constitution was, in any case, an unrealistic proposition for the time being. Hatoyama, at the bottom of his heart, believed that Japan should revise the constitution and undertake full-fledged rearmament. He disliked Yoshida's approach of carrying out rearmament incrementally, all the while denying that Japan was in fact rearming. But once in office, Hatoyama came face to face with a harsh reality: the Self-Defense Forces were an established fact, and he could hardly argue, as prime minister, that they existed in violation of the constitution as it stood.

Hatoyama's government therefore ended up equivocating on the issue of constitutionality.[15] Its interpretation of December 1954 reasoned that the Self-Defense Forces were not unconstitutional but that Article 9 of the constitution was prone to misunderstanding and that the government would consider making a revision when the time was right.[16] The right time, however, was not soon in coming.

Japan held a general election February 1955, the first since April 1953. In the 1955 election, the right-leaning wing of the Socialist Party gained 17 seats, and the left-leaning branch 1 seat. That brought the party's strength to 156 seats. Note that a majority in the 467-seat lower house required 234 votes.

We can but wonder what Shigemitsu had in mind in extolling "so much success in only three days." The foreign minister had achieved a communiqué that called for revising his nation's security treaty with the United States, but he was in no position to bring that about any time soon. He appears to have come away from the talks in Washington, DC, with little more than a scolding from Dulles. The secretary of state, it would seem, had laid down the law to the upstart foreign minister. In view of Japan's inadequate military capabilities, the time was hardly ripe for revising the security treaty.[17]

"Western Pacific"

The communiqué's reference to "peace and security in the Western Pacific" warrants careful consideration in reviewing the Shigemitsu-Dulles talks. That reference meshes with the question Dulles raised about protecting Guam if it were attacked. The reference to "Western Pacific" appears to have originated, however, with input from Shigemitsu. An advance proposal for the joint statement prepared by the State Department contained no mention of "Western Pacific" or of "mutual-defense treaty."

A trove of US diplomatic papers made public in October 1991 includes the minutes of the Shigemitsu-Dulles talks and other important documents that pertain to the talks. They reveal that Shigemitsu read a position paper about defense issues at the opening of the second session, on August 30. That paper became the focus of the subsequent discussions and is therefore crucial to understanding what transpired between the foreign minister and the secretary of state.

A copy of Shigemitsu's position paper is available in the US National Archives. That document, which matches copies subsequently declassified in Japan, has Shigemitsu proposing a revision of the security treaty.

> We feel that the time has arrived that is most beneficial for both [the United States and Japan] to conduct a reconsideration of circumstances for the purpose of concluding a new defense treaty to replace the present security treaty. At the time of the signing of the security treaty, the disarmed Japan could not stand as an equal partner in a collective security framework. In addition, concluding a bilateral treaty of military character based on a foundation of mutuality was impossible for the Japanese government on account of Japan's fiscal and economic circumstances and the prevailing constitutional interpretation at the time.
>
> However, Japan now possesses military strength superior to that of some members of [the North Atlantic Treaty Organization] and [the Southeast Asia Treaty Organization], and that will increase under the six-year plan that has been proposed, so the time is ripe for concluding a bilateral new defense treaty based on a mutual foundation to replace the present unilateral security treaty.
>
> This new treaty might be similar in form to the treaties that the United

> States has concluded with Australia, New Zealand, the Philippines, the Republic of Korea, and [Taiwan]. It might also include a stipulation in regard to mutual defense to the effect that each party to the treaty is to regard an armed attack on the territory of or territory under the administration of the other party to the treaty in the Western Pacific as a danger to its own peace and security and declare that it will take action in response to the common danger in accordance with its constitutional procedures.[18]

Shigemitsu brought to Washington, DC, a six-year plan for strengthening Japan's national defense and showed it to Dulles. The plan covered the six fiscal years to March 1962. It provided for increasing the Ground Self-Defense Force to a troop strength of 180,000 by March 31, 1959, for bolstering the Maritime Self-Defense Force to a troop strength of 34,000 and a fleet tonnage of 123,900 tons, and for growing the Air Self-Defense Force to a troop strength of 42,000 and a complement of 1,300 aircraft by March 31, 1962.

"Western Pacific" debuted at the Shigemitsu-Dulles talks in this position paper presented by the foreign minister. Shigemitsu had taken note of the treaties that the United States had concluded with other ostensibly free world nations in the Asia-Pacific. He proposed replacing the security treaty with a mutual-defense pact modeled on the lines of those treaties. Either party, as noted, would respond to an attack on the other's territory as an attack on their own territory.

Critics of Shigemitsu have portrayed him as approaching the talks with a barely coherent notion for revising the security treaty. We see here, however, that he held an ever-so-clear vision of the geographical scope of the proposed treaty and of the mutual military obligations under the new treaty. Shigemitsu's reference to "Western Pacific" furnished the background for the subsequent query by Dulles about a hypothetical attack on Guam.[19]

Simply reading a short position paper didn't constitute, of course, presenting a concrete proposal for a mutual-defense treaty. The paper excerpted here, albeit of unquestionable importance, did little more than broach the subject. Shigemitsu, however, had conveyed a proposal for a new treaty to the State Department before traveling to Washington, DC. He submitted the proposal on a personal and informal basis through Ambassador John Allison.[20]

The attention that Shigemitsu's proposal received became evident in another proposal for a new Japanese-US treaty. Douglas A. MacArthur II succeeded Allison as the US ambassador to Japan in February 1957, and he floated a proposal in February 1958 for revising the security treaty. MacArthur accompanied each section of his draft proposal with notes about how the content compared with that in Shigemitsu's proposal.[21]

As we have seen, the traditional understanding of the talks ran as follows: Shigemitsu proposed replacing the security treaty with a defense pact based on mutuality, and Dulles rejected the idea out of hand: "If you want a mutual treaty, then be prepared at least to contribute to maintaining peace and security in the Western Pacific." We now know, however, that the talks were less one-sided than this traditional version of events suggests.

Shigemitsu took the initiative in presenting Dulles with a concrete policy proposal for revising the security treaty, and a core element of his proposal, "Western Pacific," ended up, albeit undefined, in the joint statement. The foreign minister also deserves credit for infusing the communiqué with a prescient acknowledgement: the likely eventuality where "it would be appropriate to replace the present Security Treaty with one of greater mutuality." Shigemitsu's exuberant "so much success in only three days" seems less boastful and more justified in view of these achievements.

Although Shigemitsu deserves higher grades than he has traditionally received for his performance in Washington, DC, the tangible results were nil. He would have liked to begin negotiating a new treaty immediately, but Admiral Arthur Radford, the chairman of the Joint Chiefs of Staff, criticized Shigemitsu's six-year plan for strengthening Japan's defense as woefully inadequate.[22] Dulles, meanwhile, dismissed a mutual-defense treaty that did not provide for dispatching Japanese troops overseas as meaningless for the United States. The secretary of state thought enough of the exchange with Shigemitsu, however, to take his pen to fine-tuning the communiqué.[23]

Secondary documentation suggests that Dulles's editing centered on the portion of the communiqué that pertained to revising the security treaty. The secretary was extremely wary of revising the treaty at that stage, and his editing reflects an effort to save face for Shigemitsu while rejecting the foreign minister's proposal. Yasukawa, in his memoir, describes the portion of the communiqué in question as the product of compromise.

> This part of the joint statement was a strained effort to reconcile Shige-

> mitsu's call for revising the treaty with the US position [in opposition to the revision]. Uncharitably, you could regard the text as a façade.[24]

Shigemitsu had perhaps scored a coup indeed by his reckoning. He had secured a communiqué that mentioned the potential need for revising the security treaty, that spoke of a Japan that could and would "assume primary responsibility for the defense of its homeland and be able to contribute to the preservation of international peace and security in the Western Pacific," and that left unspecified the "conditions such that Japan could, as rapidly as possible" attain that capability. The joint statement, in that sense, left the Japanese government with immense latitude for interpretation.[25]

Ōmori Minoru, a reporter for the *Mainichi Shimbun*, covered the Shigemitsu-Dulles talks. He writes of press conference remarks by Robert McClurkin, the director of the State Department's Office of Northeast Asian Affairs. Ōmori reports that McClurkin characterized the reference to preserving Western Pacific peace and security as denoting Japanese readiness to dispatch troops abroad. McClurkin's remarks, according to Ōmori, impinged briefly on the generally positive feeling that Kishi and Kōno had gleaned from the talks. Ōmori writes that Kishi expressed satisfaction with the outcome.

"We've gotten past first base," observed Japan's UN ambassador Kase Toshikazu in Ōmori's account.[26] Japan was still an observer at the United Nations, but Kase was a trusted confidant of Shigemitsu and had participated in drafting the proposal for replacing the security treaty with a mutual-defense pact. In the absence of other commentary, his evaluation might well have carried the day in Japanese public opinion. That was not to be, however, as coverage of McClurkin's remarks and other output from the talks reached Japan.

2 A US Military Withdrawal

Pressure to forge a conservative coalition quickly

Dulles might have demonstrated some consideration in his editing of the communiqué to saving face for Shigemitsu. But McClurkin, intentionally or otherwise, put the foreign minister in a difficult position with his comments about Japan dispatching troops abroad. And follow-up output from the State Department was notably insensitive to Shigemitsu. US State Department officials continued to insist that the subject of Japan's dispatching troops overseas had arisen in the talks and that it could become an issue in the future, though other, seemingly contrary output from the department kept things somewhat confused.[27]

What emerged clearly from the talks was that formal negotiations for revising the security treaty would not begin anytime soon. The US government had taken a hard line, and Shigemitsu's camp had come up short in its optimistic expectations of the talks. Dulles's aversion to renegotiating the security treaty is understandable in the light of his political and geopolitical instincts, as we will see. The outright rejection of Shigemitsu's overture is puzzling nonetheless.

Shigemitsu, in pursuit of a mutual treaty, had proposed that Japan take more responsibility for its national defense. Still unsettled was the issue of how far Japan should go in strengthening its defense capacity. But Shigemitsu had offered, in principle, what the US government had been demanding since the days of the Yoshida government. We would think that his proposal would elicit a more favorable response.

Allison was amenable to the notion of revising the security treaty with an eye to fortifying Japanese-US ties.[28] Shigemitsu held multiple discussions secretly with him before traveling to Washington, DC. He emerged from those discussions confident of achieving a positive outcome in the talks with Dulles. Shigemitsu was realistic enough to realize that formal negotiations for revising the security treaty were unlikely to begin immediately, but he had good reason to believe that his talks with Dulles could be a first step in that direction. Kōno writes in his memoir that Shigemitsu was extremely upbeat at a meeting of the Japanese delegation before the talks.[29]

Dulles's firm rejection of the proposal for renegotiating the security treaty thus took Allison and Shigemitsu by surprise. Allison, in his memoir, attributes that rejection to Dulles's abhorrence of the thought of shepherding a treaty through congressional debate.[30] The geopolitical outlook had remained uncertain since a July 18, 1955, summit in Geneva among the US, Soviet, UK, and French leaders, and Dulles was loath to complicate his dealings with Congress further.

Another reason for Dulles's resistance to Shigemitsu's proposal was his concern about Japan's unsettled domestic politics and the frailty of Shigemitsu's political position.[31] The Hatoyama government's political foundation was weak, and the government had blundered repeatedly in legislative management. Dulles doubted that Hatoyama's government possessed the ability to secure the passage of a revised treaty in the Diet. The Americans knew, too, that Hatoyama's health was questionable and that his government was unlikely to last long.

Japan's political landscape was rife with instability. The Americans were concerned that any treaty commitments made by the Hatoyama government might not survive under a successor government.[32] Even the Democratic Party was beset with all manner of factional infighting and policy disputes. Opposition groups that advocated neutralism in foreign policy and leftist agendas were also political forces to be reckoned with.

Hatoyama's cabinet had compounded its difficulties with a serious diplomatic error. The error occurred in negotiating a reduction in Japan's share of the financial burden of maintaining US forces in Japan.[33] Japanese and US government representatives met in Tokyo on March 25, 1955, to begin the negotiations in earnest. The talks ran aground immediately on US inflexibility. That alarmed the members of the Hatoyama cabinet, since it threatened to prevent them from finalizing their budget. In response, the cabinet decided on April 1 to go over the heads of the negotiators. It resolved to dispatch Shigemitsu to Washington, DC, to take up the matter directly with the secretary of state. The cabinet reached that decision, however, without vetting the visit in advance with the US government.

Shigemitsu asked Allison on April 1 to help arrange a meeting with Dulles within two weeks. The ambassador cautioned the foreign minister that setting up a meeting on such short notice would be difficult and that the visit would be politically risky. Traveling to Washington, DC, and returning empty-handed, he noted, would be a political black eye for Shigemitsu and for the Hatoyama government. Allison nevertheless pledged, reluctantly, to explore the possibility of arranging a meeting, accompanying his pledge with a "solemn caution against premature publicity." He was therefore livid to find on April 2 that the Japanese press had trumpeted the news of the planned visit.[34]

Sure enough, the State Department formally declined on April 3 to receive Shigemitsu. It couched the refusal in terms of the impossibility of reworking the secretary's schedule and providing him with sufficient briefing in a fortnight. The opposition parties in the Diet demanded that the Hatoyama government take responsibility for the humiliation. They tabled a reprimand on April 6 that accused the government of conduct that had been "gravely injurious to international confidence in [Japan]."

The mishandling of the defense-spending negotiations had indeed damaged Japan's prestige. Equally troubling, however, was the gist of Shigemitsu's argument in the August talks with Dulles. Shigemitsu essentially based his case on the fragility of the Hatoyama government's political standing. The security treaty required revision, he argued, because: (1) it was widely perceived in Japan as inequitable; (2) the Communists and other leftist elements seized on that perception to foster anti-government sentiment; and (3) negotiating the allocation of defense costs and the resolution of frictions occasioned by US bases was politically disruptive.[35]

Shigemitsu's argument might well have been long on sincerity, but it was short on persuasiveness. Dulles took aim at the most glaring flaw in the foreign minister's argument. A new treaty wouldn't mean much, he suggested, if the socialists and other leftists wielded a destabilizing influence in Japanese politics. What they opposed, Dulles observed, was not the inequality of the treaty but the very act of cooperating with the United States.[36]

Whereas Shigemitsu sought to blame Japan's domestic political instability on the inequitable security treaty, Dulles questioned the value of revising the treaty on an unstable political foundation. The fundamental problem in the eyes of the secretary of state was the weakness of Japan's government and trying to blame that weakness on an allegedly inequitable treaty was mere rationalization. What Shigemitsu and his cohorts needed to do, Dulles believed, was cement a conservative coalition. That belief is evident in the following excerpt from a September 1 letter from Dulles to Eisenhower.

> The Japanese conference has gone really well. I gave them some straight talk which was, I believe, wholesome. The fact that Kono and Kishi were also present was good, because they represent much political power. The important thing for us is to get the right-wing parties to consolidate and not tear each other apart and seek popularity by joining in the

> "American go home" theme. I believe our talks impressed them with the need to consolidate on a platform of cooperation with the United States. I hope the impression will survive long enough for it to produce some political results.[37]

Dulles's stern attitude toward Shigemitsu in Washington, DC, was, in other words, a matter of tough love. It was an admonishment to put Japan's domestic politics in order and to move swiftly toward putting a resilient conservative coalition in place. Dulles and his colleagues in the US government were well aware of the weak political position of the Hatoyama administration and of the weak standing of Shigemitsu in the government.

A State Department position paper prepared for the talks characterized Shigemitsu as a politician of ambition disproportionate to his ability. The Americans appraised him as a pathetic politician who elicited neither respect nor loyalty from the larger conservative groups. Hatoyama had signaled his lack of confidence in Shigemitsu by sending Kishi and Kōno along to monitor the talks with Dulles, and their clashes of policy and personality with the foreign minister were well understood at the US embassy in Tokyo.[38]

The Americans recognized that Shigemitsu's political future hinged on his establishing himself as a coordinator of Japanese-US cooperation.[39] Shigemitsu's negotiating position deteriorated at the Dulles talks, however, when he exposed the cracks in the Democratic Party's foundation and was unable to control Kishi and Kōno. Kishi, Kōno, and Deputy Chief Cabinet Secretary Matsumoto Takizō met, sans Shigemitsu, with the Deputy Assistant Secretary for Far Eastern Affairs, W. J. Sebald, and with McClurkin and Allison and a US embassy staffer on the morning of August 31. The Japanese took the opportunity to stab their foreign minister in the back.

Parrying the Communist threat was fundamental to the case that Shigemitsu had made to Dulles the previous day. He had emphasized that threat in calling for revising the security treaty as a means of stabilizing Japanese domestic politics and nurturing a conservative coalition. Kishi expressed the view, however, that Shigemitsu had misrepresented the Communist threat, as recorded in a State Department memorandum.

> With regard to Japan's internal situation, Mr. Kishi said that he personally

> disagreed with the Foreign Minister as to the extent of the Communist threat. He felt that in discussions with the Secretary yesterday the Foreign Minister had greatly exaggerated the danger. The threat could certainly not be ignored, but it was not as serious as the Foreign Minister had depicted it.[40]

Shigemitsu had perhaps exaggerated the threat posed by the Communists and other leftist groups to emphasize the need for revising the security treaty. And he had perhaps been amiss in not coordinating his talking points better with Kishi and Kōno in advance. But for delegation members to refute the delegation leader's remarks of the previous day was stunning, and it largely negated whatever weight the Japanese delegation might have otherwise brought to the talks.[41]

A concept for forcing change in US Far Eastern strategy

Dulles had ample reason for irritation. Here was the foreign minister of a nation that had, in American eyes, neglected its defense, in military capability and constitutional provisions. Yet Shigemitsu was bringing forth a proposal for mutual assistance in defense in utter disregard for Japan's reality and, equally disturbing, utter disregard for his government's and his own political weakness. And the secretary's reason for irritation went further still.

The proposal for revising the security treaty that Shigemitsu was preparing to bring to Washington, DC, was problematic for Dulles. As we have seen, it addressed the US demand for Japan to shoulder a greater share of its defense burden. Yet the military buildup that Shigemitsu was offering in exchange for greater mutuality was woefully inadequate from the American perspective.

Shigemitsu broached his proposal with the US government through Allison, as also noted, on a personal and informal basis. The ambassador summarized Shigemitsu's reasoning as follows in a July 25, 1955, telegram to Dulles: repositioning the treaty as a more equitable arrangement would deflect domestic criticism from the left of alleged subservience to the United States, Japan's defense buildup would occasion an orderly withdrawal of US forces from Japan, and the US withdrawal would end the annual haggling over allocating the cost of maintaining the US military presence.

The Shigemitsu proposal aimed unabashedly at reasserting Japanese independence. Allison interpreted the proposal as reflecting the feelings of a vast majority of the Japanese. He perceived broad sentiment that Japan would never be an independent sovereign state under the security treaty as then configured. Shigemitsu insisted, Allison wrote, that Article 9 of the constitution was not an obstacle to concluding a collective defense agreement, and the foreign minister claimed that the other members of the Hatoyama cabinet shared that view. Japan could conclude a pact with the United States, Allison reported Shigemitsu as suggesting, similar to the Australia, New Zealand, United States Security Treaty (ANZUS).[42]

We have seen Shigemitsu's references in the copy of his proposal available for perusal to ANZUS and to US mutual-defense treaties with the Philippines, the Republic of Korea, and Taiwan.[43] And we have seen that he envisioned

> a stipulation in regard to mutual defense to the effect that each party to the treaty is to regard an armed attack on the territory of or territory under the administration of the other party to the treaty in the Western Pacific as a danger to its own peace and security and declare that it will take action in response to the common danger in accordance with its constitutional procedures.[44]

The foreign minister interpreted this text as obliging Japan to defend US forces if the latter were attacked in Japan; in Okinawa (then under US control, returned to Japanese sovereignty in 1972); on the Ogasawara Islands (then under US control, returned to Japanese sovereignty in 1968); or in Guam, but not if they were attacked in the Republic of Korea, in the Philippines, in Taiwan, or in any other venue further afield. He regarded this obligation as subject to the approval of the Diet, and in the event of an emergency where there is no time to seek Diet approval ahead of time, then after the fact. Shigemitsu proposed an initial term of 25 years, to 1980, to overlap with the Sino-Soviet Treaty of Friendship, Alliance and Mutual Assistance, which spanned from 1950 to 1979, and subsequent renewal in five-year increments.

Shigemitsu accompanied the foregoing core elements of his proposed treaty with an annex of supplementary provisions. Some of those provisions had important implications, some of which were unacceptable to the Americans. Archival evidence reveals that Shigemitsu initially planned to incorporate some of them in the body of his proposed treaty text.

Walter Robertson, the US assistant secretary of state for the Far East, provided the following commentary on Shigemitsu's proposal in a July 28, 1955, memorandum to Dulles:

1. Transitional arrangements for the withdrawal of United States ground forces within six years.

Comment: This is in accord with present [National Security Council] policy which provides for "a phased withdrawal from Japan of United States forces as consistent with United States and Japanese security interests". (Paragraph 51, Tab B [see note, below]) The difficult problem would be for us to retain the right—if Defense considered it necessary or desirable to do so—to send our forces back in case of emergency.

2. Mutual agreement on the date of withdrawal of United States air and naval forces, but at the latest six years after completion of the withdrawal of the ground forces.

Comment: General thinking here had been that United States air and naval bases would be retained in Japan indefinitely. Subject to advice from Defense, this is a point on which we would want a good deal more favorable arrangements than contained in this Japanese proposal.

3. United States bases in Japan and United States forces there to be utilized for mutual defense purposes only, under arrangements similar to those with the NATO countries.

Comment: The explicit limitation on the use of the bases which the present security treaty allows us to use "to contribute to the maintenance of international peace and security in the Far East" is clearly undesirable.

4. No further Japanese contribution to the support of United States forces in Japan.

Comment: Paragraph 51 of the [National Security Council] paper (see Tab B) provides that we should accept reductions of the Japanese contribution in relation to the buildup of the Japanese defense

> forces and the withdrawal of our own forces. Here it would probably be possible to negotiate a specific phased reduction over a period of years which would avoid the annual wrangle about the Japanese defense budget. We could also probably set some understanding that the amounts thus released would be devoted to the development of the Japanese defense forces.[45]
>
> *Note:* Tab B, a series of pertinent quotations from NSC 5516/1, Document 28, is not printed.[46]

Robertson thus highlights the principal sticking points for the US government in Shigemitsu's proposal. Especially problematic are the proposal's calls for withdrawing US air and naval forces and for narrowing the strategic role of US bases in Japan. Under the 1952 security treaty, Japan ensured its military security by lending bases to the United States and by cooperating with US military strategy for the Far East. Shigemitsu was proposing to replace that arrangement with a fundamentally different mutual-defense framework.

The US bases in Japan fulfilled a comprehensive role in US military strategy. That role encompassed functions far more extensive than just defending Japan. The bases were for providing operational, logistical, and maintenance support for US army, air, and naval forces throughout the Far East and for launching strikes against Communist forces on the Asian continent in the event of attack. Their role is clear in a research report prepared at the time by the US embassy in Tokyo as "US Defense Policy in Japan."[47]

US policymakers were hardly likely to look kindly on Shigemitsu's proposal. It essentially called on the United States to discard key strategic assets and rewrite its military strategy for the Far East. His proposal called for withdrawing US air and naval forces, as well US army forces, from Japan in the near future. It called, too, for limiting the function of the bases while they remained. US military forces in Japan would be unable to respond automatically to an emergency in the Republic of Korea, for example, or in Taiwan.[48]

Allison and his counterparts in the State Department's Bureau of Far Eastern Affairs were alert to the difficulties posed by Shigemitsu's proposal but nonetheless found aspects worthy of approval. Most notably, they credited Shigemitsu for proposing that Japan and the United States undertake responsibility for mutual defense. They knew, meanwhile, that the security treaty as then configured could not ensure the US military rights in Japan indefinitely. Even if the treaty remained in place, the Japanese could neuter it through the passive resistance of an uncooperative stance.

The possibility that popular dissatisfaction with the treaty in Japan could strengthen neutralist forces was a serious concern for Allison, and he feared that the United States risked losing a valuable ally if it mishandled the treaty discussions.[49] His counterparts in the Bureau of Far Eastern Affairs were eager to engage Japan in a broad collective security arrangement in the Pacific, and they welcomed Japanese participation in a mutual-defense arrangement with the United States as a step toward that goal.

Dulles signed off on the following three recommendations that Robertson included in his memorandum:

> 1. that copies of [the Japanese proposal reported in telegram No. 201 from the Tokyo embassy] be given to Secretary [of Defense Charles] Wilson, [Joint Chiefs of Staff chairman] Admiral [Arthur] Radford and [army chief of staff] General [Maxwell] Taylor;
> 2. that we discuss the whole question carefully with them in the near future; and
> 3. if they agree, that we authorize Ambassador Allison to continue informal and personal discussions with Foreign Minister Shigemitsu.[50]

Although Dulles signed off on Robertson's recommendations, he was decidedly cooler to Shigemitsu's proposal than his subordinates were, including Allison.

The secretary of state was extremely wary about withdrawing US forces and narrowing the functionality of US bases in Japan. He had expressed that wariness at an April 7 meeting of the National Security Council, a meeting discussed in Chapter 2. The policy paper adopted there, NSC 5516/1, was the second basic exposition of Japan policy under the Eisenhower administration. An early draft of the paper (NAS 5516) included the following paragraph (paragraph 35):

> Indicate [at a suitable early date and mutually advantageous time] will-

> ingness to negotiate replacement of the present United States-Japan Security Treaty by a treaty of mutual defense which would include the right to maintain forces in Japan and the right upon Japan's request to aid Japan in resisting subversion or infiltration by unfriendly forces.[51]

Dulles declared his opposition at the security council meeting to including the above paragraph in the paper. The content of the paragraph in question had originated in the State Department, and Eisenhower was therefore bemused at Dulles's opposition. Dulles reiterated his opposition, however, as described in the minutes of the meeting.

> Secretary Dulles [argued that supplanting the United States'] present treaty with Japan with a new one . . . could not be done without a grave loss of advantage to the United States. If we suggest a new mutual defense treaty to the Japanese they will certainly want to model such a treaty on the existing mutual defense treaties between the US and South Korea and the US and the Philippines. This would mean that the United States would have to forgo its *right* [italics in original] to maintain forces and bases in Japan, and the privilege of doing so would be dependent on the agreement of the Japanese Government. Moreover, the treaties for mutual defense ran for a much shorter time than is desirable in the light of the present situation. Such mutual defense treaties were subject to termination in a year's time at the behest of either partner. Accordingly, concluded Secretary Dulles, unless pressure in Japan for a new treaty became a great deal stronger than it was at the present time, he was firmly opposed to the proposal set forth in paragraph 35 of NSC 5516.[52]

The National Security Council honored Dulles's views and deleted the paragraph in question from the position paper. Dulles was concerned that a treaty revision, even if it stipulated US rights to retain bases in Japan, would restrict US scope in using the bases. Shigemitsu's proposal had earned the secretary's opposition with its clause for a 12-year horizon on US bases in Japan. Dulles could not accept the proposal as long as it contained that clause. His opposition was firm even if the Japanese held out the prospect of retaining US base rights in some form, even if the Hatoyama government displayed a longer life expectancy than it did, even if Shigemitsu's political position was stronger than it was, even if Japan acquired a substantially stronger defense capacity based on a revised constitution.

Dulles wrote to Allison on August 1 that he could "see both pros and cons to moving in direction replacing present US-Japan Security Treaty with mutual defense pact," but that "we would have to be certain Japanese Government could deliver Diet ratification which would be true only if there were firm assurance both Democrats and Liberals would support it. I do not want to open up the treaty we have when we are not sure of a treaty to replace it." The secretary instructed the ambassador to "tell Shigemitsu this obviously [is a] most important and difficult subject which will require careful thought." Allison reported to Dulles on August 3 that he had spoken with Shigemitsu that day and that he had "discouraged any thought it might be possible for final action to be taken" during the foreign minister's scheduled visit to Washington, DC.[53]

A week before the Shigemitsu-Dulles talks began, Sebald, the deputy assistant secretary for Far Eastern affairs, submitted commentary on Shigemitsu's proposal to Dulles. Sebald granted that the proposal was a step toward achieving the collective security framework that the US government desired. He complained, however, that it failed to ensure the unrestricted base rights in and around Japan that the US government also desired. Sebald urged putting off negotiating a mutual-defense treaty until "it has become clear that a new agreement is indispensable for maintaining US-Japanese cooperation in defense matters."[54]

Shigemitsu's proposal, though floated in the vein of a personal perspective, transcended its ostensible focus on the Western Pacific. The proposal contained profound implications for US military strategy throughout the Far East. Those implications presumably accounted for Dulles's wary response. They were, in their immense scope, far out of proportion to the political standing and capabilities of Shigemitsu and the Hatoyama government. The proposal surely struck Dulles as brash to the point of impudence.

No call for troop withdrawals

Shigemitsu ultimately declined to call for a complete withdrawal of US troops from Japan at the talks with Dulles. We gain some insight into a possible reason from the following entry in the former's memoir. The passage relates an incident three days before Shigemitsu was to leave for Washington, DC.

> August 20, Saturday. Sunny and hot.
> Leave Ueno at 9 a.m. on a train for Nasu.
> Met at the station by an Imperial Household Ministry [*sic*; correctly Imperial Household Agency since 1949] car, which takes me to imperial villa. Bathe and change clothes in anteroom. Receive lunch. Enter [emperor's] quarters shortly after 1 o'clock for audience. Deliver detailed summary of [upcoming] mission to United States. Emperor expresses view that Japanese-US cooperation is necessary in resisting Communists and that withdrawal of [US] forces stationed in Japan is impossible [emphasis added] and gives me friendly messages for conveying to his acquaintances.
> Leave at 3:30 and arrive at Ueno at 6:30. Enter hotel and head [next morning] for Hirogawara.[55]

We surmise from this passage that Shigemitsu provided the emperor with a highly detailed account of his US plans. Of special note, of course, is the emperor's comment about the impossibility of the removal of US troops from Japan. We assume that the comment was in response to Shigemitsu's explanation of his proposal for revising the security treaty, but we cannot be certain and must be careful about evaluating the possible implications. The opinion of the emperor alone, who constitutionally had no political power at all, would not necessarily prompt Shigemitsu to abandon his call for a complete withdrawal of US troops.

According to Yasukawa, Shigemitsu still intended to propose the troop withdrawal to Dulles. Yasukawa describes in his memoir a discussion among Shigemitsu and other Foreign Ministry officials on the eve of the talks with Dulles. The discussion took place at the Japanese delegation's hotel in Hot Springs, Virginia. Shigemitsu's materials for submission to Dulles included the phrase, "When Japan has completed the [proposed] strengthening of its defense capability, centered on [an increase to] ground forces of 180,000 troops, the US military should withdraw completely from Japan [emphasis added]." Yasukawa reports that he recommended deleting that phrase.

> Shigemitsu argued that we Japanese should make our case frankly at this juncture, regardless of whether our US counterparts find it acceptable. I objected that to call for a complete withdrawal would impart to our US counterparts the impression that Japan's foreign minister was out of touch with reality. I still remember the sour expression [that my objection brought] to Shigemitsu's face.[57]

Kase, we learn from Yasukawa, edited the text of Shigemitsu's proposal after the discussion at the hotel and, though his changes were generally minor, deleted the passage that called for a complete withdrawal of US forces. Shigemitsu appears to have agreed at the last minute to refrain from calling for complete withdrawal. The position paper that he submitted at the talks retained a reference, however, to withdrawal "starting with" army forces.[58] That phrasing implies that the withdrawal is to continue with the removal of air and naval forces.

Regardless of what was said or submitted at the Shigemitsu-Dulles talks, Allison had conveyed Shigemitsu's thinking in advance and in full to Dulles. The decision as to whether to raise the question of complete withdrawal overtly was a matter of negotiating tactics. Shigemitsu made a carefully considered tactical decision in accepting Yasukawa's advice about deleting the complete withdrawal reference.

It is to be suspected that Shigemitsu's feelings about deleting the problematic reference were more complex than even Yasukawa imagined. Yasukawa attributed the "sour expression" on the foreign minister's face to the mention of his seeming "out of touch with reality." One wonders if Shigemitsu wasn't perhaps in touch with a larger reality brought home at his audience with the emperor.

3 A Step Toward Revision

Shigemitsu's "failure" and Kishi's "success"

Following a brief administration by Ishibashi Tanzan, Kishi became prime minister in February 1957 and traveled to the United States for talks with

Eisenhower and Dulles four months later. Those talks, held nearly two years after the Shigemitsu-Dulles talks, yielded a joint statement that contained the following affirmation: "The President and the Prime Minister affirmed their understanding that the Security Treaty of 1951 was designed to be transitional in character and not in that form to remain in perpetuity." Kishi had succeeded in securing US agreement, in principle, to revising the security treaty.[59]

Witnessing the Shigemitsu-Dulles talks had imparted important lessons to Kishi, who judged his rival's performance in Washington, DC, a failure. He recognized the importance of convincing the US government that a solid conservative coalition was taking shape in Japan. That coalition acquired a platform with the November 1955 establishment of the Liberal Democratic Party, and Kishi moved to position himself in the eyes of the Americans as a figure who could unify the coalition. He presented himself as a leader who could steer Japanese politics in a direction consistent with US government expectations. His courting of the Americans included cultivating dialogue with the US embassy in Tokyo, starting in autumn 1953, and he used that interchange effectively in advancing his cause.[60]

Accompanying Shigemitsu to Washington, DC, provided an opportunity that Kishi used to portray himself as a power in the Democratic Party. Shigemitsu, as we have seen, called persistently for revising the security treaty to deflect leftist criticism of the treaty's inequitableness and thereby earned Dulles's ire. In contrast, Kishi argued that the best way to counter the Communists and others on the left would be to achieve economic growth and strengthen the conservative coalition. And he appears to have made a good impression on the Americans with that argument.[61]

Kishi reiterated his differences with Shigemitsu two years later in his meeting with Eisenhower.

> The year before last, the Prime Minister continued, as Mr. Dulles will remember, Mr. Shigemitsu asked that the Security Treaty be revised into an "equal" agreement, because he believed that Japan was in a "subjugated" position under the Treaty. I do not have that feeling. There are, nevertheless, some matters which we would like to see reconsidered.[62]

As prime minister, Kishi avoided the clumsy tack of Shigemitsu's that had triggered a heated rebuttal by Dulles. Shigemitsu had suggested that "the Japanese people do not believe that they are being treated as equals under the present arrangements" and had sought assurance "that the United States did not intend to keep Japan in a semi-independent position." Dulles had fired back "that Japan had made a treaty which had been overwhelmingly approved by the Diet," "that this did not mean a semi-independent position," "that every treaty involves a partial surrender of sovereignty and that interdependence and cooperation rather than independence are the requirements," and that "for Japan to consider itself as unequal is wrong; this is not the way the United States treats Japan."[63]

Kishi was extremely circumspect in his approach to his 1957 talks with Dulles and Eisenhower. What he proposed to Dulles after emphasizing his differences with Shigemitsu warrants consideration in comparing his "success" with Shigemitsu's "failure." To wit, his 1957 proposal for revising the security treaty was far less ambitious than Shigemitsu's proposal. Kishi confined his proposed revisions to three changes: make decisions about changes in the deployment of US forces in Japan subject to prior consultation with the Japanese government, clarify the positioning of the treaty in the context of Japan's rights and responsibilities as a member of the United Nations, and specify a duration for the treaty.[64]

The Kishi proposal stopped far short of Shigemitsu's call for reshaping the security treaty as a mutual-defense pact between equals. Ambassador MacArthur had apprised Dulles of Kishi's stance in a letter of May 25, 1957. He wrote that, in their discussions, the prime minister had "never supported nor opposed the concept of a mutual defense treaty." According to MacArthur, Kishi had simply said of the notion of a mutual-defense treaty that it "is not contemplated." MacArthur's report to Dulles continued with an analysis of Kishi's reasoning.

> He is perhaps reluctant to propose it now because of Japanese domestic political considerations, and perhaps more importantly because he thinks our terms might involve Japanese troops having to be deployed elsewhere in Asia or even defending the US continent or its territories. This would *not* [italics in original] be politically possible for him.[65]

Kishi, like Shigemitsu, called for a US troop withdrawal from Japan but, unlike Shigemitsu, confined his call to ground troops. He had opined to Allison in February 1955 that the withdrawal of US ground troops was desirable but that long-term reliance on US air force protection would be necessary.[66] MacArthur wrote in his letter to Dulles of May 25, 1957, that Kishi "has indicated that his basic views on the world situation, the Communist threat in the Far East, and Japan as a major Communist target, are the same as ours" and that the prime minister "shares our concept of mobile striking forces held in readiness against aggression."[67]

That the US government intended to maintain air and naval forces in Japan over the long term was eminently clear to Kishi. He suspected Dulles would regard his proposal for revising the security treaty as a ploy to evict the US military, and he therefore went out of his way in explaining his proposal to relieve Dulles of that notion. Kishi emphasized "that he had no thought whatever of seeking to abolish the Security Treaty in its basic sense."[68]

The prime minister had learned well the lessons of what he regarded as Shigemitsu's failed talks with Dulles. Kishi approached the 1957 talks with the secretary as a figure who had put his political house in order and strengthened his personal standing there, and he avoided irritating Dulles with complaints about the alleged inequality of the treaty. That strategy made a success of Kishi's first state visit to the United States as prime minister.

Kishi's proposal for revising the treaty was immensely more acceptable to the US government than Shigemitsu's had been. The US acceptance of his proposal, however, was less than total, as we will see in the next chapter.

Twofold value

Shigemitsu the diplomat was a paragon of integrity and professionalism. He brought to his work a coolheaded objectivity and persuasive logic that contrasted with the ad hoc tendencies that characterized Japanese diplomacy. Shigemitsu endeavored to manage Japan's foreign relations in reference to concrete objectives. He was notably successful during the chaotic wartime years in shaping a new China policy and a new policy for Greater East Asia as coherent frameworks.

Meanwhile, Shigemitsu exercised an outspoken and penetrating realism in criticizing Japan's foreign policy during his ambassadorial postings in Moscow and in London. He had been especially vociferous in his criticism of Japan's participation in the Tripartite Pact with Germany and Italy. Diplomatic historian Sakai Tetsuya writes of that criticism that it was "absolutely perfect in its grasp of the facts and in its logical structure."[69]

Diplomatic competence was exactly what the Japanese people and party politicians expected of Shigemitsu. Skill in managing foreign relations was rare among Japan's postwar politicians and therefore carried a premium. Yoshida epitomized the political capital that accrued from diplomatic acumen. The need for managing international dialogue was especially pressing in Japan's relationship with the United States. Three of Japan's five prime ministers under the occupation were former diplomats. To be sure, the occupation had ended by the time Shigemitsu entered the political realm but managing the relationship with the United States remained a task of paramount importance for Japan.

The political adversaries of Yoshida were surely happy to gain an ally who possessed impressive diplomatic credentials. Shigemitsu, for his part, had a strong sense of rivalry with Yoshida and had great expectations for the work ahead as he took on the foreign affairs portfolio in the Hatoyama government. He confided to Foreign Ministry officials that he had inherited the job of "cleaning up the mess left by Yoshida."[70]

Shigemitsu's talks with Dulles in Washington, DC, took place in the 10th summer after the humiliating surrender ceremony on the USS *Missouri.* He possibly relished the opportunity to rewrite what he regarded as the unequal treaty signed by Yoshida in San Francisco.[71] He might have viewed the talks, as Allison suggested, as an opportunity to register a diplomatic coup and thereby raise his political standing.[72] Both views conflict, however, with our understanding of the upright diplomat who served the Empire of Japan with integrity and distinction.

Rather than speculating about possible motivation in settling scores or fulfilling ambition, we would be on firmer ground interpreting Shigemitsu's intentions at face value. We have every reason to conclude that Shigemitsu believed that Japanese-US cooperation in military security mustn't and needn't injure Japanese pride and that his proposal for revising the security treaty grew out of that belief.

Whatever Shigemitsu's intentions and whatever we think of his appraisal of the outcome of the talks with Dulles, that his proposal for revising the security treaty ran aground is undeniable. He was proposing a mutual-defense treaty that covered the Western Pacific, that provided for withdrawing all US military forces from Japan within 12 years, and that narrowed the operational scope of the US bases in Japan in the meantime. Such a proposal was, in retrospect, a nonstarter.

Implementing Shigemitsu's proposal would have entailed fundamental change in US military strategy for the Far East. For that reason alone, the proposal never had a chance of earning US acceptance. It was destined for failure irrespective of Japan's lack of international clout, insufficient preparation, or Shigemitsu's weak political standing and despite Shigemitsu's personal commitment and considerable diplomatic competence.

Shigemitsu displayed a curious lack of objectivity with regard to Japan's and his individual standing in the eyes of the Americans. That is possibly attributable to an idealistic preoccupation with rectifying the inequality that he perceived in the security treaty. But it unquestionably contributed to his failure to achieve a meeting of minds with Dulles.

Even in failure, Shigemitsu achieved a step toward fulfilling his goal, as Yasukawa writes:

> If we were to view the Shigemitsu-Dulles talks as a game, we would have to concede that Dulles had won a sweeping victory, and I couldn't bring myself at the time to accept what had transpired. But in reflection, the talks were a valuable step toward the revision of the security treaty that occurred later [emphasis added]. I held nothing against Foreign Minister Shigemitsu. If anything, I held the greatest respect for his commitment to advancing Japan's foreign relations.[73]

We can understand Yasukawa's reference to a "step toward the revision of the security treaty" in terms of twofold value. One, the Shigemitsu-Dulles talks yielded lessons that served Kishi well in his negotiations as prime minister with Dulles. Two, the foreign minister's calling for a US military withdrawal, even in an ostensibly personal and informal proposal, was a wake-up call. It alerted the US government to the potential danger posed by mounting discontent with the security treaty in Japan.

The very boldness of Shigemitsu's proposal cast the subsequent request from Kishi for a treaty revision in a moderate light. Shigemitsu's judgment "that we Japanese should make our case frankly at this juncture, regardless of whether our US counterparts find it acceptable," proved prescient. We need to note, however, the important differences between what Shigemitsu envisioned and what Kishi settled for. Those differences figure crucially in the process that led to the 1960 revision of the security treaty as the Treaty of Mutual Cooperation and Security between the United States and Japan.

Kishi, to be sure, staked his political life on revising the security treaty of 1952, and the revision that he achieved rectified several shortcomings in the eyes of Japan. As a result, the 1960 treaty struck the Japanese as substantially more equitable than its predecessor. Kishi's security treaty was identical to Yoshida's, however, in a decisive respect: Japan would continue to lend base sites to the United States in exchange for military protection. Shigemitsu's failed proposal is a lasting reminder of the compromises that underlay both of those treaties.

Chapter Notes

1 Kishi Nobusuke, *Kishi Nobusuke kaikoroku: Hoshu gōdō to Anpo kaitei* [Kishi Nobusuke Memoir: The Conservative Coalition and the Revision of the Security Treaty] (Tokyo: Kōsaidō Shuppan, 1983), 205.

2 The present work focuses on Shigemitsu's treaty-revision proposal to the exclusion of other subjects also discussed at the Shigemitsu-Dulles talks. It does not deal, for example, with the negotiations under way at the time for restoring Japanese-Soviet diplomatic ties. Shigemitsu was dubious about those negotiations, partly because of his disaffection with the Hatoyama confidants who were spearheading the Japanese participation but more because of his concern that they could affect the talks with Dulles adversely. Tanaka Takahiko addresses this point in Chapter 3 of his excellent commentary on Shigemitsu's perspective on the Soviet negotiations, *Nis-So kokkō kaifuku no shiteki kenkyū: Sengo Nis-So kankei no kiten, 1945–1956* [A Historical Study of the Restoration of Japanese-Soviet Relations: The Starting Point for Postwar Japanese-Soviet Ties, 1945–1956] (Tokyo: Yuhikaku, 1993).

Also worthy of consideration in connection with Shigemitsu's proposal are the ramifications of other geopolitical events; for example, the April 1955 Bandung Conference, where representatives of 29 African and Asian nations affirmed the nonaligned movement at the eponymous Indonesian venue, and the July 1955 Geneva Summit of US, Soviet, UK, and French leaders, which led to a thaw in Soviet-US relations.

3 This chapter is an expansion of the author's "Shigemitsu hōbei to Anpo kaitei kōsō no zasetsu" [Shigemitsu's US Visit and the Collapse of His Proposal for Revising the Security Treaty], *Hōkei ronsō* [Journal of Law and Economics] 10, no.

2 (December 1992). For pioneering and exhaustive research findings regarding the revision of the security treaty, see Hara Yoshihisa, *Nichi-Bei kankei no kōzu: Anpo kaitei o kenshō suru* [The Mechanics of the Japanese-US Relationship: An Examination of the Revision of the Security Treaty] (Tokyo: NHK Books, 1991).

4 Itō Takashi and Watanabe Yukio, eds., *Zoku Shigemitsu Mamoru shuki* [Shigemitsu Mamoru Diary, Sequel] (Tokyo: Chuokoronsha, 1988).

5 US Department of State, *Foreign Relations of the United States* (*FRUS*), 1955–1957 (Washington, DC: Government Printing Office, 1991), Document 92.

6 Kishi, *Kaikoroku*; Kishi, Yatsugi Kazuo, and Itō Takashi, *Kishi Nobusuke no kaisō* [Kishi Nobusuke's Reminiscences] (Tokyo: Bungeishunjū, 1981); Kōno Ichirō, *Ima dakara hanasō* [What I Can Now Say] (Tokyo: Shunyodo Shoten, 1958).

7 Memorandum of Conversation by Windsor Hackler, 22 September 1955, US Department of State, Lot 58 D 118; Shigemitsu Trip, RG 59, National Archives.

8 US Department of State, *Department of State Bulletin* (September 12, 1955), 419–420.

9 *Asahi Shimbun*, September 3, 1955, evening edition.

10 Hara, *Nichi-Bei kankei no kōzu*, 40–42.

11 US Department of State, *FRUS*, 1955–1957, Document 45. Foreign Ministry documents on Shigemitsu's visit to the United States contain the following Japanese language account of a conversation between Shigemitsu and US secretary of state John Dulles.

Shigemitsu: Japan's self-defense capabilities are already organized. We think the current mechanisms should be modified based on the fact that Japan already has a self-defense force.

Dulles: We could look into new avenues if Japan's self-defense capabilities were in place and the constitution were amended accordingly. Does the current constitution allow for a mutual-defense treaty?

Shigemitsu: Yes. Japan can protect itself.

Dulles: But could Japan also protect the United States? What if Guam were to be attacked, for instance?

Shigemitsu: In that type of situation, we would just need to consult with you.

Dulles: I was under the impression that only the broadest interpretation of the Japanese constitution gives Japan the ability to maintain defense capabilities to defend itself.

Shigemitsu: Correct. The objective must be self-defense, but we can consult with you on the use of military force.

Dulles: But isn't "consulting" about protecting the United States a moot point if the constitution doesn't allow it in the first place?

Shigemitsu: Our interpretation is that the matter is open to consultation if the objective is self-defense.

Dulles: That's news to me. I had no idea that Japan could send troops abroad upon consultation.

Shigemitsu: Is consultation a requirement for the United States?

Dulles: No.

Shigemitsu: Japan can consult with the United States about sending troops abroad provided that the objective is self-defense. Whether or not Japan approves sending the troops abroad is another matter, of course, and you may not agree with what the Japanese government decides to do, but Japan already has self-defense capabilities and is prepared to expand that capacity further. We expect our position to be given proper consideration. We want to be seen on equal standing with the United States. Under the current treaty, we are not equal with but rather dependent on you. Our hope is to be an equal partner. You say that the time is not yet ripe for a new defense treaty, but as I explained at our meeting yesterday, we have made the decision to follow through on firming up our self-defense capabilities. We are also prepared to accept the joint committee's proposal on defense issues.

Dulles: We could put something in the joint communiqué to express our shared beliefs, I suppose.

Shigemitsu: We want equality.

Source: "Gaimu daijin Kokumu chōkan kaigi memo (dainikai)" [Notes on the Second Meeting between the Foreign Minister and the Secretary of State], August 30, 1955 ("Nichi-Bei Anpo jōyaku kaisei ni kakawaru keii (8)" [Developments Concerning Revisions to the Japanese-US Security Treaty (8)], 0611-2010-0791-08, H22-003, collection of the Diplomatic Archives of the Ministry of Foreign Affairs). Accompanying the above records are notes (in English) that Shigemitsu read at the start of the day's meeting to propose replacing the existing security treaty with a "new defense treaty" with jurisdiction in the Western Pacific, the content of which is the same as the US State Department documents quoted in the main text.

12 *Mainichi Shimbun*, September 2, 1955, evening edition; *Asahi Shimbun*, September 2, 1955, evening edition.

13 Kimura Tokutarō, speaking as the Yoshida cabinet's director general of the National Safety Agency, answered a question as follows in the Diet on April 12, 1954: "We are clearly prohibited [by Article 9 of the constitution] from resorting to the threat or use of force as means of settling international disputes. Our self-defense forces have been established within the realm of Japan's right to self-defense. The self-defense forces are for protecting our nation's independence and for ensuring our security, and we are not considering dispatching troops abroad." Nakamura Akira, *Sengo seiji ni yureta kenpō 9-jō: Naikaku hōsei-kyoku no jishin to tsuyosa* [Postwar Political Threats to Article 9 of the Constitution: The Confidence and the Power of the Cabinet Legislation Bureau] (Tokyo: Chūōkeizai-sha, 1996), 145.

14 Nakamura, *Sengo seiji ni yureta kenpō 9-jō*, 9.

15 Tanaka Akihiko, *Anzen hoshō: Sengo 50-nen no mosaku* [Military Security: Fifty Postwar Years of Searching] (Tokyo: Yomiuri Shimbunsha, 1997), 141–144.

16 Nakamura, *Sengo seiji ni yureta kenpō 9-jō*, 9.

17 Kishi, Yatsugi, and Itō, *Kishi Nobusuke no kaisō*, 130.

18 The Defense Problem, 29 August 1955, US Department of State, Lot 66 D 70,

Japan, RG 59, National Archives.

19 The notes that furnished the basis for the US minutes of the talks provide clarification of this point. According to the notes, Dulles mentioned Guam as an example after first asking Shigemitsu a more general question. He asked if Japan, under the present constitution, could come to the aid of the United States in the event of an attack on US territory in the treaty geography. US Department of State, *SHV*.

20 In Diplomatic Archives of the Ministry of Foreign Affairs of Japan, accessible online at the University of the Ryukyus Repository, http://ir.lib.u-ryukyu.ac.jp/bitstream/20.500.12000/43890/1/RC001_05_01_08_01.pdf.

21 "Treaty of Mutual Cooperation and Security between Japan and the United States," US Department of State, Central Files (CF) 794.5/2-1858, RG 59, National Archives. See endnote 43 for more information.

22 One reason for Radford's harsh assessment: The six-year Japanese plan didn't address the support function performed by half of the 70,000 US army troops in Japan. US Department of State, *FRUS*, 1955–1957, Document 45.

Japan's approach to strengthening national defense under the Hatoyama government was not significantly different from that under the Yoshida government. For insight into this issue, see Uemura Hideki, *Saigunbi to 55-nen taisei* [Rearmament and the 1955 Framework] (Tokyo: Bokutakusha, 1995), 249–259.

Matsumoto Takizō, a member of the Japanese delegation at the Shigemitsu-Dulles talks, was critical of Shigemitsu's presentation. Back in Japan, he complained to his Liberal Party colleague Ashida Hitoshi that Shigemitsu had failed to distinguish between combat units and support units and that his explanation was therefore unconvincing. Matsumoto, who spoke fluent English, also made fun of Shigemitsu's speaking style, which he characterized as "pretentious." Entry for October 4, 1955, Shindō Eiichi and Shimokōbe Motoharu, eds., *Ashida Hitoshi nikki* [Ashida Hitoshi Diary], vol. 6 (Tokyo: Iwanami Shoten, 1986), 12.

23 Kōno, *Ima dakara hanasō*, 102. The *Mainichi Shimbun* quoted Kishi as saying, "At the end, Dulles read the proposal carefully, section by section, and then reflected our opinions in some handwritten changes." September 10, 1955, evening edition.

24 Yasukawa Takeshi, *Wasureenu omoide to korekara no Nichi-Bei gaikō: Pāruhābā kara hanseiki* [Indelible Memories and the Future of Japanese-US Relations: A Half Century since Pearl Harbor] (Tokyo: Sekai-no-Ugoki-sha, 1991), 50.

25 The joint statement contains the following passage: "With the conclusion of such a treaty [of greater mutuality] as an objective, it was further agreed that consultations would take place in Tokyo between Japanese and United States representatives on defense problems. . . ."

26 Ōmori Minoru, *Tokuhain 5-nen: Nichi-Bei gaikō no butaiura* [Five Years as a News Correspondent: Behind the Scenes of Japanese-US Diplomacy] (Tokyo: Mainichi Shimbunsha, 1959), 92, 96.

27 The *Asahi Shimbun* reported in its evening edition of September 7, 1955, that a State Department spokesperson had made remarks to this effect on September 3 but that another spokesperson for the department had declared on September 6

that the subject didn't warrant attention.

28 John M. Allison, *Ambassador from the Prairie; or, Allison Wonderland* (New York: Houghton Mifflin, 1973), 275.

29 Kōno, *Ima dakara hanasō*, 96–97. Ōmori writes that Shigemitsu understood from his talks with Allison that the US government was receptive to his ideas and that the rejection from Dulles therefore took him by surprise. *Tokuhain 5-nen*, 97–99.

30 Allison, *Ambassador from the Prairie*, 276.

31 For insight into the fragility of the Hatoyama government, see Hiwatari Yumi, *Sengo seiji to Nichi-Bei kankei* [Postwar Politics and Japanese-US Relations] (Tokyo: University of Tokyo Press, 1990), 121.

32 For this reason, Allison urged Shigemitsu to secure support for his proposal from the Liberal Party before traveling to Washington, DC. US Department of State, CF 794.5/8-455 (tel. 300); *FRUS*, 1955–1957, Document 38.

33 The Japanese government had pledged formally to share the cost of maintaining US forces in Japan, as mentioned in Chapter 1. That pledge was under a provision in Article 25 of an administrative agreement based on the security treaty. The Japanese and US governments agreed that Japan would initially pay ¥55.8 billion annually and that the amount would decline as Japan strengthened its defense capabilities gradually. Japan's contribution toward funding the US military presence declined about ¥2.5 billion, for example, in the fiscal year to March 1955.

Hatoyama's cabinet moved on taking office in December 1954 to cap Japan's defense expenditures at the previous year's level. It announced defense spending of ¥137.2 billion for the upcoming fiscal year, little changed from the current fiscal year. That amount included Japan's contribution toward funding the US military presence, and the Hatoyama cabinet announced that a reduction in that contribution would offset an increase in autonomous military spending. The government, in other words, had determined an overall defense budget before entering into negotiations about funding the US bases.

General elections in Japan delayed the start of formal negotiations until March 25, 1955, and the negotiations ran aground immediately. The US government balked at the Japanese proposal for reducing Japan's share of the cost of funding the US bases. On April 19, the negotiators arrived at a compromise. They agreed on a ¥17.8 billion reduction, subject to conditions, in Japan's contribution toward funding the US military presence. That compares with the reduction of about ¥20 billion that the Japanese were seeking, and it reduced Japan's contribution toward funding the bases to about ¥38 billion annually.

The negotiations that led to the compromise were tough, nerve-racking, and occasionally heated. "[The Americans] reproached the Japanese severely," Shigemitsu writes in his diary entry for April 13, 1955, "and the mood became extremely foul, the air tense. I reported that evening to [Hatoyama at his home in] Otowa that the situation was dire." *Zoku Shigemitsu Mamoru shuki*, 695.

Ichimada Hisato, the finance minister, was uncompromising in his stance toward the US demands. On the day of the entry cited in Shigemitsu's diary, he had gone so far as to offer his resignation to Hatoyama. US Department of State, *FRUS*, 1955–1957, Document 32.

Ichimada's resignation, which Hatoyama refused, would have threatened to bring down the government. "We'd hold a cabinet meeting, and we'd hear all manner of bad news. We'd won the election and formed a government, I thought, but we were on the verge of being unable to draft a budget and therefore needing to throw in the towel. That's how bad things had become." Hatoyama Ichirō, *Hatoyama Ichirō kaikoroku* [Hatoyama Ichirō Memoir] (Tokyo: Bungeishunjū Shinsha, 1957), 159.

34 US Department of State, *FRUS*, 1955–1957, Document 23.

35 Frictions caused by US bases raised new questions about the handling of the bases in the security treaty and occasioned heated debate between Japan's ruling party and opposition parties in 1955 before Shigemitsu's US trip. The frictions arose in connection with the proposed expansion of an airbase and the prospect that the US military might bring nuclear weapons into Japan. They were becoming serious political and social issues.

In the more political of the issues, plans for expanding Tachikawa Airfield, in western Tokyo, were drawing fierce opposition. Residents of the airbase's host community were staging large protests to prevent the expansion. In an issue of broader social impact, the US military deployed MGR-1 Honest John surface-to-surface rockets in Japan in August. Those rockets were capable of carrying nuclear warheads, and their deployment occasioned intense and widely monitored debate in the Diet in July and August. Hatoyama had made comments to non-Japanese journalists on March 14, 1955, that were interpreted as countenancing Japanese storage of US nuclear weapons and that also triggered debate in the Diet.

Shigemitsu fielded questions from opposition lawmakers about the nuclear issue in the Diet on June 27. He replied that Allison had assured him that the US forces then in Japan did not possess nuclear weapons and that they would never bring nuclear weapons into Japan without Japanese government approval. Allison, however, delivered a protest to Shigemitsu on July 2 in which he denied having offered such assurance. Shigemitsu defended his remarks as a means of parrying criticism from the political left and preventing damage to the Japanese-US relationship and asked that the Americans refrain from going public with their stance.

Allison delivered his protest in person and orally to avoid the risk of leaks, so no original documentation remains, but US archival materials summarize the salient content as follows. They record Allison as indicating that the US government did not interpret the Japanese-US security agreements as prohibiting the introduction of nuclear weapons into Japan. "Introduction of Atomic Weapons, 23 August 1955" (position paper), US Department of State, *SHV*; cf. CF 711.5611/6-2755 (dep. tel. 2711), 711.5611/7-155 (tel. 187), 711.5611/7-255 (tel. 751).

36 US Department of State, *FRUS*, 1955–1957, Document 45.

37 US Department of State, *FRUS*, 1955–1957, Document 49.

38 Hatoyama describes a lack of confidence in Shigemitsu in his memoir, *Hatoyama Ichirō kaikoroku*, 162–165. We don't know how thoroughly Shigemitsu briefed Hatoyama in advance on his proposal for revising the security treaty, but some

insight is available in US government archives. The archives include input from the head of the Japanese Foreign Ministry's Treaties Bureau, Shimoda Takesō, to the US embassy in Tokyo. Shimoda reported that Shigemitsu told Hatoyama on August 4, 1955, of his plan to discuss defense issues during his visit to Washington, DC, and that Hatoyama agreed to the idea. However, the two did not discuss in detail what Shigemitsu would propose, according to Shimoda, and Shigemitsu did not show Hatoyama his proposal for revising the security treaty. US Department of State, CF 794.5/8-1255 (tel. 400).

39 "Conservative Merger, 22 August 1955" (position paper), US Department of State, *SHV*. Also interesting is the memorandum of an August 10, 1955, conversation between the deputy chief cabinet secretary, Matsumoto Takizō, and J. Graham Parsons, a counselor at the US embassy in Tokyo. The memorandum records Matsumoto as providing a detailed account of the personal dynamics among the members of the Japanese delegation for the scheduled trip to Washington, DC. Memorandum of Conversation, 11 August 1955, US Department of State, Lot 58 D 118; Shigemitsu Trip, RG 59, National Archives.

40 US Department of State, *FRUS*, 1955–1957, Document 46.

41 The *Mainichi Shimbun*'s Ōmori writes that Kōno became concerned that the heated exchange between Dulles and Shigemitsu would drag on, that he therefore moved to bring the argument to an end, and that his attempted intervention earned the contempt of the American participants as a "breach of diplomatic common sense." September 6, 1955.

42 US Department of State, CF 794.5/7-2555 (tel. 201). This telegram suggests that the Foreign Ministry's Treaties Bureau participated in drafting Shigemitsu's proposal; cf. CF 794.5/8-455 (tel. 300).

However, another Allison telegram reports evidence to the contrary. It reports that Shimoda, the head of the bureau, questioned the wisdom of presenting the proposal to the US government. CF 794.5/8-1255 (tel. 400).

43 Ministry of Foreign Affairs records indicate that Article 4 of Shigemitsu's treaty proposal contained the following stipulations on "invoking mutual defense."

> Each Contracting Party recognizes that an armed attack in the West Pacific Area directed against the territories, or the areas under the administrative jurisdiction, of the other Contracting Party would be dangerous to its own peace and safety and declares that it would act to meet the common danger in accordance with its constitutional processes.

Article 5 of the draft stipulates the withdrawal of US armed forces.

1. Armed forces of the United States of America disposed in Japan pursuant to the Security Treaty between Japan and the United States of America of September 8, 1951, shall commence their withdrawal from Japan upon the coming into force of this Treaty.
2. All land forces of the Army and Navy of the United States of America shall complete their withdrawal from Japan not later than ninety days after the close of the Japanese fiscal year when the long-term defense program of

Japan shall have been fulfilled.

The date by which air forces, and sea forces of the Navy, of the United States of America shall have completed their withdrawal from Japan shall be determined subsequently through consultation between the Governments of both Contracting Parties. (Provided, however, that such date shall be not later in any even than six years after withdrawal of the land forces shall have been completed pursuant to the preceding sub-paragraph.)

Source: "Nihonkoku to Amerika Gasshūkoku to no aida no sōgo bōeki jōyaku (shian)" [Treaty of Mutual Defense between Japan and the United States of America (Draft)], July 27, 1955 ("Nichi-Bei Anpo jōyaku kaisei ni kakawaru keii (8)" [Developments concerning revisions to the Japanese-US security treaty (8)], 0611-2010-0791-08, H22-003, collection of the Diplomatic Archives of the Ministry of Foreign Affairs).

44 US Department of State, Lot 66 D 70, Japan, RG 59, National Archives.

45 The six-year time span is implicitly in sync with the six-year defense plan.

46 US Department of State, *FRUS*, 1955–1957, Document 37; Memorandum of Sebald to the Secretary of State, CF 794.5/8-2355.

47 "US Defense Policy in Japan," US Department of State, Lot 58 D 637, International Security, RG 59, National Archives.

48 Richard Finn, a State Department Japanese affairs staffer, described the Japanese position at a meeting held in advance of Shigemitsu's visit. US Department of State, *FRUS*, 1955–1957, Document 42.

In that context, the reference in the joint statement to "conditions such that Japan could . . . contribute to the preservation of international peace and security in the Western Pacific" takes on a striking weightiness. The open-ended phrasing can be interpreted as addressing broad US interests, including the Philippines, the Republic of Korea, and Taiwan, as well as the narrower focus of Shigemitsu's proposal on Japanese and US territory in the Western Pacific and territory under US administration there.

According to Foreign Ministry records, the complete withdrawal of the US military that Shigemitsu's proposal called for also appeared to imply changing the nature of the US presence in Japan from "constant" to "emergency" stationing. The Foreign Ministry addressed that issue in a prepared response to an anticipated question.

Question: After the US forces withdraw, will they be unable to use bases in Japan in any form whatsoever?

Answer: If US forces come to the assistance of Japan in an emergency in the name of mutual defense, they will, of course, need to have access to bases in our territory. We believe, however, that working out practical arrangements through bilateral discussion for the US forces to use Japanese bases in the event of a military emergency is preferable to establishing guidelines that provide for the continuing right to use bases, even in peacetime.

Source: "Nichi-Bei sōgo bōei ni kansuru gimon gitō" [Responses to Possible

Questions Concerning the Japanese-US Mutual-Defense Treaty], August 23, 1955 ("Nichi-Bei Anpo jōyaku kaisei ni kakawaru keii (8)" [Developments Concerning Revisions to the Japanese-US Security Treaty (8)], 0611-2010-0791-08, H22-003, collection of the Diplomatic Archives of the Ministry of Foreign Affairs).

It remains unclear how Shigemitsu saw connections between the complete withdrawal of US military forces from the Japanese mainland and the return of the administrative rights over Okinawa to Japan.

49 US Department of State, CF 794.5/7-2555 (tel. 201).
50 US Department of State, *FRUS*, 1955–1957, Document 37.
51 US Department of State, *FRUS*, 1955–1957, Document 22.
52 US Department of State, *FRUS*, 1955–1957, Document 26.
53 US Department of State, *FRUS*, 1955–1957, Document 38.
54 Memorandum of Sebald to the Secretary of State, US Department of State, CF 794.5/8-2355.
55 Shigemitsu, *Zoku Shigemitsu Mamoru shuki*, 732. Iwami Takao writes in *Heika no goshitsumon: Shōwa Tennō to sengo seiji* [Imperial Questions: The Shōwa Emperor and Postwar Politics] (Tokyo: Mainichi Shimbunsha, 1992), 21–23, that this episode was the subject of a brief round of questioning in the Diet on May 26, 1988, right after the publication of the Shigemitsu book.
56 Yasukawa, *Wasureenu omoide*, 45.
57 Yasukawa, *Wasureenu omoide*, 46.
58 The Defense Problem, 29 August 1955, US Department of State, Lot 66 D 70, Japan, RG 59, National Archives.
59 US Department of State, *Department of State Bulletin* (July 8, 1957), 51.
60 Allison, *Ambàssador from the Prairie*, 270–273. The former US ambassador writes that Kishi proved a reliable source of insight into the development of the conservative coalition. For additional information about Kishi's interchange with the US embassy, see US Department of State, CF 794.00/12-754 (desp. 675).
61 US Department of State, *FRUS*, 1955–1957, Document 45.
62 US Department of State, *FRUS*, 1955–1957, Document 183.
63 US Department of State, *FRUS*, 1955–1957, Document 45.
64 US Department of State, *FRUS*, 1955–1957, Document 187.
65 US Department of State, *FRUS*, 1955–1957, Document 159.
66 US Department of State, CF, 794.00/2-2455 (desp. 1003).
67 US Department of State, *FRUS*, 1955–1957, Document 159.
68 US Department of State, *FRUS*, 1955–1957, Document 187.
69 Sakai Tetsuya, "Gaikōkan no shōzō: Shigemitsu Mamoru" [Portrait of a Diplomat: Shigemitsu Mamoru], pt. 2, *Gaikō Forum* 11 (August 1989): 79. The author of the present work has relied extensively on Sakai's text for insight into Shigemitsu's prewar and wartime activity.
70 Yasukawa, *Wasureenu omoide*, 43.
71 Ōmori, *Tokuhain 5-nen*, 120–121.
72 US Department of State, CF 794.5/7-2555 (tel. 201).
73 Yasukawa, *Wasureenu omoide*, 51

Chapter 4

The Irony of the Treaty Revision

Kishi Nobusuke and the Treaty of Mutual Cooperation and Security

Prime Minister Kishi Nobusuke (*center left*), signing the Treaty of Mutual Cooperation and Security; President Dwight D. Eisenhower (*center right*); and flanking Kishi and Eisenhower, Foreign Minister Fujiyama Aiichirō (*left*) and Secretary of State Christian Herter (*right*), in Washington, DC. January 19, 1960. Photo from Jiji Press

Ishibashi Tanzan succeeded Hatoyama Ichirō as prime minister on December 23, 1956, but illness forced him from office barely two months later, on February 25, 1957. Succeeding Ishibashi as prime minister was Kishi Nobusuke. Kishi served as the minister of commerce and industry in the Tōjō government during the war, and the occupation authorities took him into custody as a suspected perpetrator of Class A war crimes. They held him in Sugamo Prison for more than three years but released him in December 1948 without bringing formal charges.

Kishi had honed his political skills as an elite member of Japan's government bureaucracy and had gone on to become a highly effective elected politician. He returned to politics after the occupation authorities released him from prison and from the ban on public service and won election to the lower house of the Diet in April 1953. Kishi joined Miki Bukichi in forming a conservative coalition opposed to Yoshida. He served as the secretary general of the Liberal Party and became in November 1955 the inaugural secretary general of the Liberal Democratic Party (LDP). Kishi was instrumental in tending the relations between the LDP and an array of pressure groups and thereby solidifying Japan's conservative dynamics.

As prime minister, Kishi sought to steer Japan's domestic politics out of the occupation mode and to reinstate mechanisms and attitudes appropriate to an independent nation. He strove vigorously in his foreign policy to reassert a respected position for Japan in the international community. Achieving the long-sought revision of the security treaty by concluding the Treaty of Mutual Cooperation and Security in 1960 was a tremendous achievement. Kishi's crowning achievement encompassed, however, a striking paradox.

The revised treaty, to be sure, exhibited a greater mutuality than its predecessor and at least implied a pairing of equals as a treaty between two sovereign nations. It stipulated that the United States was responsible for protecting Japan militarily and that Japan was responsible for hosting US military bases.

Proponents of the revised treaty could argue that it redressed the principal failings cited by critics of its predecessor: that the treaty was something that the United States had imposed on Japan unilaterally and that it was nothing more than a base-hosting agreement. The revised treaty, its proponents could argue, placed Japan on an equal footing with the United

States. Yet the revised treaty was identical to its predecessor in that it did not oblige Japan to defend US territory. (We could say, rather, that it implicitly acknowledged Japan's inability to provide such assistance.)

The new treaty remained inadequate with regard to establishing a framework for interaction as equals between two independent nations. That the drafters of the treaty would acknowledge the vast differential in military capabilities between Japan and the United States is readily understandable, but we wonder why they would decline to provide that the signatories each be prepared to help defend the other.

More troubling than the 1960 treaty's inadequacy with regard to mutual-defense provisions was the built-in obstruction to redressing that inadequacy. In heightening superficial mutuality and in resolving minor sources of friction, the drafters obstructed potential revisions that might have achieved structural gains in mutuality.

This chapter examines the process that led to Kishi's decision in summer 1958 to endeavor to revise the security treaty and analyzes the paradoxical outcome of the revision. We will question why Kishi sought a treaty revision before Japan could hold its own in a truly mutual pact; that is, why he acted before Japan had revised its constitution and strengthened its military enough to play a meaningful role in mutual defense.

We will discover that the answer is surprisingly simple and that the key to the paradoxical outcome resides in that simple answer. Kishi's decision, we will find, exerted a decisive influence on Japanese-US relations and on the political process in Japan. The circumstances of that decision are therefore well worth consideration.[1]

1 Kishi's 1957 US State Visit and the Two-Stage Treaty Revision

A crucial juncture

Witnessing the Shigemitsu-Dulles talks in August 1955 imparted important lessons to Kishi, as we saw in the previous chapter. Dulles's argument was sound, Kishi later acknowledged, but "I came away with the strong feeling that the US-Japanese security treaty needed to be an agreement between equals."[2] Kishi was alert to the public sentiment in Japan in favor of revising the treaty. He also retained vivid memories, however, of how Dulles had shot down Shigemitsu's proposal. The Shigemitsu-Dulles talks had sensitized him to the need for revising the security treaty but had also impressed on him the need for proceeding carefully and for making careful preparations. "We couldn't blithely raise the issue of revising the treaty," he wrote in his memoir, "without ascertaining the Americans' intentions."[3]

Kishi declared a "new era" in Japanese-US relations as he undertook a state visit to the United States in June 1957. His visit would center on three days of talks in Washington, DC, with Eisenhower, Dulles, and other US officials from the 19th to the 21st. The prime minister would use those talks as an opportunity to call for revising the security treaty. He would carefully contrast his stance, as described in the previous chapter, with Shigemitsu's.

> Mr. Shigemitsu asked that the Security Treaty be revised into an "equal" agreement, because he believed that Japan was in a "subjugated" position under the Treaty. I do not have that feeling. There are, nevertheless, some matters which we would like to see reconsidered.[4]

And he would confine his proposed revisions, as also described in the previous chapter, to three: clarify the positioning of the treaty in the context of Japan's rights and responsibilities as a member of the United Nations, require prior consultation with the Japanese government with regard to changes in the deployment of US forces in Japan, and provide for the termination of the treaty.[5]

Observing the Shigemitsu-Dulles talks had revealed to Kishi the folly of demanding a mutual-defense pact. Any such proposal from Japan would elicit a US demand that Japan be prepared to dispatch troops abroad, and that was politically impossible in Japan at the time. Kishi appears to have decided on two alternative stratagems to evince equal standing in the treaty relationship sans mutual-defense provisions. One was to accompany the treaty with a supplementary agreement to suggest mutuality, starting with modifications in how the treaty operated, while leaving the treaty framework structurally unchanged.[6] The other was to provide for possible future revisions that would place the signatories on a truly equal standing.

Positioning the treaty in the context of Japan's UN rights and responsibilities and requiring advance consultation with regard to the deployment of US forces were Kishi's ideas for modifying how the treaty operated. Since returning to politics, he, like Hatoyama and Shigemitsu, had espoused the aim of undoing Yoshida's occupation governance and establishing a governance framework indicative of Japan being an independent nation. For Kishi, that meant exercising "our constitution, based on the free will of the people," in shaping an "autonomous economy based on [rational] planning," in dispensing with "the stance of defenseless neutrality" and the policy of the "hosting of foreign military forces," and in asserting "a capacity for self-defense."[7]

Kishi appears to have regarded autonomous self-defense and the complete withdrawal of US forces as desirable. He was a realist, however, who understood that achieving those goals in the short term was not feasible. Kishi recognized that Cold War considerations mandated the continuation of a US military presence in Japan. He acknowledged that presence as essential for the time being in the context of the Japanese-US security agreement and in the context of US naval and air strategy for the Far East.

The prime minister would ask the US government to reduce the US military presence in Japan as much as possible, but he would confine his call for total withdrawal to ground forces.[8] That approach proved successful, as far as it went. Eisenhower and Kishi's communiqué of June 21, 1957, included the US pledge to "reduce the numbers of United States forces in Japan within the next year, including a prompt withdrawal of all United States ground combat forces." That pledge was part of the US military's ongoing reappraisal of optimal force deployment in support of its Far Eastern strategy.

As mentioned in the previous chapter, US ambassador Douglas MacArthur II reported to Dulles in a telegram of May 25, 1957, that Kishi "has indicated that his basic views on the world situation, the Communist threat in the Far East, and Japan as a major Communist target, are the same as ours" and that he "shares our concept of mobile striking forces held in readiness against aggression." The ambassador added in the same telegram that Kishi "has in the last week [May 20] had the National Defense Council approve a defense policy for Japan which frankly and publicly states its purpose 'to cope with aggression with recourse to the joint security system with the United States of America.'" MacArthur opined that "I think we can do business with him but we won't really know until we sit down with him and *really explore* [italics in original] the various possibilities and ways to make the necessary readjustments in the relations between the two countries."[9]

Kishi recognized that the US military presence in Japan was bound to persist as long as the Cold War continued. He and his advisors in the Foreign Ministry naturally reasoned that Japan ought to secure the best-possible terms for accommodating US forces and hosting US bases.[10] Negotiating an even somewhat more equitable treaty, they realized, would help defuse domestic criticism of the US military presence. Calling for positioning the treaty in the context of Japan's UN rights and responsibilities was part of the effort to preempt criticism. That positioning would reinforce awareness that the purpose of the US military presence was to protect Japan. It would defuse fears that arbitrary action in the Far East by Japan-based US forces could draw Japan into a conflict.[11]

Linkage with the UN regime was a Foreign Ministry goal of long standing, as described in Chapter 1. We can well understand that Japan's accession to UN membership in December 1956 would kindle heightened interest in asserting that linkage. The US government agreed to the Japanese demand that the revised security treaty function in conformance with the UN charter, and the two governments concluded an agreement to that effect on September 14, 1957, after Kishi's state visit to Washington, DC.[12]

Prior consultation was another measure for deflecting criticism of the US military presence in Japan. Japanese critics of that presence argued that the US military could use the bases however it pleased. Requiring prior consultation for substantive changes in force deployment established a visible control mechanism. That included prior consultation with regard to bringing nuclear weapons into Japan. The *Daigo Fukuryu-maru* incident of March 1954 (see Chapter 2) had heightened Japanese sensitivity to nuclear weapons (triggering latent anger about the atomic bombing of Hiroshima and Nagasaki), and they became a serious irritant in the Japanese-US security relationship.[13]

Japanese newspapers reported in early 1957 that the US military was considering the deployment of nuclear weapons personnel in Japan. That became the subject of heated debate in the Diet, where Kishi faced questioning from opposition lawmakers. He repeated the response by then foreign minister Shigemitsu Mamoru to similar questioning in the Diet on June 27, 1955: that then US ambassador John Allison had pledged that the US forces then in Japan did not possess nuclear weapons and that they would never bring nuclear weapons into Japan without Japanese government approval.[14] That was an outright falsification, however, and had drawn a protest as such from Allison, as described in the previous chapter (see Chapter 3, endnote 35).

Clearly, the Japanese government needed to make a more convincing case to the populace that Japan would remain nuclear free. The US military, however, was disinclined to offer unconditional assurance that it would not bring nuclear weapons into Japanese territory. Kishi needed to swallow a conditional, face-saving US pledge that provided no real guarantee of refraining from introducing nuclear weapons.[15] He did win, however, a significant concession with regard to managing the deployment of US forces in Japan. The communiqué issued after his June 1957 talks with Eisenhower and Dulles mentioned a committee that would take shape as the Japanese-American Committee on Security:

> It was agreed to establish an intergovernmental committee to study problems arising in relation to the Security Treaty including consultation, whenever practicable, regarding the disposition and employment in Japan by the United States of its forces.[16]

Kishi's third request, to provide for the termination of the treaty, took a curious course. Initially, Kishi sought to allow either party to terminate the treaty after it had been in force for five years. Either party could give notice of the termination after five years, and the treaty would expire one year after the notification. Kishi apparently intended this request to express the Japanese intention to revise the treaty in the future. That is clear from MacArthur's comments in a 1966 interview.

According to MacArthur, Kishi envisioned a two-stage process for revising the treaty. The first stage would consist of expunging obligations regarded by the Japanese as inequitable, and the second stage would consist of Japan undertaking additional obligations to fulfill its side of an equitable relationship.[17] Kishi apparently expected Japan to acquire sufficient self-defense capabilities within five years to carry its weight in a mutual-defense arrangement. Conversely, he apparently viewed the first five years as a period for assembling domestic support for the necessary military buildup. Kishi planned to use that period, we assume, to make operational improvements in the treaty aimed at pacifying domestic criticism. He told MacArthur that revising Japan's constitution was necessary to enable Japan to fulfill its part of a mutual-defense arrangement, that winning elections was necessary to garner sufficient legislative support for revising the constitution, and that his proposed changes to the treaty were necessary to marshal public opinion to that cause.[18]

Dulles explained to Kishi in Washington, DC, that he

> did not think, however, that . . . the Treaty could be altered to provide an expiration date. This would require submission to the United States Senate of an amendment to the Treaty, which would require a two-thirds vote of the Senate for passage. The Secretary thought that this would be difficult to obtain because we would be unable to explain in a way satisfactory to the Senate what the relationship would be between the United States and Japan in the event that the Treaty ceased to exist.

As an alternative to incorporating a termination provision in the treaty, Dulles suggested addressing the issue in the communiqué. The two parties could declare as "the view of the United States Government that the Treaty was never designed to operate in perpetuity" and the "hope that coming circumstances or other arrangements will permit its termination."[19] Indeed, the communiqué declared, "The President and the Prime Minister affirmed their understanding that the Security Treaty of 1951 was designed to be transitional in character and not in that form to remain in perpetuity."[20]

The significance of Kishi's 1957 US visit

Kishi observes in his memoir and elsewhere that his 1957 US visit was an important step toward revising the security treaty and that it differed fundamentally from Shigemitsu's 1955 visit. In retrospect, we can agree that Kishi's talks with Eisenhower and Dulles were an important step in the treaty-revision process. We need to exercise restraint, however, in comparing the results of Kishi's June 1957 visit and Shigemitsu's 1955 visit.

One consideration in comparing the two visits is Kishi's decision to refrain from proposing such sweeping changes as Shigemitsu had. Kishi, as we have seen, sought no structural changes in the treaty except the addition of an expiration provision. Unlike Shigemitsu, he did not propose a mutual-defense pact.

Another consideration in comparing the two visits is that neither visit produced immediate results of substance. The joint statement issued after the Eisenhower-Kishi discussions "affirmed [the president and prime minister's shared] understanding that the Security Treaty of 1951 was designed to be transitional in character and not in that form to remain in perpetuity." We note that the 1951 treaty characterized the treaty in its preamble as "a provisional arrangement for [Japan's] defense." The treaty's positioning as "transitional in character and not in that form to remain in perpetuity" was therefore already enshrined in the treaty's text and hardly required reaffirmation. Reaffirming that positioning in 1957 was an exercise more political than diplomatic in its intent and in its effect.

We recall that the joint statement issued after the Shigemitsu-Dulles talks expressed a mutual commitment to establishing "conditions such that Japan could . . . be able to contribute to the preservation of international peace and security in the Western Pacific" and the agreement "that when such conditions are brought about it would be appropriate to replace the present Security Treaty with one of greater mutuality." Judging solely from the communiqués, we can hardly conclude that Kishi's 1957 visit was more productive than Shigemitsu's 1955 visit. We also need to recognize, however, that the US government perceived Kishi to be a more capable leader than Shigemitsu. It was therefore more responsive to Kishi's entreaties with regard to possible treaty revisions than it had been to Shigemitsu's.[21]

Kishi had hammered together a conservative coalition. He had brought a stability to the conservative side of Japanese politics that the US government had desired since the tumultuous closing days of the Yoshida government. Dulles advised Eisenhower before the talks with Kishi that "Mr. Kishi gives every indication of being the strongest Government leader to emerge in postwar Japan" and "that the time has come to take the initiative in proposing a readjustment of our relations with Japan and to suggest to Mr. Kishi that we work toward a mutual security arrangement which could, we would hope, replace the present Security Treaty."[22]

However highly US government leaders might have regarded Kishi, his 1957 state visit did not kick-start the treaty-revision process. The prime minister brought to Washington, DC, a proposal for rethinking, not revising, the treaty. Kishi writes in his memoir that the Japanese-American Committee on Security, established after his 1957 visit, took up the matter of treaty revision, but Tōgō Fumihiko disputes that recollection. Tōgō took part in negotiating the revision of the treaty as the director of the Japan-US Security Treaty Division in the Foreign Ministry's North American Affairs Bureau. He later served as the vice minister in the ministry and, from 1976 to 1980, as Japan's US ambassador. In his memoir, Tōgō notes that the Japanese-American Committee on Security dealt solely with such matters as military conditions in the Far East, issues associated with the withdrawal of US army troops from Japan, and administrative and nonmilitary personnel issues in connection with the US bases in Japan. He asserts that it did not take up the issue of revising the security treaty.[23]

Dulles felt "that the time [had] come to take the initiative in proposing a readjustment of [US] relations with Japan," but he judged "that this is not the time to renegotiate any of the specific provisions of the present Treaty." He believed that such renegotiation would require the "most careful study and preparation if it is not to precipitate strong Japanese public and Socialist Party demands for such sweeping revisions in the Treaty that our entire security relationship with Japan could be placed in jeopardy."[24]

Kishi overhauled his cabinet on July 10, 1957, less than a month after returning from the United States. That included appointing Fujiyama Aiichirō as foreign minister. Fujiyama was not a Diet member, but the Japanese constitution allows nonmembers of the Diet to serve as government ministers. The newly named foreign minister, a wealthy businessman, was an old friend of Kishi's and a leading donor to the prime minister's political war chest. Kishi clearly intended to play a hands-on role in foreign policy, and that intention presumably figured in the appointment of Fujiyama as foreign minister.[25]

The Kishi government waited until 1958 to begin moving toward revising the security treaty. Nearly a year after Kishi's US state visit, the prime minister and his government began lobbying MacArthur for a treaty revision.[26] Fujiyama held talks with Dulles in Washington, DC, on September 11, 1958, and the US government informed Kishi through MacArthur on October 4 that it was amenable to "replacing present treaty with mutual treaty."[27] That breakthrough occurred not because Japan had fulfilled the conditions for pulling its weight in a mutual-defense pact but because the US government had lowered the bar.[28]

US government leaders had reached the conclusion that revising the security treaty was essential to maintaining and strengthening the alliance with Japan, and they had determined that swift action was in order. Japanese readiness to dispatch troops abroad had been a condition for concluding a mutual-defense arrangement, and Japanese reticence in that regard had precluded progress toward achieving such an arrangement. The US government saw fit, however, to drop that condition. And it appears to have acted unilaterally, Kishi's treaty-revision overtures aside, in doing so.

2 Change in the US Stance and the Role of MacArthur's Recommendations

The urgency of acting while Kishi remained in office

US policy makers' biggest Japan-related concern after the peace treaty signing was that the nation might leave the US orbit and assume a nonaligned stance.[29] No moves in that direction ever gained serious momentum in Japanese policy, but the US diplomatic establishment remained sensitive to the perceived threat. They feared that any Japanese tilt toward nonalignment would spread, domino-like, through the region and that it would undermine the welcome for US bases in Japan. The United States' bases in Japan were bulwarks of the US military presence in the Far East. And the members of the US diplomatic establishment therefore cringed at each incident that caused friction with the Japanese populace and stimulated anti-US sentiment.

Concern among US policy makers had attained a fever pitch in early 1957, driven by fears that Japanese-US ties were fraying and that the bilateral relationship was entering an adjustment phase.[30] Engendering that concern was what they perceived as Japan's weakening dependence on the United States. The Japanese economy was waxing, the nation had restored diplomatic ties with the Soviet Union in October 1956, and it had acceded to full membership in the United Nations in December. Against this backdrop occurred an incident that was precisely the sort of irritant for Japanese-US relations that US diplomats deplored.

The incident occurred on January 30, 1957, on a firing range at Camp Weir, a US army base in Gunma Prefecture. Japanese residents in the base vicinity would gather shell casings during breaks in the shooting to sell as brass scrap. Among the scavengers on the fateful day was Sakai Naka, a forty-six-year-old mother of six. Specialist 3rd Class William Girard fired an empty cartridge from a grenade launcher fitted to his M1 rifle in the direction of Sakai. Whether he was aiming directly at the woman is unclear, but the cartridge struck her in the back, ripped her aorta, and killed her instantly.[31]

What became known as the Girard Incident triggered a dispute over whether the serviceman should be tried in a Japanese or US court. Ultimately, the US army waived jurisdiction, and a Japanese court tried Girard, convicted him of manslaughter, and handed down a suspended sentence. The Girard Incident and similar incidents fueled public dissatisfaction in Japan with the base-hosting arrangements. Calls for revising the security treaty became increasingly strident and figured in Kishi's decision to propose changes in the treaty.

Japanese-US relations warmed somewhat with the announced withdrawal of US ground forces after Kishi's June meeting with Eisenhower.[32] Concern about the bilateral relation continued to weigh on US policy makers, however, and Japan received prominent mention in a survey of world affairs that Dulles sketched in a memorandum of January 19, 1958. The secretary cautioned that the US stance on Japan and Okinawa was becoming untenable.

> If we try merely to sit on our treaty rights, we shall end by being blown out by popular sentiment, spearheaded by a Japanese government of hostile and neutralist, if not pro-communist, sentiments.[33]

He called for readjusting the US stance while the capable and US-friendly Kishi was prime minister.

Dulles wrote this memorandum with a sense of urgency about addressing diplomatic priorities in a post-Sputnik world. The Soviet Union had orbited Sputnik, the world's first artificial Earth satellite, on October 4, 1957, and that had been hugely inspirational for people there and throughout the socialist world. Nikita Khrushchev, the Soviet premier, called on November 6 for an East-West summit. Mao Zedong evoked the Eastern bloc's mounting confidence in a widely quoted speech at the Moscow Meeting of Communist and Workers' Parties on November 18. Alluding to a Chinese proverb, Mao famously asserted in that speech "that the east wind is prevailing over the west wind."

The US government hastened to alleviate the domestic shock at the Soviet assertion of technological might and to parry the Sputnik-fueled surge in the Soviets' international standing. That included moving to strengthen the solidarity among the members of the Western camp, including Japan. Eisenhower appeared at a North Atlantic Treaty Organization (NATO) summit in Paris in December 1957 and secured an agreement in principle for deploying intermediate-range ballistic missiles in Europe. Dulles, meanwhile, ordered every bureau in the State Department to develop measures to counteract the psychological fallout from Sputnik.[34]

Mounting anti-US sentiment in Okinawa

Developments in Okinawa presented Dulles with worries over Japan more compelling than the Girard Incident or the negative public relations of the Sputnik fallout. Residents all across Okinawa had staged protests, beginning in June 1956, to express opposition to the US bases there and anti-US sentiment in general.[35] Triggering the protests was the June 20 release of a report by a special subcommittee of the Armed Services Committee in the US House of Representatives.

Securing the rights to land for the US bases and related facilities in Okinawa had become an issue, and the house had dispatched a special subcommittee to Okinawa in October 1955 to study how best to proceed. Headed by Charles Price (D-IL), the committee's "Price Report" made two recommendations that agitated the Okinawans greatly. One, it called for acquiring permanent title to the real estate in question with a lump-sum payment. And two it called for acquiring additional property as necessary, though it accompanied this recommendation with the caveat that the

United States should restrain additional land acquisition "to an absolute minimum."[36]

Frictions in Okinawa fermented through 1957 and into 1958. They propelled Kaneshi Saichi to victory in the mayoral election in Naha, the Okinawan capital, on January 12, 1958. That was exactly a week before Dulles wrote the memorandum cited above.

Kaneshi ran as the candidate of a leftist coalition organized under the banner of the Liaison Conference for the Defense of Democracy. He was the political heir of Senaga Kamejirō, a candidate of the leftist Okinawa Jinmintō [Okinawa People's Party] who had been elected mayor in December 1956. The US Civil Administration of the Ryukyu Islands had engineered the removal of Senaga by the city council in November 1957 and thereby necessitated the January 1958 election. Voters perceived Kaneshi as more anti-American than his opponent in the election, and his victory occasioned considerable consternation for Okinawa's American overseers.

The day before Dulles wrote his memorandum, C. L. Sulzberger posted a pithy editorial about Okinawa in the *New York Times*. That paper was a prominent voice for internationalism in American discourse, and Sulzberger, a scion of the family that owned the *Times*, was its lead foreign correspondent. Entitled "An American 'Cyprus' in the Pacific?" the editorial noted the parallel between the United Kingdom's difficulty in administering Cyprus, then a crown colony, and the United States' difficulty in administering Okinawa.

Sulzberger pointed out the contradiction between the US recognition under the 1951 peace treaty of Japanese "residual sovereignty" over Okinawa and the stipulation under the same treaty "that we can administer the islands as a military strong point for as long as we deem necessary." He attributes the strained distinction to "philosophical opposition to the ideal of maintaining our own colonial empire." And he observes cynically that the Japanese are unlikely "to recognize the difference between such de facto administration and de jure renunciation of ownership rights."

Retaining control of Okinawa, argued Sulzberger, "poisons our relationship with the Japanese." He concludes that the United States has "only one course" to avoid the sort of impasse that the United Kingdom encountered in Cyprus: "negotiate new security arrangements with Tokyo, complementing those which already exist to insure sufficient retaliatory bases in Japan," and "relinquish political control over [Okinawa] and [the Bonin (Ogasawara) islands]."[37]

Dulles took the Okinawan surge in anti-US sentiment, epitomized by the outcome of the Naha mayoral election, seriously. He and his State Department team had gone to work on a proposal for reshaping the US-Japanese relationship and returning Okinawa to Japanese administration became a central plank in that proposal. US bases occupied numerous sites across Okinawa. Dulles and his team proposed grouping them at sites fewer in number and less obtrusive in geography. The United States would secure the property rights under the base sites in perpetuity or near perpetuity, and it would return the rest of Okinawa to Japanese administration.

Eisenhower expressed support for the proposal from the Dulles State Department. Like Dulles, the president was alert to the fiascos unfolding for the United Kingdom in Cyprus and for France in Algeria. He believed that the United States should avoid problems in Okinawa by making generous and well-considered concessions sooner rather than later.[38]

The proposal proved not feasible, however, in the short term. On careful consideration, the US bases in Okinawa were too disparate to group at just a couple of sites. Another problem was that the proposal did not specify sites for accommodating the possible deployment of intermediate-range nuclear missiles.[39]

The Japanese and US governments ultimately began negotiating the revision of the security treaty in October 1958. Whether the negotiations could have gotten under way then if the Dulles State Department's proposal had taken hold is questionable. Contrasting dynamics are evident in a telegram of June 23, 1958, from the State Department to Ambassador MacArthur.

> [At the] time you were recommending consideration [of] revision [of the] Security Treaty with Japan we were exploring within Department possibility discussing with Prime Minister reversion of administrative rights in Ryukyus with bases being reserved as military enclaves over which US would retain complete jurisdiction.
>
> Both these considerations were directed at a determination of what action US might be advised take to encourage Japanese move toward more satisfactory mutual security relationship with US.[40]

Returning Okinawa, albeit partly, to Japanese administration while agreeing to revise the security treaty would have been, in the eyes of the US government, conceding too much. On top of this, the existence of nuclear weapons in Okinawa clouded the picture. The ability to retain them and/or maintain the free use of bases in Okinawa would have complicated the treaty revision negotiations further if Okinawa had already reverted partly to Japanese administration.[41]

A proposal from Ambassador MacArthur

The prospects faded for a partial return of Okinawa to Japanese administration and revising the security treaty became the focus of discussions in the US government about reshaping the US-Japanese relationship.[42] A chief proponent of treaty revision was Ambassador MacArthur, as alluded to in the Dulles telegram quoted above. He sent Dulles a proposal for a revised treaty that he had prepared with his Tokyo embassy staff on February 18, 1958. That proposal bore the same name as but differed in important respects from the treaty that Japan and the United States concluded in 1960.

An exchange of telegrams about revising the security treaty ensued between MacArthur and the State Department. The ambassador expanded on his thinking in an April 18, 1958, message to Walter J. Robertson, then the assistant secretary of state for Far Eastern affairs. MacArthur observed that, although Japan was "now in practice aligned with the United States, it is not yet a dependable alignment *because of the feeling of many Japanese that the alignment was forced on them by us in a one-sided manner for our own purposes rather than for mutual benefit* [italics in original]." He suggested that "a fundamental objective of treaty revision would be to define this alignment in a form which will not have attached to it the stigmas and disadvantages now associated in Japan with the present Security Treaty in order to give the alignment durability and dependability."[43]

Ambassador MacArthur had provided context for the treaty revision in a May 25, 1957, message to Dulles and Robertson. He wrote that message in connection with Kishi's upcoming state visit to Washington, DC, and underlined Japan's importance to the United States in reference to Germany's.

> In terms of our vital interests, Japan occupies in Asia a position similar to that of Germany in Western Europe. Just as the course that Germany fol-

> lows in Western Europe will vitally affect where Western Europe goes, so the course that Japan chooses to follow will vitally influence the road that the free nations of the Far East and Asia follow. Japan has the only great industrial complex in Asia which in a sense is comparable to the Ruhr-Western Europe complex. If it were ever harnessed to Communist power, we would be in a desperate situation. It is every bit as important to us as Germany.[44]

The ambassador acknowledged that bringing Japan into alignment with US interests would entail challenges not experienced with Germany.

> In Japan we do not have the same favorable factors we had in Germany. Geography is against it. There are no common ties of religion, culture, philosophy or civilization with the United States, nor with some of Japan's free Asian neighbors. . . . Therefore, as contrasted with Germany where we could use the NATO umbrella and European collective devices in the economic and security fields to tie Germany with the free world, we do not have those possibilities here. . . . Japan has had neither the leavening influence of close association with dependable free world neighbors which Germany has had nor Germany's first hand exposure to Soviet brutality. The Japanese people have in fact been living largely in semi-isolation since 1941 and most are quite unaware of the nature of the world in which we live.[45]

MacArthur cited the value of the United States' Japan ties from a military perspective in his April 18, 1958, message to Robertson.

> Japan is of major importance to the proper deployment and logistical support of our deterrent forces. For example, Admiral [Felix] Stump told me that if we did not have the two large fleet facilities at Yokosuka and Sasebo and the other naval facility in the Philippines, it would take two-and-a-half times as many ships and men to maintain the 7th Fleet at its present strength in Far Eastern waters. This would involve a terrific additional defense appropriation.[46]

The ambassador thus made his case forcefully for Japan's immense importance to the United States in a politico-economic sense and in a military sense. He cited in his May 25, 1957, message to Dulles the need

> *to at least firmly align and, if possible, to knit Japan so thoroughly into the fabric of the free world nations that it will not in the next few years be easily tempted to take an independent course leading either to non-alignment or neutralism (at best of the Swiss-Swedish type or at worst of the Nehru brand) or worst of all some form of accommodation with the Communist bloc* [italics in original].

MacArthur argued that the best way to accomplish that alignment and, "if possible," knitting, would be to revise the treaty and treat Japan as a full and equal partner, like any other aligned nation. And he warned of the alternative, that the "risk may increase that Japan would come to believe its interests best served by termination of treaty without any replacement."[47]

The ambassador noted that the US-Japanese security treaty accorded more extensive base-usage rights than did US treaties with other nations. He criticized the resistance of some members of the US military leadership to relinquishing any portion of those rights. MacArthur insisted that any US rights in Japan hinged on maintaining a sound overall relationship between the two nations.[48] He opined that Japanese perceptions of the treaty as inequitable were the biggest obstacle to propagating a sound relationship. And he expressed agreement with those perceptions: "This is not an 'alleged' inequality. . . . There is, as we all recognize, actual inequality."

Cosmetic, supplementary measures aimed at allaying Japanese dissatisfaction with the treaty, cautioned MacArthur, would be counterproductive. He suggested that a US willingness to make fundamental revisions in the treaty would "wipe out resentment of the 'one-sided' Security Treaty and greatly improve the climate of public opinion on security and defense matters."[49]

MacArthur warned that simply tweaking the treaty and leaving it basically intact would "only be postponing inevitable and perhaps to [a] time when circumstances are less favorable, and pressures build up for disengagement." He pushed strongly for undertaking the revision of the treaty while Kishi—US friendly, anti-Communist, politically adroit—was in power. The United States, MacArthur advised, could optimize the outcome by taking the initiative in proposing a truly mutual treaty.[50]

"Our willingness to effect treaty revision," MacArthur predicted, "will strengthen the position of those who believe in Japan's alignment with the United States. Early treaty revision is, therefore, very much in our own enlightened self-interest."[51]

"I think it is tremendously important," reflected the ambassador, "for us to have the initiative in this matter. I feel that if we have the initiative, our prospect of obtaining what we can reasonably expect in a mutual security arrangement is good; whereas if we lose the initiative and the pressure builds up, we may, over a period of the next several years, lose what we have now."[52]

Mutuality in the hosting of US bases in Japan

The notion of taking the initiative in proposing a treaty revision presented US policy makers with a conundrum. That was because of a long-standing emphasis in the US negotiating stance. The US negotiators had long insisted that Japanese readiness to help defend US territory was a prerequisite for treaty mutuality. That meant a readiness to dispatch troops abroad. Japan and the United States could not conclude a mutual-defense treaty as long as the US negotiators adhered to that stance.

Positioning Japan to dispatch troops abroad would require revising the nation's constitution and fortifying its military. A two-thirds majority in both houses of the Diet would be necessary to amend the constitution. That would require, as a practical matter, the introduction of single-member constituencies through a change in Japan's electoral law. And that would take a couple of years, as Ambassador MacArthur wrote in an August 1, 1958, telegram to the State Department.

> It now seems clear electoral law will not be modified till 1960 at earliest and next elections for lower house do not have to be held till 1962. Even then, we cannot be sure that Govt will obtain two-thirds majority or if it does that circumstances will permit amendment of constitution.[53]

MacArthur recommended abandoning the insistence on Japanese readiness to dispatch troops abroad as a condition for a mutual-defense treaty. That was the central thrust of his treaty-revision advocacy. He explained the need for that abandonment in his February 18, 1958, message to Dulles.

> The crux of the matter will probably be the definition of the treaty area. In the past, some of our people have suggested that, for such a treaty to be really mutual, Japan would have to agree to come to the aid of the United States if the continental United States or its territories elsewhere in the Pacific were attacked. Given the present Japanese interpretation of Japan's Constitution and the political facts of life in this country, any such condition would prevent the conclusion of a mutual security treaty. If we are to have Japan as a partner and thus be able to continue to use certain of her military and logistical facilities which are very important to us, it is *not* [italics in original] essential for Japan to be committed to come to our aid except within a fairly limited area.[54]

The ambassador viewed Japan's obligations to the United States under treaty reciprocity as consisting principally of hosting US bases. From that standpoint, Japanese readiness to dispatch troops overseas was not an absolute condition for revising the treaty. Neither too was a revision of the constitution nor an increase in defense capacity. The geographical coverage of mutual defense under the treaty (the "treaty area") could be of limited scope.[55]

MacArthur's recommendations did not gain traction right away in Washington, DC. Richard L. Sneider, a Japan desk officer at the State Department who worked on the treaty revision, explained why in his book. Recommendations from MacArthur and the embassy staff, Sneider writes, constituted proposals for compromise based on anticipated, rather than an actual, crisis in Japanese-US relations, and those proposals went down poorly with the US military.[56]

Dulles was reticent to begin negotiating a revision of the treaty. He responded to MacArthur's recommendations in a March 23, 1958, telegram to the ambassador.

> The essential, it seems to me, is that the Japanese should accept the basic premise that their future lies in close cooperation with the United States to create a balance of power as against the Soviet Union and Communist China.[57]

Dulles expressed concern about the possibility of Japan seeking to play off the United States against the Sino-Soviet bloc. He suggested that revising the treaty would be acceptable, however, if it promised to strengthen Japan's US alignment.

The secretary sought MacArthur's judgment with regard to this matter, and the ambassador opined that demonstrating receptivity to revising the treaty would reinforce Japan's cooperative stance vis-à-vis the United States. He expressed that judgment in a telegram of April 18.

> I am . . . convinced that if we simply try indefinitely to temporize or stall on the issue of treaty revision, such action can only lead to a serious deterioration in our relations with Japan and will also encourage those elements in Japan which seek to shift Japan's orientation away from the United States. As things now stand, the conservative party in Japan still has support for its policy of alignment with the United States despite the basic and growing desire of all Japanese for a revision of the Security Treaty. Our willingness to effect treaty revision will strengthen the position of those who believe in Japan's long-term security alignment with the United States and will deny to neutralist and leftist elements a powerful argument for a disengagement policy on the part of Japan.[58]

"Assuming something better would take its place"

The negotiations toward "mutualizing" the security treaty gained momentum after the May 1958 general election for the Diet's lower house. Dulles and his State Department devoted heightened attention to the negotiations after receiving an informal feeler from the Japanese government. MacArthur notified the State Department on June 5 of a request from the foreign minister for renewed talks. He accompanied the notification with a strong recommendation that the US government respond in a positive manner to the Japanese request and an equally strong warning that failing to do so could have undesirable results.

> Fujiyama has alerted me that following the formation of the new Japanese Cabinet, he and Kishi wish to have serious, confidential discussions with me regarding basic security problems, including revision of the US-Japan Security Treaty. . . . I would like to emphasize very strongly that the present atmosphere for constructive discussions with the Japanese is

> most favorable. . . . While the situation is now favorable, it will not remain so indefinitely if we are unable or unwilling to take constructive action.[59]

Dulles replied to MacArthur on June 23. He told the ambassador to feel "free [to] enter into exploratory talks [with Kishi and Fujiyama] on these matters without of course committing the US in any way." Dulles instructed MacArthur to secure input from the Japanese to help decide how to approach the security relationship.

> Accordingly, before making any firm decisions in Washington as to which of various means might be chosen to stimulate Japan in development firmer alignment with free world and greater participation in defense responsibilities Pacific area, you should probe possibilities with Foreign Minister and Prime Minister.[60]

The May 1958 general election was the first since the Kishi-led conservative coalition had taken power in February 1957. Dulles and his people at the State Department could only speculate how the election results would affect Japanese foreign policy. They knew, however, that the conservative coalition's strong showing in the election had strengthened Kishi's political standing. The LDP had suffered a net loss of 3 seats and emerged from the election with 287 seats, but the number of unaffiliated conservative lawmakers increased.

Meanwhile, the Socialist Party managed an increase of just 8 seats, to 166. The party's leaders had expected a substantially bigger gain, so the result registered as a defeat. Even that disappointing result would prove to be the high watermark for the Socialist Party. Never again would the party claim as many seats in the lower house.

Embellishing the election campaign were flagrant efforts by the Chinese and the Soviets to influence the Kishi government. The Chinese government responded furiously to what it perceived as an affront to its national pride in Nagasaki on May 2. A department store there was holding an exhibition of Chinese stamps sponsored by the Japan-China Friendship Association. Hanging at the entry to the exhibition space was the flag of the People's Republic of China (PRC). A Japanese rightist charged in and tore down the flag.

Japan still recognized the Taiwan-based Republic of China and did not yet have formal diplomatic relations with the PRC, so the Japanese government declined to prosecute the case on the basis of debasing a national flag. That infuriated Beijing, which accused the Kishi government of displaying hostility to mainland China and sacrificing Japanese interests out of blind allegiance to the United States. The PRC foreign minister, Chen Yi, declared on May 11 that the PRC government was suspending economic and cultural interchange with Japan.

As for the Soviets, Moscow inquired of the Japanese government on May 15 if any nuclear weapons were in Japanese territory. It warned the Japanese that any such weaponry would be a threat to peace and security in the Far East and would not go unaddressed.[61]

That the conservative coalition prevailed in the Japanese election despite the Chinese and Soviet pressure was encouraging for the US government.[62] Thus did MacArthur characterize "the present atmosphere for constructive discussions with the Japanese" as "most favorable." And thus did Ambassador MacArthur's recommendation earn acceptance by Dulles and his State Department, by the Defense Department and the Joint Chiefs of Staff, and by Congress and become the US government's roadmap for revising the security treaty.

The US government welcomed the Japanese government's hardline stance against the Communists. Here is an illustrative episode.

Nikolai Bulganin, the Soviet premier, sent a letter dated December 10, 1957, to the leaders of the United States, the United Kingdom, France, and the Federal Republic of Germany (West Germany). The letter was in advance of the NATO summit mentioned in this chapter, which took place from December 16 to 19. In it, Bulganin deplored the summit as provocative, cited the threat of nuclear war, and called for reducing arms and defusing international tensions.

The Soviet government also delivered a verbal note to the Japanese government through Japan's Moscow embassy. That note carried the same date as the letter to the Western leaders and expressed the same sentiment.

On February 24, 1958, the Japanese government delivered its response to the Soviet message. It expressed support for NATO and suggested that the Soviets' commitment to arms reduction was insufficient. That response impressed Eisenhower, who praised the Japanese government's stance in a March 4 telephone discussion with Dulles. The secretary suggested that the time had come for the Japanese government to possess more self-respect. Eisenhower agreed and pledged to do everything possible in that regard. On Dulles's recommendation, he sent a letter to Kishi dated March 8. The president praised Kishi in that letter for the moral strength evinced in the Japanese response to the Soviets.

MacArthur traveled to Washington, DC, and met with Dulles, Robertson, and other State Department officials on September 8. That was in advance of a visit by Fujiyama, and MacArthur had come to explain the need for revising the treaty.[63]

> The Secretary said he was less interested in what we might get technically in a mutual security treaty than what we could win in Japanese psychological alignment with the free world. Japan had been slower than Germany in regaining its pride and national spirit. He had felt for a long time that when the spirit did re-emerge the Japanese would recognize the indispensability of a security relationship with the United States against the neighboring Communist area.
>
> Ambassador MacArthur pointed out differences between Japan and Germany. It had been possible to bring Germany into alliance through a collective approach both economically and militarily. Japan was historically isolated not only from the West but also from the remainder of Asia. With the recent experience of alienation from other Asians by its military adventure preceding and during World War II Japan was not susceptible to (and would not be drawn into the free world orbit militarily speaking through) a collective approach. The only possible approach was through alignment with the United States.
>
> The Secretary expressed his concurrence and remarked that he would have to proceed with the practical arrangements for getting a unified United States position.[64]

Dulles and Fujiyama met three days later. At their meeting, the secretary "noted that the present Security Treaty had been negotiated with himself as negotiator," that he took "some satisfaction in the fact that it has served well the purposes for which it was designed under the conditions then obtaining," but that, as "the father of the Treaty . . . he was not so devoted to it that he would be unwilling to consider changing it, assuming something better would take its place." Dulles added that the treaty "had never been designed to be a permanent and perpetual formula for the regulation of [US-Japanese] security arrangements" and that "the Treaty itself stated that it was a 'provisional' arrangement."[65]

Ambassador MacArthur would steer the US government toward revising the security treaty with Japan and leave an indelible mark on the Japanese-US relationship. His predecessor, John Allison, had been culturally and linguistically familiar with Japan. MacArthur, on the other hand, had earned his stripes as a diplomat in Europe.

Douglas MacArthur II was the nephew of General Douglas MacArthur. He earned a commission in the army after graduating from Yale College in 1932 but joined the State Department in 1935. MacArthur was a member of the US embassy staff in Paris when France fell to the Germans in June 1940, and he was part of the US liaison team in Vichy until November 1942. That was when the Germans seized the US consulate and held MacArthur and the other members of the consulate staff as prisoners of war. MacArthur's German captors exchanged him and his colleagues in March 1944 for Germans who had been captured by the Allies in North Africa. He then worked as an assistant political advisor to Eisenhower, then the head of the Supreme Headquarters Allied Expeditionary Force, in London and in Normandy.

MacArthur resumed work at the US embassy in Paris after the city's liberation and, after brief service in Brussels, became the chief of the State Department's Division of Western European Affairs. He thereupon undertook postings that would earn him the unwavering confidence of Eisenhower and Dulles and underlie his influence in shaping the revised security treaty with Japan. MacArthur served as Eisenhower's political advisor after the latter became NATO's supreme commander in December 1950, and Eisenhower appointed him to the post of counselor at the State Department after taking office as president in January 1953. He served as State Department counselor for four years, working closely with Dulles and traveling the world with the secretary.

The MacArthur name surely figured in the decision to name the nephew ambassador to Japan, but the younger MacArthur had clearly established solid diplomatic credentials in his own right. He headed the Tokyo embassy for four years, to 1961, and subsequently served as US ambassador to Belgium, Austria, and Iran. In Tokyo, MacArthur was an entirely worthy successor to the highly regarded Allison. He performed every bit as well as his predecessor in conveying insightful information about developments in Japan to Washington, DC, and he was even more effective with regard to mobilizing US government support for the policies that he favored.

3 Kishi's Decision

A mutual treaty compatible with the Japanese constitution

Fujiyama met with MacArthur on July 30, 1958 and explained the thinking in the Japanese government about revising the security treaty. MacArthur reported that the foreign minister offered as a reason for revising the treaty that the

> USSR has announced success in development of missiles and satellites and has launched major psychological offensive aimed at creating doubts regarding advisability of depending on US deterrent power.[66]

The Soviets had indeed endeavored during the election campaign, as noted, to influence the Kishi government. In the event, the security treaty did not become an important issue in the election, but opposition to the treaty became central to the Japan Socialist Party's political agenda. Sputnik had prompted a shift in the party's stance to one of advocating abrogation, rather than revision, of the treaty.

Japan's Socialists argued that choosing sides between the United States and the Soviet Union was dangerous in the post-Sputnik era of intercontinental ballistic missiles. They proclaimed a formal commitment to dissolving the security treaty with the United States and to establishing a collective-security arrangement that would include the Soviet Union and China, as well as the United States and Japan. The Socialist Party was preparing post-election agitation to spark a people's movement for banning nuclear weapons from Japanese territory.[67]

Kishi was alert to the smoldering opposition to the security treaty.

Extinguishing that opposition was part of his strategy for reinforcing the Japanese-US relationship. It was therefore clearly in mind for Kishi as his government moved to revise the treaty. Tōgō writes that Fujiyama spoke to MacArthur of the need for a bilateral discussion of fundamental changes in the security treaty. According to Tōgō, Fujiyama acknowledged that the security treaty remained fundamental to Japan's national security but explained that Japanese perceptions of the treaty were changing:

> A sense of autonomy has finally awakened among the Japanese as the postwar years have gone by. As Japan nurtures the Self-Defense Forces and as plans proceed for the withdrawal of US military forces from Japan, the treaty is becoming inconsistent in some aspects with Japanese sentiment.[68]

Fujiyama and the Foreign Ministry were thinking, however, in terms of reconciling the treaty with Japanese sentiment through a supplementary agreement, not through wholesale revision. Tōgō writes that

> [our] side was dealing with constitutional limitations. We couldn't simply float an idea for a treaty of the mutual defense and assistance variety. That wasn't [constitutionally] possible, even if it was what we really wanted.

Exactly what sort of supplementary agreement Tōgō and his colleagues had in mind is unclear. Tōgō writes, however, that the text under consideration contained two key provisions: (1) for Japan-based US forces to cooperate with the Japanese Self-Defense Forces and (2) for the US government to consult with the Japanese government in advance of deploying Japan-based forces beyond Japanese territory or introducing nuclear weapons into Japanese territory.

The provisions cited by Tōgō addressed two domestic criticisms of the treaty: one, that it did not specify a US obligation to defend Japan, and two, that it imposed no restrictions on the operation of the US bases in Japan. The latter criticism reflected concerns that the treaty's reference to "the maintenance of international peace and security in the Far East" could draw Japan unknowingly into a war and that the US military could introduce nuclear weapons into Japanese territory.[69]

Ambassador MacArthur responded to the overtures from Fujiyama and the Foreign Ministry with an indirect suggestion that revising the treaty would be preferable. According to Tōgō, the ambassador touched at the July 30 meeting with Fujiyama on the possibility of a mutual-assistance treaty and offered to work to bring about such a treaty if requested by the Japanese government. Fujiyama replied that he would talk with Kishi and let MacArthur know if the prime minister opted for a supplementary agreement or a treaty revision.[70]

Tōgō's account of the July 30 meeting between Fujiyama and MacArthur differs in nuance from the US archival documentation. MacArthur reported in a July 31, 1958, telegram to the State Department that Fujiyama had acknowledged that

> if, as in past, US continues to insist that to enter a mutual security treaty Japan must obligate herself to send her troops abroad, then such a mutual security treaty is not feasible at this time.

Fujiyama, according to MacArthur, had explained that the Foreign Ministry "had looked into other possibilities." Those included, as Tōgō has written, leaving the treaty intact and redressing its shortcomings with a supplementary agreement. Such an agreement, MacArthur reports Fujiyama as explaining,

> in effect would accomplish de facto revision of treaty to provide for full equality and consultation, meaning mutual agreement, on all major decisions affecting Japan's defense and security interests.
>
> Fujiyama felt that objections to existing treaty could be to considerable extent removed by such adjustments placing US-Japanese security relations on de facto equal basis.

MacArthur adds here, however, that Fujiyama volunteered that another option had received "some consideration in [the Foreign Ministry]":

> [a] mutual security treaty not requiring Japan send its forces outside "Japan area" [including Okinawa and the Ogasawara Islands]. Such treaty would not seem to pose constitutional difficulties for Japan and would be in many respects desirable alternative. Fujiyama stated that, due pre-

viously expressed US views on mutual security treaty, (i.e., Japan must commit itself to send its troops abroad) [the Foreign Ministry] hesitated put forth this alternative in any formal sense.

The ambassador asked Fujiyama

which of two alternatives for adjusting existing US-Japan security arrangements [prime minister] Kishi and [foreign minister] Fujiyama really preferred (i.e., adjustments without changing present security treaty or new mutual security treaty for "Japan area").

And MacArthur explained that he

did not have instructions which would enable me to discuss these alternatives with [Fujiyama] and did not know what Washington's reactions would be to specific suggestions he had made, I was sure Kishi's preference re suggested alternatives would be important.[71]

Tōgō implies that MacArthur made the first mention of a mutual-security treaty that didn't oblige Japan to dispatch troops abroad, whereas the ambassador attributes the first mention of that option to Fujiyama. Whatever the reason for that discrepancy, the Fujiyama-MacArthur exchange preceded and presumably influenced Kishi's decision to opt for revising the treaty—to opt, in other words, for concluding a mutual treaty.[72]

Kishi met with MacArthur sans Fujiyama, apparently in mid-August, and announced that he wanted to conclude a new and mutual treaty. He emphasized, however, that the treaty would need to abide with Japan's constitutional prohibition on dispatching troops abroad.[73] Kishi had maintained a cautious approach all along to the matter of revising the treaty, and whether he would have pursued a mutualized treaty consonant with the Japanese constitution without MacArthur's urging is doubtful. MacArthur presumably had some basis for confidence that the prime minister would take his hint.[74] We have no direct evidence, however, that Kishi had indicated formerly that he was interested in revising the treaty.[75] The first record of Kishi indicating such an interest is an August 18, 1958, telegram from MacArthur to the State Department.[76]

Two options

Kishi determined that revising the security treaty was the best approach to addressing the treaty's issues and acted accordingly. He veered sharply away from his original idea of amending the constitution and fortifying Japan's military and then revising the treaty. That course correction suggests convincingly that Kishi was attentive to US government intentions. He had not committed himself irrevocably, however, to treaty revision. Witness his remarks in an August 25, 1958, meeting with MacArthur, accompanied by Fujiyama and Foreign Ministry staffers. Tōgō recounts those remarks as follows:

> I expected intense debate to ensue in the Diet once we moved ahead with undertaking a fundamental revision of the treaty, but I believed that working our way through that debate would serve to place the Japanese-US relationship on a truly stable foundation and that revising the existing treaty fundamentally was, if possible, desirable. On the other hand, we would have no choice, if getting a new treaty would take an inordinate amount of time, but to leave the existing treaty in place and resolve the individual issues with a supplementary agreement.[77]

The prime minister declared his intention of concluding a revised treaty but retained the fallback position of improving the treaty with a supplementary agreement. Keeping his options open came naturally to Kishi as a skilled politician, but this stratagem was more than just a means of getting something done for the sake of getting it done. Kishi felt strongly about curtailing US latitude to deploy Japan-based forces beyond Japanese territory and to introduce nuclear weapons into Japanese territory, and that was a more pressing priority for him than securing a revised security treaty.

MacArthur reported the gist of his August 25 meeting with Kishi at the September 8 State Department meeting in Washington, DC. He explained

> that two courses of action were open to the Japanese: (1) to retain the present security treaty with all its unilateral aspects and to have a side arrangement covering consultation prior to the introduction of nuclears and to the operation of United States forces from bases in Japan; or (2) to

> negotiate a new mutual security treaty with provision in exchange of notes or a communiqué to take care of the same two points.[78]

Notes to the US records of the September 8 discussions cite an earlier, telegraphic exchange that reported that

> Kishi preferred the second alternative, principally on the ground that the one-sided nature of the existing treaty made it a vulnerable target for Socialist attacks.[79]

We see in the Japanese and the US records that (1) Kishi preferred revising the security treaty fundamentally to "fixing" it with a supplementary agreement and that (2) he was in a hurry. The prime minister wanted to negotiate the treaty revision promptly with the US government, submit a treaty proposal at the next regular session of the Diet, and let the lawmakers debate the proposal fully before the June 1959 elections for the Diet's upper house. If that schedule did not prove feasible, Kishi would feel obliged to leave the treaty in place and conclude a supplementary agreement to address two issues: the introduction of nuclear weapons into Japan and the mobilization of US military forces based in Japan for purposes other than defending Japan. Failing to address those two issues in the next regular Diet session, Kishi felt, would weaken the Japanese-US relationship.[80] Addressing those issues took precedence in his priorities over revising the treaty fundamentally.

The decision in the context of domestic politics

Kishi's reason for deciding in summer 1958 to opt for revising the security treaty is something of a mystery. One possibility is that he was complying with Ambassador MacArthur's wishes. The ambassador regarded revising the treaty as preferable to redressing the treaty's shortcomings with a supplementary agreement. Kishi and MacArthur maintained close communication, and the prime minister might have sensed or been informed of that preference and accepted the ambassador's judgment. We have no evidence, however, of such influence. And even if MacArthur's views were a factor in Kishi's decision to opt for revising the treaty, that need not diminish our appraisal of the role of Kishi's independent judgment in the decision.

In retirement, Kishi told biographer and international relations specialist Hara Yoshihisa in an interview that his main reason for deciding to revise the treaty was twofold: establish in writing the US obligation to defend Japan and heighten the Japanese people's awareness of the need to defend their nation.[81] That explanation is convincing, as far as it goes. We need to view Kishi's decision, however, more in the context of his domestic political program than of his foreign-policy goal of equalizing the Japanese-US security relationship. That is evident in the confidence he gained from the lower-house elections of May 1958.

The LDP won an absolute majority in the lower house of the Diet in the 1958 elections. That electoral victory, Kishi's first since becoming prime minister, emboldened him greatly. It encouraged him to adopt an aggressive stance against the Socialist Party and the Communist Party; against the General Council of Trade Unions of Japan; against the Japan Teachers' Union, which had fought his proposed system for evaluating teacher performance; and against the All-Japan Federation of Students' Self-Governing Associations.

Kishi met privately with MacArthur on July 11, a month before he decided to revise the treaty. He explained his postelection political plans to the ambassador on the condition of strict confidentiality. Those plans, Kishi confided, included several legislative initiatives that would entail taking on the opposition parties and leftist forces in Japan. They included strengthening public security by passing a counterintelligence (secrets protection) law and by strengthening the Police Duties Execution Act and upgrading social welfare by passing what became the National Pension Act and the Minimum Wage Act.[82]

The security treaty would of course become a subject of dispute in the sort of political confrontation that Kishi had in mind. MacArthur reported at the State Department meeting on September 8, 1958, in Washington, DC, that the Socialist Party

> was preparing two draft resolutions for the forthcoming regular session of the Diet, one concerning the non-introduction of nuclears without the agreement of the Japanese Government and the other concerning the operational use of United States bases in Japan without Japanese consent.[83]

Japanese were sensitive to the nuclear and operational issues targeted by the Socialist Party, and a resolution to those issues was presumably possible through a supplementary agreement to the treaty. In that sense, Kishi would have been happy to deal with the treaty by modifying the supplementary agreement. Taking MacArthur's hint, however, and tackling a fundamental revision of the treaty offered greater rewards. It would allow for securing a written commitment from the US government to defending Japan, and that would negate the complaints from the left about the treaty's inequality and underline the soundness of Kishi's pro-US policy in the eyes of the people. Kishi had acknowledged in a discussion with MacArthur on August 25 that the treaty's "one-sided nature" was problematic. He noted that it rendered the Japanese government's security policy vulnerable to attacks from socialists as deferential to the United States and that it would continue to do so as long as its "one-sided nature" persisted.[84]

The prime minister wanted, if possible, to sign a new Japanese-US security treaty, to have it debated thoroughly in the Diet, and to leave no doubt that it had secured the support of the lawmakers and the citizenry. Fujiyama and his Foreign Ministry would have preferred to avoid confrontation with the opposition parties in the Diet. For that reason, they would have preferred to deal with the treaty through supplementary measures for resolving individual issues. Kishi, on the other hand, welcomed the treaty revision as an opportunity for carrying the battle to the treaty opponents.[85]

Kishi's decision to undertake a revision of the security treaty meshed with his moves after the general election to take on the Socialist Party and the Communist Party. Those moves benefited from cash funding provided by the US government through the Central Intelligence Agency. Kishi's younger brother and finance minister, Satō Eisaku, figured in a well-documented episode. Satō met with a US embassy staffer on July 25 and requested secret cash funding from the US government to fight Japan's Communist movement.[86]

Formal negotiations over revising the security treaty got under way on October 4 with talks between Fujiyama and MacArthur. At the ambassador's insistence, the negotiations began with the submission of a US draft proposal. The Japanese and US negotiators soon worked out core elements of the revised treaty, such as the treaty area. (See Chapter 5 for a detailed discussion of the negotiations over the geographical scope of the treaty.) Political unrest in Japan forced the suspension of the negotiations, however, from mid-December to mid-April 1959. The unrest erupted in response to the Kishi government's attempt to broaden police powers under the Police Duties Execution Act. It escalated into massive demonstrations, which obliged the government to withdraw its proposed amendment to the law in November 1958 and reverberated well into 1959.

The bill for bolstering the Police Duties Execution Act had been a core element in Kishi's legislative onslaught against the left. It reached the floor of the Diet on October 8, just four days after Fujiyama and MacArthur began negotiating the security-treaty revision. The bill proved a cruel indication for Kishi that his public support was less robust than he thought. Its introduction sharpened the public perception of the prime minister as a reactionary throwback to prewar authoritarianism, and that perception would weigh heavily on the process of passing the revised security treaty. The very association with Kishi, as much as the bill's content, triggered wariness.

Kishi's political leadership suffered from the disorder occasioned by the Police Duties Execution Act debacle. Competing LDP factions smelled blood. They began positioning themselves to secure increased clout in the next government. And that, too, would impede the legislative progress of the treaty revision.

While the treaty-revision negotiations were suspended, Ikeda Hayato, Kōno Ichirō, Miki Takeo, and other anti-mainstream lawmakers in the LDP called for rewriting the treaty's administrative agreement. They based their demand on the wide-ranging effect of that agreement on the lives of numerous Japanese. Revising the administrative agreement was not part of the original agenda for the treaty-revision negotiations, but the government yielded to the intraparty pressure and agreed to seek an extensive revision of the agreement.

Ambassador MacArthur was dubious about undertaking a wholesale revision of the administrative agreement, but he could see that it had become a condition for securing Japanese acceptance of the treaty revision and went along with the Japanese government's request. The negotiations over revising the administrative agreement began at the end of March 1959, before the treaty-revision negotiations resumed. They proceeded, in Tōgō's words, "with the stumbling gait that was to have been expected." All manner of issues arose, and the negotiations dragged on to the end of 1959.

The negotiations over the treaty itself resumed on April 13 and produced a document that was more or less ready for signing by the end of June. The negotiations over the administrative agreement had likewise progressed and awaited only a consensus among the Japanese to finalize. The Japanese government, however, requested a delay in the treaty-revision signing.

Kishi's government had signed a reparations agreement in May with the Republic of Vietnam (South Vietnam), and that agreement was bound to encounter resistance in the Diet from the opposition parties. Fujiyama explained the request for a delay as necessary to avoid "entangling new treaty with acrimonious debate over Vietnamese reparations." MacArthur conveyed the request to the State Department in a telegram of July 14, 1959. His detailed explanation of how constitutional considerations figured in "parliamentary tactics and time schedule" is interesting, and I have therefore reproduced here at length.

> Fujiyama asked to see me yesterday afternoon in order to give detailed report of meeting of key party and cabinet leaders last week, especially with respect to timing of signature and ratification of new Mutual Security Treaty and related documents. . . .
>
> Consensus of meeting, Fujiyama said, was that while it was most important that no announcement re timing should be made at this time (since it would only give aid and comfort to Socialists), new treaty and related documents should be introduced not into extraordinary Diet session but into subsequent regular Diet session which will be convened in December. This is necessary for reasons of parliamentary tactics and time schedule necessitated by constitutional provisions. Fujiyama said Vietnamese reparations agreement, which was signed May 13, must take precedence in ratification process over new security treaty. Cabinet and party leaders have decided that it would be most unwise for [the government] to sign treaty or introduce it into Diet while Vietnamese agreement is being debated. In view strong Socialist opposition to any agreement with South Vietnam, extraordinary Diet session in autumn will inevitably spend considerable time on that agreement and [the govern-

> ment] wishes that issue to be safely out of the way before engaging final battle over security treaty.
>
> In terms of parliamentary calendar, Fujiyama said, [the government's] strategy has in mind article 61 of constitution which provides that a treaty becomes effective 30 days after passage by lower house, regardless whether it has been approved by upper house. [The government] is calculating that for Vietnamese reparations agreement to become effective it must allow 40 days for lower house debate, followed by period of 30 days during which it can be debated in upper house. Since extraordinary Diet must close by December 10 or December 15 at the very latest, Vietnamese reparations agreement must therefore be introduced toward end of September at the latest. In light of fact that ratification of Vietnamese agreement will thus take about 70 days if the US-Japan security treaty were to be introduced into extraordinary Diet, session would have had to be convoked very shortly after Kishi's return and even then might not complete action on both Vietnamese accord and security treaty by mid-December. Furthermore, party leaders have judged that such extended extraordinary session would be unwise and that such tight schedule might have involved excessive risk of being upset by opposition maneuvers. It would be better, Fujiyama reported, to introduce new treaty and Admin Agreement into regular Diet session which will be convoked latter half Dec, which will then recess for one month and get down to business in latter half of January.
>
> Under this time schedule, Fujiyama said, it is envisioned that new treaty and related agreements could be signed some time between end of extraordinary Diet in early or mid-December and convocation of regular Diet later that month or possibly during Diet recess from late December to late January. Signature during extraordinary session would risk entangling new treaty with acrimonious debate over Vietnamese reparations.[87]

Tōgō offers a different reason for the Japanese government's request to delay the signing and ratification of the treaty revision. He attributes it to the need to accommodate "intraparty circumstances."[88] Whatever the actual reason or reasons for the Japanese request, the US government complied, and the signing ended up taking place in January 1960.

The Japanese returned to some formerly settled issues after the Americans agreed to delay the signing, and that necessitated further negotiation. Those issues included the time span of the treaty, the requirement for prior consultation (discussed in Chapter 5), and the provisions of the administrative agreement.

With regard to the treaty time span, Kishi sought "a provision for reviewing the treaty" during its 10-year span. MacArthur explained the request in a November 30, 1959, telegram to the State Department.

> Kishi was not of course suggesting that the treaty draft which we have agreed can be changed, but he did feel a provision, in the form of an agreed minute re treaty review, which could be made public if necessary in Diet debates, was extremely important. In particular it would enable him to deal with Kono or any other anti-mainstreamers who wanted to make difficulties over the duration or other elements of the treaty.

Fujiyama had submitted to MacArthur a proposed text for the provision that Kishi sought, and the ambassador included that text in his telegram.

> While the Treaty of Mutual Cooperation and Security is of indefinite duration the period after which either party may give notice for termination has been fixed at ten years. No explicit provision was made for reviewing the treaty because in the agreed opinion of the two governments stability is a very important factor in the security relationship between the two countries. Obviously, if either party should so request at any time while the treaty is in force, the two parties would consult together for the purpose of reviewing any aspect of the treaty or its related arrangements having regard for the factors then affecting peace and security in the Far East.

MacArthur concluded the telegram with the recommendation that the US government agree to Kishi's request.

> Foregoing proposed minute will unquestionably greatly strengthen Kishi's position, and permit government to deal with criticism which has potentially most damaging appeal inside LDP and with public. I urge its acceptance since it seems entirely consistent with position we have taken re

> our European Allies in NATO and also since it merely reflects fact that if either party at any time wishes to review any aspect of the treaty the two parties would be obliged to consult together.[89]

The State Department, however, rejected the request.

Signing the treaty was just the beginning of what proved to be a traumatic path to ratification. Kishi had secured a pledge by Eisenhower to visit Japan in 1960. The visit was ostensibly to coincide with the centennial of the ratification of the Japanese-US Treaty of Amity and Commerce. It was to take place from June 19 to 22, and Kishi was determined to get the new security treaty ratified by that date. As MacArthur noted, "article 61 of constitution . . . provides that a treaty becomes effective 30 days after passage by lower house, regardless whether it has been approved by upper house." So meeting Kishi's target date meant passing a treaty-ratification motion in the lower house of the Diet by May 20.

The treaty faced unprecedented resistance on the streets of the nation and in the halls of the Diet. Public demonstrations rocked Japan, the demonstrators shouting for an end to the security treaty and for the overthrow of the Kishi government. Parliamentarians resorted to extraordinary measures to block the ratification of the treaty. Opposition lawmakers went so far as to confine the speaker of the house of representatives, Kiyose Ichirō, to prevent him from calling a vote. Police swarmed the Diet to release him, however, in the late-night hours of May 19, and he made his way into the house chamber, escorted by burly LDP parliamentarians. Kiyose called the house to order just after midnight, and the conservative coalition used its majority to ratify the treaty.

People throughout Japan regarded the conservative coalition's unilateral ratification of the treaty as an abuse of democratic process, and the demonstrations against the treaty increased in order of magnitude. Epitomizing the Anpo [security treaty] rancor was the so-called Hagerty Incident of June 10. James Hagerty, Eisenhower's press secretary, had arrived in Japan to take part in preparations for Eisenhower's scheduled visit and was leaving Tokyo's Haneda Airport in a car with MacArthur. A mob surrounded the car, some of the members of the mob climbing onto the vehicle's hood and roof, and the US military needed to dispatch a helicopter to rescue the presidential press secretary.

Civil order deteriorated further. A clash between demonstrators and police on the periphery of the Diet building claimed the life of Kanba Michiko, a University of Tokyo student, on June 15. Kanba was part of a group that was trying to break through a police cordon and enter the building. Accounts differ as to how she died in the encounter. The next day, the Japanese government asked the US government to delay Eisenhower's visit on account of the public disorder.

The May 20 treaty-ratification vote in the lower house of the Diet was to take effect at 12:00 midnight. Kishi awaited the hour in the prime minister's residence with his younger brother and finance minister, Satō. Outside was pandemonium. Kishi half expected an attack on his person sooner or later. He would announce five days later, on June 23, that he would resign after Japan and the United States had exchanged ratifications and the treaty had taken effect.[90]

Heavy in the air in the prime minister's residence was the determination with which Kishi had brought about the treaty revision and the social disruption that his decision had occasioned. As Kishi and Satō well knew, the protests were, first and foremost, an outpouring of anti-Kishi sentiment. People were rising up in opposition to Kishi and to the continuation of the prewar authoritarian nationalism that he represented. Their passion would abate quickly once he had left office.[91] That happened on July 15.

4 The Shape of the Revised Treaty

Obstacles to future treaty revision

The 1960 Treaty of Mutual Cooperation and Security between Japan and the United States of America, born amid the violent trauma of the Anpo protests, inherited the basic structure of the 1952 Security Treaty Between Japan and the United States of America. It incorporated, however, several important changes, summarized below. Some of those changes ameliorated aspects of the 1952 treaty that had engendered perceptions of treaty inequity and otherwise occasioned friction in Japan.

a. *Linkage with the UN charter (preamble and Articles 1, 5, and 7 of the treaty)*
Demonstrate that the treaty is consistent with the aims of the UN charter and that it is an agreement based on the right to collective self-defense enshrined in that charter.
b. *Mutual commitment to strengthening both nations' free institutions and promoting political and economic cooperation (Article 2)*
Position the treaty as an agreement that, like the NATO treaty, would transcend military considerations.
c. *Continued strengthening of self-defense capabilities (Article 3)*
Oblige Japan to continue strengthening its self-defense capacity, subject to constitutional provisions.
d. *Consultation (Article 4)*
Provide for consultation at the request of either party with regard to implementing the treaty when the security of Japan or international peace and security in the Far East is threatened.
e. *US obligation to defend Japan (Article 5)*
Oblige the United States to defend Japan from attack.
f. *Japanese obligation to defend the United States (Article 5)*
Oblige Japan to defend US forces from attack in territory under Japanese administration.
g. *Prior consultation (Article 6)*
Provide for consultation in advance of changes in the deployment of US military forces in Japan or, as the treaty would be interpreted by both governments, in advance of the introduction of nuclear weapons.
h. *Expiration (Article 10)*
Provide for termination of the treaty. Whereas the security treaty of 1952 was of an open-ended time span, the treaty of 1960 allowed either party to terminate the pact after it had been in force for ten years. Giving notice would result in the treaty's expiration one year after the notification.
i. *Domestic unrest*
Eliminate the provision for US military engagement in putting down domestic unrest. The revised treaty dispensed with a clause in article 1 of the security treaty of 1952 that provided for the United States to provide military "assistance given at the express request of the Japanese Government to put down large-scale internal riots and disturbances in Japan,

caused through instigation or intervention by an outside power or powers."

j. *Revision of the administrative agreement (Article 6)*
Replace the administrative agreement concluded under article 3 of the security treaty of 1952 with a status of forces agreement. The status of forces agreement took shape as the Agreement under Article VI of the Treaty of Mutual Cooperation and Security between Japan and the United States of America, Regarding Facilities and Areas and the Status of United States Armed Forces in Japan. It granted rights and privileges to US military personnel and their dependents that were comparable to those granted under base-hosting arrangements in NATO member nations. The status of forces agreement dispensed, meanwhile, with the administrative agreement's provisions for Japanese financial outlays for base upkeep, which had caused intergovernmental frictions.[92]

Improvements notwithstanding, the new treaty retained its predecessor's structure in a fundamental respect: it basically provided for leasing sites to the United States for bases in exchange for the assurance of military security.[93] Kishi, who had sought to mutualize the treaty, was undoubtably less than fully satisfied with that outcome. He was also surely aware, however, that a truly mutual pact had never been a realistic possibility. The enormous differential in the nations' might—military, economic, industrial, diplomatic, and otherwise—meant that any mutuality would be, at most, a matter of phrasing and not of substance.

Kishi believed that fortifying Japan's position through strengthened ties with Southeast Asian nations would help achieve greater parity with the United States.[94] That might have been a reasonable hope for the future, but no amount of bridge building with nations anywhere could have overcome Japan's gaping disadvantage vis-à-vis the United States in 1960. In that context, securing written affirmation of US responsibility for defending Japan and thereby infusing the treaty with an increased measure of mutuality was an impressive accomplishment.

Even the revised treaty failed, however, to engage Japan and the United States in a mutual commitment to defending one another. That didn't sit well, of course, with the nationalist Kishi. He clung to the goal of forging a Japanese-US relationship of equality, and he viewed the revised security treaty of 1960 as a work in progress.

The 1960 treaty revision was, for Kishi, a means of broaching the principle of mutuality in the Japanese-US security relationship. He anticipated that Japan and the United States could enter into an alliance later to confront the Communist world. That would happen when Japan could deal with the United States on a more equal footing—after Japan had strengthened its military capabilities, revised its constitution, and otherwise put its house in order.

Kishi acknowledged after leaving office that he had envisioned the treaty revision as a step toward revising the constitution. He had envisioned, he told Hara Yoshihisa, revising the constitution to allow for dispatching troops abroad and thereupon concluding "a truly mutual defense treaty in the sense of Japanese-US equality."[95]

That things did not proceed as Kishi had envisioned is attributable largely to an ironic aspect of the treaty revision. The revision, however limited in scope, strengthened the treaty's foundation greatly. It enunciated the principle of mutuality and improved the overall appearance of the treaty in the eyes of the Japanese. That lessened the motivation for revising the treaty further. The 1960 revision resulted in a treaty that would be more difficult to change than its predecessor had been. That was more the result, however, of how events happened to play out than of intentional design.

Circumstances, for example, could conceivably have prompted a US military withdrawal from Japan soon after the revision of the treaty. That would have necessitated further revision or even revocation of the agreement.

Meanwhile, no bilateral consensus had solidified in summer 1958 with regard to a goal for the final form of the security treaty. Aiming for a treaty on the order of a mutual-assistance agreement consonant with Japan's constitution was hardly a done deal.

A further revision of the treaty could have resulted from the treatment of Okinawa and the Ogasawara Islands. Kishi had wanted to include those territories in the Japanese geography covered by the revised treaty of 1960, though that didn't happen on account of opposition from multiple quarters.

Okinawa and the Ogasawara Islands were officially Japanese territory, but they were under US administration. Kishi had called during his 1957 visit to Washington, DC, for restoring Okinawa and the Ogasawara Islands to Japanese administration in 10 years. Including them in the geographical coverage of the revised treaty would have suggested joint defense, and it could have set the stage for concluding a mutual-defense pact. The subsequent process of Okinawa's reversion to Japanese administration, meanwhile, would have followed a different course from what it did. The reversion might, for that matter, have occasioned a further revision of the security agreement.

US initiative

Kishi made the decision to put the process of revising the treaty in motion, but he doesn't appear to have had a clear vision for the shape of the revised treaty at that time. Such is the impression, at least, from the findings of historical research to date and from US archival documents that have become public. Kishi's thinking on treaty revision has remained a mystery despite the progressive declassification of Japanese government documents over the years.[96] Not even the dramatic disclosure in 2010 of formerly classified secret agreements between Fujiyama and MacArthur (see Chapter 5) illuminated this mystery significantly.

Prudence dictates that we withhold judgment for the time being on Kishi's goals and motivation. We are entitled to wonder, however, why Kishi, who died in 1987, decided to move ahead with the treaty revision when he did. We are entitled to question why he acted before Japan was in a position to conclude a truly mutual defense pact—before the Japanese had revised their constitution to permit the dispatching of troops abroad, before they had strengthened their military sufficiently to pull their weight in a mutual-defense arrangement.

A key enabling condition for the treaty revision was the US government's decision to lower the bar for "mutuality." The Americans, at MacArthur's urging, dropped their insistence on Japan being prepared to dispatch troops abroad. That enabled MacArthur to hint to the Japanese that a mutual-assistance treaty compatible with the Japanese constitution might be possible. Without those developments, any revision sought by the Kishi government after the conservative coalition's electoral victory would have been more modest. The bilateral negotiations over substantive revisions in the treaty that commenced in October 1958 wouldn't have happened. We can therefore regard the 1960 treaty revision as the result of US initiative.

MacArthur and his colleagues in the US government had high regard for Kishi. And the ambassador apparently had good reason for confidence that Kishi would respond positively to the US proposal. Hara Yoshihisa writes that MacArthur had sounded out Fujiyama and other Foreign Ministry officials in summer 1958 about a mutual treaty. The ambassador, according to Hara, had already secured the beginnings of an agreement with Kishi for a new treaty. That treaty would incorporate substantive changes that would establish mutuality without obliging Japan to be prepared to dispatch troops abroad.[97]

US initiative was a crucial factor in the treaty revision, but the increasingly vocal Japanese discontent with the inequitable treaty played a big role in motivating US action. Kishi's decisiveness also played a big role. His decisiveness, however, was an after-the-fact development, as far as we can determine from presently available information. The prime minister's involvement in shaping the treaty revision was more a matter of responding to a US proposal than of initiating change. Any initiative exercised by Kishi came only after he had ascertained the US intentions. And that was only natural, we need to acknowledge, in view of the power dynamics in the Japanese-US relationship. Kishi worked tirelessly, meanwhile, to mobilize support for the treaty revision in the Japanese government once he had made his decision.

We can well understand Kishi's decision to support the treaty revision in view of his political position. Securing a formal US commitment to defend Japan would make the revised treaty more beneficial for Japan than its predecessor. That promised to help allay Japanese criticism of the treaty's inequity and to place Japanese-US relations on a steadier footing. Kishi could then proceed with his plans for moving against the leftist forces on Japan's political landscape.

Although Kishi's decision to go ahead with the treaty revision on offer possessed an undeniable logic, that decision strikes us as somewhat inconsistent with his goal of balancing Japanese and US security obligations. He might have regarded the 1960 revision as a step toward achieving a more balanced mutual-security arrangement through a future revision. But how or even if he hoped to arrive at a truly mutual security treaty consistent with Japan's constitution is unclear. If he didn't possess a mental roadmap for attaining an equalized treaty before hearing the US proposal, he certainly came to terms quickly with its terms and possibilities.

Kishi's accommodation with the US proposal was most likely something of an ad hoc response to evolving circumstances. That is, MacArthur suggested that the US government might accept a mutualization of the security treaty within the bounds of Japan's constitution, and Kishi mulled that suggestion in reference to domestic political considerations and his political program and accepted the US pledge to defend Japan as the biggest step toward treaty equality feasible at the time.

A compelling obstacle to revising the constitution

Kishi reemerged on the political scene in postwar Japan and laid claim to the office of prime minister almost as a matter of course. He marshalled a razor-sharp intellect; unbounded energy; an extensive network of personal connections, including ties to funding cultivated since his prewar days in the Ministry of Agriculture and Commerce and Ministry of Commerce and Industry; a readiness to take the bull by the horns; astounding good fortune; and political acumen that put experienced party politicians to shame.[98]

An air of cool detachment born of Kishi's background as an elite bureaucrat shaped his persona throughout his political career, and he never enjoyed the popularity that accrued to more approachable politicians, such as Hatoyama. Kishi brought more to politics, however, than just an elite bureaucrat's capacity for performing work flawlessly. He had a clear agenda of political goals, centered on revising the constitution and dispensing with the trappings of the occupation.

Kishi sympathizers established the Japan Reconstruction Federation in April 1952 in advance of the lifting that month of his purge from public service. The federation was a political organization designed to support Kishi's political resurgence. Its platform included the pledge to "Revise the Constitution in accordance with the will of the people and restore a political framework suitable to an independent nation." Kishi accompanied a commitment to fulfilling that goal with capabilities that would have seemed fully up to the task at hand. The Anpo chaos obliged him, however, to resign on July 15, 1960, his supreme political goal unfulfilled. Ikeda Hayato, a disciple of Yoshida, and his successor, Satō Eisaku, were unwilling to pursue it.

Actually, Kishi did worse than simply fail to achieve the revision of the constitution. He left a political environment in which revising the constitution had become more difficult and thus more unlikely than ever. Kishi envisioned the revised security treaty, meanwhile, as a step toward concluding a truly mutual defense pact with the United States. And that goal, too, went unfulfilled.

Kishi commented in an interview with political scientist Itō Takashi on why the LDP couldn't revise the constitution after he left office.

> The individuals most responsible for wasting the opportunity to revise the constitution were Ikeda Hayato and my younger brother, [Satō] Eisaku. They decided to let the constitution take hold and not to tackle changes on their watch. That's why talk of revising the constitution ended with me."[99]

This is, tone aside, true, but it is a somewhat one-sided interpretation.

The Ikeda and Satō governments had good reasons for choosing the courses that they took. Both sought to avoid all-out confrontations with the opposition parties and leftist forces, as occurred in the Anpo disturbances. Both also sought to avoid the kind of schisms in the LDP that had destabilized politics under Kishi. They sought instead to apply the dividends yielded by rapid economic growth to solidifying the conservative orientation of Japanese politics. That meant moving away from such divisive issues as revising the constitution, strengthening the military, or dividing Japan's electoral districts into single-member constituencies.

Kishi's political stance had been a decisive factor in triggering the Anpo disturbances. That served as a backhanded reminder of the value of tolerance and patience and thus engendered a less-assertive stance among his successors. Kishi's own stance, in other words, had heightened the difficulty of revising the constitution. Ikeda and Satō strove to distance themselves and Japan's conservative politics from Kishi and the throwback to prewar politics that he represented. To blame them for failing to achieve the revision of the constitution is disingenuous. For that matter, to suggest that the Anpo disturbances made revising the constitution more difficult is a bit tautological.

That revising the security treaty would cause such a calamitous backlash as the Anpo disturbances surely never occurred to Kishi. He presumably envisioned a straightforward scenario something like this: revise the security treaty, normalize Japanese-US relations, secure the broad backing of public opinion, expand his party's majority, win the next general election, switch the electoral map to a system of single-member districts, and revise the constitution. This scenario, notwithstanding its air of inevitability, harbors a serious logical flaw.

Even if the Anpo disturbances had not occurred, revising the security treaty would not necessarily have segued into constitutional revision. Simply redressing the perceived inequity of the security treaty would greatly diminish the motivation for revising the constitution. Conversely, amending Article 9 of the constitution would not necessarily be a requirement for mutualizing the treaty. Revisions other than that of permitting the dispatching of Japanese troops abroad would make the security treaty more equitable and thus more palatable to the Japanese public.

Kishi thought that mutualizing the security treaty while leaving the constitution unchanged would open a path to constitutional revision later, but he got things backwards. Revising the security treaty functioned more to impede than spur constitutional revision. Kishi's decision to press ahead in the manner that he chose seemed at the time to advance his political program, but we can see in hindsight that it set his program back. The prime minister's formidable political instincts failed him, and he misread the ramifications of his decision. This is perhaps a valuable reminder of the inevitable limitations of any politician, no matter how astute.

Chapter Notes

1 This chapter is an expansion of Sakamoto Kazuya's "Kishi Shushō to Anpo kaitei no ketsudan" [Prime Minister Kishi and the Decision to Revise the Security Treaty], *Handai hōgaku* [Osaka Law Review] 45, no. 1 (June 1995).

2 Hara Yoshihisa, *Kishi Nobusuke: Kensei no seijika* [Kishi Nobusuke: A Politician of Influence] (Tokyo: Iwanami Shoten, 1995), 186–187.

3 Kishi Nobusuke, *Kishi Nobusuke kaikoroku: Hoshu gōdō to Anpo kaitei* [Kishi Nobusuke Memoir: The Conservative Coalition and the Revision of the Security Treaty] (Tokyo: Kōsaidō Shuppan, 1983), 298.

4 US Department of State, *Foreign Relations of the United States* (*FRUS*), 1955–1957 (Washington, DC: Government Printing Office, 1991), Document 183.

5 US Department of State, *FRUS*, 1955–1957, Document 187.

6 This was the mainstream preference in the Foreign Ministry on account of the perceived difficulty of revising the treaty fundamentally. Hara Yoshihisa, *Nichi-Bei kankei no kōzu: Anpo kaitei o kenshō suru* [The Mechanics of the Japanese-US Relationship: An Examination of the Revision of the Security Treaty] (Tokyo: NHK Books, 1991), 60–61.

7 Hara, *Kishi Nobusuke*, 156–157.
8 US Department of State, *Department of State Bulletin* (July 8, 1957), 52.
9 US Department of State, *FRUS*, 1955–1957, Document 159. MacArthur is referring to the fourth of the four objectives cited in Japan's Basic Policy for National Defense. The Japanese government's official translation of the Basic Policy reads as follows:
1. To support the UN activities and promote international cooperation to achieve world peace;
2. To stabilize the livelihood of the people, promote their patriotism, and establish the foundations required for national security;
3. Within the limits required for self-defense, to progressively establish efficient defense capabilities in accordance with the nation's strength and situation;
4. To deal with external acts of aggression based on the Japan-U.S. Security Arrangements, until the United Nations can provide sufficient functions to effectively prevent such acts in the future.

Tanaka Akihiko observes that Kishi hewed to the Yoshida doctrine of increasing Japan's defense capacity gradually in the framework of the Japanese-US security treaty and that he did so "despite his background and his former propensity for rightist rhetoric." *Anzen hoshō: Sengo 50-nen no mosaku* [Military Security: Fifty Postwar Years of Searching] (Tokyo: Yomiuri Shimbunsha, 1997), 158–159.
10 Yasukawa Takeshi, who worked in the Foreign Ministry's European and American Affairs Bureau, gives Kishi credit for being willing, unlike Shigemitsu, to take advice. Yasukawa Takeshi, *Wasureenu omoide to korekara no Nichi-Bei gaikō: Pāruhābā kara hanseiki* [Indelible Memories and the Future of Japanese-US Relations: A Half Century since Pearl Harbor] (Tokyo: Sekai-no-Ugoki-sha, 1991), 55, 59.
11 Tōgō Fumihiko, *Nichi-Bei gaikō 30-nen: Anpo, Okinawa to sono go* [Thirty Years of Japanese-US Diplomacy: The Security Treaty, Okinawa, and Later] (Tokyo: Chuokoronsha, 1989), 53–54.
12 Exchange of Notes regarding the Relationship between the Japan-United States Security Treaty and the Charter of the United Nations, https://www.mofa.go.jp/mofaj/gaiko/treaty/pdfs/A-S38(3)-241.pdf. The governments affirmed through this exchange that "[the] Security Treaty does not affect and shall not be interpreted as affecting in any way the rights and obligations of the two Governments under the Charter of the United Nations or the responsibility of the United Nations for the maintenance of international peace and security." They also affirmed that as "set forth in the Charter of the United Nations, both Governments are obliged to settle any international disputes in which they may be involved by peaceful means in such a manner that international peace and security, and justice, are not endangered and to refrain in their international relations from the threat or use of force against the territorial integrity or political independence of any state, or in any other manner inconsistent with the purposes of the United Nations."
13 For an analysis of public attitudes in Japan toward nuclear weapons, see US Department of State, Office of Intelligence Research, *The Relationship of Japan to*

Nuclear Weapons and Warfare, Intelligence Report No. 7466 (April 22, 1957).

14 *Mainichi Shimbun*, January 17, 1957, evening edition; *Asahi Shimbun*, February 11, 1957, evening edition; US Department of State, *FRUS*, 1955–1957, Document 118.

15 US Department of State, *FRUS*, 1955–1957, Document 187.

16 US Department of State, *Department of State Bulletin* (July 8, 1957), 52.

17 Interview with Douglas MacArthur, II, 16 December 1966, The John Foster Dulles Oral History Collection, Mudd Library, Princeton University.

18 US Department of State, *FRUS*, 1955–1957, Documents 159 and 177.

19 US Department of State, *FRUS*, 1955–1957, Document 187.

20 US Department of State, *Department of State Bulletin* (July 8, 1957), 52.

21 For a discussion of the high regard for Kishi in the US government, see Hara, *Nichi-Bei kankei no kōzu*, 92–95.

22 US Department of State, *FRUS*, 1955–1957, Document 173.

23 Kishi, *Kaikoroku*; Kishi, Yatsugi Kazuo, and Itō Takashi, *Kishi Nobusuke no kaisō* [Kishi Nobusuke's Reminiscences] (Tokyo: Bungeishunjū, 1981), 234; Tōgō, *Nichi-Bei gaikō 30-nen*, 50.

24 US Department of State, *FRUS*, 1955–1957, Document 173.

25 Kitaoka Shinichi, "Kishi Nobusuke: Yashin to zasetsu" [Kishi Nobusuke: Ambition and Foundering], in *Sengo Nihon no saishōtachi* [The Prime Ministers of Postwar Japan], ed. Watanabe Akio (Tokyo: Chuokoronsha, 1995), 138.

26 US Department of State, *FRUS*, 1958–1960 (Washington: Government Printing Office, 1994), Document 3.

27 US Department of State, *FRUS*, 1958–1960, Document 31.

28 For example, commencing negotiations in Tokyo for mutualizing the security treaty did not signify US satisfaction with the Kishi government's defense plan. Uemura Hideki observes that revising the security treaty did not require any military preparations. "Anpo kaitei to Nihon no bōei seisaku" [The Security-Treaty Revision and Japan's Defense Policy], *Kokusai seiji* [International Relations] 115 (May 1997): 31–32.

29 For further discussion of this issue, see Ishii Osamu, *Reisen to Nichi-Bei kankei: Pātonāshippu no keisei* [The Cold War and Japanese-US Relations: The Formation of a Partnership] (Tokyo: Japan Times, 1989).

30 US Department of State, *FRUS*, 1955–1957, Document 115.

31 For further discussion of the Girard Incident, see Mark Schreiber, "Death by Firing Range," *Number 1 Shimbun*, August 2016, Foreign Correspondents' Club of Japan, http://www.test.fccj.or.jp/number-1-shimbun/item/836-death-by-firing-range/836-death-by-firing-range.html.

32 "US-Japanese Security Relations: July–December 1957," US Department of State, Central Files (CF) 794.5/2-1458 (desp. 938), RG 59, National Archives. This report includes the caution, however, that pressure in Japan to revise the security treaty was likely to mount after the general election in 1958. A 1958 book critical of the Japanese-US security treaty cited the following statistics about crimes committed by US military personnel in Japan from October 1953 to December 1956:

Cases accepted by the public prosecutors' office	25,000
Traffic infractions not resulting in accidents	10,000

Traffic accidents	4,000
Violent acts	2,500
Theft or damage of physical property	1,000
Fraud	800
Robbery	272
Robbery-murder	211
Rape	143
Arson	26
Murder	11

Hayashi Katsuya, Andō Toshio, Kimura Kihachirō, *Misairu to Nihon: Kichi no kyōfu* [Missiles and Japan: The Terror of the Bases] (Tokyo: Tōyō Keizai Shinpōsha, 1958), 40.

33 Memorandum of Howe to Robertson, 24 January 1958, Lot File 61 D 68, US Foreign Policy, 1957–58, RG 59, National Archives; cf. US Department of State, *FRUS*, 1958–1960, Document 3.

34 Comments by Marshall Green, a State Department official responsible at the time for Far Eastern affairs, quoted by NHK reporting teams, *NHK Supesharu, sengo 50-nen, sono toki Nihon wa* [NHK Special, 50 Years after the War, Japan Back Then], vol. 1 (Tokyo: NHK, 1995), 251–252.

35 For further discussion of the US administration of Okinawa for the first 20 years after the war, including the US government response to the protests, see Miyazato Seigen, *Amerika no Okinawa tōchi* [US Rule of Okinawa] (Tokyo: Iwanami Shoten, 1966).

36 Report of a Special Subcommittee of the Armed Services Committee, House of Representatives, Following an Inspection Tour October 14 to November 23, 1955 (Washington, DC: Government Printing Office, 1956).

37 C. L. Sulzberger, "An American 'Cyprus' in the Pacific?" *The New York Times*, January 18, 1958.

38 US Department of State, *FRUS*, 1958–1960, Document 7.

39 US Department of State, *FRUS*, 1958–1960, Documents 10 and 16. For further discussion of the concept of returning Okinawa partially to Japanese administration, see Gabe Masaaki, *Nichi-Bei kankei no naka no Okinawa* [Okinawa in Japanese-US Relations] (Tokyo: San-Ichi Shobo, 1996), 117–130.

40 US Department of State, *FRUS*, 1958–1960, Document 16.

41 Okinawa warrants attention in any consideration of the process of negotiating the revision of the security treaty. Kōno Yasuko writes, for example, that letting the US military continue to use its Okinawa bases freely figured crucially. Kōno Yasuko, *Okinawa henkan o meguru seiji to gaikō: Nichi-Bei kankeishi no bunmyaku* [The Politics and Diplomacy of the Return of Okinawa: The Historical Context of Japanese-US Relations] (Tokyo: University of Tokyo Press, 1994), 185.

42 Marshall Green asserts that Sputnik and the Okinawa election were influential in steering the security treaty from the unilateral instrument of the occupation in the 1950s to the mutual agreement concluded in 1960. NHK reporting teams, *NHK Supesharu*, 254.

43 US Department of State, *FRUS*, 1958–1960, Documents 11 and 15; CF 611.94/8-

1858 (tel. 357). For further discussion of MacArthur's initiative in pursuing a revision of the security treaty, see Hara, *Nichi-Bei kankei no kōzu*, ch. 4. MacArthur, soon after becoming ambassador, advocated revising the treaty to Dulles in advance of Kishi's US visit in June 1957. *FRUS*, 1955–1957, Document 159.

On the other hand, the ambassador felt that the time was not right to begin returning Okinawa to Japanese administration. US Department of State, *FRUS*, 1958–1960, Document 9; Gabe, *Nichi-Bei kankei no naka no Okinawa*, 126.

44 US Department of State, *FRUS*, 1955–1957, Document 159.

45 US Department of State, *FRUS*, 1955–1957, Document 159.

46 US Department of State, *FRUS*, 1958–1960, Document 11.

47 US Department of State, *FRUS*, 1958–1960, Document 3; 1955–1957, Document 159.

48 US Department of State, *FRUS*, 1958–1960, Documents 11 and 20; MacArthur to Dulles, 3 March 1958, CF 794.5/3-858.

MacArthur is critical of the "U.S. military view . . . that the Japanese can have 'equal' treaty status when they have 'equal' military forces." He insists that such equality "can never happen because of the disparity in the strength and resources of Japan and the United States." *FRUS*, 1958–1960, Document 11.

49 US Department of State, *FRUS*, 1958–1960, Document 11.

50 US Department of State, *FRUS*, 1958–1960, Documents 3, 11, 15, and 20; cf. Document 171.

51 US Department of State, *FRUS*, 1958–1960, Document 11.

52 US Department of State, *FRUS*, 1958–1960, Document 11.

53 US Department of State, *FRUS*, 1958–1960, Document 20.

54 US Department of State, *FRUS*, 1958–1960, Document 4.

55 For further discussion of MacArthur's basic stance, see US Department of State, *FRUS*, 1955–1957, Document 159; 1958–1960, Documents 4, 12, 15, 20, 42; and CF 794.5/3-858, 794.5/11-1658 (tel. 1049).

56 Richard Sneider, *US-Japanese Security Relations: A Historical Perspective* (New York: Columbia University Press, 1982), 31.

57 Memorandum for Robertson, 23 March 1958, JFD Chronological, March 1958 (2), The John Foster Dulles Papers, Eisenhower Library (Abilene, Kansas); cf. US Department of State, *FRUS*, 1958–1960, Document 5.

58 US Department of State, *FRUS*, 1958–1960, Document 11.

59 US Department of State, *FRUS*, 1958–1960, Document 15.

Kishi met with MacArthur on other business on June 19, 1958, and he took that opportunity to request a meeting to discuss modifications to the security treaty. CF 611.94/6-1958 (tel. 3354); cf. *FRUS*, 1958–1960, Document 16.

MacArthur suggested to Kishi that tackling basic security issues before the general election would be unwise. He cautioned that, on doing so, the issue "would inevitably become enmeshed in the emotional atmosphere of a political campaign." *FRUS*, 1958–1960, Document 15.

60 US Department of State, *FRUS*, 1958–1960, Document 16.

61 *Asahi Shimbun*, May 16, 1958.

62 Telephone Call from the President, March 4, 1958, 4:05 p.m., Telephone Conver-

sation Series, John Foster Dulles Papers, Mudd Library, Princeton University; Memorandum for the President, March 7, 1958; and Eisenhower's letter to Kishi, March 8, 1958, Japan 1957–59 (3), International Series, Ann Whitman File, Eisenhower Library (Abilene, Kansas).

63 US Department of State, *FRUS*, 1958–1960, Document 23. Some portions of the discussions omitted from the *FRUS* file are available in CF 794.5/9-858.

64 US Department of State, *FRUS*, 1958–1960, Document 23. Also interesting is MacArthur's explanation of the proposed treaty revision to representatives of the Defense and State Departments on September 9. Some portions of the discussions omitted from the *FRUS* file are available in CF 794.5/9-958.

65 US Department of State, *FRUS*, 1958–1960, Document 26. Ministry of Foreign Affairs records quote Dulles's response as follows. All the Japanese records of Dulles's remarks and the other discussions at the meetings (quoted in endnotes 72, 77, and Chapter 5's 'Floating a "Personal Proposal"' and endnote 13) were prepared by (then) American Affairs Bureau Security Division Director Tōgō Fumihiko, who interpreted for the attending parties.

> The present Security Treaty had been negotiated with himself [Dulles] as negotiator. I take some satisfaction in the fact that it has served well the purposes for which it was designed under the conditions then obtaining. As the father of the treaty, however, I am not so devoted to it that I would be unwilling to consider changing it, assuming something better would take its place. Of course, it had never been designed to be a permanent and perpetual formula for the regulation of our security arrangements. The treaty itself stated that it was a "provisional" arrangement. I think that the United States is quite prepared to accept the view of the Foreign Minister. . . . The preamble of the treaty indicated that Japan would increasingly assume the responsibility for its own defense against direct and indirect aggression, but that forecast had changed. I do not want to say that the United States considers that what Japan has done has been adequate, but I recognize the limitations of budget which Japan, like others, faces. But even if Japan had done the maximum which might have been expected, I do not believe that in world conditions today any single nation, including the United States, could feel secure without interdependence and unity with the other free nations. We had hoped at the time the Treaty was made, we have hoped since, and we hope today for limitation of arms. But in order to be secure, we must stand together, since demilitarization has not yet happened and is not in prospect. The Foreign Minister has said that matter concerning the world situation would also come out during the conversation. To me, the most disturbing basic fact in the international situation is the stubborn unwillingness of the Soviet Union to do anything which might lead to a reduction in armaments or effectively eliminate nuclear weapons. The Soviet Union concentrates its propaganda on the single item of discontinuing nuclear tests, but this is not a measure which would affect the production or limitation of armaments. The United States, on the other hand, with its Western Allies, has sought the cessation of the use of fissionable materials for weapons and the siphoning off of weapons stocks to peaceful stocks

to diminish the threat, but the Soviet Union rejects this. The Soviet Union increasingly threatens the use of nuclear weapons and missiles. That occurred during the Suez crisis, later on in Syria, and at the time of the threat in Lebanon. The latest letter from Khrushchev to President Eisenhower contains a veiled threat to use nuclear weapons to destroy navies. In the present trouble in the Formosa area, too, the Soviet Union has told the Chinese Communists that the United States is frightened of Soviet nuclear and missile power that the Soviet Union says it will use to aid the Chinese Communists. In the face of that Soviet power and their apparent willingness to threaten its use to impose their will, there is no alternative for the free non-communist nations but to unite their strength. Any nation that wants to remain master of its own destiny needs security relations with others, so that a single pool of power to which each contributes can in total be pledged to protect all. The United States believes that we need dependable relations with Japan, assuming that Japan wants to retain genuine independence and remain master of its own destiny. In the light of these considerations, I am happy that the Japanese Government wants to continue mutual security relations with the United States, and that the question presented by the Foreign Minister is not whether, but how, these relations will evolve. He has mentioned three alternatives and indicated that the preference of the Japanese government is for the first choice: a fresh, new treaty. The United States is quite prepared to accept [that] in principle, with the possibility of reserving the other alternatives to fall back upon if serious difficulty is encountered in reaching a new treaty.

Source: "9-gatsu 11-nichi Fujiyama Daijin–Daresu Kokumu chōkan kaidanroku" [Minutes of the September 11 Meeting between Minister Fujiyama and Secretary of State Dulles] (September 11, 1958), which is included in the "Iwayuru 'mitsuyaku' mondai ni kansuru chōsa, sonota kanren bunsho" [The Investigation into the So-Called Secret Agreements, Other Pertinent Documents], no. 1-15: 160–189, https://www.mofa.go.jp/mofaj/gaiko/mitsuyaku/pdfs/k_1960kaku1.pdf.

Important note about the "secret agreement" documents that the Japanese Foreign Ministry disclosed on its website as PDFs in 2010: No page numbers accompany the PDFs for the investigative reports because those PDFs do not include multiple documents. Therefore, files should not be opened in the browser but rather exported, allowing for reference of the page numbers indicated.

Framing the just weeks-old Second Taiwan Strait Crisis as an example of the Soviet threat, Dulles underscored the need for unity among the nations of the free world in the face of that menacing presence. In that context, he welcomed Japan's hopes for a dependable mutual-security relationship between Japan and the United States and expressed his openness to the possibility of forging a new security treaty.

66 US Department of State, *FRUS*, 1958–1960, Document 18.

67 Kishi takes note of this policy shift by the Socialists in his memoir. Kishi, *Kaikoroku*, 344–351. For further discussion of this subject, see Ōhinata Ichirō, *Kishi seiken: 1241-nichi* [The Kishi Government: 1,241 Days] (Tokyo: Gyōsei Mondai Kenkyūjo, 1985), 120–129.

68 Tōgō, *Nichi-Bei gaikō 30-nen*, 62. Fujiyama writes in his memoir that he urged

Kishi after the general election to undertake the revision of the security treaty. Fujiyama Aiichirō, *Seiji, wagamichi: Fujiyama Aiichirō kaisōroku* [Politics, My Path: Fujiyama Aiichirō Memoir] (Tokyo: Asahi Shimbunsha, 1976), 58–61.

69 Tōgō, *Nichi-Bei gaikō 30-nen*, 58–63.

70 Tōgō, *Nichi-Bei gaikō 30-nen*, 62–63.

71 US Department of State, *FRUS*, 1958–1960, Document 18. Notions of including Okinawa and the Ogasawara Islands in the security treaty were percolating in the Foreign Ministry's Treaties Bureau by early 1957. The idea was to conclude a mutual-defense treaty with the United States that would include those territories. That would exempt them from the constitutional ban on dispatching troops abroad and would neuter constitutional objections to Japanese mainland-based US forces defending the US bases in Okinawa and the Ogasawara Islands. CF 794.5/3-1257 (tel. 1996); CF 794.5/4-557 (desp. 1060).

This recalls a debate that arose among the Japanese negotiators when working out the security treaty of 1952. The question then was whether such action by US forces would constitute collective defense. Portions of MacArthur's telegraphic reporting on his exchanges with Fujiyama remain classified in the US diplomatic archives. The chronology suggests that the redacted portions describe Japanese ideas for de facto treaty revision with a supplementary agreement.

72 After Foreign Minister Fujiyama gave his opening presentation on security issues, he and Ambassador MacArthur shared the following exchange (originally recorded in Japanese).

MacArthur: Thank you for your presentation, Foreign Minister Fujiyama. Let me begin my response by offering my personal reaction to the points you made. Please understand that these are not official remarks on any instruction from the government. First, would I be correct in assuming that Japan believes it would be necessary to establish some kind of long-term security arrangement with the United States? My understanding of your presentation is that, given the major shifts in the global balance of power since the end of World War II and the significant dual threat posed by the Soviet Union and the Chinese Communists, Japan feels it would be unable to ensure its own safety in the current climate and thus wants to form some kind of security framework with the United States with a view to the long term. Is that correct?

Fujiyama: Yes. There have been no changes in that regard. Our basic stance would shift if the global dynamics were to change in the event of a massive worldwide disarmament, for example, but our standpoint will remain the same as long as the Soviet Union and the Chinese Communists have the enormous military might that they currently wield.

MacArthur: US government officials also believe that the safety of Japan represents a benefit not only for Japan itself but also for the United States and all the other free nations of the world. The circumstances would obviously change if the UN were able to establish an effective system for maintaining global peace or countries around the world were to embrace disarmament, for instance, but we believe that the free nations of the world need to continue to maintain a security framework that is dependable and mutually acceptable. Considering the current state of Japanese-US relations, the one-sided nature of the existing security treaty between our two countries poses problems that have become a point of contention in both these meetings and the court of public opinion. I am prepared to do whatever I can to bring this issue to a resolution, but there is something I want to confirm with you first—on a completely personal basis—so that we can start making progress on that front. What I would like to know is whether or not Japan sees mutual-aid arrangements as the best way of ensuring durable Japanese-US security relations. Does Japan want a mutual-aid arrangement but feel unsure about its ability to comply with the corresponding requirements? Or does Japan want to make side arrangements within the structure of the existing treaty to deal with issues as they emerge instead of pursuing the mutual-aid route? If mutual aid is the best route but something is preventing you from committing to that framework, we have to determine what that issue is. There are two options, essentially: we could lay out all the issues and try to create a system that would be durable enough to meet the full scope of corresponding needs over the long term, or we could keep things in a less stable state and continue to take stopgap measures whenever the need arises. Your presentation seemed to leave room for both approaches, so I just first want to know which side your basic preference lies on. Another question I have is if [whether] Japan is looking for a treaty similar to the United States' mutual-aid treaties with other countries, which include provisions on offering mutual aid in accordance with constitutional stipulations and defined treaty periods.

Fujiyama: In terms of revising the existing security treaty into one stipulating mutually equal obligations, the constitutional restrictions in Japan would make it impossible to create a completely equal treaty. We are therefore not seeking to make the existing treaty completely equal. However, the existing treaty contains numerous provisions whose stipulations or the implementation thereof were established unilaterally by the United States. The fact that the treaty was created at a time when Japan had no self-defense capabilities makes its one-sided nature even more problematic, too. We find it unsatisfactory that the treaty functions under the unilateral intentions of the United States alone. If we were able to find a way to implement the treaty in a way that incorporates Japan's intentions through equal dialogue, that would effect, to some extent, a substantive revision. And if both sides were to reach a basic understanding of that arrangement, I believe that we would be able to arrive at a rather durable solution that would eliminate the need to address problems individually, as they arise.

MacArthur: Do the "constitutional restrictions" you mentioned mean issues concerning Japan's dispatching troops overseas?

Fujiyama: The constitutional restrictions prevent Japan from sending its self-defense forces to the United States. We cannot dispatch them to Korea, either. The very existence of the self-defense forces, for that matter, is only possible under the broadest constitutional interpretation.

MacArthur: Just to clarify, would it be constitutionally possible to limit the geographical scope of the treaty to the Japan area and thereby enable mutual aid without obligating Japan to send forces abroad? Would that sort of arrangement raise any other issues outside of the constitutionality question?

Fujiyama: The self-defense forces cannot leave Japan. Are you referring to having US and Japanese forces do joint operations in Japan, without the self-defense forces leaving the country?

MacArthur: It was just a hypothetical example. At any rate, it sounds as if the obstacle complicating the mutual-aid approach is the issue of sending troops abroad, which would only be possible through revisions to the Japanese constitution. Of course, a constitutional amendment is something that only the country concerned can undertake. The process of revising the constitution obviously depends on the political climate of the time and other specific circumstances affecting the country in question, so the United States thus has no intention to have any say on that point. On an entirely personal basis, my question is this: assuming that the Japanese constitution did allow for the mutual-aid approach, would Japan see mutual aid as the optimal solution? Or, even if the possibility of a mutual-aid approach were in play, would Japan prefer to keep the existing treaty as is or make minor adjustments to the wording and continue handling issues as they come up? What would be your general preference at this stage?

Fujiyama: A completely equal mutual-aid agreement would naturally entail provisions for dispatching Japan's self-defense forces to the United States, and that would be impossible without amending the Japanese constitution. In that sense, we will not be able to make the treaty completely mutual, regardless of the arrangements we make. Japan's aim is to eliminate the one-sidedness of the existing treaty. To do that, we would need either to revise the treaty or to keep it as is and establish side arrangements accordingly. However, given the potential political challenges of revising the treaty, the side-arrangement approach would appear to be the more appropriate option.

MacArthur: Just to be clear, would the mutual-aid approach be possible under the terms of the Japanese constitution?

Fujiyama: Yes.

MacArthur: Understood.

MacArthur thus sought to determine exactly how Japan envisioned establishing a long-term security relationship with the United States under a security treaty absent of any one-sided characteristics: revising the treaty into a constitutionally feasible mutual-aid agreement or opting for an approach involving supplementary arrangements. In response, Fujiyama told MacArthur that the latter was the more suitable choice. In the line and tone of MacArthur's questioning, however, one can see signs that he was hoping Fujiyama would opt for the revision approach. Apparently unsatisfied with Fujiyama's answers, MacArthur went through another round of questions after this initial exchange. A member of MacArthur's team, Richard L. Sneider, suggested that the ambassador might need to make his views clearer, prompting MacArthur to float the same question one more time.

MacArthur: Let me ask you again: Assuming that it were possible to conclude a mutual security treaty that would not contractually bind Japan to sending troops abroad, would Japan be willing to consider a new treaty?

Fujiyama told MacArthur that, while a new treaty would be ideal from a political perspective, Japan would need time to weigh the advisability of the approach. Telling his counterpart that the matter was "extremely important" and would require a "political judgment," Fujiyama said that he would discuss the issue with Prime Minister Kishi and hoped to have a three-way discussion with MacArthur and Kishi if necessary.

Sources: "7-gatsu 30-nichi Fujiyama Daijin zaikyō Bei taishi kaidanroku" [Minutes of July 30 Meeting between Minister Fujiyama and US Ambassador to Tokyo], July 31, 1958; "Sonota kanren bunsho" [Other Pertinent Documents], no. 1-9: 96–108, https://www.mofa.go.jp/mofaj/gaiko/mitsuyaku/pdfs/k_1960kaku1.pdf.

The presentation that Fujiyama gave at the beginning of the meeting to explain Japan's basic stance was from a script prepared by administrative staff members. The script contains the following passage:

> Next, I would like to take a look at the issues that you want to see addressed in the existing security-treaty framework—issues that would obviously come into play in discussions of a new, mutual-aid treaty after we make our way through the more pressing problems at hand. The key question is whether the United States would deem it sufficient for Japan to make three guarantees—providing defense cooperation within the scope of its constitution, lending bases, and offering backup cooperation—as its responsibilities in a mutual-aid treaty. That type of arrangement would also require close and careful attention, as it would also have significant political ramifications for Japan.

Sources: "Anzen hoshō ni kansuru tōmen no shomondai ni tsuite (Daijin setsumeian)" [Current Issues Pertaining to Security (Draft of the Foreign Minister's Remarks)], July 26, 1958; "Sonota kanren bunsho," no. 1-8: 90–95, https://www.mofa.go.jp/mofaj/gaiko/mitsuyaku/pdfs/k_1960 kaku 1.pdf.

As explained previously, American records indicate that Fujiyama noted at the start of the meeting that the Foreign Ministry had discussed the option of signing a mutual security treaty not involving Japan sending its forces overseas. The above section of Fujiyama's address was probably referring to those discussions. Officials at the Ministry of Foreign Affairs were actually discussing different proposals: one involved making adjustments to establish a security treaty based on a mutual-aid arrangement, and the other was a draft of a brand-new treaty rooted in the concept of mutual security, "Anzen hoshō jōyaku" (A-an)" [Security Treaty (Draft A)].

Article 1 of the latter proposal (Draft A) was as follows:

> Should the peace of the Far East be breached by an armed attack against Japan and an armed attack against the United States, either simultaneously or subsequently, the governments of both countries shall provide each other with the necessary assistance.

Article 2 read:

> Should an imminent threat to the peace of the Far East arise, the governments of both countries must consult with one another.

Article 4, meanwhile, stipulated the following provisions:

1. To achieve the objectives stipulated in Article 1 promptly and effectively, the US government shall deploy troops in the Japan area at the request of the government of Japan.
2. The number of US troops deployed in Japan, the primary equipment thereof, and the facilities and areas in Japan provided for the use thereof shall be determined based on the agreement of the governments of both countries.
3. The status of US troops deployed in Japan shall be stipulated in a separate agreement.

The mutual-treaty proposal has the same core essentials as the new security treaty that took shape through the process of revising the security treaty: mutual aid, considerations for emergencies in the Far East, and the lending of bases to the United States (with the deployment and equipment of US troops requiring a separate agreement between Japan and the United States), for example. The proposal did not, however, include the political and economic clauses in Article 2 of the new security treaty or the "Vandenberg clause" in Article 3.

Source: "Anzen hoshō jōyaku" (A-an)," July 8, 1958, "Sonota kanren bunsho," no. 1-6: 78–89, https://www.mofa.go.jp/mofaj/gaiko/mitsuyaku/pdfs/k_1960kaku1.pdf.

Fujiyama's scripted address at the meeting ("Anzen hoshō ni kansuru tōmen no shomondai ni tsuite (Daijin setsumeian)" [Current Issues Pertaining to Security (Draft of the Foreign Minister's Remarks)]) included a description of the Foreign Ministry's ideas for making adjustments via mutual-aid arrangements.

73 Tōgō, *Nichi-Bei gaikō 30-nen*, 66; CF 611.94/8-1858 (tel. 357).

74 MacArthur reported to the State Department in a telegram of June 5, 1958, that "Fujiyama has alerted me that following the formation of the new Japanese Cabinet, he and Kishi wish to have serious, confidential discussions with me regarding basic security problems, including revision of the US-Japan Security Treaty."

He expressed the view that only two courses of action were open to the US government. "The first," wrote MacArthur disparagingly, "would be to resist revising the security treaty and make piecemeal adjustments in our security arrangements, (i.e., on nuclears, deployment and use of US forces in Japan, etc.) giving in reluctantly inch by inch as the pressure and public opinion mount against us. This, I think, would be a disastrous course to follow and could lead to steady erosion of our position in Japan as forces favoring neutralism gain ground by appealing to public sentiment against the inequalities in the present security treaty. The alternative course of action," MacArthur offered affirmatively, "would be for US to take constructive initiative, when Kishi raises this matter with me, looking toward a new treaty."

MacArthur accompanied his analysis with a caveat and an optimistic prognosis: "Until this matter is discussed with Kishi, I cannot of course say with certainty what his reaction will be to a new treaty even with the limited treaty and concept. However, I think that there is a good prospect of success and, in any event, the very fact that we have offered such a mutual defense treaty will have beneficial effect on those Japanese who were convinced we intend to hold onto our treaty rights to the bitter end." US Department of State, *FRUS*, 1958–1960, Document 15.

75 We have indirect evidence in a comment by MacArthur in the September 8, 1958, discussion in Washington, DC, with Dulles, Robertson, and other members of the State Department in Washington, DC. The minutes of the discussion summarize that comment in the third person as follows: "Prime Minister Kishi himself proposed such a treaty a month or two after Ambassador MacArthur, on the basis of the Secretary's instructions, had opened the matter with him last spring." US Department of State, *FRUS*, 1958–1960, Document 23.

MacArthur's comment, if accurate, suggests that Kishi had proposed revising the treaty to the ambassador at least by the end of July. No documentation remains, however, of Kishi having made such a proposal to MacArthur in that time frame. If he had, the ambassador surely would have reported it to the State Department, and a record of that report would remain. MacArthur was fastidious about reporting any exchanges with Kishi, as in his telegrams of August 18 (CF 611.94/8-1858, tel. 357) and August 26 (CF 611.94/8-2658, tel. 444).

As noted, the ambassador received instructions from Dulles on June 23 to "probe possibilities with Foreign Minister and Prime Minister." MacArthur might have misspoken in referring to "summer" instead of "spring" in his September 8 comment. We know that he met privately with Kishi on July 11 (see endnote 81) and that the prime minister mentioned at that time having devoted consideration to revising the security treaty but that he did not offer a concrete proposal. CF 611.94/7-1358 (tel. 86).

76 MacArthur dispatched this telegram on August 1 after meeting with Fujiyama on July 30. In it, he describes the two options of preparing a supplementary agreement to redress the treaty's shortcomings and revising the treaty fundamentally and outlines the pros and cons of each option. US Department of State, *FRUS*, 1958–1960, Document 20.

MacArthur subsequently discussed the issues unofficially with Kishi, with

Fujiyama, and with other members of the Foreign Ministry to ascertain their positions and reported his findings to the State Department in a telegram of August 18. The ambassador explained that Kishi was considering the two options, that he was leaning toward that of revising the treaty fundamentally, and that dropping the US demand that Japan be prepared to dispatch troops abroad would encourage that choice. CF 611.94/8-1858 (tel. 357).

77 Tōgō, *Nichi-Bei gaikō 30-nen*, 64. According to Foreign Ministry records, Prime Minister Kishi, Foreign Minister Fujiyama, and Ambassador MacArthur had the following discussion at a meeting at the foreign minister's official residence on the evening of August 25, 1958.

Kishi: . . . I understand that you will be departing (temporarily returning to the United States) on September 1, Mr. Ambassador.

MacArthur: The plan is to leave on the first, yes, but there are two or three matters that I would like to discuss with the both of you before that. First is the issue of how to progress with adjustments to the Japan-US security agreement. Foreign Minister Fujiyama and I reached the conclusion at our recent discussion [July 30] that there are two possible ways of approaching the issue at hand, and it would be extremely helpful to hear your thoughts on which of the approaches would be more advisable. Foreign Minister Fujiyama's visit to the United States [Fujiyama eventually met with Dulles in the United States on September 11; see endnote 65] was too short for actual negotiations, but we believe that we were able to lay a foundation for progress by establishing the two methods for consideration. One is to keep the existing one-sided treaty as is and make supplementary side arrangements to address individual issues as they arise. The other is to make radical changes to the one-sided treaty and create a new, mutual treaty that conforms to the Japanese constitution and does not obligate Japan to send troops abroad. Foreign Minister Fujiyama and I were unable to reach a final conclusion on the optimal solution, and I, personally, cannot make a definitive statement at this point on whether either proposal would be feasible. If possible, we would like to hear what you think, Mr. Prime Minister.

Kishi: (To Fujiyama) Where do the discussions at the Ministry stand?

Fujiyama: (Responding to Kishi) The issue is on hold because we need your approval to make a final decision, sir. I have told officials at the Ministry that I would bring the matter up for discussion with you in attendance, and I will report back to them with whatever you have to add today. Opting for a new treaty would create some challenges in dealing with the Diet, for example, but everything would come out on a fresh, clean slate if we were to clear that hurdle. The other option would involve "mutual-aid arrangements" via exchanges of notes, an approach with no political burden but also no real sense of a fresh slate. Either way, the Ministry understands that we need to hear your stance on the issue before anything can happen.

Kishi: This is what I think. If possible, it would be best to overhaul the existing treaty. Radical revisions would surely prompt heated debate in the Diet, just as it would stir controversy in the US Congress. But I think that debate would be a good thing. Things today are different from what they were when the security treaty first took effect. My cabinet's basic policy is to make the security treaty the foundation of a new relationship of understanding and cooperation in Japanese-US relations. From that standpoint, then, I think it would be best to put the issues up for discussion. Yes, the debate will be heated—but once we make it past that stage, I think we'll be able to put Japanese-US relations on a stable foundation over time. Discussion is the first step toward making a new treaty possible. The Socialist Party will fling barbs at the Conservative cabinet over defense issues, but I think a new treaty system would be able to help the Japanese people's prepare for a new future. I think this is the right way to build up a firm basis for Japanese-US relations. However, rebuilding the treaty from square one could take quite a bit of time, especially considering the challenges that could emerge on the American side. If that process proved prohibitive, we would have to go with agreements via exchanges of notes or some kind of measure that would avoid involving the Security Committee. I like the idea of creating a new treaty, which I think would be good for Japanese-US relations on the whole–but if that would take too much time, the only option we have would be to adopt a mid-range perspective and handle two or three issues first.

MacArthur: By "two or three issues," do you mean the points that the Foreign Minister brought up about using the US forces in Japan and introducing nuclear weapons?

Kishi: Correct.

[Remainder of the exchange omitted]

Source: "8-gatsu 25-nichi sōri, gaimu daijin, zaikyō Bei taishi kaidanroku" [Minutes of August 25 Meeting between the Prime Minister, Foreign Minister, and US Ambassador to Tokyo], August 25, 1958, "Sonota kanren bunsho," no. 1-12: 116–133, https://www.mofa.go.jp/mofaj/gaiko/mitsuyaku/pdfs/k_1960kaku1.pdf.

78 US Department of State, *FRUS*, 1958–1960, Document 23.

79 US Department of State, *FRUS*, 1958–1960, Document 23.

80 CF 611.94/8-2658 (tel. 444).

81 Hara, *Nichi-Bei kankei no kōzu*, 123–124.

82 CF 794.00/7-1258 (tel. 83). The US archival documentation records that Kishi, accompanied only by Matsumoto Takizō as interpreter, met privately with MacArthur on the night of July 11.

83 US Department of State, *FRUS*, 1958–1960, Document 23; CF 794.00/8-2258 (tel. 407).

84 CF 611.94/8-2658 (tel. 444).

85 CF 611.94/8-1858 (tel. 357).

86 MacArthur to Parsons, 29 July 1959, CF 794.00/7-2958. This matter later received coverage in all leading Japanese newspapers; for example, *Mainichi Shimbun*, October 10, 1994. It also became a subject of lawmakers' comments in the Diet. The US historian Michael Schaller writes that cash payments from the CIA to the LDP began after Japan's 1958 general election and continued for at least 10 years and that some opposition parties also received cash payments from the CIA. Michael Schaller, *Altered States: The United States and Japan since the Occupation* (Oxford: Oxford University Press, 1997), 135–136.

The cash payments from the US government to Japanese politicians are testimony to the era's blurred lines between domestic politics and international relations. Satō believed that Communist elements in Japan were receiving financial support from China and the Soviet Union. He regarded the Japanese and US governments as comrades in the struggle against Communism and surely saw nothing extraordinary in securing US financial assistance for the struggle. Satō assured the embassy staffer, of course, that any payments would remain strictly confidential and would not become an embarrassment to the US government.

87 US Department of State, *FRUS*, 1958–1960, Document 89.

88 Tōgō, *Nichi-Bei gaikō 30-nen*, 95.

89 US Department of State, *FRUS*, 1958–1960, Document 110. For further discussion of the process of negotiating the revision of the security treaty and its administrative agreement, see Tōgō, *Nichi-Bei gaikō 30-nen*, 86–101, and Hara, *Nichi-Bei kankei no kōzu*, ch. 5.

90 For further discussion of how the treaty-revision negotiations interacted with Japan's domestic political dynamics and of how the treaty revision came to determine Kishi's political fortunes and to shape the subsequent political process in Japan, see Hara Yoshihisa, *Sengo Nihon to kokusai seiji: Anpo kaitei no seiji rekigaku* [Postwar Japan and International Relations: The Political Dynamics of the Security-Treaty Revision] (Tokyo: Chuokoronsha, 1988). For the classic research work on the security-treaty revision, see George Packard, *Protest in Tokyo: The Security Treaty Crisis of 1960* (Westport: Greenwood Press, 1966). For a highly readable contemporary account of the Anpo disturbances, see Hidaka Rokurō, ed., *1960, 5-gatsu 19-nichi* [May 19, 1960] (Tokyo: Iwanami Shoten, 1960).

For a more recent account of the disturbances, see NHK reporting teams, *NHK Supesharu*. For an analytical perspective on the attempted revision of the Police Duties Execution Act, see Hatakeyama Hirobumi, "Keishokuhō kaisei to seijiteki rīdāshippu" [The Revision of the Police Duties Execution Act and Political Leadership], in Ōtake Hideo, ed., *Nihon seiji no sōten: Jirei kenkyū ni yoru seiji taisei no bunseki* [The Issues in Japanese Politics: Analyzing the Political System through Research on Concrete Examples] (Tokyo: San-Ichi Shobo, 1984).

91 In regard to the character of the Anpo disturbances as a fundamentally anti-Kishi phenomenon, Iwanaga Kenkichirō writes as follows: "The pros and cons of revising the security treaty were difficult for ordinary people to understand and elicited a suspension of rational judgment. When the government needed to press ahead with the revision before people's doubts had been resolved, the people felt instinctively that they needed to halt the [legislative process], and they responded

by calling for Kishi's resignation and for the dissolution of the Diet." *Sengo Nihon no seitō to gaikō* [Political Parties and Diplomacy in Postwar Japan] (Tokyo: University of Tokyo Press, 1985), 153.

Kōsaka Masataka writes that protesting the diplomacy of the treaty revision allowed Japanese to express their hopes and concerns for their nation. He cites four elements in the protests: pacifism and other kinds of idealism, a nationalistic urge to speak up to the United States, the influence of the Marxist-Leninist worldview, resistance to the Kishi government's moves to shape a strong nation-state on the prewar model. Kōsaka argues that the fourth of these elements was the most influential. "Kishi Nobusuke to sengo seiji" [Kishi Nobusuke and Postwar Politics], *Voice*, November 1987; also in Iokibe Makoto, Sakamoto Kazuya, Nakanishi Hiroshi, and Sako Susumu, eds., *Kōsaka Masataka chosakushū*, vol. 4 (Tokyo: Toshi Shuppan, 2000).

Kishi reflected humorously in his later years on the tendency of people at the time to oppose anything that he proposed. "I recall a comment by an editorial writer at the *Asahi Shimbun* whose name I've forgotten. He said he'd been a proponent of revising the constitution but felt obliged to oppose the revision as long as Kishi was behind it. That was pretty irritating to hear at the time, but in retrospect, what he was saying sort of makes sense [laughs]. Sometimes, things require a change in personalities." Kishi, Yatsugi, and Itō, *Kishi Nobusuke no kaisō*, 277.

92 Japan Ministry of Foreign Affairs, Agreement under Article VI of the Treaty of Mutual Cooperation and Security between Japan and the United States of America, https://www.mofa.go.jp/mofaj/area/usa/sfa/pdfs/fulltext.pdf. For further discussion of the revision of the administrative agreement, see Aketagawa Tōru, *Nichi-Bei gyōsei kyōtei no seijishi*, ch. 5.

Some LDP members opposed deleting the passage that had authorized US troops to participate in quelling domestic unrest. They were concerned about leaving Japan exposed to "indirect aggression." Representatives of the Japanese and US governments discussed preparing a record of separate understanding to address that concern, but they abandoned that idea in the end. US Department of State, *FRUS*, 1958–1960, Documents 101, 106, 112, 126, 128, and 129.

93 The "quid pro quo" (base access in exchange for security) remained in place. Looking back from the current vantage point, however, one can appreciate just how significant it was that the treaty revisions made the security treaty a mutual one. The shift unquestionably laid the groundwork for what would transpire between the Japanese and US governments, which worked together to cultivate the mutuality of their cooperative security relationship and forge an alliance as "equal partners" (p. 273).

In the alliance, both parties must "cooperate with each other" in a manner that is "with and for each other": for mutual security and benefit. The treaty revisions thus gave the pact a degree of mutuality in verbalizing the element of acting in the interest of "each other." Several portions of the new treaty underscore the governments' commitment to working "with and for each other." In the preamble, for example, is a passage declaring that Japan and the United States "have a common concern in the maintenance of international peace and security in the

Far East." The point of this stipulation was to make it clear that the treaty was a pact binding Japan and the United States "with and for each other" instead of having the United States simply protect Japan, as the former treaty stipulated, and reframe the agreement as serving the shared objective of the "maintenance of the peace and security of the Far East."

In addition, Article 5 of the new treaty stipulates that the United States recognizes an armed attack against Japan as "dangerous to its own peace and safety"; if the safety of Japan is one and the same as the safety of the United States, it follows that protecting Japan is a means of Japan and the United States acting "with and for each other." Article 6 of the new treaty defines the use of bases by the US military as contributing to the "security of Japan" and "the maintenance of international peace and security in the Far East," thereby connoting that the lending of bases is a form of cooperation "with and for each other."

In terms of "cooperating with each other," the countries had already established what amounted to a mutual-cooperation system in the form of a quid-pro-quo framework, as I explain elsewhere in the text. Articles 5 and 6 of the new treaty present the United States' obligations to defend Japan and Japan's obligations to provide bases to the United States, respectively. While Article 5 may confine the scope of armed attacks warranting action to "territories under the administration of Japan," it nonetheless positions the corresponding responses of the self-defense forces and American military as mutual-defense obligations against the "common danger" of any attack "against either party." The former quid (bases) pro quo (American military) had become quid (self-defense forces) pro quid (American military), so to speak.

After the revisions to the treaty were complete, the Japanese and US governments proceeded to flesh out the concept of mutuality central to the security pact by acting "with and for each other" and maintaining a commitment to "cooperate with each other." The history of the Japanese-US alliance is essentially the history of how these two dimensions of mutuality have developed.

94 Kishi, *Kaikoroku*, 312. For further discussion of this strategic notion and of its failure, see Hiwatari Yumi, "Kishi gaikō ni okeru Tōnan Ajia to Amerika" [Southeast Asia and the United States in Kishi Diplomacy], in Kindai Nihon Kenkyūkai [Society of Modern Japanese Studies], ed., *Nenpō kindai Nihon kenkyū* [Journal of Modern Japanese Studies], vol. 11, *Kyōchō seisaku no genkai: Nichi-Bei kankeishi, 1905–1960* [The Limits of Collaboration-Oriented Policy: The History of Japanese-US Relations, 1905–1960] (Tokyo: Yamakawa Shuppansha, 1989).

95 Hara, *Nichi-Bei kankei no kōzu*, 124–125, 198–199; Hara, *Sengo Nihon to kokusai seiji*, 184, 594.

96 As I have noted elsewhere, a wealth of Foreign Ministry records on revisions to the security treaty have become available after this book's first publication via requests to the Foreign Ministry for information disclosure, documents that the Ministry of Foreign Affairs released through its 2009–2010 "Iwayuru 'mitsuyaku' mondai ni kansuru chōsa" [The Investigation into the So-Called 'Secret Agreements'] ("Hōkoku taishō bunsho" [Documents Covered by the Report], "Sonota kanren bunsho"), and scheduled releases. However, none of the documents that I

have seen present any evidence offering new interpretations of Kishi's stances on the issues.

97 Hara, *Nichi-Bei kankei no kōzu*, 123.

98 For a biographical discussion of Kishi, see Yoshimoto Shigeyoshi, *Kishi Nobusuke den* [A Biography of Kishi Nobusuke] (Tokyo: Tōyō Shokan, 1957); Kōsaka Masataka, *Saishō Yoshida Shigeru* [Yoshida Shigeru as Prime Minister] (Tokyo: Chuokoronsha, 1968), in *Kōsaka Masataka chosakushū*, vol. 4, 108–128; Kōsaka, *Kishi Nobusuke to sengo seiji*; Hara, *Kishi Nobusuke*; Kitaoka, *Kishi Nobusuke*; Shiota Ushio, *Kishi Nobusuke* (Tokyo: Kodansha, 1996); and Iwami Takao, *Kishi Nobusuke: Shōwa no kakumeika* [Kishi Nobusuke: Showa Revolutionary] (Tokyo: Gakuyo Shobo, 1999).

99 Kishi, Yatsugi, and Itō, *Kishi Nobusuke no kaisō*, 123. Putting in place a national framework suitable to an independent state was part of LDP founding policy. That policy called for revising the constitution autonomously; changing or eliminating legal features of the occupation; acquiring the capacity for self-defense, including a revised security treaty with the United States; and ensuring civil order.

Chapter 5

Issues for the New Treaty

Geographical scope and prior consultation

Foreign Minister Fujiyama Aiichirō (*left*) in conversation with Ambassador Douglas MacArthur II (*right*) at the Japanese Foreign Ministry. May 1959. Photo from Mainichi Shimbunsha

A lack of reciprocity marred the Treaty of Mutual Cooperation and Security, which Japan and the United States concluded in 1960. That treaty was a revised incarnation of the Security Treaty Between the United States and Japan, concluded in 1951. The original treaty had entitled the United States to maintain military bases in Japan without formally obliging it to defend Japan. That imbalance had earned opprobrium for the treaty among the Japanese people.

An obvious solution to the first treaty's unilateral framing would have been for the two nations to undertake balanced obligations. The United States would pledge to defend Japan from third-party aggression, and Japan would pledge to defend the United States if the latter's homeland were attacked by a third party. As we saw in Chapter 4, that was not feasible. Japan could not undertake such a pledge, even on a pro forma basis. Domestic resistance to wholesale rearmament was implacable, and resistance from Japan's neighbors, who had suffered mightily from Japanese aggression, was equally stubborn.

US strategic objectives and a tolerant acknowledgement of Japan's strategic limitations underlay the US's acquiescence to the 1960 compromise that was the Treaty of Mutual Cooperation and Security. The United States agreed to undertake the obligation to defend Japan in exchange for Japan's agreement to host US military bases. That pretense of reciprocity wilted, however, under scrutiny.

The 1960 Japanese-US treaty compares poorly with regard to reciprocity with, for example, the North Atlantic Treaty and the mutual defense treaty between the Philippines and the United States. That occasioned spirited debate in the US Senate, though the treaty ultimately won passage by a large, 90–2 margin.[1] Even more challenging were the tasks of rationalizing the treaty in the context of Japan's constitution and winning over Japanese public opinion to the pact.

In this chapter, we will focus on two issues central to the treaty revision: geographical scope and prior consultation. We will examine those issues in reference to the question of reciprocity.[2]

1 The Significance of Geographical Scope

From "Western Pacific" to "Pacific"

US ambassador to Japan Douglas MacArthur II submitted the aforementioned original proposal for a revised Japanese-US security treaty to Secretary of State John Foster Dulles on February 18, 1958. His proposal called for the United States and Japan to undertake obligations to come to the defense of the other. Each would regard an armed attack on specified territory of the other as a threat to its own peace and security. It provided that either nation should respond accordingly to such an attack in accordance with its "constitutional processes."[3]

MacArthur's specified territory was "all territory under the administrative control of Japan and the island territories in the Western Pacific which are referred to in Article III of the Treaty of Peace with Japan and which are under the administrative control of the United States of America." The Article 3 territories of the peace treaty were "Nansei Shoto [Southwest Islands] south of 29° north latitude (including the Ryukyu [Okinawa] Islands and the Daito Islands), Nanpo Shoto south of Sofu Gan (including the Bonin [Ogasawara] Islands, Rosario Island and the Volcano Islands) and Parece Vela and Marcus Island."[4] A note to MacArthur's proposal cites the US-Philippine mutual defense treaty and Shigemitsu Mamoru's treaty proposal (see Chapter 3) as reference sources for geographical scope.

That MacArthur would have submitted such a proposal on his own initiative is somewhat curious, for the implicit call for Japan to be prepared to dispatch troops abroad is counter to his expressed stance. MacArthur had opined that a revised security treaty should position Japan as a geopolitical partner for the United States in Asia. He had argued additionally that Japan could fulfill its role in the partnership fully by hosting US military bases. MacArthur believed, in other words, that Japanese readiness to dispatch troops abroad needn't be a condition for mutuality in a new treaty.

The Philippine-US security treaty and the Shigemitsu proposal were mutual arrangements that provided unequivocally for Japan to pledge to defend US territory. MacArthur's reference to "Western Pacific" mirrored the geography of the Shigemitsu proposal and seemed at first glance to stretch Japan's defensive obligations across a vast swath of territory. In fact, the ambassador had delineated those potential obligations narrowly.

Western Pacific "territory under the administrative control" of Japan meant the four main Japanese islands; smaller islands that had remained under Japanese control; and the Amami Islands, which had reverted to Japanese sovereignty in 1953. It did not include, of course, the Southern Kurile Islands, which Japan claimed but which were under the control of the Soviet Union.

The Western Pacific "territory under the administrative control" of the United States meant only Okinawa and the Ogasawara Islands. Ambassador MacArthur had inserted a caveat that exempted permanent US territory, such as Guam, from the scope of Japan's defensive obligations. He did so in the belief that limiting Japan's defensive obligations narrowly would avoid a conflict with the Japanese constitution.

MacArthur's judgment reflected his understanding of thinking in the Japanese government. Officials in the Treaties Bureau of Japan's Foreign Ministry had formulated an idea for a revised security treaty in early 1957 and had submitted it to the US embassy in March for consideration.[5] That idea included broadening the scope of the joint Japanese-US defense obligations to include Okinawa and the Ogasawara Islands, in addition to Japan's four main islands and the smaller islands that were unambiguously Japanese territory.

The Treaties Bureau officials explained that their idea offered the advantage of preempting objections from Japan's opposition parties. Those parties would reject any treaty revision that provided for dispatching Japanese troops abroad as a violation of Japan's constitution. They were unlikely, however, to regard the past and future Japanese territories of Okinawa and the Ogasawara Islands as "abroad."

MacArthur believed in the possibility of concluding a mutual defense treaty with Japan that would cover "the Japan area," and he expressed that belief in a letter to Dulles of May 25, 1957. In State Department parlance, "the Japan area" included Okinawa and the Ogasawara Islands.[6]

To be sure, MacArthur was unenthusiastic about formalizing a Japanese obligation to participate in defending Okinawa and the Ogasawara Islands. He regarded Japanese participation in the defense framework for those territories as unnecessary from the standpoint of military strategy, and he feared that Japanese participation would impinge on the US military's latitude in using its bases. The ambassador was especially concerned about the danger of crimping US latitude in moving nuclear weapons through or into the bases.[7]

MacArthur's foremost priority was on producing a treaty that would somehow commit Japan to defending territory beyond its border. His solution was to incorporate a defensive obligation in the Western Pacific that would be acceptable to the Japanese. That, he hoped, would clear the way for future Japanese participation in a multilateral defense framework in that region.[8]

The "Western Pacific" reference in MacArthur's proposal underwent a change when the State Department went to work in earnest on a revised treaty. Officials in the department felt that MacArthur's proposal was overly deferential to Japan's circumstances at the time. They called for broadening the geographical scope of mutual defense obligations to the "Pacific," from the "Western Pacific." And they included in that scope all territory in the Pacific under the permanent ownership or then under the administrative control of either nation. That would mean obliging Japan to participate in defending Guam and Hawaii but not the continental United States. The view in the State Department was that the broadened scope of mutual defense obligations would secure Senate approval more easily.[9]

Neither MacArthur nor his State Department colleagues equated a Japanese obligation to participate in defending US territories in the Pacific with an obligation to dispatch troops abroad. All recognized the need for reconciling the treaty provisions with the Japanese constitution. That very recognition underlay, however, the difference between the ambassador and his colleagues in Washington, DC.

The State Department officials in Washington, DC, agreed that the treaty provisions should and would comply with the Japanese constitution. Any defense obligations that Japan undertook, they reasoned, would be in compliance with the constitution, so the treaty needn't confine the geographical scope of mutual defense obligations to the Western Pacific.

Japan could participate in responding to an attack on Hawaii, for example, without dispatching troops. It could fulfill its mutual defense obligation by assisting the US military response through measures permitted by the Japanese constitution. Accommodating Japan's constitutional strictures like this, reasoned the State Department officials, would accommodate its constitution for the time being, and Japan could assume broadened mutual defense responsibilities without necessitating treaty revision as its circumstances evolved.[10]

MacArthur presented Prime Minister Kishi and Foreign Minister Fujiyama with a draft proposal for a revised security treaty on October 4, 1958. That draft reflected the State Department thinking described above, as in the following passage:

> Each Party recognizes that an armed attack in the Pacific directed against the territories or areas under the administrative control of the other Party would be dangerous to its own peace and safety and declares that it would act to meet the common danger in accordance with its constitutional processes.[11]

The October 4 meeting between MacArthur, Kishi, and Fujiyama marked the beginning of formal negotiations on revising the security treaty. Thereafter, the US negotiators emphasized to the Japanese that the draft mirrored the US security pacts with the Republic of Korea, with the Philippines, and with Australia and New Zealand.[12] They insisted that, in view of congressional considerations, this was the only format to which their government could agree. The US negotiators also insisted, however, that each nation's actions under the treaty should be in compliance with its constitution.[13]

Fujiyama needed to explain the treaty proposal in the Diet and thus needed to know how the US government expected Japan to respond to an attack on US territory or on territory under US administration. He sought clarification from Ambassador MacArthur on October 22.

MacArthur responded that, as with other US security treaties, choosing how to respond was for each party to decide and that the decision would hinge on the circumstances at the time. When Fujiyama protested that this would be inadequate to parry questions from opposition members of the Diet, MacArthur elaborated further. He assured Fujiyama that hosting US bases was sufficient for Japan to fulfill its mutual defense obligation under the treaty. The bases in Japan could support a US response to armed aggression and were a substantive contribution to mutual security.[14]

In fact, the US government was counting additionally on Japanese military support not mentioned by MacArthur. It expected Japan to undertake proactive air defense: to shoot down enemy aircraft that entered Japanese air space en route to or from attacking US territory or US forces in the treaty area.[15]

The Japanese government studied the US proposal for a treaty revision carefully while maintaining close dialog with MacArthur. An issue that the Japanese raised was what they regarded as the proposal's insufficient emphasis on compliance with the Japanese constitution. Rather than simply mentioning compliance with constitutional processes, the treaty, they argued, should prescribe compliance with the war-renouncing Article 9 of the constitution. MacArthur regarded that as an entirely manageable issue, and the negotiators finessed the issue by supplementing "processes" with "provisions": "in accordance with its constitutional provisions and processes."[16]

The dilemma for the Japanese

Japan's government had decided by November 1958 that a security treaty that covered the entire Pacific would not be politically feasible. Vociferous public rejection of the Police Duties Execution Act had weakened the government's political standing, and the government was extraordinarily sensitive to public opinion and to the ebb and flow of political dynamics in the ruling Liberal Democratic Party.[17]

MacArthur was sympathetic to the Japanese government's position. He expressed his view as follows in a telegram of December 24, 1958, to the State Department:

> [Government of Japan] statements to effect that inclusion of US territory would not oblige Japanese forces to act outside of home islands would be unconvincing to Japanese public. Critics would ask why in such case such territory was included and would accuse [government] of having given secret commitment to violate constitution, or of having given secret commitment to railroad revision of constitution through Diet. There would be uproar in Japanese Diet which could bring fall of government, withdrawal of ratification bill, or both.[18]

At issue here was something more than the Japanese government's true intentions with regard to the revised security treaty. Tōgō Fumihiko, who participated in negotiating the treaty revision as a Foreign Ministry official and who later served as Japan's US ambassador, wrote of two challenges posed by territorial considerations. He detailed those challenges in the autobiographical *Nichi-Bei gaikō 30-nen: Anpo, Okinawa to sono go* (Thirty Years of Japanese-US Diplomacy: The Security Treaty, Okinawa, and Later).

One challenge, according to Tōgō, related to the broadening of the treaty's geographical scope. The security treaty of 1951 provided that the US bases in Japan were for defending Japan from external aggressors, for suppressing riots and other large-scale domestic unrest, and for contributing to maintaining peace and security in the Far East. Redefining the treaty area in the revised treaty as "the Pacific" would expand the treaty geography immensely, and that expansion would trigger rejection among the Japanese people.

The other challenge noted by Tōgō is that of collective defense. Japan's government had interpreted the nation's constitution as prohibiting Japanese participation in collective defense. The US draft proposal for the revised treaty provided, however, for behavior that would violate that prohibition. It obliged Japan to respond to aggression against US territory anywhere in the Pacific as a threat to joint security. Japanese were bound to regard that as a matter of engaging in collective defense. It was hard to swallow, writes Tōgō, no matter how the negotiators might tweak the description of Japan's obligations.[19]

In the final version of the treaty, the negotiators narrowed the scope of Japan's defense obligations greatly. What began in MacArthur's initial draft proposal as

> each Party recognizes that an armed attack in the Pacific directed against the territories or areas under the administrative control of the other Party would be dangerous to its own peace and safety and declares that it would act to meet the common danger in accordance with its constitutional processes[20]

became in the final version

> each Party recognizes that an armed attack against either Party in the territories under the administration of Japan would be dangerous to its own peace and safety and declares that it would act to meet the common danger in accordance with its constitutional provisions and processes.[21]

Even this narrowed rendering of Japan's defense obligations is subject to interpretation as engaging in collective defense. And opposition lawmakers returned repeatedly to that issue in the Diet deliberations on the revised treaty. The Kishi government argued, however, that an attack on US forces in Japanese-administered territory would be an attack on Japan and that participating in a counterattack would be entirely a matter of self-defense. Typical of the back-and-forth that ensued in the Diet was the following exchange between Ishibashi Masashi of the Socialist Party and Kishi on April 20, 1960.

> Ishibashi: The preamble [to the proposed treaty] holds that Japan and the United States recognize that both "have the inherent right of individual or collective self-defense as affirmed in the Charter of the United Nations." To interpret the Article 5 reference to a [response to an] attack on US bases as anything other than exercising the right of collective defense would be inconsistent.
>
> Kishi: The peace treaty and the Japanese-Soviet joint declaration employ similar phrasing. Japan, as a sovereign nation, possesses the right of individual and collective self-defense under Article 51 of the UN Charter. But Article 9 of our constitution prevents us from exercising the right of collective defense by going abroad to defend the territory of a treaty counterparty. At issue in Article 5 [of the draft for the revised security treaty] is an armed attack on territory under the administration of Japan, so [the response prescribed there] is entirely explainable as military action required for exercising our right of individual self-defense.[22]

This sort of explanation has the sound of rationalization for domestic consumption, and Takatsuji Masami, who took part in examining constitutional aspects of the treaty, acknowledged as much. He worked with the Foreign Ministry in analyzing the treaty as an official in the Cabinet Legislation Bureau. Takatsuji, who went on to head the bureau for eight years and to later serve briefly as Japan's justice minister, related the government's interpretive stonewalling as follows:

> Takahashi [Michitoshi, the director general of the Foreign Ministry's Treaties Bureau] and I were in agreement that the constitution did not permit dispatching self-defense forces overseas to protect the United States, even Guam. Even [responding militarily to] an armed attack on US bases in Japan would amount to exercising the right of collective defense. Japan would be acting in accordance with the treaty provision to recognize that "an armed attack against either Party in the territories under the administration of Japan would be dangerous to its own peace and safety" and to declare "that it would act to meet the common danger." What Japan would actually be doing, however, was the same thing as exercising its right of individual self-defense and did not need to be interpreted as exercising the right of collective self-defense. Prime Minister Kishi, the Legislation Bureau's Director General Hayashi [Shūzō], and others in the government stonewalled with the "exercise of the right to individual self-defense" argument. The Americans, however, regarded Japanese action in defense of US bases as exercising Japan's right of collective self-defense.[23]

The charitable reader will determine that the same phrasing meant one thing to the Japanese and something else to the Americans. A less charitable one will suspect that the Japanese government was engaging in rhetorical sleight of hand.[24] Whatever our perspective on the government's posturing, we perceive here a dilemma that the treaty revision presented for the Japanese government.

Japan's Foreign Ministry viewed the security treaty from the outset as a departure from traditional strategic alliances. It would fall in the category of undertakings expressly permitted under Article 52 of the UN charter as "regional arrangements or agencies for . . . the maintenance of international peace and security." Japan's diplomats were eager to demonstrate Japanese compliance with the UN charter, the "constitution" of the global community. They envisioned that compliance in the context of the "inherent right of individual or collective self-defense" guaranteed under Article

51 of the charter. For the Foreign Ministry, that meant collective self-defense, as we have seen in Chapter 1 of the present work.

Demonstrating a solid grounding in the principles of the UN charter would establish a clear linkage between the treaty and the Japanese constitution, and it would position Japan and the United States, at least formally, as equal partners. Frustration at the failure to achieve a treaty on these terms in 1951 lingered at the Foreign Ministry, and ministry officials were determined to assert a clearer linkage to the UN charter in the revised treaty. They pressed for formal clarification during the diplomacy that unfolded before, during, and after Kishi's state visit to the United States in June 1957.

The communiqué signed by President Dwight D. Eisenhower and Kishi at the conclusion of the state visit on June 21 provided for establishing what became the Japanese-American Committee on Security. That committee would "study problems arising in relation to the Security Treaty including consultation, whenever practicable, regarding the disposition and employment in Japan by the United States of its forces" and "also consult to assure principles of the United Nations Charter."[25] Additionally, the Foreign Ministry proposed an exchange of notes to further affirm the grounding of the treaty in the UN charter, and that exchange took place on September 14, 1957.[26]

A clear affirmation of grounding in the UN charter, accompanied by clear references to collective self-defense, also appears in the final treaty text. The preamble affirms, as did the preamble to the 1951 treaty, nations' right to engage in collective self-defense, based on the UN charter. In Article 5 of the treaty, the Japanese negotiators requested and obtained the insertion of the phrase "in accordance with the provisions of Article 51 of the [UN] Charter." That insertion was in connection with the reporting of acts taken in the name of collective self-defense to the UN Security Council. Although minor, it also reflects the Foreign Ministry's determination to demonstrate the treaty's grounding in the UN charter.[27]

Thus did the Japanese negotiators secure affirmation of their nation's commitment to collective self-defense in the treaty and in the accompanying exchange of notes. All the while, their government was reassuring the Japanese people that the Japanese constitution forbade the fulfillment of that commitment. The inherent contradictions posed a persistent dilemma for Japan's negotiators in working out the revised treaty.

Exercising the right of collective defense

Whether Japan's constitution countenanced collective self-defense had not arisen as an issue in negotiating the 1951 security treaty. To be sure, the Foreign Ministry had forcefully argued the Japanese right to engage in collective self-defense with the United States (see Chapter 1). The defense in question, however, was the defense of Japan alone. Japan's role would consist entirely of deploying police capacity to maintain domestic order and hosting US military bases to resist external foes.

The Japanese government had not developed a clear position with regard to the meaning of the right to collective self-defense or the standing of that right under the Japanese constitution.[28] In fairness, the right to collective self-defense was a new concept. Japan, meanwhile, possessed practically no military capacity at the time, so the question of how far afield it could act militarily in connection with collective self-defense might have seemed irrelevant.[29]

Japan, however, had subsequently acquired a substantive, though still modest, military capacity. The Japanese Diet passed the Self-Defense Forces Act in spring 1954. Under that act, the National Security Force became the Ground Self-Defense Force, the Coastal Safety Force became the Maritime Self-Defense Force, and the Air Self-Defense Force was born as a third branch of the Japan Self-Defense Forces.

The Diet also passed in spring 1954 the Mutual Security Agreement. That confusingly named agreement was separate from and subsidiary to the 1951 Security Treaty Between Japan and the United States of America and the 1960 Treaty of Mutual Cooperation and Security between Japan and the United States of America. Based on the US Mutual Security Act of 1951, it was a unified framework for US military and economic assistance formerly provided separately.

Japan's growing military capacity obliged the government to define explicitly the scope of its right to assert military power and to produce a working definition of collective self-defense. Diet deliberation of the Mutual Security Agreement, the Self-Defense Forces Act, and the Defense Agency Establishment Act included debate over whether Japan could assert the newly fortified military capacity overseas. The Yoshida government denied that the Self-Defense Forces could be dispatched abroad. It explained that the Self-Defense Forces would not be of such character and would not be responsible for cross-border operations. A resolution passed by the upper house of the Diet on June 2, 1954, expressed formal opposition to dispatching the Self-Defense Forces abroad.

The Diet's fierce insistence on prohibiting the overseas dispatching of Self-Defense Forces apparently affected government thinking about collective self-defense. That was evident in remarks by Shimoda Takesō, the director general of the Foreign Ministry's Treaties Bureau. He made the remarks while fielding questions in the lower house of the Diet on June 3. Shimoda offered the first formal assurance by the government that the constitution prohibited Japan from engaging in collective self-defense. The Kishi government would later reiterate that stance during Diet deliberations on the revised security treaty. It stated that the constitution prohibited engaging in collective self-defense in the sense of dispatching forces to defend another nation.[30]

On May 29, 1981, Prime Minister Suzuki Zenkō articulated the interpretation of collective self-defense that had become axiomatic for successive Japanese governments. He did so in the House of Representatives in response to a question from the Socialist Party lawmaker Inaba Seiichi.

> Under international law, a nation possesses the right to engage in collective self-defense, that is, to use military force to halt an armed attack on a foreign nation with which it has a close relationship, even if it is not itself under direct attack.
>
> Japan, under international law, clearly possesses this right of collective self-defense as a sovereign nation. However, we believe that the exercise of the right of self-defense permitted under Article 9 of our constitution should be interpreted as being confined to the minimum range necessary to defend our nation. We believe that the exercise of collective self-defense transcends that range and is not permitted by the constitution.[31]

This interpretation of the right of collective self-defense culminated decades of rhetorical pirouettes and drew criticism on several fronts. Acknowledging the Article 9 prohibition on dispatching Japanese forces abroad had presented several issues in drafting the 1960 treaty. The foremost example is in Article 3:

> The Parties, individually and in cooperation with each other, by means of continuous and effective self-help and mutual aid will maintain and develop, subject to their constitutional provisions, their capacities to resist armed attack.

Concluding a mutual security treaty with Japan was, for the United States, contingent on fulfilling the criteria prescribed in the Vandenberg Resolution (see Chapter 1, endnote 111). That resolution, passed in 1948, provided that the United States should confine any participation in "regional and other collective arrangements" to those "as are based on continuous and effective self-help and mutual aid, and as affect its national security." Inadequate capacity for "continuous and effective self-help and mutual aid" had prevented Japan from achieving a truly mutual security treaty in 1951. Article 3 of the revised treaty acknowledges Japan's attainment of that capacity and would thus seem to have been a welcome step for the Japanese.

For the US negotiators, the expressed commitment to "continuous and effective self-help and mutual aid" was indispensable. The same commitment appeared in the North Atlantic Treaty and in other collective security treaties, and its presence in the revised treaty with Japan was a condition for securing Senate passage.

Japan could not accept, however, the US draft proposal for Article 3 of the revised treaty:

> In order more effectively to achieve the objectives of this Treaty, the Parties, separately and jointly, by means of continuous and effective self-help and mutual aid will maintain and develop their individual and collective capacity to resist armed attack and to prevent and counter subversive activities directed from without against their territorial integrity and political stability.[32]

The phrase "collective capacity" implied that Japanese military capabilities would be available for defending territory other than Japan, and the reference to "separately and jointly" maintaining and developing that capacity implied engaging in collective defense beyond what was permitted by Japan's constitution. Following what Tōgō characterized as "a prolonged back-and-forth," "separately and jointly" became "individually and in cooperation with each other," "their individual and collective capacity" became simply "their capacities," the reference to subversive activities was deleted, and the article gained the clause "subject to their constitutional provisions."[33]

With regard to the phrase that became "subject to their constitutional provisions," the Japanese negotiators initially proposed different phrasing: "Nothing in this treaty shall be interpreted as imposing on either party any obligation in conflict with its constitutional provisions." That phrasing appears in the draft that MacArthur submitted to the State Department on April 29, 1959.[34] And the ambassador voiced support for the change:

> This new article is important to [the government of Japan] for domestic political reasons as it emphasizes that treaty does not impose obligations on either party conflicting with its constitutional provisions. From our viewpoint this would seem to create no problem.[35]

MacArthur's recommendation failed to sway the State Department, which rejected the proposal.

> We have serious objections to inclusion in treaty of special article on constitutionality qualifying whole treaty. First, there is no similar provision in any of our other mutual security arrangements and Congress is bound to question inclusion this article in Japanese arrangements very closely. Second, we fear other countries may raise problems with us re this Article and seek similar relief from obligations incurred in treaty arrangements on basis conflict with constitution. Third, there is problem whether under US constitutional system Executive Branch can so explicitly assert its authority to interpret constitution.[36]

The State Department was sensitive, nonetheless, to the Japanese concerns.

> We recognize, however, constitution issue very delicate and crucial point in Japan. Therefore, propose that as addition at end of Article V: "and constitutional provisions".

This proposal, as noted elsewhere, took hold in the final version of the treaty text, though not exactly in the position proposed.

> Each Party recognizes that an armed attack against either Party in the territories under the administration of Japan would be dangerous to its own peace and safety and declares that it would act to meet the common danger in accordance with its constitutional provisions and processes.

Collective security was a subject of discussion when Christian Herter testified before the Senate Foreign Relations Committee on June 7, 1960, as secretary of state. Herter succeeded Dulles in that post in April 1959 when illness sidelined the latter, who died a month later. In his testimony, Herter cited Japan's progress in achieving stand-alone sovereignty.

The secretary noted that Japan had acceded to UN membership in 1956, that it had increased its defense capabilities significantly, that it had been the second-largest market for US exports since 1957, and that it had become a nonpermanent member of the UN Security Council in 1958. Herter emphasized, too, that Japan had benefited the United States by allocating substantial territory to hosting US bases and by placing important facilities at the disposal of the US military.

Some senators responded to Herter's testimony by expressing dissatisfaction with Japan's contributions to the ostensible alliance. The tone of the objections, however, was civil, and the senators seemed to have accepted the administration's stance that Japan had attained the capacity for "continuous and effective self-help and mutual aid."[37]

Floating a "personal proposal"

Fujiyama met secretly with Ambassador MacArthur on November 26, 1958, to discuss the revision of the security treaty. He explained that defining the treaty area as "the Pacific" would not go down well in Japan. Fujiyama added that including Okinawa and the Ogasawara Islands in the treaty area would also undermine the prospects for earning Japanese acceptance.[38]

Before the meeting, a Foreign Ministry official showed a member of MacArthur's staff "a draft on consultation which he said Fujiyama was considering." The staff member qualified it as Fujiyama's personal response to the US draft that MacArthur had submitted on October 4 and emphasized that he was sharing the draft on a private, confidential, and personal basis. Belying the qualification, however, is a handwritten note on a typewritten copy of the proposal in the Foreign Ministry archives. The note, which appears atop the first page of the draft, offers a ringing affirmation of the content:

> This proposal has undergone review from 3 p.m. to 6 p.m. on November 21 at the foreign minister's official residence as optimally suited to Japanese domestic circumstances and as maximally strong from the standpoint of Japan (minister, vice minister, two directors-general, two deputy directors-general, and two directors in attendance)[39]

The Japanese proposal dispensed with what appeared in the US proposal as Articles 2 and 3. Article 2 in the US draft provided for political and economic cooperation, and Article 3 provided for each party to "maintain and develop their individual and collective capacity to resist armed attack" in accordance with the aforementioned Vandenberg Resolution. The Japanese proposal was lacking throughout, meanwhile, in any provisions for committing Japan and the United States to respond to common dangers.

MacArthur rejected Fujiyama's proposal forcefully in colorful terms. What follows is a reverse translation of the Foreign Ministry's Japanese-language record of the ambassador's comments.

> The president and secretary of state have entrusted me with the negotiation of a new treaty to the extent that it is consistent in concept with the security agreements that the United States has concluded with other allies. If a treaty were to result that was utterly different in concept [from our security agreements with other allies], it would inevitably draw criticism from our other allies and would never gain approval in Congress.
>
> As an exception, I am inclined, as someone able to understand the Japanese perspective, to recommend limiting the treaty area to Japanese territory, though that is an extremely vexing issue for the US side. I am prepared to recommend to Washington a draft proposal that differs [from our proposal] within the scope of limiting the treaty area to Japanese territory and making minor modifications in respect to other points.
>
> However, this draft proposal, though I have, of course, read it through just once, appears to differ fundamentally from the United States' other security treaties. If I were to send this draft to Washington as the Japanese proposal, the present negotiations would end there. They would be like a

baseball game that has come to an end. If I were to send this to Washington, I suspect that the uproar from the officials there would be so loud as to be audible without relying on telephone lines across the Pacific.

The US negotiators have a basic line from which they will not accept any significant deviation. I will explain some reasons that this draft is unacceptable.

First of all is the problem of basic concept. The United States does not enter into purely military alliances because such alliances lack sustainability and reliability. The basis for concluding a treaty needs to be not merely military alignment but also a community of interest, complete with common benefit and mutual purpose. A proposal that lacks provisions for demonstrating that basis is bound to draw questions about that lack in the Senate or anywhere.

A proposal that conforms as closely as possible to the standard format is thus preferable from the US standpoint. I'm not saying that this is the most important point, but you have mentioned that your proposal is under study, so I urge you to devote renewed study to this matter.

Next is Article 3 of the US proposal; that is, the provision for continuous and effective self-help and mutual aid. The proposal will not clear the Senate without this article. This is, of course, an issue in regard to the Vandenberg Resolution. The United States can do nothing for anyone who makes no effort at self-help, for any nation that would seek simply to get the United States to do something.

If the problem for Japan is the issue of collective [security], we need to recognize that problem. If that is the problem, I think that we can somehow meet your needs. However, simply deleting this article completely will anger the US officials unnecessarily.[40]

MacArthur then described his dissatisfaction with Article 4 of Fujiyama's proposal. That article began with the provision, "If an armed attack occurs against Japan, the United States of America shall take such joint measures with Japan as are necessary for the defense of the latter." MacArthur offered the following commentary:

I will offer my personal feelings on the issue of the treaty area as defined in Article 4. To limit [the treaty area] to Japanese territory is something to which I, being here and able to understand Japan's circumstances, am sympathetically disposed. The phrasing of your proposal, however, is extremely difficult to accept. To start with, the concept of common danger is completely absent. The proposal calls for the United States to undertake, willy-nilly, a commitment to defend Japan if Japan is attacked. You ought to be able to think of a suitable manner of expression.

The US proposal speaks of [each party] being prepared to "act to meet the common danger" [in the event of an attack in the Pacific on the other]. It expresses the US commitment to defending Japan in the strongest possible language. I can't understand why you have a problem with that provision. Do you have a problem with that phrasing in connection with limiting the treaty area to Japanese territory?

Your proposal is unacceptable as it stands. If I pass this on [to Washington] with this wording, that will be the end of the negotiations. I don't understand why narrowing the treaty area to Japanese territory needs to involve changing the basic concept.

MacArthur, continuing, took issue next with Article 3 of Fujiyama's proposal. That article read as follows:

Japan grants to the United States of America, subject to such conditions as may be agreed upon, the use of certain facilities and areas in Japan by the United States land, air and sea forces.

The ambassador identified fundamental flaws in the article.

Article 3 of your proposal provides that the use of [Japanese] bases [by US forces] is to be "subject to such conditions as may be agreed upon." The text needs to guarantee, however, that US forces will have at least minimal access to the bases that they require. Japan will not be undertaking defense obligations commensurate with the obligations that the United States will be undertaking to defend Japan. The treaty's mutuality basically rests on the provision of bases.

From another perspective, the United States cannot fulfill its obligation to defend Japan if it does not have access to Japanese bases. Your

> proposal, however, does not ensure that access. I assume that the Japanese side does not deny the need for an agreement that specifies facilities and areas that the US forces can use.
>
> Of course, consultation will be necessary when US forces make requests for the provision of additional facilities. I am happy to note, meanwhile, that the return of some facilities is under way. The US side will find negotiations meaningless, however, if seeking minimal access to facilities encounters challenges.

MacArthur also touched on issues with regard to the administrative agreement and prior consultation. He then concluded with a question about how to handle Fujiyama's proposal. MacArthur asked if Fujiyama wanted him to go ahead and forward the proposal to Washington, DC, or to put the draft aside and simply convey the foreign minister's thoughts on limiting the treaty area and other matters. Fujiyama replied that the latter option would be preferable.

In later years, MacArthur mentioned in a magazine interview having received a Japanese proposal for the new treaty. The proposal cited was clearly Fujiyama's, and MacArthur recalled it as having been unilaterally favorable to Japan. He described the proposal as utterly lacking in reciprocity. It placed all responsibility for defending Japan on the United States, MacArthur recalled, while obliging Japan to take no action whatsoever in its own defense.

MacArthur shed new light on the Fujiyama proposal in a 1981 interview that appeared in the monthly Japanese magazine *Chūō Kōron*. He reported that he had later learned an interesting tidbit about the background to that proposal. A government source had informed him that the proposal was the result of a push by figures in the cabinet. The idea was to run the draft by the Americans under the guise of a personal proposal by Fujiyama and see what kind of reaction it elicited. Kishi and Fujiyama, according to the source, both regarded the ploy as futile but went along with it nonetheless.[41]

Exempting Okinawa and the Ogasawara Islands

Officials in the Kishi government had apparently assumed that the revised treaty would include Okinawa and the Ogasawara Islands.[42] Including them in the treaty area would be a welcome opportunity to underline their identity as inherently Japanese territory. Kishi had said as much in the Diet on October 23, 1958. He interpreted including Okinawa in the treaty area as serving to recover territory rightly subject to Japanese administrative authority.

Kishi thus viewed including Okinawa in the treaty area as a means of securing popular support for the revised treaty. The stratagem failed to gain traction, however, with opposition lawmakers and even with a large swath of Kishi's fellow Liberal Democratic Party members. Okinawa, argued the opposition parties, would become a pivot for a de facto "Northeast Asia Treaty Organization" in the mold of the North Atlantic Treaty Organization. It would become, they feared, the linkage for drawing Japan into a web of US security arrangements that also encompassed the Republic of Korea, Taiwan, and the Philippines. They warned that including Okinawa in the treaty area would thus threaten to draw Japan into regional conflicts.

In the Liberal Democratic Party, some lawmakers called for demanding up front the restoration of Japanese administrative control over Okinawa and the Ogasawara Islands. That restoration should be a condition, they insisted, for including those territories in the treaty area. Others opposed including Okinawa and the Ogasawara Islands in the treaty area on the grounds of military strategy. They believed that the US military could better defend Japan if it was free to bring nuclear weapons there, and they feared that including those territories in the treaty area would rob the US military of that strategic option. Fujiyama cited the former prime minister Ashida Hitoshi, the former admiral and diplomat Nomura Kichisaburō, and the former admiral Hoshina Zenshirō as parliamentarians in the Liberal Democratic Party who were of that view.[43]

MacArthur determined that narrowing the treaty area would be unavoidable in concluding a revised security treaty with Japan, and he called for the US government to take the initiative in proposing to narrow the treaty area. That was in a telegram of November 3, 1958. MacArthur wrote that the Japanese wanted to narrow the treaty area but were hesitant to propose as much because they were uncertain of the US response. He acknowledged that the Japanese hesitance might seem illogical but that it was a quintessentially Japanese posture.[44]

The ambassador wrote on November 16, 1958, that he had described three possibilities for the treaty area to Senate leaders in September: "A. US- and Japanese-administered islands in Pacific; B. Japan and [Okinawa and the Ogasawara Islands]; C. Japan main islands." The senators, he reported, were amenable to any of the three as long as the major objective of aligning Japan with the United States was achieved.[45]

MacArthur reiterated his reasoning in a telegram of November 28, 1958.

> Major substantive difficulty in talks thus concerns the treaty area. . . . Inclusion of US-administered territories in treaty area does not seem essential to our purposes. As I understand it, our basic and overriding interest lies in creation of reasonably dependable and long-term military security arrangement entered into voluntarily by Japan which will: Align Japan with us and free world in military security field; which will give us use of Japanese logistic facilities and bases in peace-time thus saving us literally hundreds of millions of dollars; and which will at same time give us reasonable expectation of use of bases for logistic support if we become involved in hostilities in the Far East in which Japan is not involved, with possibility of also using them operationally. These objectives can be accomplished regardless of whether [Okinawa and the Ogasawara Islands] are in treaty area. As matter of fact, given the situation here and question of continued administration of [those territories] etc., I now believe that there is very substantial advantage to us if they are not so included. (Incidentally the [Nationalist Chinese and the South Koreans] will also be much happier if [Okinawa is] not included.) I therefore strongly recommend that we be prepared to have treaty area confined to Japanese home islands.[46]

The thinking advanced by MacArthur prevailed, and the US government agreed in early 1959 to narrow the treaty area. In its final version, the treaty defines the treaty area narrowly as "territories under the administration of Japan." That concession was in deference more to the wishes of the US military, however, than to public sentiment in Japan. As we have seen, Japanese of different stripes opposed including Okinawa or the Ogasawara Islands in the treaty area. And MacArthur worked effectively in conveying their concerns to the State Department and to the Senate. What proved more decisive, however, was the opposition of the US military.

Senior members of the US military establishment wanted the United

States to retain administrative control over Okinawa and the Ogasawara Islands. Including those territories in the treaty area, they feared, would lend momentum to moves toward restoring them to Japanese administration. The US negotiators ultimately yielded to the Japanese opposition to defining the treaty area as the Pacific, but they coupled that concession with the removal of Okinawa and the Ogasawara Islands from the treaty area. Dulles proposed redefining the treaty area as follows in a telegram of January 24, 1959, to MacArthur:

> Each party recognizes that an armed attack directed against the territory or areas under the administrative control of Japan would be dangerous to its own peace and safety and declares that it would act to meet the common danger in accordance with its constitutional processes.[47]

The treaty area as defined by Dulles became the basis for the bilateral negotiations that finalized the treaty. Those negotiations produced an interesting tweak in Dulles's phrasing. That change appears in a draft that MacArthur sent to the State Department on April 29, 1959:

> Each party recognizes that an armed attack against either party in the areas under the administration of Japan would be dangerous to its own peace and safety and declares that it would act to meet the common danger in accordance with its constitutional processes.

Here, "an armed attack directed against territory or areas under the administrative control of Japan" has become "an armed attack against either party in the areas under the administration of Japan." MacArthur writes that the draft incorporates "modifications suggested by Japanese." The Japanese negotiators presumably sought the addition of "against either party" to emphasize the mutuality of the treaty.[48]

Okinawa and the Ogasawara Islands, though deleted from the treaty area in the final treaty text, received attention in the Agreed Minute to the Treaty of Mutual Cooperation and Security.[49] Kishi and Herter signed that document on the same day as the treaty. In it, Kishi makes the following pledge on behalf of Japan:

> While the question of the status of the islands administered by the United States under Article 3 of the Treaty of Peace with Japan has not been made a subject of discussion in the course of treaty negotiations, I would like to emphasize the strong concern of the Government and people of Japan for the safety of the people of these islands since Japan possesses residual sovereignty over these islands. If an armed attack occurs or is threatened against these islands, the two countries will of course consult together closely under Article IV of the Treaty of Mutual Cooperation and Security. In the event of an armed attack, it is the intention of the Government of Japan to explore with the United States measures which it might be able to take for the welfare of the islanders.

The islands covered under Article 3 of the peace treaty were, as noted elsewhere, "Nansei Shoto [Southwest Islands] south of 29° north latitude (including the Ryukyu [Okinawa] Islands and the Daito Islands), Nanpo Shoto south of Sofu Gan (including the Bonin [Ogasawara] Islands, Rosario Island and the Volcano Islands) and Parece Vela and Marcus Island."

Herter, meanwhile, makes the following pledge in the agreed minute on behalf of the United States:

> In the event of an armed attack against these islands, the United States Government will consult at once with the Government of Japan and intends to take the necessary measures for the defense of these islands, and to do its utmost to secure the welfare of the islanders.

From "Pacific" to "Far East"

The US State Department had argued for retaining a regional reference to the Pacific in the treaty. That reflected a continuing concern in the department: that narrowing the treaty area could occasion in Japan waning interest in defending free-world interests in the Pacific and waxing pressure to restrict US latitude in using its Japanese bases.

Dulles instructed MacArthur in a telegram of September 29, 1958, to propose changing Article 6 in the treaty draft from

> for the purpose of contributing to the security of Japan and in consideration of the common concern that the two parties have in the mainte-

> nance of international peace and security in the Far East, the United States of America is granted the use by its land, air and naval forces of facilities and areas in Japan

to

> in furtherance of the objectives of this Treaty, the US has the use of certain bases in Japan. With respect to the use of these bases and the status of US forces in Japan, the Administrative Agreement signed at Tokyo on February 28, 1952, as amended, shall continue in force.[50]

The treaty wording at that time still specified the treaty area as the "Pacific." Dulles's change thus provided for using the US bases in Japan to maintain security throughout the Pacific region. Narrowing the treaty area to "the areas under the administration of Japan" would undercut that role. State Department concern about this issue is on view in a subsequent telegram from the department to the Tokyo embassy. The gist of the telegram is as follows:

> Japan needed to demonstrate a commitment to contributing to US security and to the security of the free world in the Pacific. That was the minimum condition for achieving genuine mutuality in the security treaty. The United States was pledging to ensure Japanese security. In return, the US military deserved a free hand, subject to the prior consultation formula, in using its bases in Japan. Nothing less would be acceptable to Congress or to the American people.[51]

No one seriously expected Japan to provide protection for the United States through its minuscule military capacity. But the US government could not countenance a diminution of the strategic value of its Japanese bases. Dulles instructed Ambassador MacArthur on January 24, 1959, to propose a revised opening to the preamble in exchange for narrowing the treaty area: "Recognizing that the maintenance of international peace and security in the Pacific area is a matter of mutual concern." That, reasoned Dulles, would establish a legal basis for using Japan-based US forces beyond the treaty area.[52]

MacArthur dutifully conveyed Dulles's proposal to his Japanese counterparts but met with strong resistance. He met with Fujiyama on June 9, 1959 and reported the foreign minister's response the next day in a telegram to the State Department.

> Fujiyama said he had discussed phrase with Kishi. They recognized this language would not represent substantive undertaking on the part of Japan but such provision would be subject to misrepresentation by opposition and by hostile press as constituting undefined and indefinite broadening of Japan's commitments; would confuse public opinion; and would be troublesome to [the government of Japan] out of all proportion to any benefit that could be gained by ourselves. Accordingly, he regretted [the government] could not agree to inclusion of words "and in the Pacific area".[53]

The Japanese government suggested "Far East" as an alternative to "Pacific area" for geography of concern that transcended the treaty area. "Far East" appeared in the security treaty of 1951 and was less likely, in the eyes of the Japanese government, to cause political frictions. It appears in the draft proposal that MacArthur submitted to the Department of State on April 29, 1959.[54]

In the revised draft, Article 5 defines the treaty area as "areas under the administration of Japan." The preamble cites "a common concern in the maintenance of international peace and security in the Far East." Article 4 provides for consultation "whenever the security of Japan or international peace and security in the Far East is threatened," and Article 6 grants the United States "the use by its land, air and naval forces of facilities and areas in Japan" "for the purpose of contributing to the security of Japan and in consideration of the common concern that the two parties have in the maintenance of international peace and security in the Far East."

The US government grudgingly accepted the alternative wording proposed by the Japanese.[55] Thus did the final version of the treaty refer to "peace and security in the Far East," and adopting that wording does not appear to have diminished the strategic positioning of the US bases in Japan. That is because "Far East," in the diplomatic context, denoted no geographical limitation on the deployability of the Japan-based US forces.

It had denoted no such limitation in the security treaty of 1951 and would denote none in the revised treaty. Nishimura Kumao, who played a core role in the negotiations as the director general of the Japanese Foreign Ministry's Treaties Bureau (see Chapter 1), explains:

> People usually seem to think of the Far East as the range of deployability in relation to the range of territory to be defended. Range of deployability encourages mistaken associations, however, with delineating geographical boundaries on the deployability of the US forces in Japan. On careful reading, the phrasing is specifying the purpose of US forces in Japan as maintaining peace and security in the Far East. The reader sees that the geographical limits in question are on purpose and not on deployment. As a practical matter, the two coincide. Japan-based US forces deployed for the purpose of maintaining peace and security in the Far East will presumably operate in that region. The security treaty, however, does not restrict the deployability of those forces to the Far East. They could operate elsewhere if that served the purpose of maintaining peace and security in the Far East.[56]

Article 6 in the revised treaty grants the United States "the use by its land, air and naval forces of facilities and areas in Japan" "for the purpose of contributing to the security of Japan and the maintenance of international peace and security in the Far East." Likewise, Article 1 in the 1951 treaty granted the United States the right to "dispose United States land, air and sea forces in and about Japan" "to contribute to the maintenance of international peace and security in the Far East and to the security of Japan."

"Far East" had not occasioned dispute in the context of the 1951 treaty, but it became the subject of chaotic disagreement in the Diet deliberations on the revised treaty. Lawmakers interpreted the term as denoting geographical boundaries of the deployability of the Japan-based US forces. Kishi's government aggravated the confusion with inconsistent explanations that lent fuel to the opposition's attacks. The definition of "Far East" became a focus of debate over the revision of the treaty in the Diet and among the general public.

Ambassador MacArthur, concerned about the direction of the debate, urged Kishi and Fujiyama to have the government refrain from defining Far East. He cautioned that any definition they floated might be contradicted by members of the US administration in Senate testimony.

Taking MacArthur's admonishment to heart, members of the Japanese government tempered their subsequent comments on Far East geography. They confined their remarks on the subject to the broadest outlines of previous government output. At every opportunity, they emphasized that the concept of Far East was neither exclusive nor restrictive and that it imposed no geographical limitations on the deployability of the Japan-based US forces.[57]

Kishi fielded a question about the definition of Far East on February 26, 1960, in the House of Representatives Special Committee on the Japanese-US Security Treaty. The question was from the Liberal Democratic Party lawmaker Aichi Kiichi:

> The term "Far East," as generally used, does not have a precise geographical definition. Japan and the United States have a common concern, however, in maintaining international peace and security in the Far East, as described in the security treaty. In practice, the area subject to our common concern comprises, for the purposes of this treaty, the area that US forces in Japan, using Japanese facilities and territory, can contribute to defending from armed attack. That area basically extends north from the Philippines to Japan and its periphery and includes the territories under the control of the Republic of Korea and the Republic of China. That is the basic thinking in the revised treaty. If that area came under armed attack or if developments on its periphery posed a threat to that area, the area in which the United States would act in response would depend on the nature of the attack or the threat and would not be confined to the area that I have outlined.[58]

Worthy of note in passing here is that Kishi did not include the Democratic People's Republic of Korea in the geography described. That omission wasn't to suggest that Japan-based US forces could not launch an attack on North Korea in a military emergency. It was to confirm, rather, that maintaining peace and security for North Korea was not part of the mission of those forces.

Of larger note is that whether the Pacific or the Far East served as the geographical context for the treaty made little difference. The objective parameters of the treaty lay elsewhere. Any difference between "Pacific" and "Far East" was largely a matter of subjective response by Japanese lawmakers and the Japanese public.

2 Prior Consultation

A US concession

Two concerns weighed heavily on the Japanese government in agreeing to continue hosting US military bases: the possibility of the US military bringing nuclear weapons into Japanese territory and that of it deploying Japan-based forces to respond to military emergencies beyond Japanese territory. Japanese were extremely sensitive to both of these possibilities, and their government strove to allay that sensitivity by accompanying the treaty with an agreement that provided for "prior consultation." That agreement took the form of a diplomatic exchange of notes.

Herter and Kishi signed the notes on the same day that they signed the revised security treaty, January 19, 1960. The notes bore the heading "Regarding the Implementation of Article VI of Treaty of Mutual Cooperation and Security between Japan and the United States of America," and they mandated prior consultation in the following circumstances:

> Major changes in the deployment into Japan of United States armed forces, major changes in their equipment, and the use of facilities and areas in Japan as bases for military combat operations to be undertaken from Japan other than those conducted under Article V of the said Treaty, shall be the subjects of prior consultation with the Government of Japan.[59]

The Japanese government sought to demonstrate to the public that it possessed some control over the US military bases. Prior consultation meant that the United States could not act unilaterally in bringing nuclear weapons into Japan ("major changes in their equipment") or in deploying

Japan-based forces to operations beyond Japanese territory ("military combat operations to be undertaken from Japan other than those conducted under Article V of the said Treaty"). This stratagem drew criticism in Japan on account of the absence of any formal assurance of veto power.

An example is the criticism leveled at Kishi by Socialist Party lawmaker Hoashi Kei in the House of Representatives Committee on Foreign Affairs on November 19, 1959. With a colorful turn of phrase, Hoashi noted that the results of prior consultation were not binding on the US military.

> Your foreign minister has stated in answer to questioning that anyone thinking that the US military would act irresponsibly was suffering from a misconception. . . . He assumes that the United States is an absolutely model nation and that Americans would never do anything that would cause problems for other people. . . . Hearing him is like listening to "The Maiden's Prayer." But we're not holding a recital here. We're debating a serious issue with regard to national defense. That sort of aimless answer from the foreign minister is unacceptable.[60]

The Japanese and US governments moved to forestall criticism of the lack of a formal veto in the prior consultation formula. They addressed that issue, for example, in the joint communiqué issued after the signing of the revised security treaty.

> [President Eisenhower and Prime Minister Kishi] are convinced also that the treaty will foster an atmosphere of mutual confidence. In this connection, the Prime Minister discussed with the President the question of prior consultation under the new treaty. The President assured him that the United States government has no intention of acting in a manner contrary to the wishes of the Japanese government with respect to the matters involving prior consultation under the treaty.[61]

This explanation enabled the Japanese government to argue that Japan held a meaningful right of consent or refusal through prior consultation. It was less than convincing, however, for numerous Japanese, and criticism of the lack of a formal veto in the prior consultation formula persisted. Kishi addressed a question about that issue in the aforementioned meeting of the Special Committee on the Japanese-US Security Treaty on February 26, 1960. Again, the questioner was the Liberal Democratic Party lawmaker Aichi Kiichi, who asked whether Japan wielded genuine veto power.

> The notion of veto as conventionally framed under international law is untenable in one-on-one relationships. . . . Either party can agree to a proposal with "Yes" or reject it with "No." The question then becomes one of whether the United States can ignore and act in defiance of a response of "No" from Japan. In that the United States is not free to act in that manner Japan could reasonably be said to have a veto. A shared understanding that the United States cannot casually disregard a "No" answer from Japan has underlain the negotiations on this treaty at every stage.[62]

Kishi, writing in his memoir twenty years later, discounted the significance of veto power in the context of prior consultation.

> The treaty text didn't explicitly attribute a veto to prior consultation, but the Kishi-Eisenhower joint communiqué was clear: Mutual trust was fundamental. We'd be better off not concluding a treaty if either side didn't trust the other. Whatever the treaty text might say, we wouldn't have the luxury in a real emergency of considering things carefully after going through prior consultation and then debating whether we'd be serving Japanese security best by exercising our veto and saying "No."[63]

The principle of prior consultation was of real substance, even if it didn't impart a veto. It provided Japan with at least the trappings of a sovereign say over the US bases that it hosted. The government could assure the citizenry that the US military wouldn't bring nuclear weapons into Japan unbeknownst to the government and that Japan wouldn't get drawn into US wars in the Far East.

Prior consultation was more binding on the US government, meanwhile, than its Japanese critics allowed. Neither abrogating responsibility to undertake prior consultation nor ignoring Japanese resistance to a proposed course of action was a realistic option. Either would inflict unacceptable damage on a strategic relationship of immense value to the United States.

The Japanese government therefore did possess a measure of control over the US bases. Witness the sensitivity to Japanese nuclear concerns that is evident in a National Security Council report of June 11, 1960, "NSC 6008/1, Statement of US Policy Toward Japan." Bringing any nuclear weapons into Japanese territory would be subject to prior consultation under the security treaty. NSC 6008/1 notes that Japanese approval would be "highly unlikely," except in the event of a serious military emergency. It cautions, meanwhile, against contravening Japanese wishes expressed in prior consultation unless instructed to do so by the president.[64]

Prior consultation thus served as a brake on the US deployment of nuclear weapons in Japan. On the other hand, it does not seem to have been a significant handicap for US military strategy. Okinawa, for example, was still under the administrative control of the United States. A totally free hand for the US military in operating the bases there had been a precondition for the adoption of prior consultation.[65] Indeed, the US military was preparing to deploy medium-range nuclear missiles there.

Senior US officials clung to the expectation that Japanese resistance to nuclear weapons would weaken. They envisioned a day when the US military, following prior consultation, could deploy nuclear weapons on Japan's main islands. MacArthur went so far as to suggest to US military leaders that Japan would one day arm itself with nuclear weapons.[66]

Nuclear-armed US naval vessels posed a vexing issue with regard to prior consultation. Refusing to allow them to dock at Japanese ports would, to be sure, hinder US military strategy greatly. Nuclear-armed vessels of the US 7th Fleet had unquestionably docked in Japan frequently before the adoption of prior consultation. And that practice would continue on a "don't ask, don't tell" basis.

A pair of diplomatic artifices

"Differing interpretations by the Japanese and the Americans could cause problems in administering the treaty. Do you have any plans for recording mutually agreed minutes in regard to prior consultation?"

The questioner was Tsutsumi Tsuruyo, a Democratic Socialist Party member of Japan's House of Representatives. She was questioning Kishi on April 13, 1960, about the revised treaty. Her questioning took place in a meeting of the House of Representatives Special Committee on the Japanese-US Security Treaty.

"Your suggestion is entirely reasonable," replied the prime minister. "But we will be operating in the realm of established diplomatic practice. So I will rely on the diplomatic technique of our foreign affairs people and ask them to determine whether or how to prepare agreed minutes."

Kishi and his government were indeed operating in the realm of diplomacy. They had employed a pair of somewhat obscure diplomatic artifices to reconcile the military needs inherent to the security treaty and the political value of the treaty revision. And successive Japanese governments would avoid explaining those artifices to the citizenry for half a century.

Each diplomatic artifice employed by the Kishi government and its US counterpart finessed the prior consultation mandated in the Herter-Kishi exchange of notes. The first pertained to port calls by nuclear-armed US naval vessels. It addressed the issue of whether they were subject to prior consultation between the Japanese and US governments.

The second artifice pertained to the mobilization of Japan-based US forces to participate in overseas combat operations. Any such mobilization was subject, as a rule, to prior consultation. The Kishi government's diplomatic device, however, finessed the prior consultation requirement for a mobilization under the UN flag. Notably, it cleared the way for dispatching Japan-based US forces to the Korean Peninsula in the event of a military emergency.

A third-party investigation

My discussion here of the dual artifices reflects discoveries since the original, Japanese edition of this book appeared in 2000. Most notably, it addresses the findings of an investigation by Japan's Foreign Ministry into four secret agreements between Japan and the United States. Representatives of the two nations concluded two of the agreements in question when negotiating the revision of their bilateral security treaty and two when negotiating the return of Okinawa to Japanese administration.

The so-called secret agreements were long an open secret among everyone cognizant of the workings of Japanese diplomacy. Edwin O. Reischauer, the US ambassador to Japan from April 1961 to August 1966, acknowledged "an oral agreement" [with regard to nuclear weaponry] in 1981.[67] Successive Liberal Democratic Party governments abided by an official stance, however, of denying their existence.

Official acknowledgement of the existence of the secret agreements only became possible in September 2009. That was when the Democratic Party of Japan, the People's New Party, and Social Democratic Party coalition displaced the Liberal Democratic Party and put in place a government headed by Hatoyama Yukio.

Okada Katsuya, the Hatoyama government's foreign minister, promptly launched a Foreign Ministry investigation into the secret agreements. The ministry's internal investigation segued in November 2009 into a third-party investigation by a panel of six university professors. I served on the third-party, six-person investigative panel. We submitted our report on March 9, 2010, to the Foreign Ministry, which immediately made the report public.

The third-party panel's report, the Foreign Ministry's investigation report, and a trove of related diplomatic documents are available for perusal on the Foreign Ministry's website. Unfortunately, the ministry has posted the report and the related documents only on the Japanese-language side of its website, and the report appears only in Japanese. A lot of the documents, however, are in English and appear as facsimiles.[68]

Our panel's report, discussed in more detail in the following chapter, comprised an overview and afterword by the panel chairman and five chapters, each written by one of the other five panel members:

1. US global strategy and Japan
2. Calls by nuclear-armed US naval vessels at Japanese ports
3. Military emergencies on the Korean Peninsula and prior consultation
4. The return of Okinawa and the introduction of nuclear weapons in military emergencies
5. The return of Okinawa and funding for restoring it to pre-occupation condition

I was responsible for Chapter 2, about calls at Japanese ports by nuclear-armed US naval vessels.[69]

Our third-party investigative panel dealt forthrightly with the information unearthed by the Foreign Ministry. I have drawn on that information here in my discussion of two secret agreements. Both of those agreements supplemented the revised security treaty. I have drawn here, too, on information that has become available through the declassification of US government documents. A crucial aspect of the secret agreements remained under wraps when I penned my chapter in the third-party report. Insufficient access to pertinent documents precluded a full understanding of the brilliance of the negotiators in framing their supplementary agreements—the "secret agreements"—with regard to prior consultation.

The phrasing of the agreements exhibits an ambiguity that I originally attributed to insurmountable differences between the Japanese and US negotiators. I have since recognized, however, that the negotiators were of one mind in overcoming the daunting obstacles that they faced. Those obstacles encompassed political, diplomatic, and military contradictions, detailed in this chapter, that defied straightforward, unambiguous phrasing.

In the texts of the agreements, the negotiators finessed the contradictions masterfully and furnished the security treaty with the lubricant required for real-world functionality. That the treaty has remained in force and unrevised for more than 60 years is a tribute to the negotiators' genius. I revisit the secret agreements here with an eye to highlighting the subtle sublimity of their phrasing.

Diplomatic artifice no. 1: Port calls by nuclear-armed US naval vessels

One of the two secret agreements that pertained to prior consultation was the Record of Discussion.[70] The US government has yet to declassify that agreement, and direct references to its content succumb to "source text not declassified" in the State Department's public archives.[71] What appears below is a document released by the Japanese Foreign Ministry on March 9, 2010. The original of this document is typewritten English. Accompanying it is a handwritten Japanese translation.

> CONFIDENTIAL
> TREATY OF MUTUAL COOPERATION AND SECURITY
> RECORD OF DISCUSSION
> Tokyo, January 6, 1960.
>
> 1. Reference is made to the Exchange of Notes which will be signed on January 19, 1960, concerning the implementation of Article VI of the "Treaty of Mutual Cooperation and Security between the United States of America and Japan", the operative part of which reads as follows:

"Major changes in the deployment into Japan of United States armed forces, major changes in their equipment, and the use of facilities and areas in Japan as bases for military combat operations to be undertaken from Japan other than those conducted under Article V of the said Treaty, shall be the subjects of prior consultation with the Government of Japan."

2. The Notes were drawn up with the following points being taken into consideration and understood:
   a. "Major changes in their equipment" is understood to mean the introduction into Japan of nuclear weapons, including intermediate and long-range missiles as well as the construction of bases for such weapons, and will not, for example, mean the introduction of non-nuclear weapons including short-range missiles without nuclear components. [Underlining is handwritten addition to original]
   b. "Military combat operations" is understood to mean military combat operations that may be initiated from Japan against areas outside Japan.
   c. "Prior consultation" will not be interpreted as affecting present procedures regarding the deployment of United States armed forces and their equipment into Japan and those for the entry of United States military aircraft and the entry into Japanese waters and ports by United States naval vessels, except in the case of major changes in the deployment into Japan of United States armed forces.
   d. Nothing in the Exchange of Notes will be construed as requiring "prior consultation" on the transfer of units of United States armed forces and their equipment from Japan.

Aiichiro Fujiyama
Douglas MacArthur II

Item "a" is self-explanatory. In item "b," Fujiyama and MacArthur qualified the reference to "military combat operations to be undertaken from Japan" in the notes to be exchanged. They confirmed that this pertained only to attacks launched from Japanese bases. It would not pertain, that is, to operations staged by US forces that had redeployed to positions outside Japan.

Left unmentioned in item "c" is the issue of nuclear armament on the military aircraft or naval vessels in question. The US military then, as now, abided by a policy of not disclosing the deployment of nuclear weaponry, and nuclear-armed US aircraft and vessels had landed and docked in Japan repeatedly. Exempting "present procedures" from prior consultation presumably pertained to the coming and going of US aircraft and vessels armed with nuclear weapons.

US military reservations about prior consultation were on view in a meeting between Defense Department and State Department officials, including MacArthur, on September 9, 1958. Admiral Arleigh Burke, the chief of naval operations, asked MacArthur if nuclear-armed vessels would be subject to prior consultation. The ambassador acknowledged that some Japanese newspapers had devoted coverage to that subject, but he opined that the Japanese government was unlikely to raise the issue.

MacArthur noted that Kishi was vulnerable on this point, having assured the Diet that "the 'new era' required the United States to get Japan's agreement prior to bringing in nuclears." The ambassador counseled patience, suggesting that "there was no point in our driving Kishi out of business."[72]

As for item "d," the US negotiators insisted that the US military required unfettered freedom to withdraw from any position. The exchange of notes would provide that "major changes in the deployment into Japan of United States armed forces" would be subject to prior consultation. Fujiyama and MacArthur confirmed here that the requirement for prior consultation did not pertain to the withdrawal of forces from Japan.

State Department officials had issued instructions to MacArthur about prior consultation when the security treaty negotiations began. They had instructed him to secure Japanese government authorization for exempting port calls by nuclear-armed US naval vessels from prior consultation. The order from the State Department was surely at the request of the navy high command.

MacArthur knew that requesting authorization outright for exempting prior consultation would be counterproductive, and he declined to act on the instruction. The findings of a later US government study of this stage of the treaty negotiations are revealing. According to the study report, the reply from the embassy was firm: No Japanese leader would ever sign a document renouncing the right to be consulted about incoming nuclear weapons. "No specific understanding was reached," the study found, as to whether port calls by nuclear-armed ships required prior consultation.[73]

We find the US government's stance puzzling at first glance. The US government insisted initially on securing an exemption from prior consultation for port calls by nuclear-armed US vessels. But it soon dropped that insistence, apparently without even bringing the issue to debate. We learn on further examination, however, that the Japanese and US negotiators had resolved the issue through a clear understanding.

The negotiators shared an understanding about the Herter-Kishi exchange of notes with regard to port calls by nuclear-armed US vessels; that is, they shared an understanding that the exchange of notes did not mandate prior consultation for such port calls. That understanding dated from the Dulles-Fujiyama talks held in Washington, DC, on September 11, 1958.

Prior consultation was a mechanism that had originated as a proposal by the Japanese government. And the prior consultation that Fujiyama sought in Washington, DC, did not cover port calls by nuclear-armed US naval vessels. It covered only the mobilization of Japan-based US forces for overseas combat operations and the equipment of US forces stationed in Japan.[74] Kishi's government and its successors blurred that distinction, however, in the interest of rendering the security peace treaty palatable for the citizenry. And they enjoyed the cooperation of their US counterparts.

Here is a reminder of how the Kishi government framed the prior consultation requirement with regard to nuclear-armed vessels for domestic consumption. Akagi Munenori, the then director general of the Defense Agency (now the Ministry of Defense), set the prototype for the government posture in April 19, 1960. He was responding to a question by the Socialist Party's Yokomichi Setsuo during a meeting of the House of Representatives Special Committee on the Japanese-US Security Treaty. "Port calls at Yokosuka," stated Akagi, "or at any other port in Japan by vessels of the US 7th Fleet equipped with nuclear weaponry would be subject to prior consultation."

Temperatures were rising across the nation amid swelling opposition to the security treaty, and temperatures were rising in the halls of the Diet as the treaty ratification debate escalated. Akagi, as a Kishi government representative, opted for a response clearly aimed at defusing the overheated debate in the Diet.

The US government did not take issue with Akagi's explanation. That was in keeping with well-established US policy. The Japanese and US had a strong mutual interest in concealing the arrangement that ensured access to Japanese ports for all US naval vessels. And the US government fulfilled its part of the bargain by leaving Japanese assertions of a prior consultation requirement unchallenged.

MacArthur, in retirement, offered insights into the principle of unspoken understandings in an interview for a Japanese magazine article.

> In diplomacy, we sometimes leave things intentionally vague. We leave them vague because we realize that defining things clearly is not necessarily in our interest. I am speaking of [Japan and the United States]. If we try to make things overly sharp and define them detail upon detail, that can prove harmful and can be disadvantageous for our basic national interests. Some degree of vagueness can help calm things, especially when groups of differing ideologies are seeking to turn problems into major turmoil.[75]

Diplomatic artifice no. 2: The mobilization of Japan-based US forces for overseas combat operations, notably on or around the Korean Peninsula

Let us turn now to the diplomatic artifice that pertained to mobilizing Japan-based US forces for combat operations outside Japan. Unlike port calls by nuclear-armed vessels, such mobilization was subject explicitly to prior consultation under the Herter-Kishi exchange of notes. The content of that exchange left no margin whatsoever with regard to the requirement for prior consultation. Any mobilization of Japan-based US forces to respond to a military emergency on the Korean Peninsula or anywhere else outside Japan required prior consultation. Even Fujiyama and MacArthur's Record of Discussion prescribed that requirement explicitly.

Senior US army commanders were understandably uncomfortable with the prior consultation strictures. They were especially sensitive about the potential need for responding to a military emergency on the Korean Peninsula. And they demanded unfettered latitude in mobilizing their Japan-based forces—operating under the UN flag—for that purpose.

The Japanese and US negotiators thus encountered a hugely challenging dilemma. On one side were the Japanese negotiators. They insisted on prior consultation even in military emergencies and pledged in return that their government would respond favorably to any US request for authorization for a mobilization. On the other side were the US negotiators. They argued that a military emergency on the Korean Peninsula or elsewhere would demand a prompter response than prior consultation would permit. And they therefore insisted on an exception from the requirement for prior consultation in such events.

We find the resolution of the above dilemma in a document unearthed by Japan's Foreign Ministry in 2009. The document bore the title "Minutes for Inclusion in the Record of the First Meeting of the Security Consultative Committee." That committee originated under Article 25 of the status of forces agreement, which begins as follows:

> A Joint Committee shall be established as the means for consultation between the Government of Japan and the Government of the United States on all matters requiring mutual consultation regarding the implementation of this Agreement.[76]

Foreign Ministry investigators unearthed the text of the document as four working drafts and as two copies of what appears to be the final version, though one of the two is missing a title. Below is the full text of what is presumably the final version of the proposed insertion.

> SECRET
>
> MINUTES FOR INCLUSION IN THE RECORD OF THE FIRST MEETING OF THE SECURITY CONSULTATIVE COMMITTEE
>
> At the meeting of the Security Consultative Committee today the situation in Korea was discussed and the following statements were made by Ambassador MacArthur and Foreign Minister Fujiyama respectively.
>
> Ambassador MacArthur:
>
> Fortunately, since the Armistice Agreement was reached there has been no resumption of the armed attack against the United Nations forces in Korea. It is our hope that a final settlement involving the peaceful reunification of Korea in accordance with the United Nations resolutions can be reached without a recurrence of hostilities. However, the possibility of a renewal of the armed attack cannot be ruled out. In this event, the

preservation of the Republic of Korea against aggression not only is essential to the continued effectiveness of the United Nations but has a particular importance for the security of Japan and the other nations of the Far East endangered by such aggression. While it might be possible to detect in advance preparations for a large-scale armed attack, the possibility of an emergency arising out of an attack cannot be ruled out. Thus it could happen that, unless the United States armed forces undertook military combat operations immediately from Japan, the United Nations forces could not repel an armed attack made in violation of the Armistice. I hereby request, therefore, the views of the Japanese Government regarding the operational use of bases in Japan in the event of an exceptional emergency as mentioned above.

Foreign Minister Fujiyama:

The Japanese Government shares with the United States Government the hope that a final settlement in accordance with the resolutions of the United Nations can be brought about in Korea without a recurrence of hostilities.

I have been authorized by Prime Minister Kishi to state that it is the view of the Japanese Government that, as an exceptional measure in the event of an emergency resulting from an attack against the United Nations forces in Korea, facilities and [bases] in Japan may be used for such military combat operations as need be undertaken immediately by the United States armed forces in Japan under the Unified Command of the United Nations as the response to such an armed attack in order to enable the United Nations forces in Korea to repel an armed attack made in violation of the Armistice.

Aiichiro Fujiyama
Douglas MacArthur II

Tokyo, January 6, 1960[77]

Chapter 3 of our third-party investigative committee's report, penned by Haruna Mikio, reviewed in detail the above minutes. It characterized them as follows:

The text is of the character of a secret agreement. It constitutes an exemp-

> tion from prior consultation for combat operations launched from US bases in Japan in the event of a military emergency on the Korean Peninsula.[78]

We find corroboration of the "secret agreement" characterization in two undated and unattributed documents in the US National Archives: "Summary of Unpublished Agreements Reached in Conjunction with the Treaty of Mutual Cooperation and Security with Japan" and "Description of Consultation Arrangements under the Treaty of Mutual Cooperation and Security with Japan."[79] Although the documents bear no dates, their wording places them after the signing of the security agreement and before the convening of the first meeting of the Security Consultative Committee.

The first of the two documents comprises five items, the first two of which are the Record of Discussion and the Security Consultative Committee Minutes under discussion here:

1. Consultation–Record of Discussion (Confidential)
   This is a confidential interpretation ["agreement" in typewritten original crossed out and replaced with "interpretation" in handwriting] defining more precisely the consultation arrangements combined in the public exchange of notes. This has the effect of restricting our obligations to consult on "deployment" to the introduction into Japan of nuclear weapons and large missiles and on "operations" to military combat operations that may be initiated from Japan against areas outside Japan. (See also description of consultation arrangements.)
2. Consultation–Consultative Committee Minutes (Secret–Limit Distribution)
   This is a secret arrangement for advance consultation to permit us to react immediately from Japanese bases to a renewal of the Communist attack in Korea. (See also description of consultation arrangements.)

Of note here is the straightforward characterization of the Consultative Committee Minute. The US government officials responsible for this cataloging of agreements have described it unequivocally as "a secret arrangement." As for the other three items in the "Summary of Unpublished Agreements," they cover largely administrative matters and minor matters of interpretation:

3. Agreements of the Joint Committee Established by Article XXVI of the Administrative Agreement–Minute (Limited Official Use)
   A large body of detailed arrangements [developed by the Joint Committee] implementing the Administrative Agreement. . . .
4. United States Base Rights and Waiver of Private Claims–Minute (Official Use Only)
   An interpretive minute for the guidance of the new Joint Committee clarifying the meaning of Article III, Paragraph 1, and rescinding in part an agreed view relating to Article XVIII, Paragraph 1, of the Japan Status of Forces Agreement. . . .
5. MDAA Agreement (Unclassified)
   An exchange of notes making minor technical amendments to the Mutual Defense Assistance Agreement with Japan. . . .

That brings us to the second of the National Archives documents cited above, the "Description of Consultation Arrangements under the Treaty of Mutual Cooperation and Security with Japan." That document categorizes activity under the different arrangements as: I. Consultation with Japan Required (Confidential); II. Presidential Assurance on Consultation (Unclassified); III. Consultation with Japan Not Required; and IV. Arrangements for Prior Consultation Already Completed (Secret). Of interest here is the fourth category, which is a reference to the material for inclusion in the Security Consultative Committee minutes:

> IV. Arrangements for Prior Consultation Already Completed (Secret)
>
> At the first meeting of the United States-Japan Security Consultative Committee following the entry into force of the new treaty arrangements, Foreign Minister Fujiyama will state the view of the Japanese Government that "as an exceptional measure in the event of an emergency resulting from an attack against the United Nations forces in Korea, facilities and [bases] in Japan may be used for such military combat operations as need be undertaken immediately by the United States armed forces in Japan under the unified command of the United Nations as the response to such an armed attack in order to enable the United Nations forces in Korea to repel an armed attack made in violation of the Armistice."

The operative phrase here is in the heading: "prior consultation already completed." That phrase explains MacArthur's and his fellow Japanese and American negotiators' stratagem. In the text for inclusion in the minutes of the Security Consultative Committee, MacArthur is asking Fujiyama for prior authorization for possible future operations. He is not, therefore, requesting an *exemption* from prior consultation.

MacArthur cites the potential need "in the event of an exceptional emergency [on the Korean Peninsula]" for US forces to conduct "combat operations immediately from Japan." Of crucial note here is the adverb "immediately," which clearly implies acting without further consultation. The parties have fulfilled the prior consultation requirement by concluding the "Arrangements for Prior Consultation Already Completed (Secret)."

Fujiyama responds affirmatively in the text on behalf of the Japanese government. He offers authorization for "such military combat operations as need be undertaken immediately by the United States armed forces in Japan." This exchange is doubly significant when cast in the context of the proceedings of the Security Consultative Committee. In that context, it constitutes faithful fulfillment of the requirement for prior consultation, albeit prior to the occurrence of an emergency rather than prior to a mobilization in the wake of such an occurrence.

A second minutes

The minutes presented here in full are for a virtual meeting of the Security Consultative Committee posited for January 6, 1960. Real members of the committee gathered for their first meeting on September 8, 1960, and no record of any such discussion of prior consultation remains in the Japanese or US archives. Another version of the minutes surfaced in 2008 at the Gerald R. Ford Presidential Library at the University of Michigan, in Ann Arbor, Michigan. It bears the tersely compact title "Minute" and the date June 23, 1960 but is all but identical to the Foreign Ministry's version in every other respect.

We seek here the reason for the existence of the Ford Library version of the minutes. The story begins with an incident that occurred amid the unrest in the spring and summer of 1960.

As described in Chapter 4, the ratification of the security treaty by the Diet triggered massive demonstrations throughout Japan at the time. The unrest was still swelling in intensity when the US presidential press secretary, James Hagerty, arrived in Japan on June 10. Hagerty had come to take part in preparations for President Dwight D. Eisenhower's scheduled visit and was leaving Tokyo's Haneda Airport in a car with MacArthur. A mob surrounded the car, some of the members of the mob climbing onto the vehicle's hood and roof, and the US military needed to dispatch a helicopter to rescue the presidential press secretary and the ambassador.

The Hagerty Incident spawned doubts in MacArthur's mind about the staying power of the Kishi government. He developed a sense of urgency about bringing the Security Consultative Committee minutes that Fujiyama and he had initialed in January into force. That meant holding the initial meeting of the committee. Eager to get things started, MacArthur wrote the next day, June 11, to US secretary of state Herter.[80] That telegram resided in the US National Archives and was a classified document until 2013. Its declassification thus occurred three years after the Japanese Foreign Ministry released its investigative report and our panel's report with regard to the secret agreements.

Haste was essential, emphasized MacArthur. The Kishi government's days were clearly numbered, and the minutes addition initialed in January was only valid while Fujiyama was still in place as the foreign minister. (In the event, Kishi voiced his intention of resigning on June 20, announced his resignation formally three days later, and stepped down with his entire cabinet on July 15.) MacArthur wrote that he would propose to Fujiyama that they hold the Security Consultative Committee meeting on the very day that the treaty took effect. That appeared likely to be, he added, by the end of June. For public consumption, they would characterize the purpose of the inaugural meeting as being to work out organizational and procedural matters.

The security treaty was to take effect on June 23 when the Japanese and US governments would exchange ratifications of the treaty. Kishi would announce his resignation formally on the same day. Convening a formal meeting of the Security Consultative Committee, much less the inaugural meeting, was well-nigh impossible in the circumstances. MacArthur, however, was undaunted. He and his fellow negotiators were determined to produce a record of him and Fujiyama signing off on the minutes on that date.

If a formal convocation of the Security Consultative Committee was not feasible, the negotiators would hold a "preparatory meeting." Here is how the events of June 23 appear to have unfolded.

The original schedule had called for the exchange of ratifications to take place at the Foreign Ministry. Demonstrations threatened to disrupt the ceremony there, however, so the planners shifted the venue at the last minute to the official residence of the foreign minister. MacArthur and a retinue of embassy officials arrived at 9:25 a.m. on June 23. Fujiyama and Foreign Ministry officials had gathered before the Americans arrived for a meeting and breakfast.

The parties waited in separate rooms on the second floor until the ceremony began on the first floor at 10:10 a.m. In just a matter of minutes, the ceremony was over, concluded with a champagne toast. The Americans and Japanese then departed, each party accompanied by a security detail. Demonstrators learned belatedly of the change in venues for the ceremony and didn't turn up until around 11:00 a.m., after everyone was gone.[81]

As we have seen, the Japanese and US parties were both on the second floor of the foreign minister's official residence for about thirty minutes. The Preparatory Meeting of the Security Consultative Committee took place there and then. It consisted only, however, of the initialing of the addition to the minutes by MacArthur. Fujiyama had not yet secured Kishi's approval to initial the document on account of lapses in preparations for the meeting, and a copy on which his initials accompanied MacArthur's did not arrive at the US embassy until two days later.[82]

The last-minute stumble notwithstanding, the deed was done. The US government—Ambassador MacArthur—was on record as having requested, through the prior consultation mechanism, authorization for possible future operations. And the Japanese government—Foreign Minister Fujiyama—was on record as having given authorization for the operations. The Japanese and US governments thus secured solid evidence of prior consultation with regard to a thorny issue: possible operations by Japan-based US forces in the event of a military emergency on the Korean Peninsula.

Kishi's "foreign affairs people" exercised indeed the "diplomatic technique" he had cited in his response to Tsutsumi. They finessed the matter of port calls by nuclear-armed US naval vessels by refraining from raising the issue. And they disposed of the matter of overseas mobilizations of Japan-based US forces with a before-the-fact consultation.

The exercises of diplomatic technique relied heavily on interpretations of the texts of the January 19, 1960, exchange of notes between Herter and Kishi. Those interpretations tackled the phrases "major changes in [the] equipment [of US armed forces deployed in Japan]" and "shall be the subjects of prior consultation."

Japan's negotiators managed to sidestep the issue of temporary stops in Japan by nuclear-armed ships and aircraft. But if that issue arose in connection with prior consultation, they were prepared to address it with textual interpretation. Port calls and landings by ships and aircraft bearing nuclear arms, they could argue, did not constitute deployment into Japan.

Textual interpretation also prepared the Japanese to address the question of prior consultation for overseas mobilizations of Japan-based US forces. The Japanese could argue that the "prior" of "prior consultation" could mean prior to the occurrence of an emergency. And they could cite the minutes of the inaugural meeting of the Security Consultative Committee as evidence of that consultation.

Both of the exercises of diplomatic technique were essentially opaque to the eyes of the Japanese people. Their opacity persisted for half a century, until after the end of the Cold War. And their discovery adversely affected the Japanese people's confidence in the security treaty and in the Japanese-US alliance. On the other hand, the political scope of the security treaty impinged invariably on the treaty's military function. The contradictions were irreconcilable on the logical plane and therefore precluded resolution in the public sphere. Thus was the opacity of what became known as "secret agreements" a necessary condition for effectuating the security treaty.

3 Appraisal of the Revised Treaty

The importance of presentation

Katsuobushi (dried, fermented, and smoked skipjack tuna or less-expensive bonito) is a traditional ingredient in Japanese cuisine. High-grade *katsuobushi* is a prized gift on special occasions. Nishimura employed *katsuobushi* as a metaphor in describing the presentation of the revised security treaty.

> Presenting someone with a gift of *katsuobushi* as a naked block would be crude. The original security treaty came across as a naked block of *katsuobushi*, and Japanese frowned at the presentation. Conscientious presentation means placing the *katsuobushi* in a box of paulownia wood, wrapping the box with formal white paper, tying decorative red and white string around the box, and affixing an auspicious ornament of red and white paper folded ornately around a strip of dried abalone. In presenting the revised treaty, we placed it in a paulownia box of linkage to the UN charter (Articles 1 and 7), wrapped it in the white paper of shared worldview (Article 2), tied it with the decorative string of continuing dialog (Article 4), and affixed the ornament of the potential for further improvement in 10 years (Article 10). The difference between receiving a gift of *katsuobushi* as a naked block or in a beautifully wrapped wooden box makes all the difference in the world to the recipient. We were confident that the new treaty would earn a welcome reception from sensible Japanese.[83]

The security treaty revision of 1960 addressed aspects of the 1951 treaty that had occasioned dissatisfaction among the Japanese people. It received, as Nishimura describes metaphorically, more attention to presentation than its predecessor had. Thanks partly to that attention, the revised treaty gradually took hold among the people and earned their acceptance. The treaties differed more in presentation, however, than in substance. They were essentially identical with regard to their main thrust: Japan agreed to host US military bases, and, in exchange, the United States agreed to ensure Japanese security.

In this chapter, we have examined the revision—the repackaging—of the security treaty with regard to geographical scope and prior consultation. We can admire the repackaging for the dexterity of its framers, or we can find fault with its lack of transparency.

Defining the treaty area posed an especially daunting challenge in drafting the revised treaty. Substantive joint defense arrangements prevailed in the United States' defense pacts with other nations, but constitutional restrictions on militarization prevented Japan from entering into a reciprocal defense arrangement. That crimped the negotiators' latitude in defining the treaty area.

The US negotiators initially sought to define the treaty area as the Pacific while accepting the constitutional restrictions on Japan's participation. Japan, that is, could engage in joint defense in the Pacific to the extent permitted by its constitution. That approach proved unacceptable to Japanese, however, and the final version of the treaty narrowed the geographical scope of joint defense to "territories under the administration of Japan."

Narrow geographical scope notwithstanding, the treaty provided for some sort of joint defense there, in "territories under the administration of Japan." That was a huge improvement over the 1951 treaty, which Japanese perceived as essentially just a base-hosting agreement.

The revised treaty's framers were equally dexterous in allowing for different interpretations of joint defense. Japanese were able to interpret as exercising the right of individual self-defense what the Americans interpreted as exercising the right of collective self-defense.

Establishing a perception of balance in the Japanese-US relationship had long been a challenge for Japan's treaty negotiators. On November 24, 1950, the US government unveiled a memorandum that caused consternation in the Japanese Foreign Ministry. It had circulated the memorandum among representatives of the member nations of the Far Eastern Commission since September 22. The memorandum comprised seven issues for addressing in drafting a peace treaty with Japan. What caused the consternation in the Foreign Ministry was the fourth item:

> 4. Security
> The Treaty would contemplate that, pending satisfactory alternative security arrangements such as U.N. assumption of effective responsibility, there would be continuing cooperative responsibility between Japanese facilities and US and perhaps other forces for the maintenance of international peace and security in the Japan area.[84]

The Japanese Foreign Ministry, in preparing materials for the peace treaty negotiations, took issue with this item in the US memorandum. It argued that a nation's security depends foremost on the people's patriotic commitment to maintaining their nation's peace and security. Conversely, "continuing cooperative responsibility between Japanese facilities and US and perhaps other forces" was wholly inadequate, insisted the Foreign Ministry, as assurance of Japanese security. In bilateral or multilateral security arrangements, the Japanese people would draw encouragement only from those structured as partnerships among equals.[85]

Japan's negotiators would manage to keep the text of the peace treaty free of provisions for national security. They were unable, however, to position the original security treaty as a pact between equal partners based on collective security. It was, in the event, ever so much a framework for "continuing cooperative responsibility between Japanese facilities and US and perhaps other forces."

The revised treaty repositioned the security relationship as a mutual undertaking, albeit one confined to "territories under the administration of Japan." The base-hosting agreement had grown into an alliance. The alliance, however, was an asymmetrical affair. Whereas the United States pledged to defend Japanese territory, Japan pledged only to defend its own territory. The only US assets that stood to benefit from protection by the Japanese military were the US bases in Japan. Thus did the Japanese-US treaty differ formally from the United States' other security relationships, such as the North Atlantic Treaty Organization and the Philippine-US mutual defense pact. The Japanese-US security treaty had grown into something more than just a base-hosting agreement, but the US bases in Japan remained the foundation of the treaty.

We can credit the treaty negotiators for impressive dexterity in working out the geographical scope of the security treaty. The treaty area as defined in the final draft, though imperfect, is a tribute to skill and perseverance in reconciling factors of fearsome incompatibility. In contrast, the mechanism established for prior consultation impresses us less with the dexterity of its formulation than with its lack of transparency.

Prior consultation, as noted elsewhere, was a subject of the exchanges of notes that accompanied the signing of the treaty. The US government agreed to consult with the Japanese government before undertaking "major changes in the deployment into Japan of United States armed forces, major changes in their equipment, [or] the use of facilities and areas in Japan as bases for military combat operations to be undertaken from Japan [not including Okinawa or the Ogasawara Islands]."

We encounter clear dichotomy in the dynamics of the Japanese and US approaches to the issue of prior consultation. The Japanese sought to secure the appearance of a treaty arrangement concluded on the basis of equality between sovereign states. On the other hand, the Americans were primarily interested in avoiding any diminution of the military value of their Japanese bases.

The US government accepted the prior-consultation mechanism while predicating that acceptance on the understanding that it could continue to use its Okinawa bases freely. It secured an exemption from prior consultation, as noted elsewhere, for port calls by nuclear-armed naval vessels.

Japan's negotiators, meanwhile, exercised opaque diplomatic technique in countenancing prior consultation in advance of a military emergency. That allowed for Japan-based US forces to deploy under the UN flag in response to an emergency on the Korean Peninsula.

The US government was unenthusiastic, to say the least, about prior consultation. But that was just part of the problem with the prior consultation mechanism. Also undermining the mechanism was Japan's unpreparedness to hold its own in the arrangement. The Japanese government was unprepared to respond meaningfully if the US government were to seek consultation on an important development.

Nishi Haruhiko, a recently retired diplomat at the time of the negotiations on the revised treaty, spoke out against prior consultation. He had been the vice minister for foreign affairs at the time of the attack on Pearl Harbor but had resigned that post less than a year later. Nishi returned to the diplomatic service after the war and served as Japan's ambassador to Australia and, later, to the United Kingdom. His criticism of the prior consultation mechanism appeared in the February 1960 issue of a Japanese monthly magazine.

> The new security treaty mandates prior consultation when Japan-based US forces deploy overseas for a purpose other than defending our nation. In that sense, the new treaty has narrowed the latitude of the Japan-based US forces to operate freely. Yet Japanese participation in US military planning through consultation and agreement, be it within that latitude, constitutes Japanese participation in the military action in question. Japan thus bears joint responsibility with the United States to the nation or nations subject to the action.[86]

An alliance is ordinarily a relationship in which the participating nations take coordinated action in pursuit of a common purpose and accept shared responsibility for the outcome of their action. Japan's government has demanded that the US government consult with it before undertaking any of a specified set of actions. Yet whether Japan is prepared to fulfill responsibility commensurate with its demand is unclear. That question has dogged the issue of prior consultation from the time of the earliest work on the revised security treaty to this day. The question is fundamental to the Japanese-US relationship under the security treaty, and it remains basically unanswered.

Prior consultation has been strikingly inactive since the revised security treaty took effect on June 23, 1960. Not once has it triggered a response by Japan-based US forces to a military emergency in the Far East. That is welcome and compelling evidence of restraint imposed by the security treaty.

Revising the security treaty improved its packaging, as Nishimura described, and unquestionably made the pact more palatable for the Japanese people. The revised treaty is lacking, however, in clarity and in transparency. That lack is more than apparent in just the two facets of the treaty that we have examined closely: geographical scope and prior consultation. It reflects a forced effort to present the asymmetry of the Japanese-US treaty relationship as genuine mutuality. And the diplomatic artifices employed—albeit unavoidably—in lubricating the treaty undeniably damaged the Japanese people's trust in their government.

Tōgō nonetheless placed the shortcomings of the revised security treaty in a positive light. He appraised the treaty as the good-faith result "of taking mutual defense to the very edge of what was possible without violating the [Japanese] constitution."[87] We need to understand the treaty as the best result that was possible under the circumstances of its origin. Then will we have an honest and sound basis for eyeing ways to achieve a more ideal treaty framework.[88]

Chapter Notes

1 106 Congressional Record (Bound), vol. 106, pt. 10 (June 14–22, 1960), 13518–13597 (Washington, DC: Government Printing Office, 1960), https://www.govinfo.gov/content/pkg/GPO-CRECB-1960-pt10/pdf/GPO-CRECB-1960-pt10-7-1.pdf, and US Department of State, American Foreign Policy, Current Documents, 1960, 671 (Washington, DC: Government Printing Office, 1960).

2 This chapter is an expansion of Sakamoto Kazuya's "Anpo kaitei ni okeru sōgosei no mosaku: Jōyakukuiki to jizenkyōgi o megutte" [The Striving for Mutuality in the Revision of the Security Treaty: The Treaty Area and Prior Consultation], *Kokusai seiji* [International Relations] 115 (May 1997), and Sakamoto's "Nichi-Bei Anpo jizenkyōgisei no seiritsu o meguru gimon: Chōsen hantō yūji no baai" [Doubts about the Origins of the Provisions for Prior Consultation in the Japanese-US Security Treaty: In the Event of an Emergency on the Korean Peninsula], *Handai hōgaku* [Osaka Law Review] 46, no. 4 (October 1996).

3 "Treaty of Mutual Cooperation and Security between Japan and the United States of America," US Department of State, Central Files (CF) 794.5/2-1858, RG 59, National Archives.

4 United Nations, Treaty Collection, https://treaties.un.org/doc/Publication/UNTS/Volume%20136/volume-136-I-1832-English.pdf.

5 US Department of State, CF 794.5/3-1257 and 794 5/5-457. See also endnote 71 in Chapter 4.

For example, Article 1 of the "Nichi-Bei anzen hoshō jōyaku kaiteian" [Proposal for Revision of the Japanese-US Security Treaty] accompanying the "Nichi-Bei kyōryoku kankei o kyōka hatten seshimeru tame ni toru beki seisaku" [Optimal Political Measures for Strengthening and Developing Collaborative Japanese-US Relations], a Ministry of Foreign Affairs document dated March 1957, reads:

> Japan shall grant the United States the right to deploy army, air force, and navy forces required for contributing toward the prevention of an armed attack against Japan, either in Japan or in the vicinity thereof, and the United States shall accept said right accordingly.

Article 4 then goes on to stipulate:

> Each party to the treaty is to regard an armed attack on Japan from without as a danger to its own peace and security and declare that it will act to meet the common danger in accordance with its constitutional processes.
>
> [Remainder omitted]

The only purpose for which the US military could use the bases was for the defense of Japan, and the only armed attacks subject to joint action were those against Japan (which likely also included Okinawa and the Ogasawara Islands, which were then under the administrative control of the United States). The Ministry of Foreign Affairs explained that the revision proposal incorporated the "joint-defense" approach for Japan only, not a bilateral "mutual-defense" arrangement; Japan would thus engage in joint action to protect itself and the American military stationed in Japan. "Nichi-Bei Anzen Hoshō Jōyaku no kaiteian no setsumei" [An Explanation of Revisions to the Japanese-US Security Treaty] reads as follows:

> The treaty unilaterally grants the United States the right to deploy troops, so the defense obligations are obviously one-sided. The defense of Japan is nothing but the self-defense of the US military stationed in Japan. Thus, there is no reason to go out of the way to create a 'bilateral' arrangement by expanding the geographical scope of the defense obligations to areas outside Japan.

The current security treaty stipulates mutual defense by obligating joint action against an "armed attack against either Party in the territories under the administration of Japan," a phrasing slightly different from the proposal's call for joint action against any "armed attack against Japan."

Source: "Kishi sōri daiichiji hōbei kankei ikken, Kishi-Makkāsā yobi kaidan (oite-Tōkyō), dai 1 kan" [Preliminary Talks between Kishi and MacArthur on Prime Minister Kishi's First Visit to the United States (in Tokyo), vol. 1] 16 (3), *Kaigi shiryō (1)* [Meeting Materials (1)]. This document is available on the Diplomatic Archives website, https://www.mofa.go.jp/mofaj/annai/honsho/shiryo/shozo/pdfs/2018/04_21.pdf.

6 US Department of State, *Foreign Relations of the United States* (*FRUS*), 1955–1957 (Washington, DC: Government Printing Office), Document 159.

7 US Department of State, CF 611.94/6-2058 (tel. 3380) and CF 794.5/10-1358 (tel. 792).

8 US Department of State, CF 611.94/6-2058 (tel. 3380).

9 US Department of State, *FRUS*, 1958–1960, Document 16.

10 US Department of State, *FRUS*, 1958–1960, Document 16, and CF 611.94/7-3158 (deptel. 206).

11 US Department of State, *FRUS*, 1958–1960, Document 27.

12 The signatories of the North Atlantic Treaty, however, undertook broader obligations in regard to mutual defense. They articulated those obligations in Article 5 of the treaty:

> The Parties agree that an armed attack against one or more of them in Europe or North America shall be considered an attack against them all and consequently they agree that, if such an armed attack occurs, each of them, in exercise of the right of individual or collective self-defence recognised by Article 51 of the Charter of the United Nations, will assist the Party or Parties so attacked by taking forthwith, individually and in concert with the other Parties, such action as it deems necessary, including the use of armed force, to restore and maintain the security of the North Atlantic area.

North Atlantic Treaty Organization, https://www.nato.int/cps/en/natolive/official_texts_17120.htm.

13 Tōgō Fumihiko, *Nichi-Bei gaikō 30-nen: Anpo, Okinawa to sono go* [Thirty Years of Japanese-US Diplomacy: The Security Treaty, Okinawa, and Later] (Tokyo: Chuokoronsha, 1989), 77–78. For further comments by Tōgō on the US negotiating stance, see Hara Yoshihisa, *Nichi-Bei kankei no kōzu: Anpo kaitei o kenshō suru* [The Mechanics of the Japanese-US Relationship: An Examination of the Revision of the Security Treaty] (Tokyo: NHK Books, 1991), 143. For MacArthur's summary of the October 4 meeting with Kishi and Fujiyama, see *FRUS*, 1958–60, Document 31.

At the beginning of the meeting on October 4, 1956, Ambassador MacArthur addressed Prime Minister Kishi and Foreign Minister Fujiyama as follows:

> I am well aware of how busy the both of you are, so today, if it would be all right with you, I would just like to begin by presenting our general views, a proposal, and the feasibility of the proposal. First, I am extremely happy that the time has now come to discuss adjustments to our security relationship.

> The fact that we are at this point is not only a testament to how important the United States views the issues at hand but also a tribute to the efforts of the prime minister and government of Japan, with all the parties involved working to bring a new age in Japanese-US relations to fruition. To be honest, there was significant opposition to the matter of forming a new security treaty in the United States. From our standpoint, after all, these discussions will result in the United States voluntarily placing limits on the extensive, ongoing rights that it has held under the existing treaty and assuming new obligations in the express provisions of the treaty. There was quite a bit of opposition to that premise. However, the President and the US government put their faith in the Prime Minister and Foreign Minister and began to support the idea of establishing a new, mutual treaty to strengthen Japanese-US security ties on the basis of the Prime Minister's vision and, by extension, nurture stable, enduring Japanese-US relations in all aspects. It is true, of course, that there are several issues to resolve on both the Japanese side and US side. In these negotiations, I do not want to engage in "diplomatic" dealing. Instead, my intention is to lay all my cards out on the table from the outset. I want to be as frank and open as possible, just as I have been to this point in my discussions with both of you.

MacArthur then explained the US treaty proposal. Going through the first paragraph of Article 5, which spelled out mutual defense ("Each Party recognizes that an armed attack in the Pacific directed against the territories or areas under the administrative control of the other Party would be dangerous to its own peace and safety and declares that it would act to meet the common danger in accordance with its constitutional processes"), MacArthur detailed the rationale behind the provisions:

> The text of the Article conforms to Article 4 of the mutual-defense treaty between the United States and the Republic of the Philippines. As the proposal currently reads, the geographical scope of the treaty for the Japan side would comprise the Japanese mainland, Shikoku, Kyushu, Hokkaido, and Amami Oshima, and the scope for the American side would cover the Ryukyu Islands, Ogasawara Islands, and US islands in the Pacific. The treaty, as current worded, would not need to be revised if the administrative rights over the Ryukyu Islands or Ogasawara Islands were to be returned or the Kurile Islands were to be reverted to Japanese control, nor does the wording conflict with any US rights under Article 3 of the peace treaty. The phrase "dangerous to its own peace and safety," which originated with the Monroe Doctrine, is the strongest wording that we use and the phrasing of choice in our other mutual-aid treaties. The Article also includes "in accordance with its constitutional processes," so any obligations to send troops abroad would naturally be excluded if overseas deployment were to be problematic on constitutional grounds. A completely mutual treaty would create issues for Japan, but I think this wording avoids any constitutional concerns. We feel that it takes Japan's circumstances into as much consideration as possible, and US congressional leaders have given the terms their approval.

MacArthur also offered the following explanation of the prior-consultation system.

> There are two other issues that have come up in your statements, as well as in Foreign Minister Fujiyama's presentation to Secretary Dulles: the issue of introducing nuclear weapons and the issue of using Japan-based American troops outside Japan. Foreign Minister Fujiyama said that if Japan were to be attacked, Japan would allow the US military to use Japanese bases, and in the event of an attack on the US military outside Japan, Japan would provide refueling assistance but would like to consult with the United States on permitting the strategic use Japanese bases. You also explained that though sending troops overseas would be problematic, Japan would allow the United States to use bases for the purpose of refueling. (Let me add, off the record, that Washington really struggled to iron out these issues.) We have drawn up a formula for these two issues to meet the requests on both sides.

After covering the above points, MacArthur went on to detail a tentative formula for an exchange of notes on prior consultation. (For more on the proposal, see Chapter 6, p. 337.)

> The first clause (likely "The deployment of United States forces and their equipment into bases in Japan") has to do with nuclear weapons. The United States normally groups normal weapons and nuclear weapons together, which means that we cannot treat nuclear weapons as a separate, solitary category and also explains why we have not used the term "nuclear weapons" in the phrasing. Just to be clear, this proposal applies only to nuclear weapons; regarding all other weapons, the terms of our existing agreement remain in effect. The second clause (likely "and the operational use of these bases in an emergency") deals with the strategic use of bases in emergency situations. This portion of the proposal is based on the assumption that it will not cause any impediments to the use of bases for refueling. The part stating that any invasion of a friendly nation in Asia by a member of the Communist bloc concerns Japan's own security is from Foreign Minister Fujiyama's statement to Secretary Dulles, and refueling support is extremely important to the United States.

MacArthur thus explained that the use of Japanese bases for refueling purposes would not be subject to prior consultation, a statement that helped solve the "secret agreement" question of whether temporary stops by US vessels carrying nuclear weapons would or would not be subject to prior consultation. See Chapter 6 for more information.

Source: "10-gatsu 4-ka sōri, gaimu daijin, zaikyō Bei taishi kaidanroku" [Minutes of October 4 Meeting between the Prime Minister, Foreign Minister, and US Ambassador to Tokyo], October 4, 1958, "Sonota kanren bunsho" [Other Pertinent Documents] no. 1-18: 210–234, https://www.mofa.go.jp/mofaj/gaiko/mitsuyaku/pdfs/k_1960kaku1.pdf.

14 US Department of State, CF 794.5/10–2358 (tel. 882).

15 US Department of State, CF 794.5/11-2858 (deptel. 802).

16 Japan Ministry of Foreign Affairs, "Japan-US Security Treaty," https://www.mofa.go.jp/region/n-america/us/q&a/ref/1.html.

17 US Department of State, *FRUS*, 1958–1960, Document 35.

18 US Department of State, *FRUS*, 1958–1960, Document 42.
19 Tōgō, *Nichi-Bei gaikō 30-nen*, 78.
20 US Department of State, *FRUS*, 1958–1960, Document 27.
21 Japan Ministry of Foreign Affairs, "Japan-US Security Treaty," https://www.mofa.go.jp/region/n-america/us/q&a/ref/1.html.
22 Shūgiin Gaimu Iinkai Chōsashitsu [House of Representatives Committee on Foreign Affairs, Research Office], *Shūgiin Nichi-Bei Anzen Hoshō Jōyaku Tō Tokubetsu Iinkai shingi yōkō* [Deliberations by the House of Representatives Special Committee on the Japanese-US Security Treaty] (Tokyo: Ministry of Finance Printing Bureau, 1961), 44–45.
23 Nakamura Akira, *Sengo seiji ni yureta kenpō 9-jō: Naikaku hōseikyoku no jishin to tsuyosa* [Postwar Political Threats to Article 9 of the Constitution: The Confidence and the Power of the Cabinet Legislation Bureau] (Tokyo: Chūōkeizai-sha, 1996), 184–185.
24 For a critical appraisal from the standpoint of international law of the government's interpretation, see Tabata Shigejirō, "The New Treaty of Security and the Right of Self-Defence," *Journal of International Law and Diplomacy* 59, no. 1/2 (July 1960). For an approving appraisal, see Ōhira Zengo, "Shūdanteki jieiken no hōri" [The Legal Logic of the Right of Collective Self-Defense] in Anzen Hoshō Kenkyūkai [Security Research Association], ed., *Anzen hoshō taisei no kenkyū* [A Study of the Security Framework], vol. 1 (Tokyo: Jiji Press: 1960). For historical perspective on the Japanese government's interpretation of the right of collective security, see Sakaguchi Kiyoshi, "Shūdanteki jieiken ni kansuru seifu kaishaku no keisei to tenkai" [The Development and Implementation of the Government's Interpretation of the Right of Collective Security], pts. 1 and 2, *Revue Diplomatique* 1330 (July/August 1996) and 1331 (September 1996).
25 National Graduate Institute for Policy Studies and Institute for Advanced Studies on Asia, University of Tokyo, The World and Japan database, Joint Communiqué of Japanese Prime Minister Kishi and US President Eisenhower issued on June 21, 1957, https://worldjpn.grips.ac.jp/documents/texts/JPUS/19570621.D1E.html.
25 US Department of State, *Department of State Bulletin* 37:953, 534.
27 US Department of State, *FRUS*, 1958–1960, Documents 47 and 48.
28 For more on this subject, see Sakaguchi, "Shūdanteki jieiken ni kansuru," pt. 1, 73–77.
29 For a discussion of the historical development of the right of self-defense in international law, see Taoka Ryōichi, *Kokusaihōjō no jieiken* [The Right of Self-Defense in International Law] (Tokyo: Keiso Shobo, 1981), revised edition.
30 Sakaguchi, "Shūdanteki jieiken ni kansuru," pt. 1, 79–80, 82–84.
31 House of Representatives, *Kenpō, kokusaihō to shūdanteki jieiken* [The Constitution, International law and the Right of Collective Self-Defense], https://www.shugiin.go.jp/internet/itdb_shitsumona.nsf/html/shitsumon/b094032.htm.
32 US Department of State, *FRUS*, 1958–1960, Document 27.
33 Tōgō, *Nichi-Bei gaikō 30-nen*, 75–77. For MacArthur's explanation of why the Japanese negotiators resisted the terms "jointly" and "collectively" and substituted other phrasing, see US Department of State, *FRUS*, 1958–1960, Document 48.

34 US Department of State, *FRUS*, 1958–1960, Document 47.
35 US Department of State, *FRUS*, 1958–1960, Document 48.
36 US Department of State, *FRUS*, 1958–1960, Document 56.
37 US Congress, Senate Committee on Foreign Relations, *Treaty of Mutual Cooperation and Security with Japan: Hearing Before the Committee on Foreign Relations,* United States Senate, Eighty-Sixth Congress, Second Session (Washington, DC: Government Printing Office, 1960), 8–33.
38 US Department of State, *FRUS*, 1958–1960, Document 35.
39 Japan Ministry of Foreign Affairs, "Iwayuru 'mitsuyaku' mondai ni kansuru chōsa, sonota kanren bunsho" [The Investigation into the So-Called Secret Agreements, Other Pertinent Documents], "Draft Treaty of Mutual Cooperation for Security between Japan and the United States of America," November 21, 1958, no. 1-30: 347–352, https://www.mofa.go.jp/mofaj/gaiko/mitsuyaku/pdfs/k_1960nk1.pdf.
40 Japan Ministry of Foreign Affairs, "Iwayuru 'mitsuyaku' mondai, sonota kanren bunsho," "11-gatsu 26-nichi Fujiyama Daijin zaikyō Bei taishi kaidanroku" [Minutes of November 26 Meeting between Minister Fujiyama and US Ambassador to Tokyo], November 26, 1958, 353–374, https://www.mofa.go.jp/mofaj/gaiko/mitsuyaku/pdfs/k_1960nk1.pdf.
41 Komori Yoshihisa, "Ima akasu 60-nen Anpo jōyaku kaitei no shinsō" [New Revelations about the 1960 Revision of the Security Treaty], interview with Douglas MacArthur II, *Chūō Kōron* (November 1981).
42 Tōgō, *Nichi-Bei gaikō 30-nen*, 79.
43 US Department of State, *FRUS*, 1958–1960, Document 35.
44 US Department of State, CF 794. 5/11-358 (tel. 948).
45 US Department of State, *FRUS*, 1958–1960, Document 42.
46 US Department of State, *FRUS*, 1958–1960, Document 35.
47 US Department of State, *FRUS*, 1958–1960, Document 43.
48 US Department of State, *FRUS*, 1958–1960, Document 47.
49 National Graduate Institute for Policy Studies and Institute for Advanced Studies on Asia, University of Tokyo, Database of Japanese Politics and International Relations, Agreed Minute to the Treaty of Mutual Cooperation and Security, https://worldjpn.grips.ac.jp/documents/texts/JPUS/19600119.O1E.html.
50 US Department of State, *FRUS*, 1958–1960, Document 28
51 US Department of State, CF 794.5/11-358 (deptel. 706).
52 US Department of State, *FRUS*, 1958–1960, Document 43.
53 US Department of State, *FRUS*, 1958–1960, Document 73. Also see *FRUS*, 1958–1960, Document 81.
54 US Department of State, *FRUS*, 1958–1960, Document 47.
55 US Department of State, *FRUS*, 1958–1960, Document 79.
56 Nishimura Kumao, *San Furanshisuko heiwa jōyaku: Nichi-Bei Anpo jōyaku* [The San Francisco Peace Treaty: The Japanese-US Security Treaty] (Tokyo: Chuokoron Shinsha, 1999), 65–66.
57 US Department of State, CF 611.947/2-1260 (tel. 2621, 2622, 2623) and CF 611.947/2-1560 (tel. 2637). Also see *FRUS*, 1958–1960, Document 104.

58 Shūgiin Gaimu Iinkai Chōsashitsu, *Shūgiin Nichi-Bei Anzen Hoshō Jōyaku Tō Tokubetsu Iinkai shingi yōkō*, 58–59.

59 National Graduate Institute and University of Tokyo, The World and Japan database, Exchanged Notes, Regarding the Implementation of Article VI of Treaty of Mutual Cooperation and Security between Japan and the United States of America, https://worldjpn.grips.ac.jp/documents/texts/docs/19600119.T2E.html.

60 *Shūgiin kaigiroku jōhō* [House of Representatives Minutes], Committee on Foreign Affairs, No. 11, https://kokkai.appri.me/content/60369.

61 National Graduate Institute and University of Tokyo, The World and Japan database, Joint Communiqué of Japanese Prime Minister Kishi and US President Eisenhower issued on January 19, 1960, https://worldjpn.grips.ac.jp/documents/texts/JPUS/19600119.D1E.html.

62 National Diet Library, "Kokkai kaigiroku" [Record of Diet Proceedings], Shūgiin Nichi-Bei Anzen Hoshō Jōyaku Tō Tokubetsu Iinkai, February 26, 1960, https://seijidb.com/kokkai/meetings/13816.

63 Kishi Nobusuke, *Kishi Nobusuke kaikoroku: Hoshu gōdō to Anpo kaitei* [Kishi Nobusuke Memoir: The Conservative Coalition and the Revision of the Security Treaty] (Tokyo: Kōsaidō Shuppan, 1983), 532.

64 National Archives, National Security Council (NSC) document 6008/1, Statement of U.S. Policy Toward Japan, June 11, 1960, Lot File 63 D 351.

65 Tōgō, *Nichi-Bei gaikō 30-nen*, 126.

66 US Department of State, CF 794.5/9-958 (memo, 9 September 1958).

67 *New York Times*, May 19, 1981. Reischauer was confirming remarks he had made in an interview that appeared in Japanese in the *Mainichi Shimbun* on the previous day.

68 Japan Ministry of Foreign Affairs, "Iwayuru 'mitsuyaku' mondai ni kansuru chōsa kekka" [The Investigation into the So-Called 'Secret Agreements', Findings], https://www.mofa.go.jp/mofaj/gaiko/mitsuyaku/kekka.html.

69 Japan Ministry of Foreign Affairs, "Iwayuru 'mitsuyaku' mondai ni kansuru yūshikisha iinkai hōkokusho" [Report by Panel of Experts in Regard to the So-Called 'Secret Agreements'], https://www.mofa.go.jp/mofaj/gaiko/mitsuyaku/pdfs/hokoku_yushiki.pdf.

70 National Graduate Institute and University of Tokyo, The World and Japan database, Record of Discussion, https://worldjpn.grips.ac.jp/documents/texts/JPUS/19630413.O1J.html.

71 US Department of State, *FRUS*, 1958–1960, Documents 58 and 57.

72 US Department of State, CF 794. 5/9-958 (memo, 9 September 1958) and *FRUS*, 1958–1960, Document 24. The State Department has deleted parts of this exchange as "not declassified" in the public archive memorandum of this meeting.

73 United States Army, "Comparison of U.S. Base Rights in Japan and the Ryukyu Islands," Status of Forces Agreement, Box 8, *History of the Civil Administration of the Ryukyu Islands*, Records of the Army Staff, RG 319.

74 Japan Ministry of Foreign Affairs, "9-gatsu 11-nichi Fujiyama Daijin–Daresu Kokumu chōkan kaidanroku" [Minutes of the September 11 Meeting between Minister Fujiyama and Secretary of State Dulles] (September 11, 1958), in "Iwayuru

'mitsuyaku' mondai, sonota kanren bunsho," 160–189, https://www.mofa.go.jp/mofaj/gaiko/mitsuyaku/pdfs/k_1960kaku1.pdf.

75 Komori Yoshihisa, "Ima akasu 60-nen Anpo jōyaku kaitei no shinsō."

76 "Agreement Regarding the Status of United States Armed Forces in Japan," https://www.mofa.go.jp/region/n-america/us/q&a/ref/2.html.

77 Japan Ministry of Foreign Affairs, "Minutes for Inclusion in the Record of the First Meeting of the Security Consultative Committee," in "Iwayuru 'mitsuyaku' mondai, hōkoku taishō bunsho," 29–30, https://www.mofa.go.jp/mofaj/gaiko/mitsuyaku/pdfs/t_1960nk.pdf, and in searchable format at https://worldjpn.grips.ac.jp/documents/texts/JPUS/19590509.O1J.html.

78 Japan Ministry of Foreign Affairs, "Iwayuru 'mitsuyaku' mondai ni kansuru yūshikisha iinkai hōkokusho."

79 The US National Archives document is available for viewing online at a website operated by the Research Institute for Islands and Sustainability, University of the Ryukyus: https://riis.skr.u-ryukyu.ac.jp/images/ddc_20191217-02.pdf.

80 US State Department telegram 4131 (January 11, 1960), CF 611.947/6-1160. The US government declassified this telegram on July 31, 2013, at my request.

81 *Asahi Shimbun* and *Mainichi Shimbun*, June 23, 1960, evening editions.

82 Nishimura Masahiko, "Anpo kaiteiji no jizen kyōgi seido kōshō: Chōsen gijiroku, dōi, teisatsu hikō" [Negotiation of the Prior Consultation Mechanism during the Revision of the Security Treaty: The Korea Minute, Consent, Surveillance Flights], *Hōgaku ronsō* [Kyoto Law Review] 183:6 (September 2018).

83 Nishimura, *San Furanshisuko heiwa jōyaku*, 143–144.

84 National Graduate Institute and University of Tokyo, The World and Japan database, Memorandum on the Japanese Peace Treaty Circulated by the United States to the Governments Represented on the Far Eastern Commission, https://worldjpn.grips.ac.jp/documents/texts/JPUS/19501124.O1E.html.

85 Japan Ministry of Foreign Affairs, *Heiwa jōyaku no teiketsu ni kansuru chōsho* [Documents Related to the Conclusion of the Peace Treaty], 3:73; and Nishimura, *San Furanshisuko heiwa jōyaku*, 30–32.

86 Nishi Haruhiko, "Nihon no gaikō o ureeru" [Worried about Japanese Diplomacy], *Chūō Kōron* (February 1960): 98.

87 Tōgō, *Nichi-Bei gaikō 30-nen*, 99.

88 It goes without saying that domestic circumstances in Japan at the time were a significant obstacle facing security revisions capable of "reconciling mutual defense with the Japanese constitution." Before to the start of the treaty-revision negotiations, Tōgō outlined the problematic conditions at home:

> The following domestic circumstances can be considered reasons for the current state of affairs.
>
> 1. Backlash against the militaristic, nationalistic thought and policy that took hold in the 1930s and the accompanying mistrust of government authority
> 2. A vague sense of antipathy toward the United States as the nation responsible for overseeing the occupation
> 3. A sense of danger about occupying an East-West flashpoint and an accompanying sense of helplessness with regard to self-defense

4. War-weariness and a yearning for unarmed neutrality
5. Constitutional issues and domestic politics

With these circumstances forming an undercurrent, the Japanese government has based its defense efforts on the foundation of the security treaty while dealing with internal challenges on the financial front and resisting the external challenges of the Cold War.

Source: "Nichi-Bei kan no anzen hoshō mondai ni kansuru ken" [Regarding the Japan-US Security Issues], July 21, 1958, "Sonota kanren bunsho," no. 1-7: 78–89, https://www.mofa.go.jp/mofaj/gaiko/mitsuyaku/pdfs/k_1960kaku1.pdf.

Chapter 6

Continuing to Look into Prior Consultation and the Secret Agreements

The US aircraft carrier USS *Midway* docks at her home port in Yokosuka, Japan. October 5, 1973. Photo from Asahi Shimbunsha

This book first appeared in Japanese in 2000, and this English edition reflects subsequent discoveries about the events described. Most notably, Chapter 5 addressed the findings of an investigation by Japan's Foreign Ministry into four secret agreements between Japan and the United States. Representatives of the two nations concluded the agreements in question when negotiating the revision of their bilateral security treaty and the return of Okinawa to Japanese administration. The Foreign Ministry launched an internal investigation into the agreements in September 2009 with the start of a new government comprised of former opposition parties eager to look into the policies adopted by the former ruling Liberal Democratic Party since 1955. They established a third-party panel in November to examine and flesh out the findings of its internal investigation.

I served on this panel, and was responsible for Chapter 2, about calls at Japanese ports by nuclear-armed US naval vessels.[1] Inspiring this additional chapter here is a realization that has dawned on me in recent years. I have drawn on information unearthed by the Foreign Ministry in my discussion of the secret agreements in Chapter 5 of this book. I have drawn, too, on information that has become available through the declassification of US government documents. A crucial aspect of the secret agreements evaded my attention, however, in my examination of the newly available information. Namely, I failed to recognize the brilliance of the negotiators in framing their supplementary agreements—the "secret agreements"—with regard to prior consultation.

My discussion of the secret agreements focuses on the two that pertained to prior consultation: before the introduction of nuclear weapons into Japanese territory and before the deployment of Japan-based American troops to respond to military emergencies elsewhere in the Far East. I revisit the secret agreements here with an eye to highlighting the subtle sublimity of their phrasing.

Japanese foreign minister Fujiyama Aiichirō and US ambassador to Japan Douglas MacArthur II initialed the prior consultation secret agreements, as noted in Chapter 5, on January 6, 1960. As also noted, they initialed a third agreement on that day. It remains classified but apparently pertained to US rights under the status of forces agreement, formally titled the "Agreement under Article VI of the Treaty of Mutual Cooperation and Security between Japan and the United States of America, Regarding

Facilities and Areas and the Status of United States Armed Forces in Japan." Let us examine here in detail the two secret agreements that pertained to prior consultation.

1 Port Calls by Nuclear-Armed US Naval Vessels

We begin our examination with the secret agreement that pertained to calls at Japanese ports by nuclear-armed US naval vessels. The Japanese and US governments left that issue outside the realm of formal debate and negotiation and declined to subject it to any formal agreement. Notwithstanding the absence of a formal agreement, a Herter-Kishi exchange of notes addressed the issue, albeit obliquely.

The Herter-Kishi exchange, formally titled "Regarding the Implementation of Article VI of Treaty of Mutual Cooperation and Security between Japan and the United States of America," was between US secretary of state Christian Herter and Japanese prime minister Kishi Nobusuke. It was one of multiple exchanges of notes that Herter and Kishi signed along with the revised security treaty on January 19, 1960. This exchange, introduced earlier on page 291 in Chapter 5, is the one meant here in all subsequent references to "the Herter-Kishi exchange of notes."

The phrase "operations . . . conducted under Article V of the said Treaty" is in reference to Article 5's provision for "an armed attack against either Party in the territories under the administration of Japan." Notably absent in the text are any references to US naval vessels or to nuclear weapons. Yet the Japanese government has insisted consistently that port calls by nuclear-armed US naval vessels are subject to prior consultation. It has made that insistence since the signing of the revised treaty and even since the formal acknowledgement of the existence of the secret agreements.

The Japanese government's explanation has referred to an oral understanding. Fujiyama and MacArthur affirmed a shared understanding of key provisions of the revised security treaty while it was under negotiation from 1958 to 1960. And the Japanese government maintains that their oral understanding reflected the positions of both governments.

Below is the Japanese Foreign Ministry's interpretation of the Fujiyama-MacArthur oral understanding. This interpretation appears in English in a Foreign Ministry document written later titled "On 'prior consultation' under the US-Japan Security Treaty" and dated April 25, 1968.

> The Japanese Government understands that prior consultation under the Japan-US Security Treaty will be held in the following cases:
> 1. When "major changes in the deployment into Japan of United States Armed forces" which means deployment of U.S. forces the minimum size of which would be about one divisional strength in the case of land forces, a comparable air force unit and a navy task force, is made.
> 2. When "major changes in their equipment" which means introduction into Japan of nuclear warheads or intermediate and long range missiles and the construction of bases for such weapons, is made.
> 3. When the use is made of facilities and areas in Japan as bases for military combat operations to be undertaken from Japan other than those conducted under article V of the Treaty.[2]

The above interpretation is inconsistent with the US military's policy of neither confirming nor denying the presence of nuclear weapons anywhere. Reconciling this interpretation of prior consultation with the "neither confirm nor deny" policy would require a special provision for nuclear-armed naval vessels. The implication is that the Japanese and US governments concluded a confidential agreement to deal with that issue. No evidence of any such special provision came to light, however, in the Foreign Ministry's investigation of the secret agreements.

Lending credence to the Japanese government's insistence that introducing nuclear weapons was subject to prior consultation is the January 6, 1960, "Record of Discussion."[3] As noted in Chapter 5, the Japanese Foreign Ministry released that formerly classified document on March 9, 2010. It confirms a mutual interpretation of the Herter-Kishi exchange of notes to be conducted 13 days later. Paragraph "2a" in that document expressly links "major changes in . . . their equipment" to nuclear weapons.

> "Major changes in their equipment" is understood to mean the introduction into Japan of nuclear weapons, including intermediate and long-

> range missiles as well as the construction of bases for such weapons, and will not, for example, mean the introduction of non-nuclear weapons including short-range missiles without nuclear components.[4]

The Japanese Foreign Ministry reflected the content of the above paragraph in its formal interpretation of the Fujiyama-MacArthur oral understanding. That content buttresses, as noted, the government's insistence that the introduction of nuclear weapons was subject to prior consultation. Less supportive of the government's stance in that regard, however, was paragraph "2c" in the Record of Discussion, repeated here.

> "Prior consultation" will not be interpreted as affecting present procedures regarding the deployment of United States armed forces and their equipment into Japan and those for the entry of United States military aircraft and the entry into Japanese waters and ports by the United States naval vessels, except in the case of major changes in the deployment into Japan of United States armed forces.

Even before the Japanese government disclosed the Record of Discussion, declassified US diplomatic documents had hinted at its existence. That had invited suspicions that a secret Japanese-US agreement exempted port calls by nuclear-armed US naval vessels from prior consultation. The formal disclosure of the Record of Discussion by the Japanese government in 2010 confirmed those suspicions. And it invited a compelling new suspicion: that the Japanese Foreign Ministry had intentionally omitted the "present procedures" caveat from its interpretation of the Fujiyama-MacArthur oral understanding.

If nuclear-armed vessels had made port calls under the procedures established to administer the original security treaty, they could continue to do so under "present procedures" exemption. And that would undermine the Japanese government's insistence that introducing nuclear weapons by any means was subject to prior consultation.

A crucial linkage

The Foreign Ministry's internal investigation found that the Japanese negotiators regarded the Record of Discussion as linking the Herter-Kishi exchange of notes and the status of forces agreement. More precisely, they recognized paragraph "2c" of the Record of Discussion as linking the exchange of notes and Article 5 of the status of forces agreement. Article 5 prescribes procedures for handling the coming and going of US naval ships and military aircraft at Japanese ports and airfields.[5]

Japan's treaty negotiators believed that paragraph "2c" of the Record of Discussion ensured that port calls by nuclear-armed US naval vessels were subject to prior consultation. My reading of the related documents persuades me that the US negotiators at the time were of the same view.

To be sure, the Foreign Ministry's investigation exposed disagreement between the Japanese and US negotiators with regard to paragraph "2c" of the Record of Discussion.

> We found several documents that refute the notion that Japanese and US negotiators agreed that the Record of Discussion exempted nuclear-armed naval vessels from prior consultation when passing through Japanese territorial waters or calling at Japanese ports. The fact is that the Japanese and US negotiators disagreed on that matter.[6]

The disagreement in question appears to have been something that arose after the revised security treaty took effect. It does not appear to have figured in the treaty negotiations.

The US negotiators made a proposal in May 1959, when the revised treaty was taking shape, for creating the Record of Discussion. They proposed conducting a confidential exchange of notes to serve as a shared interpretation of the public exchange of notes. Tōgō Fumihiko, a Japanese diplomat introduced in Chapter 5, commented on the creation of the Record of Discussion in a June 1960 memorandum.

At the time, Tōgō was the director of the Japan-US Security Treaty Division in the Japanese Foreign Ministry's North American Affairs Bureau. He writes in the memorandum that the proposed Record of Discussion was to confirm a shared understanding of four items:

> (1) The procedures then in effect for handling the deployment of US forces into Japan would remain unchanged, (2) The reference to equipment meant nuclear weapons, (3) The withdrawal of US forces from

> Japan would not be subject to prior consultation, and (4) The requirement for prior consultation in regard to the operation of US military bases in Japan would apply only to the mobilization of Japan-based US forces for combat operations outside Japan.[7]

Tōgō reports that the format of the written understanding was a subject of dispute between the Japanese and US negotiators. A formal protocol would ordinarily be the natural choice for the purpose at hand, but the US negotiators opposed that option because it would require congressional approval. They therefore preferred to frame the understanding in an exchange of notes. The Japanese negotiators, on the other hand, were wary of the confidential format. They feared that any secret agreement would ultimately come to light and trip up government ministers when they were fielding questions in the Diet.

Ambassador MacArthur cautioned that the exchange of notes that would accompany the revised treaty could become subject to bilateral misunderstanding. He argued that a written, shared interpretation of the content of that exchange of notes was essential to prevent misunderstanding. And he noted that political considerations would preclude an honest expression of mutual understanding in a public format. In response, the Japanese negotiators tabled a proposal for what became the Record of Discussion.

The Record of Discussion included all four confirmations sought by the US negotiators: "1" in paragraph "2c," "2" in paragraph "2a", "3" in paragraph "2d," and "4" in paragraph "2b." Thus did the Record of Discussion confirm in paragraph "2c" that US military deployments into Japan would remain exempt from prior consultation.

Tōgō writes that the Japanese and US negotiators were "in verbal agreement" from the outset with regard to all four items.[8] Curiously, the Japanese government designated the Record of Discussion as a classified document but allowed for the disclosure of its content.[9] The "classified" designation was presumably in compliance with US government wishes; that is, the preference that the Japanese government would not release any bilateral diplomatic documents that contained the term "nuclear weapons."

As for the Japanese negotiators, they voiced opposition to paragraph "2d," which pertained to "the transfer of units of United States armed forces and their equipment from Japan." They felt, Tōgō reports, that espousing the right of withdrawal in what was essentially an exchange of notes was inappropriate.[10]

The Record of Discussion was a document for preventing future misunderstanding of the Herter-Kishi exchange of notes. Its text was hardly anything that would admit to significant differences in understanding among the Japanese and their American counterparts. In it, the negotiators put in writing what had been an oral understanding since the start of the treaty negotiations. The Record of Discussion, meanwhile, contained nothing that would be discomfiting to either government if disclosed publicly.

Some in the US military feared that prior consultation would impair the logistical value of the US bases in Japan. That concern had mounted in the wake of the Second Taiwan Strait Crisis in August 1958. Ambassador MacArthur regarded paragraph "2c" as a means of putting military minds at ease.

State Department officials, incidentally, had issued instructions to MacArthur about prior consultation when the security treaty negotiations began. They had instructed him to secure Japanese government authorization for exempting port calls by nuclear-armed US naval vessels from prior consultation. The order from the State Department was surely at the request of the navy high command.[11]

MacArthur knew that requesting authorization outright for exempting prior consultation would be counterproductive, and he declined to act on the instruction. The findings of a later US government study of this stage of the treaty negotiations are revealing. According to the study report, the reply from the embassy was firm: No Japanese leader would ever sign a document renouncing the right to be consulted about incoming nuclear weapons. "No specific understanding was reached," the study found, as to whether port calls by nuclear-armed ships required prior consultation.[12]

This US government study finding meshes with Tōgō's version of events. He offered perspective on the negotiations in an internal ministry report of 1968, eight years after the treaty signing: "I have no special recollection of having debated the issue [with the US government negotiators]," stated Tōgō, "and no record exists of any such debate."[13]

We note that Tōgō is not denying that any discussion of port calls by nuclear-armed vessels and prior consultation arose. In fact, Fujiyama acknowledged in a 1981 newspaper interview that the subject came up in the negotiations.[14] MacArthur, meanwhile, commented in later years that he had discussed the issued with Kishi, Fujiyama; Vice Minister for Foreign Affairs Yamada Hisanari, and Tōgō. MacArthur stated in the interview that he had explained to the Japanese side that prior consultation for port calls by nuclear-armed vessels would be impossible.[15]

Fujiyama and MacArthur thus both verified that the treaty negotiators discussed prior consultation for port calls by nuclear-armed vessels. However, their comments and Tōgō's both suggest, as the US government study found, that the negotiators reached no specific understanding.

We can confidently assume that nuclear-armed US naval vessels called at Japanese ports frequently during the Cold War, and the US government oversaw those port calls without engaging in prior consultation with the Japanese government. It did so despite having pledged to consult in advance with the Japanese government about the following:

- "major changes in [the] equipment [of US armed forces] deployed into Japan"—a pledge made publicly in the Herter-Kishi exchange of notes—and
- "the introduction into Japan of nuclear weapons"—a pledge made confidentially in the Record of Discussion.

"Home porting"

The US navy thus apparently engaged on a continuing basis in conduct seemingly counter to the above pledges. That suggests that its overseers had grounds for believing in the justifiability of that conduct.

One possible justification is the exemption for "present procedures" in paragraph 2c of the Record of Discussion. That exemption covers "the entry into Japanese waters and ports by United States naval vessels." This argument is subject to the objection, however, that it does not specify vessels equipped with nuclear weapons.

Ambassador MacArthur, as we have seen, had addressed the subject firmly with Kishi, Fujiyama, and other senior Japanese officials. He had told them that port calls by nuclear-armed vessels would not be subject to prior consultation. Some in the US government may have regarded that as grounds for confidence in docking nuclear-armed ships at Japanese ports. But that is unlikely. An ambassadorial admonishment in conversation hardly qualified as a basis for diplomatically and militarily important strategic moves.

The US navy's overseers surely had stronger grounds for feeling confident about having nuclear-armed vessels make port calls in Japan. They perhaps found those grounds in the two words "their equipment" in the reference to "major changes in their equipment" (Herter-Kishi exchange of notes). Let us examine possible interpretations for those two words.

Japanese government officials have insisted since the treaty signing in 1960 that "their equipment" refers to any and all kinds of equipment. In their public pronouncements, they have asserted that port calls by nuclear-armed vessels are subject to the prior consultation requirement.

However, a simple and honest reading of "major changes in their equipment" yields a different understanding of "their equipment." The natural and unforced understanding of those two words would seem to be obvious: equipment in the hands of troops on the ground in Japan. Indeed, the Japanese government, before concluding the revised security treaty, had implicitly accepted that interpretation with regard to port calls. Government officials had insisted that port calls by ships of the US 7th Fleet did not constitute "deployment" in Japan. And the US government surely interpreted "major changes in their equipment" in the simple and straightforward manner.

The two governments confirmed in writing their mutual understanding that "present procedures" would not be subject to prior consultation. That, as we have seen, was in the Record of Discussion. Diplomats in both governments wanted to have that confirmation on hand as necessary to justify some deployment as "present procedures."

We can thus conclude with confidence that the Japanese government—notwithstanding public pronouncements to the contrary—and the US government have a shared understanding, that port calls are not deployments. A complication for this shared understanding arose, however, in 1973. That was when the US navy began to use Yokosuka as a home port for aircraft carriers.[16]

Some officials in the US government were concerned that "home porting" would trigger renewed friction in connection with prior consultation. The officials feared that Japan's political left would assert that the home-ported aircraft carriers were subject to prior consultation. They perceived an opening for the Japanese left to claim that the Japan-based aircraft carriers constituted "major changes in the deployment into Japan of United States armed forces [and] major changes in their equipment."[17]

The US government ultimately stonewalled the issue. It denied stubbornly that the aircraft carriers' new relationship with Yokosuka corresponded to the "major changes" in question. The navy even adopted the term "extended visits," rather than home porting, for the aircraft carriers' stays in Yokosuka.

Home porting inevitably occasioned speculation that the Japanese and US governments had reached some sort of special and secret agreement. The Foreign Ministry, in its secret agreements investigation, looked into that possibility. It found no evidence, however, of special treatment for home porting under the prior consultation requirement. It did find evidence, though, of voices in the Foreign Ministry arguing that home porting should be subject to prior consultation.[18]

Unmentionable weapons

The notion that the Japanese government has always interpreted "their equipment" as including port calls by nuclear-armed vessels is untenable. We can be certain that the Japanese negotiators never thought that the Americans adhered to that interpretation. We can be certain, too, about another aspect of the Japanese approach to the negotiations: They never asked the US government to make port calls by nuclear-armed US naval vessels subject to prior consultation. Tōgō's "no special recollection . . . no record exists" is a striking, albeit oblique, denial.

Nor did the issue arise in the talks between Fujiyama and then US secretary of state John Foster Dulles in Washington, DC, on September 11, 1958. In the Dulles-Fujiyama talks, the Japanese foreign minister explained his government's stance on the revision of the security treaty. He broached the subject of Japan-based US military operations in response to an attack on a third nation.

Fujiyama conveyed his government's expectation of the US government to consult with it before undertaking such operations. Fujiyama's wording of those expectations, however, was porous.

> We perceive no problem in continuing the relationship under the pres-

> ent security treaty in regard to cooperation in resupplying. . . . When the US military stations forces in Japan, we would hope, for the purpose of resupplying and other considerations, to be consulted in regard to the [positioning and troop strength] and the [armament] of those forces.[19]

This text would seem to exempt port calls by US naval vessels from the request for consultation. Calling at ports in Japan for resupplying does not, after all, constitute being stationed in Japan.

As noted in Chapter 4 of this book, "Fujiyama and the Foreign Ministry were thinking . . . in terms of reconciling the treaty with Japanese sentiment through a supplementary agreement, not through wholesale revision." They maintained that stance until summer 1958. That was when "Kishi determined that revising the security treaty was the best approach to addressing the treaty's issues and acted accordingly."

Nuclear weapons were an issue that Fujiyama and senior Foreign Ministry diplomats wanted to address with a supplementary agreement. They wanted to make the introduction of nuclear weapons subject to prior consultation. That included making port calls by nuclear-armed vessels subject to prior consultation, as we see in a document of July 2, 1958.

The document is a Japanese proposal with regard to the deployment of US forces in Japan and the employment of those forces. Below is the pertinent passage from the proposal:

> The United States shall not introduce nuclear weapons into Japan, including ships and aircraft that [dock or land] in Japan temporarily, as well as United States forces deployed in Japan, without the express prior agreement of the Japanese government.[20]

The Japanese demand for prior consultation with regard to "ships and aircraft that [dock or land] in Japan temporarily" subsequently vanishes from the negotiations. We find no explanation of the disappearance in the archives. It presumably had something to do with the shift in approach to revising the treaty, rather than tweaking it with supplementary agreements. The Japanese surely recognized that seeking to include port calls by nuclear-armed ships in a revised treaty was a nonstarter.

Ambassador MacArthur had discussed the issue of mentioning nuclear weapons in official discussions on October 4, 1958. Those discussions were the first official session held to negotiate the revision of the security treaty. The US negotiators proposed an exchange of notes, though they would later dub the proposal "Formula," as in a formula for handling prior consultation. Their proposal makes no mention of nuclear weapons, and MacArthur explained why:

> In the United States, we ordinarily regard conventional weapons and nuclear weapons in the same light and therefore cannot discuss nuclear weapons separately. We therefore avoid the term "nuclear weapons."[21]

The US ambassador presented a US "Draft Treaty of Mutual Cooperation and Security Between Japan and the United States of America" to Kishi, Fujiyama, and Foreign Ministry officials on October 4, 1959. That was about three weeks after the Dulles-Fujiyama talks. He accompanied that draft proposal with the previously mentioned "Formula," with regard to prior consultation:

> Formula
>
> Under arrangements made for the common defense, the United States has the use of certain bases in Japan. The deployment of United States forces and their equipment into bases in Japan and the operational use of these bases in an emergency would be a matter for joint consultation by the Japanese Government and the United States Government in the light of circumstances prevailing at the time.

Ambassador MacArthur explained orally that this proposed exchange of notes encompassed nuclear weapons.

"Their equipment"

Japan's negotiators would have understood "their equipment" to mean the equipment of US forces stationed at bases on Japanese soil. Just three weeks earlier, Fujiyama had expressed Japan's wishes to Dulles in a manner that clearly exempted port calls by ships afloat. The Japanese negotiators would not have assumed that the US government was offering something that they were not seeking.

By all accounts, "their equipment" meant the same thing to the Japanese and the US negotiators. Nowhere in the archives do we find any evidence of differing interpretations of that phrase in the Herter-Kishi exchange of notes. The negotiators all understood the equipment in question to be that in the hands of troops stationed at bases in Japan. "Major changes in equipment," as stated in the Herter-Kishi exchange of notes, explicitly cited that equipment and implicitly included the introduction of nuclear weapons. And any such changes were to be subject to prior consultation.

Fujiyama would later insist that the negotiations had left unspecified whether nuclear-armed port calls were subject to prior consultation. He recalled, for example, in a 1981 newspaper interview that the negotiators "didn't make that clear."[22] Fujiyama was saying that the Herter-Kishi exchange of notes didn't necessarily mandate prior consultation for port calls by nuclear-armed vessels. We need to be careful, however, in interpreting his remark. Interpreted precisely, Fujiyama was saying that the negotiators did not reach clear agreement that prior consultation was unnecessary.

Prior consultation for port calls by nuclear-armed vessels was not a subject of debate in the security treaty negotiations. The issue would have been on the negotiators' minds. As we have seen, it had arisen repeatedly before the treaty negotiations began formally. Note the previously cited foreign ministry proposal of July 2, 1958. The negotiators avoided the subject, however, in their bilateral discussions. And they confined their agreement on nuclear weapons and related prior consultation to a narrowly delineated scope: the requirement for prior consultation with regard to the introduction of nuclear weapons by US forces deployed in Japan; that is, by US forces stationed at bases there.

The negotiators stopped short of a clear agreement on port calls by nuclear-armed vessels, which were not "stationed" in Japan. And the Herter-Kishi exchange of notes did not mandate prior consultation on such port calls. All evidence suggests that the Japanese and US negotiators were in full agreement on that point.

To be sure, Japanese-US disagreements have arisen as to the precise meaning of the Herter-Kishi exchange of notes. Those disagreements arose, however, after the signing of the revised security treaty. They were not in play during the treaty negotiations.

Japanese government ministers have consistently maintained in the

Diet and elsewhere that port calls by nuclear-armed vessels are subject to prior consultation. Successive Japanese governments have maintained that no Japanese government has agreed to dispense with prior consultation for such port calls. The Japanese and US governments had refrained from reaching a clear decision with regard to the matter. Perhaps the Japanese wanted to retain the option of requesting prior consultation if a nuclear-armed vessel needed to make port. That was aside from any interpretation of the Herter-Kishi exchange of notes. And Japanese governments have seen fit to misrepresent that exchange for 60 years.

Akagi Munenori, the then director general of the Defense Agency, set the prototype for the government stance in April 19, 1960. He was responding to a question by the Socialist Party's Yokomichi Setsuo during a meeting of the House of Representatives Special Committee on the Japanese-US Security Treaty. "Port calls at Yokosuka," stated Akagi, "or at any other port in Japan by vessels of the US 7th Fleet equipped with nuclear weaponry would be subject to prior consultation."

Temperatures were rising across the nation amid swelling opposition to the revised security treaty, and temperatures were rising in the halls of the Diet as the treaty ratification debate escalated. We can only speculate as to Akagi's motivation, but we can well imagine why he would assert the supposed requirement for prior consultation. Akagi, with an eye to defusing the overheated debate in the Diet, surely saw that as the most prudent response. Earlier that month, he had also used an analogy in the Diet that Japan was not a puppet of the United States, so it is likely that national pride was at stake for him.

The US government, meanwhile, did not take issue with Akagi's explanation. That was in keeping with well-established US policy. The Japanese and US had a strong mutual interest in concealing the arrangement that ensured access to Japanese ports for all US naval vessels. And the US government fulfilled its part of the bargain by leaving Japanese assertions of a prior consultation requirement unchallenged.

Exactly when the unspoken agreement took hold is uncertain. Ambassador MacArthur assured Tōgō, however, on September 5, 1958, that the US government would not challenge Japanese assertions under that agreement. The two were discussing the peripheral issue of whether prior consultation occasioned veto rights.[23] MacArthur, in retirement, offered insights into the principle of unspoken understandings in an interview for a Japanese magazine article.

> In diplomacy, we sometimes leave things intentionally vague. We leave them vague because we realize that defining things clearly is not necessarily in our interest. I am speaking of [Japan and the United States]. If we try to make things overly sharp and define them detail upon detail, that can prove harmful and can be disadvantageous for our basic national interests. Some degree of vagueness can help calm things, especially when groups of differing ideologies are seeking to turn problems into major turmoil.[24]

2 Mobilization of Japan-Based US Forces in Response to Military Emergencies on the Korean Peninsula

A stratagem for fulfilling the prior consultation requirement in mobilizing Japan-based US forces turned up in the secret agreements investigation. That stratagem surfaced as material that appeared in the records of the first meeting of the Japan-US Security Consultative Committee. The existence of a document that contained that material had long been implicit.[25] Thus did the original, 2000 edition of this book include the following observation in Chapter 5:

> US diplomatic documents declassified in recent years . . . suggest that Japanese and US negotiators had addressed the need for prior consultation in the event of an emergency on the Korean Peninsula.

The stratagem emerges in a text unearthed in the Foreign Ministry's secret agreements investigation. Ministry investigators unearthed the text as four working drafts and as two copies of what appears to be the final version, though one of the two is missing a title. The full text of what is presumably the final version of the proposed insertion was included on pages 302–303 in Chapter 5.

The draft was characterized as "a" final version of the proposed insertion. That characterization reflects the existence of a slightly different draft that also appears to have served as a final version. As noted earlier, that version resides in the Gerald R. Ford Presidential Library at the University of Michigan, in Ann Arbor, Michigan. It differs from the Foreign Ministry's copy in that it bears the tersely compact title "Minute" and the date June 23, 1960, and opens with the phrase, "At the Preparatory Meeting of the Security Consultative Committee today Ambassador MacArthur tabled draft Terms of Reference for the Committee." The two versions are identical in every other respect.[26] Neither bears the initials or signatures that would appear on the official version.

The reason for the differences in the date and opening phrase—and the reason for believing the Ford Library's version to also be a final version—becomes clear when we examine how events unfolded chronologically. But before exploring the chronology, let us examine the meaning and implications of the text.

In our investigative committee report on the Foreign Ministry's secret agreement, Haruna Mikio's chapter, as noted in Chapter 5 of this book, covered military emergencies on the Korean Peninsula and prior consultation. He characterized the material prepared for inclusion as minutes of the inaugural meeting of the Security Consultative Committee as "of the character of a secret agreement" and functioning as "an exemption from prior consultation" for the US to conduct military operations out of Japan if an emergency arose on the Korean Peninsula.[27]

Haruna's "secret agreement" characterization is corroborated in the "Summary of Unpublished Agreements Reached in Conjunction with the Treaty of Mutual Cooperation and Security with Japan" and the "Description of Consultation Arrangements under the Treaty of Mutual Cooperation and Security with Japan" located in the US National Archives.[28] Both documents can be found in section 2 of Chapter 5, along with further discussion of their content. Though undated, the wording of the documents places them after the signing of the security agreement and before the convening of the first meeting of the Security Consultative Committee.

To recap, the "Summary of Unpublished Agreements" encompasses five topic items, of which the first two, the Record of Discussion and the Security Consultative Committee Minutes, are of immediate relevance.

Notably, in the Consultative Committee Minutes the discussion is unequivocally described as "a secret arrangement." The remaining three topic items cover largely administrative matters and minor matters of interpretation.

The "Description of Consultation Arrangements under the Treaty of Mutual Cooperation and Security with Japan" categorizes activity under the different arrangements in four categories. The fourth, "Arrangements for Prior Consultation Already Completed (Secret)," is a reference to the material for inclusion in the Security Consultative Committee Minutes. As previously discussed in Chapter 5, its phrasing implies authorization for US forces to act without further consultation ("immediately") "as an exceptional measure in the event of an emergency [on the Korean Peninsula]," based on the premise that the requirement for prior consultation has been fulfilled by the conclusion of the "Arrangements for Prior Consultation Already Completed (Secret)." In the context of the proceedings of the Security Consultative Committee, it constitutes faithful fulfillment of the requirement for prior consultation, ahead of the occurrence of the "emergency" in question.

Note that Article 4 of the Treaty of Mutual Cooperation and Security between Japan and the United States of America (see Documents appendix) provides that "The Parties will consult together from time to time regarding the implementation of this Treaty." And Article 6 of the security treaty provides that "the use of [the US bases in Japan] as well as the status of United States armed forces in Japan shall be governed by a separate agreement." That "separate agreement," initialed by Herter and Kishi on the same day as the signing of the security treaty, was the Agreement under Article VI of the Treaty of Mutual Cooperation and Security between Japan and the United States of America (the status of forces agreement).

The status of forces agreement provided in Article 25 that "a Joint Committee shall be established as the means for consultation between the Government of Japan and the Government of the United States on all matters requiring mutual consultation regarding the implementation of this Agreement." That committee is what became the Security Consultative Committee.[29]

Handling the Fujiyama-MacArthur exchange in another format, such as an exchange of notes, would have contravened the prior consultation requirement and would thus have been unconvincing and ineffective.

Handling the exchange as part of the Security Consultative Committee was thus a stroke of brilliance. Rather than contravening the prior consultation requirement, it complied with that requirement to the letter.

A US government representative, Douglas MacArthur II, ambassador of the United States to Japan, had engaged in prior consultation with a representative of the Japanese government, Fujiyama Aiichirō, Japan Minister for Foreign Affairs. MacArthur, going through proper channels, had secured advance authorization for potential military operations in the event of narrowly specified circumstances.

Let us turn now to the chronology of the drafting and implementation of the Fujiyama-MacArthur exchange. Tōgō writes of the origins of that exchange in the previously mentioned memorandum of June 1960.

1. Japanese-US discussion of the [standing of the] Yoshida-Acheson exchange of notes had proceeded no further since the Japanese proposal floated on May 8 [1959]. Out of the blue, the US ambassador made a request on July 6 [1959] for a meeting with the prime minister. The US government was concerned, he explained, about the possibility of renewed aggression [by North Korea], and attached immense importance to ensuring that Japan-based US forces could respond immediately to any such emergency. MacArthur wanted to seek the understanding of the prime minister on this matter. The Yoshida-Acheson exchange of notes implicitly countenanced the overseas deployment of Japan-based US forces in support of UN operations. MacArthur offered assurance, however, that the US government would interpret the exchange as confining such action to the Korean Peninsula.
2. In the event of renewed aggression in Korea by the Communists, we naturally should countenance action by Japan-based US forces as UN forces. Such support would, if anything, be natural from the standpoint of ensuring our own national security and from the standpoint of cooperating with the United Nations. We are preparing a new exchange of notes, however, in regard to prior consultation, and complying with the US request would undermine the positive effect on domestic public opinion of that exchange. The US request was therefore difficult to accept.[30]

Kishi was preparing to leave on a series of state visits to nations in Europe and in Latin America on July 11. He promised to meet with MacArthur again before his departure, but the demands of dealing with party matters made that impossible. Instead, Yamada conveyed Kishi's response to the ambassador on July 10.[31]

Yamada reported that the US proposal touched on extremely serious issues but that Kishi and Fujiyama would do everything possible to help work out a bilateral solution. MacArthur pledged in response that he and his colleagues would respond in good faith. They would strive, if the Japanese accepted the Americans' basic conditions, to avoid creating a quandary for Kishi or the Japanese government. Yamada assured MacArthur that he would convey the ambassador's message to Kishi. He volunteered the personal and unofficial impression that the stance evinced by MacArthur augured well for achieving a mutually satisfactory solution.[32]

No public record exists, unfortunately, of what sort of formal response emerged from the Japanese government after Kishi's return or of how the US government reacted. We know, however, that below-the-radar dialog unfolded between the governments through the latter half of 1959. The dialogue culminated in a solution that became public in December.

According to Tōgō's memorandum, Fujiyama submitted a proposal to MacArthur on August 22, 12 days after Kishi's return. The proposal addressed US concerns about a potential emergency on the Korean Peninsula. It was a proposed addition to the upcoming exchange of notes that would express a pledge by the Japanese government. The pledge was to "give positive consideration" to the US military's use of Japanese bases in response to such an emergency. To be sure, the Japanese government would still insist on prior consultation, but it would essentially promise in advance a "Yes" answer.

The Americans rejected this proposal. They expressed understanding of the Japanese position but insisted that some sort of allowance was necessary for situations where time did not allow for consultation.

This is where the idea debuts for devising a solution in the minutes of the first meeting of the Security Consultative Committee. Tōgō reports that the Japanese and US negotiators thereupon went to work on preparing the minutes of the committee's inaugural meeting.

The US negotiators submitted a proposal on October 6 for material to include in the minutes. After what Tōgō describes as "agonizing deliberation," the Japanese responded with a counterproposal on November 28. Negotiations unfolded through three meetings over the following three weeks. The negotiators finally reached agreement on a draft on December 23, and Fujiyama and Ambassador MacArthur initialed the document on January 6. That was the same day that the foreign minister and the ambassador initialed the Record of Discussion.

A Foreign Ministry memorandum of September 18, 1959 summarizes comments by MacArthur on the idea of advance authorization.

> [The ambassador] opined that securing advance authorization through the new committee would prove acceptable to Washington. He emphasized the need for finding a solution that would not impinge on the value of the formula [of prior consultation to be addressed in the upcoming exchange of notes].[33]

Tōgō's reference to preparing minutes for the first meeting of the Security Consultative Committee and MacArthur's reference to advance authorization highlight the character of the minutes. Here was a convergence of the thinking of the Japanese and the American negotiators. They had arrived mutually at the idea of preparing a beforehand agreement that would qualify, when necessary, as prior consultation.[34]

One could object that prior consultation cannot take place before a crisis or emergency arises. The Japanese and US governments presumably preempted that objection, however, with their interpretation of the texts of the exchange of notes. Their interpretation surely provided that "prior" could mean "before an emergency occurred," as well as "before the US military launched an operation from its Japanese bases" [after an emergency had occurred].

The perseverant and masterfully nuanced efforts of the Japanese and US negotiators culminated on January 6, 1960. Fujiyama and MacArthur initialed the Minutes for Inclusion in the Record of the First Meeting of the Security Consultative Committee. The document joined the Record of Discussion, the Herter-Kishi exchange of notes, and other documents, nonpublic and public, that accompanied the security treaty when it was signed on January 19. It was thus ready to take effect as soon as circumstances allowed for convening the meeting. Alas, that was not to be until eight months later, on September 8.

Second minutes

We turn now to the matter of the second final version of the minutes. That version, as noted, bears the date June 23, 1960—the date the treaty took effect—and refers to "the Preparatory Meeting of the Security Consultative Committee." To understand the reason for that version, we need to begin with the reason for the timing of the first version. The story begins with an incident that occurred amid the so-called Anpo unrest.

As described in Chapter 5, the June 10 Hagerty Incident spawned doubts in MacArthur's mind about the staying power of the Kishi government, and he wrote the text of a telegram on June 11, which was declassified at my request under the US Freedom of Information Act. That was in 2013, three years after the Japanese Foreign Ministry released its investigative report and our panel's report with regard to the secret agreements.

Given that Kishi's government was nearing its end and the January minutes addition was only valid while Fujiyama was still foreign minister, haste, McArthur emphasized, was essential. Public unrest made convening a formal meeting of the Security Consultative Committee well-nigh impossible. Undaunted, MacArthur planned a meeting on the very day that the treaty took effect, June 23, under the guise of a "preparatory meeting." As related in Chapter 5, the exchange of ratifications was intended to take place at the Ministry of Foreign Affairs, but a last-minute switch shifted the venue to the official residence of the foreign minister.

The ceremony itself took a matter of minutes. By the time the demonstrators turned up, everyone was gone.[35] During the thirty-minute period while both parties were on the second floor, the Preparatory Meeting of the Security Consultative Committee took place. Only MacArthur initialed the addition to the minutes, as Fujiyama had not yet secured Kishi's approval. It was not until two days later that a copy with Kishi's initials alongside MacArthur's arrived at the US embassy.[36]

With this the US government was on record as having requested, through the prior consultation mechanism, authorization for possible future operations. Likewise, the Japanese government was on record as having given authorization for the operations. It was solid evidence of prior consultation between the governments regarding a divisive issue: possible operations by Japan-based US forces in the event of a military emergency on the Korean Peninsula.

Remaining questions

Let us note that this account of the Preparatory Meeting of the Security Consultative Committee requires a couple of asterisks. For one thing, prior consultation and authorization for a response to a hypothetical event are unexplored territory in the realm of diplomacy. Whether a generally accepted procedure exists is questionable, as is the diplomatic standing of the result.

Another question about this account pertains to the awareness of the minutes in the Japanese and US governments. We find in the US diplomatic archives a reference to a Security Consultative Committee meeting on June 23, 1960, but that reference includes no mention of the Fujiyama-MacArthur exchange.[37] No reference to the June 23 meeting has surfaced in the Japanese Foreign Ministry documents that have been made public. Further, we have no idea, of course, what surprises lurk in the Japanese and US government vaults of still-classified documents.

Yet another question pertains to the whereabouts of the signed documents, both the January 6 and June 23 versions. The January 6 version of the Minutes for Inclusion in the Records of the First Meeting of the Security Consultative Committee that the Foreign Ministry's investigation unearthed was an unsigned copy. Still unknown are the whereabouts of the original, initialed by Fujiyama and MacArthur. As noted, the June 23 version of the Minute in the Ford Library is also an unsigned copy.

Also missing are the initialed copies of the Fujiyama-MacArthur Record of Discussion. The loss of important diplomatic documents is more than a hindrance to historical research. It is a serious breach of public trust.

These two important documents, which we know from secondary sources to have been initialed by the Japanese foreign minister and the US ambassador to Japan, have disappeared. Something went grievously wrong in the Japanese Foreign Ministry's document-management system (and possibly in the same function in the US State Department). Japan's Foreign Ministry launched a committee on April 6, 2010, to investigate the problem of missing diplomatic documents, and that committee issued its report about two months later, on June 4. Below is an excerpt from the committee's concluding remarks:

> Progress in resolving the problems with the framework for document management described in this report has proceeded gradually since the Act on Access to Information Held by Administrative Organs [enacted in May 1999, taking effect in April 2001] took effect. Further progress is necessary, however, and the Public Records and Archives Management Act [enacted in July 2009, taking effect in April 2011], which will take effect next fiscal year, will demand stepped-up measures and effort across the entire sequence of drafting, storing, managing, and disclosing documents.
>
> In the Foreign Ministry, we followed up the investigations into secret agreements with the formulation of the Rules Regarding the Disclosure of Diplomatic Archives. We have laid a foundation for those rules by establishing the Diplomatic Archives Disclosure and Document Management Headquarters, by adopting the 30-year automatic disclosure rule, and adopting clear criteria for classifying documents.[38]

3 Conclusion

Our panel for examining the Foreign Ministry's investigative findings with regard to secret agreements employed the following definition of a "bilateral secret agreement": an important agreement or understanding between two governments that the governments do not reveal to the people of either nation and that differs from a publicly disclosed agreement or understanding. In the narrow sense of that definition, the two allegedly secret agreements discussed here were not, strictly speaking, secret.

Let us recall how we have seen that the Japanese and US governments handled the requirement for prior consultation in each case. Regarding port calls by nuclear-armed navy vessels, the two governments handled the issue by not reaching an agreement. Since the Japanese and US governments had not reached an agreement with regard to the need for prior consultation, no secret agreement existed.

Nor did the two governments resort to a secret agreement to avoid prior consultation with regard to the other issue: operations by Japan-based US forces in response to a military emergency on the Korean Peninsula. The governments addressed the issue in a public, though admittedly idiosyncratic, manner. They documented the process of prior consultation for possible future operations in the public minutes of the Security Consultative Committee.

Furthermore, let us recall here the exchange between Kishi and the Socialist Party lawmaker Yokomichi, described in Chapter 5. That exchange took place in a session of the House of Representatives Special Committee on the Japanese-US Security Treaty on April 26, 1960. Yokomichi cited the possibility of Japan-based US forces deploying in response to renewed hostilities on the Korean Peninsula and asked Kishi if such a deployment would be subject to prior consultation. Kishi replied in the affirmative.

The veracity of Kishi's response was long questionable in the face of US government sources that indicated otherwise. We saw two instances of such sources in Chapter 5. One was US National Security Council document NSC 6008/1, "Statement of US Policy toward Japan." That document stated forthrightly that "combat operations in immediate response to an attack against the UN forces in Korea" were exempt from prior consultation. Similarly, we saw that the State Department's J. Graham Parsons had assured Senator William Fulbright that such an exemption was in place.

Both of the above instances hinted strongly at the existence of a secret agreement for bypassing prior consultation. We initially thought that the secret agreement had emerged when the minutes to the Preparatory Meeting of the Security Consultative Committee were found. But we now know, as described above, that those minutes were not, strictly speaking, a secret agreement. More importantly, we now know that they did not actually provide for bypassing prior consultation. Kishi, we now know, was speaking truthfully in his response to Yokomichi.

The very edge of the possible

Our analysis has acquitted the Japanese government of violating the prior consultation requirement with regard to nuclear weapons and the mobilization of Japan-based US forces. In each case, interpretation of the Herter-Kishi exchange of notes figured in the manner of addressing the requirement for consultation.

The option of eschewing agreement with regard to prior consultation for port calls by nuclear-armed vessels hinged on semantics: whether nuclear-armed ships, docked in harbors, counted as changes in the equipment of US forces stationed in Japan. Semantics also figured in fulfilling the prior consultation requirement for dispatching Japan-based US forces to fight on the Korean Peninsula. As described, the negotiators interpreted "prior" broadly enough to cover consultation prior to the occurrence of a military emergency.

So, neither of the dispositions of prior consultation discussed here qualifies under our narrow definition for "secret agreement." Both, however, were highly obscure. In any case, from the perspective of ordinary citizens, each was, for all intents and purposes, a secret agreement. The fact they were not disclosed certainly gives that impression.

Foreign relations and national security inherently entail dealings that require confidentiality. We recoil, however, at the long-term obscurity accorded to the agreements in question here. In Japan, the government declined throughout the Cold War to disclose and explain the agreements to the citizenry. And it continued after the fall of the Berlin Wall to keep the agreements essentially under wraps.

The obscurity of the prior consultation arrangements undermined the Japanese people's trust in the security treaty and in the Japanese-US alliance. Especially disconcerting for some was the uncertainty with regard to port calls by nuclear-armed US naval vessels.

That such unfortunate results accrued from the Japanese government's chosen approach is clear. Let us acknowledge, however, that at least the negotiators avoided overtly dishonest arrangements regarding prior consultation. They declined, for example, to have the government pledge in a mere *pro forma* manner to prior consultation while agreeing behind the scenes to dispense with such dialogue.

Adopting the mechanism of prior consultation in connection with the revised security treaty was a necessary step for Japan. It enabled Japan to assert a voice as an independent nation in the employment of US bases on Japanese soil. In addition, it provided Japan with at least the appearance of cooperation between sovereign nations in hosting US bases.

Abiding faithfully by the mechanism of prior consultation was important, meanwhile, for the United States. To renege on the promise to engage in prior consultation, or to engage in prior consultation but ignore the wishes expressed by the Japanese government and people, could inflict irreparable damage to the Japanese-US political linkage.

Thus, both the Americans and the Japanese wanted to avoid an arrangement that would correspond to our panel's definition of "secret agreement." Avoiding such a potentially problematic arrangement took precedence over the military benefits that the arrangement might bestow. That is why the negotiators provided for fulfilment of the prior consultation requirement on the basis of public domain information: the Herter-Kishi exchange of notes.

Tōgō characterized the security treaty, as noted in Chapter 5, as the good-faith result "of taking mutual defense to the very edge of what was possible without violating the [Japanese] constitution."[39] In that sense, the negotiators took diplomacy to the very edge of the possible. They did so by devising the obscure artifice of the two instances of prior consultation discussed here. Let us admire at their ingenuity in reconciling the military utility of the security treaty with the political value of the treaty revision. Let us marvel at how, under trying circumstances, they carried that reconciliation to the very edge of the possible. And let us remember that this new security treaty has not required a revision for more than sixty years.

CHAPTER NOTES

1 Japan Ministry of Foreign Affairs, "Iwayuru 'mitsuyaku' mondai ni kansuru yūshikisha iinkai hōkokusho" [Report by Panel of Experts in Regard to the So-Called 'Secret Agreements'], https://www.mofa.go.jp/mofaj/gaiko/mitsuyaku/pdfs/hokoku_yushiki.pdf.

2 Included as an attachment to "Zaikyō Beikoku taishikan Shūsumisu kōshi to no kaidan yōshi" [Summary of Discussion with US Embassy's Deputy Chief of Mission Shoesmith] (February 22, 1975) in Japan Ministry of Foreign Affairs, "Iwayuru 'mitsuyaku' mondai ni kansuru chōsa, sonota kanren bunsho" [The Investigation into the So-Called Secret Agreements, Other Pertinent Documents], https://www.mofa.go.jp/mofaj/gaiko/mitsuyaku/pdfs/k_1960kaku3.pdf.

3 Japan Ministry of Foreign Affairs, "Iwayuru 'mitsuyaku' mondai, hōkoku taishō bunsho" [The Investigation into the So-Called Secret Agreements, Documents Covered by the Report], https://www.mofa.go.jp/mofaj/gaiko/mitsuyaku/pdfs/t_1960kaku.pdf, in searchable format at National Graduate Institute and University of Tokyo, The World and Japan database, Record of Discussion, https://worldjpn.grips.ac.jp/documents/texts/JPUS/19630413.O1J.html.

4 Japan Ministry of Foreign Affairs, "Iwayuru 'mitsuyaku' mondai, hōkoku taishō

bunsho."

5 Japan Ministry of Foreign Affairs, "Sōbi no jūyō na henkō ni kansuru jizenkyōgi no ken" [The Matter of Prior Consultation in Regard to Major Changes in Equipment] (January 27, 1968) in "Iwayuru 'mitsuyaku' mondai, hōkoku taishō bunsho," and in searchable format at https://worldjpn.grips.ac.jp/documents/texts/JPUS/19680127.O1J.html. Handwritten notes on this copy reveal referencing for prime ministers and foreign ministers from the time of the Satō government (1964–1972) to at least the time of the Uno Sōsuke government (1989).

6 Japan Ministry of Foreign Affairs, "Iwayuru 'mitsuyaku' mondai ni kansuru chōsa hōkokusho" [The Investigation into the So-Called Secret Agreements, Findings], https://www.mofa.go.jp/mofaj/gaiko/mitsuyaku/pdfs/hokoku_naibu.pdf.

7 Japan Ministry of Foreign Affairs, "Nichi-Bei sōgō kyōryoku oyobi anzen hoshō jōyaku kōshō keii" [Japanese-US Mutual Cooperation and the Negotiation of the Security Treaty] in "Iwayuru 'mitsuyaku' mondai, hōkoku taishō bunsho," in searchable format at https://worldjpn.grips.ac.jp/documents/texts/JPUS/19600600.O1J.html.

8 Japan Ministry of Foreign Affairs, "Nichi-Bei sōgō kyōryoku oyobi anzen hoshō jōyaku kōshō keii."

9 Japan Ministry of Foreign Affairs, "Jōyaku dai-6-jō no jisshi ni kansuru kōkan kōbun sakusei no keii" [The Drafting of the Exchange of Notes in Regard to the Implementation of Article 6 of the Treaty] (January 6, 1960), in "Iwayuru 'mitsuyaku' mondai, hōkoku taishō bunsho," in searchable format at https://worldjpn.grips.ac.jp/documents/texts/JPUS/19600106.O1J.html.

10 Japan Ministry of Foreign Affairs, "Nichi-Bei sōgō kyōryoku oyobi anzen hoshō jōyaku kōshō keii."

11 Japan Ministry of Foreign Affairs, "Nichi-Bei sōgō kyōryoku oyobi anzen hoshō jōyaku kōshō keii."

12 United States Army, "Comparison of U.S. Base Rights in Japan and the Ryukyu Islands," Status of Forces Agreement, Box 8, *History of the Civil Administration of the Ryukyu Islands*, Records of the Army Staff, RG319.

13 Japan Ministry of Foreign Affairs, "Sōbi no jūyō na henkō ni kansuru jizenkyōgi no ken."

14 *Mainichi Shimbun*, May 20, 1981.

15 Iiyama Masashi, "Nihon wa 'kakumitsuyaku' o meikaku ni rikai shiteita" [Japan Knew Clearly What the 'Nuclear Secret Agreements' Were All About], *Chūō Kōron* (December 2009).

16 *Japan Press Weekly*, "45 years of Yokosuka, the homeport of US aircraft carrier," October 13, 2018, https://www.japan-press.co.jp/modules/news/?id=11779.

17 Robert A. Wampler, ed., "Nuclear Noh Drama: Tokyo, Washington and the Case of the Missing Nuclear Agreements," National Security Archive (October 13, 2009), https://www.gwu.edu/~nsarchiv/nukevault/ebb291/index.htm. See especially the comments on Documents 8 and 9.

18 Japan Ministry of Foreign Affairs, "Iwayuru 'mitsuyaku' mondai, sonota kanren bunsho," https://www.mofa.go.jp/mofaj/gaiko/mitsuyaku/pdfs/k_1960kaku4.pdf.

19 Japan Ministry of Foreign Affairs, "9-gatsu 11-nichi Fujiyama Daijin–Daresu

Kokumu chōkan kaidanroku" [Minutes of the September 11 Meeting between Minister Fujiyama and Secretary of State Dulles] (September 11, 1958) in "Iwayuru 'mitsuyaku' mondai, sonota kanren bunsho," https://www.mofa.go.jp/mofaj/gaiko/mitsuyaku/pdfs/k_1960kaku1.pdf.

20 Japan Ministry of Foreign Affairs, "Bei-gun no haibi oyobi shiyō ni kansuru Nihon gawa shokan an" [Japanese Written Proposal in Regard to the Deployment and Use of US Forces] in "Iwayuru 'mitsuyaku' mondai, hōkoku taishō bunsho," in searchable format at https://worldjpn.grips.ac.jp/documents/texts/JPUS/19580702.O1J.html.

21 Japan Ministry of Foreign Affairs, "10-gatsu 4-ka sōri, gaimu daijin, zaikyō Bei taishi kaidanroku" [Minutes of the October 4 Meeting among the Prime Minister, Foreign Minister, and US Ambassador], October 4, 1958, in "Iwayuru 'mitsuyaku' mondai, sonota kanren bunsho" no. 1–18: 210–234. https://www.mofa.go.jp/mofaj/gaiko/mitsuyaku/pdfs/k_1960kaku1.pdf.

22 *Mainichi Shimbun*, May 20, 1981.

23 Japan Ministry of Foreign Affairs, "Makkāsā Taishi naiwa no ken" [The Matter of the Confidential Discussion with Ambassador MacArthur] (September 8, 1958) in "Iwayuru 'mitsuyaku' mondai, sonota kanren bunsho," https://www.mofa.go.jp/mofaj/gaiko/mitsuyaku/pdfs/k_1960kaku1.pdf.

24 Komori Yoshihisa, "Ima akasu 60-nen Anpo jōyaku kaitei no shinsō" [New Revelations about the 1960 Revision of the Security Treaty], interview with Douglas MacArthur II, *Chūō Kōron* (November 1981).

25 A description of evidence for the existence of the document appears in Sakamoto Kazuya, "Nichi-Bei Anpo jizenkyōgisei no seiritsu o meguru gimon: Chōsen hantō yūji no baai" [Doubts about the Origins of the Provisions for Prior Consultation in the Japanese-US Security Treaty: In the Event of an Emergency on the Korean Peninsula], *Handai hōgaku* [Osaka Law Review] 46, no. 4 (October 1996).

26 Haruna Mikio, the author of Chapter 3 of our panel's report and then a professor at Nagoya University, has a copy of the version in the Ford Library. I extend thanks to him for showing it to me.

27 Japan Ministry of Foreign Affairs, "Iwayuru 'mitsuyaku' mondai ni kansuru yūshikisha iinkai hōkokusho."

28 The US National Archives document is available for viewing online at a website operated by the Research Institute for Islands and Sustainability, University of the Ryukyus, https://riis.skr.u-ryukyu.ac.jp/images/ddc_20191217-02.pdf.

29 National Graduate Institute and University of Tokyo, "Anzen hoshō kyōgi iinkai no setchi ni kansuru ōfuku shokan" [Exchange of Notes in Regard to the Establishment of the Security Consultative Committee], The World and Japan database (January 19, 1960), https://worldjpn.grips.ac.jp/documents/texts/JPUS/19600119.O2J.html.

30 Japan Ministry of Foreign Affairs, "Iwayuru 'mitsuyaku' mondai, hōkoku taishō bunsho."

31 US Department of State, Central Files (CF) 794.5/7-659 (tel. 43), RG 59, National Archives.

32 US Department of State, CF 794.5/7-1059 (tel. 95).

33 Japan Ministry of Foreign Affairs, "9-gatsu 18-nichi zaikyō Bei taishi naiwa no ken" [The Matter of the September 18 Confidential Discussion with the US Ambassador] (September 18, 1959), "Iwayuru 'mitsuyaku' mondai, sonota kanren bunsho."

34 For a detailed treatment of this subject, see Sakamoto Kazuya, "Anpo kaitei to jizen kyōgi: Chōsen gijiroku wa mitsuyaku ka" [The Revision of the Security Treaty and Prior Consultation: Was the Korea Minute a Secret Agreement?], *Handai hōgaku* [Osaka Law Review] 63, no. 3 (November 2013): 4.

35 *Asahi Shimbun* and *Mainichi Shimbun*, June 23, 1960, evening editions.

36 Nishimura Masahiko, "Anpo kaiteiji no jizen kyōgi seido kōshō: Chōsen gijiroku, dōi, teisatsu hikō" [Negotiation of the Prior Consultation Mechanism during the Revision of the Security Treaty: The Korea Minute, Consent, Surveillance Flights], *Hōgaku ronsō* [Kyoto Law Review] 183, no. 6 (September 2018).

37 US State Department, CF 611.947/9-1260.

38 Japan Ministry of Foreign Affairs, "Chōsa hōkokusho" [Investigation Report], Gaikō Bunsho no Ketsuraku Mondai ni Kansuru Chōsa Iinkai [Investigative Committee in Regard to the Issue of Missing Diplomatic Documents] (June 4, 2010), https://www.mofa.go.jp/mofaj/gaiko/pdfs/ketsuraku_hokokusyo.pdf.

39 Tōgō Fumihiko, *Nichi-Bei gaikō 30-nen: Anpo, Okinawa to sono go* [Thirty Years of Japanese-US Diplomacy: The Security Treaty, Okinawa, and Later] (Tokyo: Chuokoronsha, 1989), 99.

Afterword

The Japanese-US security treaty took effect in 1952 and received a facelift and some minor structural reinforcement in 1960. That it has since remained in force for sixty years without undergoing any subsequent revision is a marvel. While marveling at the treaty's prodigious durability, we need to acknowledge the role of Japanese and US political circumstances in its longevity.

Adopting the revised security treaty in 1960 occasioned massive, prolonged protests throughout Japan. That taught a lesson to the Liberal Democratic Party, which has held power since 1955 with only two brief interruptions. The party has subsequently steered clear of divisive initiatives, such as revising the constitution or strengthening the military, and has focused on nurturing economic growth and ensuring a more or less even distribution of wealth.

Meanwhile, the United States stumbled into the quagmire of the Vietnam War in the 1960s. The US government became more interested in maintaining its Japanese staging ground for military operations than in pressuring the Japanese to strengthen their military. Japan also became increasingly important as a US ally through its growing economic might. Direct investment by Japanese companies in Southeast Asia, for example, helped lay a capitalist foundation for development in that region.

Japan also expanded its value as a US ally in more overtly military ways. It increased its financial contribution toward the upkeep of the US forces in Japan. And the Japanese military engaged in expanded cooperation with the US navy and air force, as in operations for defending sealanes. Japan's military remained subject to the same constraints, however, that had vexed the negotiators of the revised treaty.

We examined on the preceding pages the evolution of the Japanese-US security relationship from around 1950 to 1960. Something that emerged from the material covered was the Japanese government's unpreparedness to tackle the 1960 treaty revision. The government was unprepared, that is, to deal with a fundamental contradiction: it sought to base the security treaty on the right of collective defense, and it approached the treaty revision as an opportunity to exercise that right, but it needed to explain the treaty in the context of a constitution that prohibits engaging in collective defense arrangements. Sadly, that situation persists to this day.*

This book consists of updated expansion of my writings over the years on the subjects at hand. Some issues deserve fuller treatment than I have been able to provide in this context. I have devoted only minimal coverage, for instance, to the influence of domestic politics on foreign policy in Japan and in the United States. And a subject pertinent to this book but barely covered here is the significance of the reversion of Okinawa to Japanese sovereignty.

I pray that this book, for all its shortcomings, will occasion renewed attention to the workings of Japanese-US security and to the broader dynamics of our nations' bilateral relationship. That relationship needs to be, as Ambassador Douglas MacArthur II emphasized to Foreign Minister Fujiyama Aiichirō in 1958, more than a military alliance. It needs to be "a community of interest, complete with common benefit and mutual purpose."

I dedicate this book to the memory of Professor Kōsaka Masataka (1934–1996). He was an inspiration to me and to countless other students at Kyoto University as a teacher and as a human being. His inquiring mind lives on, I dare to think, in the lines of this book.

Sakamoto Kazuya
April 2020
Osaka

* On July 1, 2014, the Japanese government issued a cabinet decision on the "Development of Seamless Security Legislation to Ensure Japan's Survival and Protect its People" officially approving the limited use of collective self-defense (https://www.mofa.go.jp/fp/nsp/page23e_000273.html). However, there has been no change in how the government has traditionally interpreted the constitution as prohibiting the "overseas deployment" of the Self-Defense Forces (dispatching armed troops to foreign territories, waters, or airspace for the purpose of using force).

Documents

Security Treaty Between Japan and the United States of America (Former US-Japan Security Treaty)

Signed in San Francisco, September 8, 1951
Ratified, September 18, 1951
Exchange of instruments of ratification in Washington, April 28, 1952
Effective date, April 28, 1952
Official announcement (Sixth Revision), April 28, 1952

Japan has this day signed a Treaty of Peace with the Allied Powers. On the coming into force of that Treaty, Japan will not have the effective means to exercise its inherent right of self-defense because it has been disarmed.

There is danger to Japan in this situation because irresponsible militarism has not yet been driven from the world. Therefore Japan desires a Security Treaty with the United States of America to come into force simultaneously with the Treaty of Peace between Japan and the United States of America.

The Treaty of Peace recognizes that Japan as a sovereign nation has the right to enter into collective security arrangements, and further, the Charter of the United Nations recognizes that all nations possess an inherent right of individual and collective self-defense.

In exercise of these rights, Japan desires, as a provisional arrangement for its defense, that the United States of America should maintain armed forces of its own in and about Japan so as to deter armed attack upon Japan.

The United States of America, in the interest of peace and security, is presently willing to maintain certain of its armed forces in and about Japan, in the expectation, however, that Japan will itself increasingly assume responsibility for its own defense against direct and indirect aggression, always avoiding any armament which could be an offensive threat or serve other than to promote peace and security in accordance with the purposes and principles of the United Nations Charter.

Accordingly, the two countries have agreed as follows:

ARTICLE I

Japan grants, and the United States of America accepts, the right, upon the coming into force of the Treaty of Peace and of this Treaty, to dispose United

States land, air and sea forces in and about Japan. Such forces may be utilized to contribute to the maintenance of international peace and security in the Far East and to the security of Japan against armed attack from without, including assistance given at the express request of the Japanese Government to put down large-scale internal riots and disturbances in Japan, caused through instigation or intervention by an outside power or powers.

ARTICLE II

During the exercise of the right referred to in Article I, Japan will not grant, without the prior consent of the United States of America, any bases or any rights, powers or authority whatsoever, in or relating to bases or the right of garrison or of maneuver, or transit of ground, air or naval forces to any third power.

ARTICLE III

The conditions which shall govern the disposition of armed forces of the United States of America in and about Japan shall be determined by administrative agreements between the two Governments.

ARTICLE IV

This Treaty shall expire whenever in the opinion of the Governments of Japan and the United States of America there shall have come into force such United Nations arrangements or such alternative individual or collective security dispositions as will satisfactorily provide for the maintenance by the United Nations or otherwise of international peace and security in the Japan Area.

ARTICLE V

This Treaty shall be ratified by Japan and the United States of America and will come into force when instruments of ratification thereof have been exchanged by them at Washington.

IN WITNESS WHEREOF the undersigned Plenipotentiaries have signed this Treaty.

DONE in duplicate at the city of San Francisco, in the Japanese and English languages, this eighth day of September, 1951.

FOR JAPAN:
Shigeru Yoshida

FOR THE UNITED STATES OF AMERICA:
Dean Acheson
John Foster Dulles
Alexander Wiley
Styles Bridges

Notes Exchanged between Prime Minister Yoshida and Secretary of State Acheson at the Time of the Signing of the Security Treaty between Japan and the United States of America

September 8, 1951

Excellency:

Upon the coming into force of the Treaty of Peace signed today, Japan will assume obligations expressed in Article 2 of the Charter of the United Nations which requires the giving to the United Nations of "every assistance in any action it takes in accordance with the present Charter".

As we know, armed aggression has occurred in Korea, against which the United Nations and its members are taking action. There has been established a unified command of the United Nations under the United States pursuant to Security Council Resolution of July 7, 1950, and the General Assembly, by Resolution of February 1, 1951, has called upon all states and authorities to lend every assistance to the United Nations action and to refrain from giving any assistance to the aggressor. With the approval of SCAP, Japan has been and now is rendering important assistance to the United Nations action in the form of facilities and services made available to the members of the United Nations, the Armed Forces of which are participating in the United Nations action.

Since the future is unsettled and it may unhappily be that the occasion for facilities and services in Japan in support of United Nations action will continue or recur, I would appreciate confirmation, on behalf of your Government, that if and when the forces of a member or members of the United Nations are engaged in any United Nations action in the Far East after the Treaty of Peace comes into force, Japan will permit and facilitate the support in and about Japan, by the member or members, of the forces engaged in such United Nations action, the expenses involved in the use of Japanese facilities and services to be borne as at present or as otherwise mutually agreed between Japan and the United Nations member concerned. In so far as the United States is concerned the use of facilities and services, over and above those provided to the United States pursuant to the Administrative Agreement which will implement the Security Treaty between the United States and Japan, would be at United States expense, as at present.

Accept, Excellency, the assurances of my most distinguished consideration.

Dean Acheson

His Excellency
Shigeru Yoshida,
Prime Minister of Japan

September 8, 1951

Excellency

I have the honor to acknowledge the receipt of Your Excellency's Note of today's date in which Your Excellency has informed me as follows:

(American note deleted)

With full cognizance of the contents of Your Excellency's Note, I have the honor, on behalf of my Government, to confirm that if and when the forces of a Member or Members of the United Nations are engaged in any United Nations action in the Far East after the Treaty of Peace comes into force, Japan will permit and facilitate the support in and about Japan, by the Member or Members of the forces engaged in such United Nations action, the expenses involved in the use of Japanese facilities and services to be borne as at present or as otherwise mutually agreed between Japan and the United Nations Member concerned. In so far as the United States is concerned the use of facilities and services, over and above those provided to the United States pursuant to the Administrative Agreement which will implement the Security Agreement between Japan and the United States would be at United States expense, as at present.

I avail myself of this opportunity to renew to Your Excellency the assurance of my highest consideration.

Shigeru Yoshida
Prime Minister and concurrently
Minister for Foreign Affairs of Japan

His Excellency
Dean Acheson,
Secretary of State
of the United States of America.

Treaty of Mutual Cooperation and Security between Japan and the United States of America

Japan and the United States of America,
Desiring to strengthen the bonds of peace and friendship traditionally existing between them, and to uphold the principles of democracy, individual liberty, and the rule of law,
Desiring further to encourage closer economic cooperation between them and to promote conditions of economic stability and well-being in their countries,
Reaffirming their faith in the purposes and principles of the Charter of the United Nations, and their desire to live in peace with all peoples and all governments,
Recognizing that they have the inherent right of individual or collective self-defense as affirmed in the Charter of the United Nations,
Considering that they have a common concern in the maintenance of international peace and security in the Far East,
Having resolved to conclude a treaty of mutual cooperation and security,
Therefore agree as follows:

ARTICLE I

The Parties undertake, as set forth in the Charter of the United Nations, to settle any international disputes in which they may be involved by peaceful means in such a manner that international peace and security and justice are not endangered and to refrain in their international relations from the threat or use of force against the territorial integrity or political independence of any state, or in any other manner inconsistent with the purposes of the United Nations. The Parties will endeavor in concert with other peace-loving countries to strengthen the United Nations so that its mission of maintaining international peace and security may be discharged more effectively.

ARTICLE II

The Parties will contribute toward the further development of peaceful and friendly international relations by strengthening their free institutions, by bringing about a better understanding of the principles upon which these institutions are founded, and by promoting conditions of stability and well-being. They will seek to eliminate conflict in their international economic policies and will encourage economic collaboration between them.

ARTICLE III

The Parties, individually and in cooperation with each other, by means of continuous and effective self-help and mutual aid will maintain and develop, subject to their constitutional provisions, their capacities to resist armed attack.

ARTICLE IV

The Parties will consult together from time to time regarding the implementation of this Treaty, and, at the request of either Party, whenever the security of Japan or international peace and security in the Far East is threatened.

ARTICLE V

Each Party recognizes that an armed attack against either Party in the territories under the administration of Japan would be dangerous to its own peace and safety and declares that it would act to meet the common danger in accordance with its constitutional provisions and processes. Any such armed attack and all measures taken as a result thereof shall be immediately reported to the Security Council of the United Nations in accordance with the provisions of Article 51 of the Charter. Such measures shall be terminated when the Security Council has taken the measures necessary to restore and maintain international peace and security.

ARTICLE VI

For the purpose of contributing to the security of Japan and the maintenance of international peace and security in the Far East, the United States of America is granted the use by its land, air and naval forces of facilities and areas in Japan. The use of these facilities and areas as well as the status of United States armed forces in Japan shall be governed by a separate agreement, replacing the Administrative Agreement under Article III of the Security Treaty between Japan and the United States of America, signed at Tokyo on February 28, 1952, as amended, and by such other arrangements as may be agreed upon.

ARTICLE VII

This Treaty does not affect and shall not be interpreted as affecting in any way the rights and obligations of the Parties under the Charter of the United Nations or the responsibility of the United Nations for the maintenance of international peace and security.

ARTICLE VIII

This Treaty shall be ratified by Japan and the United States of America in accordance with their respective constitutional processes and will enter into force on the date on which the instruments of ratification thereof have been exchanged by them in Tokyo.

ARTICLE IX

The Security Treaty between Japan and the United States of America signed at the city of San Francisco on September 8, 1951 shall expire upon the entering into force of this Treaty.

ARTICLE X

This Treaty shall remain in force until in the opinion of the Governments of Japan and the United States of America there shall have come into force such United Nations arrangements as will satisfactorily provide for the maintenance of international peace and security in the Japan area. However, after the Treaty has been in force for ten years, either Party may give notice to the other Party of its intention to terminate the Treaty, in which case the Treaty shall terminate one year after such notice has been given.

IN WITNESS WHEREOF the undersigned Plenipotentiaries have signed this Treaty.

DONE in duplicate at Washington in the Japanese and English languages, both equally authentic, this 19th day of January, 1960.

FOR JAPAN:
Nobusuke Kishi
Aiichiro Fujiyama
Mitsujiro Ishii
Tadashi Adachi
Koichiro Asakai

FOR THE UNITED STATES OF AMERICA:
Christian A. Herter
Douglas MacArthur 2nd
J. Graham Parsons

Exchanged Notes, Regarding the Implementation of Article VI of Treaty of Mutual Cooperation and Security between Japan and the United States of America

Excellency :

I have the honour to refer to the Treaty of Mutual Cooperation and Security between Japan and the United States of America signed today, and to inform Your Excellency that the following is the understanding of the Government of Japan concerning the implementation of Article VI thereof:

Major changes in the deployment into Japan of United States armed forces, major changes in their equipment, and the use of facilities and areas in Japan as bases for military combat operations to be undertaken from Japan other than those conducted under Article V of the said Treaty, shall be the subjects of prior consultation with the Government of Japan.

I should be appreciative if Your Excellency would confirm on behalf of your Government that this is also the understanding of the Government of the United States of America. I avail myself of this opportunity to renew to Your Excellency the assurance of my highest consideration.

Washington, January 19, 1960

Nobusuke Kishi

His Excellency
Christian A. Herter,
Secretary of State
of the United States of America.

Excellency:

I have the honor to acknowledge the receipt of Your Excellency's Note of today's date, which reads as follows:

(Japanese note deleted)

I have the honor to confirm on behalf of my Government that the foregoing is also the understanding of the Government of the United States of America.

Accept, Excellency, the renewed assurances of my highest consideration.

January 19, 1960

Christian A. Herter,
Secretary of State
of the United States of America

His Excellency
Nobusuke Kishi,
Prime Minister of Japan

Exchanged Notes, Regarding Exchanged Notes between Prime Minister Yoshida and Secretary of State Acheson

I have the honor to refer the Security Treaty between the United States of America and Japan signed at the city of San Francisco on September 8, 1951, the exchange of notes effected on the same date between Mr. Shigeru Yoshida, Primed Minister of Japan, and Mr. Dean Acheson, Secretary of State of the United States of America and the Agreement Regarding the Status of the United Nations Forces in Japan signed at Tokyo on February 19, 1954, as well as the Treaty of Mutual Cooperation and Security between the United States of America and Japan signed today. It is the understanding of my Government that:

1. The above-mentioned exchange of notes will continue to be in force so long as the Agreement Regarding the Status of the United Nations Forces in Japan remains in force.
2. The expression "those facilities and areas the use of which is provided to the United States of America under the Security Treaty between Japan and the United States of America" in Article V, paragraph 2 of the above-mentioned Agreement is understood to mean the facilities and the areas the use of which is granted to the United States of America under the Treaty of Mutual Cooperation and Security.
3. The use of the Facilities and areas by the United States armed forces under the Unified Command of the United Nations established pursuant to the Security Council Resolution of July 7, 1950, and their status in Japan are governed by arrangements made pursuant to the Treaty of Mutual Cooperation and Security.

I should be grateful if Your Excellency could confirm on behalf of your Government that the understanding of my Government stated in the foregoing numbered paragraph is also the understanding of your Government and that this understanding shall enter into operation on the date of the entry into force of the Treaty of Mutual cooperation and Security signed at Washington of January 19, 1960.

Accept, Excellency, the renewed assurances of my highest consideration.

Christian A. Herter,
Secretary of State
of the United States of America

His Excellency
Nobusuke Kishi,
Prime Minister of Japan.

I have the honour to acknowledge the receipt of Your Excellency's Note of today's date, which reads as follows:

(American note deleted)

I have the honour to confirm of behalf of my Government that the foregoing is also the understanding of the Government of Japan.

I avail myself of this opportunity renew to Your Excellency the assurance of my highest consideration.

Nobusuke Kishi

His Excellency
Christian A. Herter,
Secretary of State
of the United States of America.

Chronology

1946	May 22	First Yoshida Shigeru cabinet takes office (serves until May 24, 1947)
	Nov. 3	Japan promulgates new constitution, to take effect on May 3, 1947
1947	Jan. 21	George Marshall succeeds James Byrnes as secretary of state
	Mar. 12	US president Harry Truman announces eponymous doctrine
	Mar. 17	General Douglas MacArthur, commander of allied occupation forces, calls for swift action in concluding peace treaty with Japan
	May 24	Katayama Tetsu cabinet takes office (serves until March 10, 1948)
	Aug. 5	US State Department's Division of Northeast Asian Affairs floats proposal for peace treaty with Japan
	Aug. 12	George Kennan, head of what would become US State Department's Policy Planning Staff, expresses concerns about treaty proposal to Undersecretary of State Robert Lovett and recommends putting proposal on hold
	Sep. 2	William Sebald becomes political advisor to General MacArthur, later assuming additional title of US ambassador to Japan
	Sep. 13	Japanese foreign minister Ashida Hitoshi sketches potential Japanese stance on national security after conclusion of peace treaty and submits it to senior occupation officer General Robert L. Eichelberger
1948	Mar. 1	Kennan visits Japan and, after returning to Washington, DC, on March 25, calls for adopting more robust military positioning for Japan in occupation policy
	Mar. 10	Ashida Hitoshi cabinet takes office (serves until October 19, 1948)
	Jun. 11	US Senate passes Vandenburg Resolution, which predicates security treaties on self-defense effort by treaty counterparties
	Oct. 19	Second Yoshida cabinet takes office (serves until February 16, 1949)
1949	Jan. 21	Dean Acheson succeeds George Marshall as US secretary of state
	Feb. 16	Third Yoshida cabinet takes office (serves until October 30, 1952)
	Mar. 7	Joseph Dodge, General MacArthur's economic advisor, announces retrenchment plans for Japanese economy
	Apr. 4	United States, Canada, and 10 Western European nations sign treaty that establishes North Atlantic Treating Organization (NATO), effective August 24, 1949

1949	Sep. 13	Acheson and UK foreign minister Ernest Bevin meet in Washington, DC, and discuss plans for peace treaty with Japan
1950	Jan. 15	Peace Study Group, which comprises several dozen Japanese scholars, issues statement calling for including China and Soviet Union in peace treaty
	Apr. 19	John Foster Dulles becomes consultant to US secretary of state Acheson
	Apr. 25	Yoshida dispatches Finance Minister Ikeda Hayato to United States to observe US economic and fiscal practices firsthand and to convey Yoshida's thoughts on Japanese national security to US officials (offering United States bases in Japan after peace treaty goes into effect)
	Jun. 18	Louis Johnson, US secretary of defense, and Omar Bradley, chairman of Joint Chiefs of Staff, visit Japan and hear from General MacArthur about need for moving ahead with concluding peace treaty with Japan
	Jun. 21	Dulles visits Japan and meets on June 22 with Yoshida
	Jun. 25	Korean War erupts
	Aug. 10	Japanese government, on orders from MacArthur, establishes National Police Reserve as lightly armed paramilitary force about 75,000 strong
	Nov. 24	US government unveils memorandum that comprises seven issues for addressing in drafting peace treaty with Japan
1951	Jan. 25	Dulles returns to Japan for further talks with Yoshida
	Apr. 11	Truman relieves General MacArthur of command, replacing him with General Matthew Ridgway
	Sep. 8	Yoshida signs peace treaty and Japanese-US security treaty in San Francisco, both to take effect on April 28, 1952
1952	Feb. 28	Japanese and US governments conclude administrative agreement for implementing security treaty
	May 9	Robert Murphy assumes post of US ambassador to Japan
	Oct. 15	Japanese government expands and reorganizes National Police Reserve as National Safety Forces
	Oct. 30	Fourth Yoshida cabinet takes office (serves until May 21, 1953)
1953	Jan. 20	Dwight D. Eisenhower takes office as US president
	Jan. 21	Dulles becomes secretary of state
	May 21	Fifth Yoshida cabinet takes office (serves until December 10, 1954)
	May 23	John Allison assumes post of US ambassador to Japan

1953	Oct. 2–30	"Ikeda-Robertson Talks": Japanese delegation headed by former finance minister Ikeda, then chair of Liberal Party's Policy Research Council, and US delegation headed by Walter Robertson, assistant secretary of state for Far East, hold wide-ranging talks on military, economic, and other aspects of Japanese-US relationship
	Dec. 24	Japanese and US governments conclude agreement for return of Amami Islands to Japanese sovereignty, effective next day
1954	Mar. 1	Japanese fishing vessel *Daigo Fukuryu-maru* (No. 5 Lucky Dragon) suffers radioactive contamination from US thermonuclear test on Bikini Atoll
	Mar. 8	Japanese and US governments conclude agreement for aid to Japan under US Mutual Security Act, effective May 1, 1954
	Jun. 2	Japan's Diet passes Self-Defense Forces Act and Defense Agency Establishment Act, resulting in reorganization of National Safety Forces as Japan Self-Defense Forces and creation of Defense Agency, effective July 1, 1954
	Nov. 7	Yoshida makes state visit to United States and meets with Eisenhower in Washington, DC, on November 9
	Dec. 10	First Hatoyama Ichirō cabinet takes office (serves until March 19, 1955)
1955	Mar. 19	Second Hatoyama cabinet takes office (serves until November 22, 1955)
	May 8	Citizen protests against announced expansion of US airbase in western Tokyo district of Tachikawa begin
	Aug. 29	Japanese foreign minister Shigemitsu Mamoru visits Washington, DC, and presents proposal for revised security treaty to Dulles, who rejects it out of hand
	Nov. 15	Liberal Party and Japan Democratic Party merge to form Liberal Democratic Party
	Nov. 22	Third Hatoyama cabinet takes office (serves until December 23, 1956)
1956	Jun. 9	"Price Report": US congressional subcommittee calls for US acquisition of permanent title to Okinawa real estate used by US military with lump-sum payment and of additional property as necessary; report provokes frictions in Okinawa
	Aug. 24	Shigemitsu meets with Dulles in London and discusses Japanese peace negotiations with Soviet Union
	Oct. 19	Hatoyama and Soviet premier Nikolai Bulganin sign Japanese-Soviet Joint Declaration in Moscow, marking restoration of diplomatic relations

1956	Dec. 18	UN members unanimously approve Japan's accession to UN membership
	Dec. 23	Ishibashi Tanzan cabinet takes office (serves until February 25, 1957)
1957	Jan. 30	"Girard Incident": empty cartridge fired from grenade launcher hits and kills Japanese woman scavenging shell casings on US firing range in Gunma Prefecture
	Feb. 15	Douglas MacArthur II assumes post as US ambassador to Japan
	Feb. 25	First Kishi Nobusuke cabinet takes office (serves until June 12, 1958)
	Jun. 16	Kishi makes state visit to United States and meets with Eisenhower in Washington, DC, on June 19
	Jul. 10	Kishi revamps cabinet, installing Fujiyama Aiichirō as foreign minister
	Aug. 1	US Defense Department announces withdrawal of US ground forces from Japan (completes withdrawal on February 8, 1958)
	Sep. 14	Fujiyama and MacArthur conduct exchange of notes to confirm linkage between security treaty and UN Charter
	Oct. 4	Soviet Union places world's first artificial satellite, Sputnik, in orbit
1958	Jan. 12	Opponent of US military presence in Okinawa wins mayoral election in Naha
	Feb. 18	MacArthur submits original proposal for revised Japanese-US security treaty to Dulles
	May 2	Japanese rightist tears down Chinese flag at exhibition of Chinese postage stamps at Nagasaki department store, sparking bilateral diplomatic incident
	May 15	Soviet government inquires of Japanese government if any nuclear weapons are in Japanese territory and warns that any such weaponry would provoke response
	Jun. 12	Second Kishi cabinet takes office (serves until July 19, 1960)
	Jul. 30	Fujiyama meets with MacArthur in Tokyo and explains Japanese thinking on revision of security treaty
	Aug. 25	MacArthur meets with Kishi and Fujiyama in Tokyo and discusses treaty
	Sep. 8	MacArthur meets with Dulles and Walter Robertson, assistant secretary of state for Far Eastern affairs, in Washington, DC, and emphasizes need for revised treaty
	Sep. 11	Dulles and Fujiyama meet in Washington, DC, and discuss treaty

1958	Oct. 4	Treaty revision negotiations begin in Tokyo; US negotiators submit draft proposal
	Nov. 26	Fujiyama and MacArthur meet secretly to discuss treaty revision; before meeting, Japanese Foreign Ministry staffer submits draft proposal to US embassy counterpart as Fujiyama's "personal response" to US draft
1959	Apr. 15	Dulles resigns as secretary of state on account of illness; Christian Herter succeeds him on April 22
	Jul. 6	MacArthur explains US government stance on response to possible military emergency on Korean Peninsula to Kishi and Fujiyama
1960	Jan. 6	Fujiyama and MacArthur sign secret agreements as corollaries to revised treaty
	Jan. 19	Kishi, Herter, and other Japanese and US senior officials sign revised treaty in Washington, DC
	May and Jun.	Massive demonstrations occur throughout Japan against revised security treaty
	Jun. 16	Japanese government requests postponement of state visit by President Eisenhower (travels to Philippines, Taiwan, Okinawa, and South Korea)
	Jun. 23	Revised security treaty takes effect as Treaty of Mutual Cooperation and Security
	Jul. 14	Assassination attempt against Kishi (stabbed in leg)
	Jul. 15	Kishi cabinet resigns *en masse*
	Jul. 19	First Ikeda cabinet takes office (serves until December 8, 1960)

References

Primary sources

Hosoya Chihiro, Aruga Tadashi, Ishii Osamu, and Sasaki Takuya, eds. *Nichi-Bei kankei shiryōshū, 1945–1947* [Collected Works on Japanese-US Relations, 1945–1997]. Tokyo: University of Tokyo Press, 1999.

Japan Ministry of Foreign Affairs. Diplomatic records disclosure A'1.5.2.1-1. *Honpō tokuha shisetsu oyobi shinzen shisetsudan, Beishū shokoku hōmon kankei, Ikeda tokushi kankei* [Japanese Envoys Extraordinary and Goodwill Missions, Visits to the United States and Europe, Ikeda Special Emissary]. Diplomatic Archives of the Ministry of Foreign Affairs of Japan.

——. Microfilm reel B'.4.0.0.1. *Tai-Nichi heiwa jōyaku kankei* [Japan Peace Treaty], *Junbi ken kankei* [Preliminary Research], vol. 3. Diplomatic Archives of the Ministry of Foreign Affairs of Japan.

——. "Iwayuru 'mitsuyaku' mondai" [The So-Called 'Secret Agreements'] documents. Diplomatic Archives of the Ministry of Foreign Affairs of Japan. https://www.mofa.go.jp/mofaj/gaiko/mitsuyaku/kekka.html.

Japan Ministry of Foreign Affairs, Treaties and Conventions Bureau, Legal Division. *Heiwa jōyaku no teiketsu ni kansuru chōsho* [Documents Related to the Conclusion of the Peace Treaty]. Vol. 3, *Daiichiji Nichi-Bei kōshō no tame no junbi sagyō* [Preparations for the First Japanese-US Negotiations], December 1966. Vol. 4, *1951-nen 1–2-gatsu no daiichiji kōshō* [First Negotiations, January–February 1951], October 1967. Vol. 5, *Shōwa 26-nen 2–4-gatsu* [February–April 1951], September 1968. Vol. 6, *Shōwa 26-nen 5–8-gatsu* [Documents Related to the Conclusion of the Peace Treaty VI–May–August 1951], September 1969. Originally in Dōba Hajime Papers, Aoyama Gakuin University's School of International Politics, Economics and Communication. Published in five volumes as *Nihon gaikō bunsho: Heiwa jōyaku no teiketsu ni kansuru chōsho* [Japanese Diplomatic Documents: Documents Related to the Conclusion of the Peace Treaty] (Tokyo: Rokuichi Shobo, 2002). (Page numbers in citations refer to those in parentheses on the copy of the original available at https://www.mofa.go.jp/mofaj/annai/honsho/shiryo/archives/mokuji.html. Vol. 3 refers to "Book 1" online; vols. 4 and 5 in "Book 2"; and vol. 6 in "Book 3.")

Kamikawa Hikomatsu, ed. *Amerika jōin ni okeru shin anpo jōyaku no shingi: Gijiroku zen'yaku* [US Senate Deliberations on the New Security Treaty: Full Translation of the Complete Minutes]. Tokyo: Japan Institute of International Affairs, 1960.

Ministry of Finance. *Suzuki Gengo bunsho* [Suzuki Gengo Documents]. Takemae Eiji collection.

Niihara Shōji, ed. and trans. *Bei seifu anpo gaikō himitsu bunsho: Shiryō, kaisetsu* [US Government-Classified Documents on Security-Treaty Diplomacy: Resources and Commentary]. Tokyo: Shinnihon Shuppansha, 1990.

Ōtake Hideo, ed. *Sengo Nihon bōei mondai shiryōshū* [Archives of Postwar Japanese Defense Issues]. Vol. 1, *Higunjika kara saigunbi e* [From Demilitarization to Rearmament] (1991). Vol. 2, *Kōwa to saigunbi no honkakuka* [Peace and Full-Scale Rearmament] (1992). Vol. 3, *Jieitai no sōsetsu* [Creation of Self-Defense Forces] (1993). Tokyo: San-Ichi Shobo, 1991–1993.

Saitō Makoto, Nagai Yōnosuke, and Yamamoto Mitsuru, eds. *Sengo shiryō: Nichi-Bei kankei* [Postwar Resources: Japanese-US Relations]. Tokyo: Nippon Hyōronsha, 1970.

Shūgiin Gaimu Iinkai Chōsashitsu [House of Representatives Committee on Foreign Affairs, Research Office]. *Shūgiin Nichi-Bei Anzen Hoshō Jōyaku Tō Tokubetsu Iinkai shingi yōkō* [Deliberations by the House of Representatives Special Committee on the Japanese-US Security Treaty]. Tokyo: Ministry of Finance Printing Bureau [now the National Printing Bureau], January 1961.

US Department of State. Diplomatic Records: Central Files (CF), RG 59, National Archives.

——. Diplomatic Records: Lot Files, RG 59, National Archives.

——. *Foreign Relations of the United States* (*FRUS*). 1946, Eastern Europe, The Soviet Union, Vol. VI (1969). 1947, The Far East, Vol. VI (1972). 1948, The Far East and Australasia, Vol. VI (1974). 1949, The Far East and Australasia, Vol. VII (1976). 1950, East Asia and the Pacific, Vol. VI (1976). 1951, Asia and the Pacific, Vol. VI (1977). 1952–54, China and Japan, Vol. XIV (1985). 1955–57, Japan, Vol. XXIII (1991). 1958–60, Japan, Korea, Vol. XVIII (1994). Washington: Government Printing Office, 1969–1994.

(In addition to the citations above, my primary sources from the US side also included numerous documents from the Mudd Library at Princeton University and the Eisenhower Library in Abilene, Kansas.)

Books

Akagi Kanji. *Betonamu Sensō no kigen: Aizenhawā seiken to daiichiji Indoshina Sensō* [The Origins of the Vietnam War: The Eisenhower Administration and the First Indochina War]. Tokyo: Keio University Press, 1991.

Aketagawa Tōru. *Nichi-Bei gyōsei kyōtei no seijishi: Nichi-Bei chii kyōtei kenkyū josetsu* [A Political History of the Japanese-US Administrative Agreement: An Introduction to Research into the Japan-US Status of Forces Agreement]. Tokyo: Hosei University Press, 1999.

Allison, John M. *Ambassador from the Prairie; or, Allison Wonderland.* Boston: Houghton Mifflin, 1973.

Ambrose, Stephen E. *Eisenhower: The President.* New York: Simon and Schuster, 1984.

Asahi Shimbun Anzen Hoshō Mondai Chōsakai, ed. *Asahi shimin kyōshitsu: Nihon no anzen hoshō* [Asahi Citizens' Classroom: Japan's National Security]. Vol. 9, *Nihon no bōei to keizai* [National Defense and the Japanese Economy]. Vol. 10, *Nichi-Bei anpo jōyaku no shōten* [The Focus of the Japanese-US Security Treaty]. Tokyo: Asahi Shimbunsha, 1967.

Buckley, Roger. *US-Japan Alliance Diplomacy, 1945–1990.* Cambridge: Cambridge University Press, 1992.

Dower, John. *Empire and Aftermath: Yoshida Shigeru and the Japanese Experience, 1878–1954.* Cambridge: Harvard University Asia Center, 1979.

Dunn, Frederick S. *Peacemaking and the Settlement with Japan.* Princeton: Princeton University Press, 1963.

Finn, Richard B. *Winners in Peace: MacArthur, Yoshida, and Postwar Japan.* Berkeley: University of California Press, 1992.

Kowalski, Frank. *An Inoffensive Rearmament: The Making of the Postwar Japanese Army.* Annapolis: Naval Institute Press, 2013.

Fujiyama Aiichirō. *Seiji, wagamichi: Fujiyama Aiichirō kaisōroku* [Politics, My Path: Fujiyama Aiichirō Memoir]. Tokyo: Asahi Shimbunsha, 1976.

Gabe Masaaki. *Nichi-Bei kankei no naka no Okinawa* [Okinawa in Japanese-US Relations]. Tokyo: San-Ichi Shobo, 1996.

Gaddis, John L. *Strategies of Containment: A Critical Appraisal of Postwar American National Security Policy.* New York: Oxford University Press, 1982.

——. *The United States and the Origins of the Cold War, 1941–1947.* New York: Columbia University Press, 1972.

Gotō Motoo, Uchida Kenzō, and Ishikawa Masumi. *Sengo hoshu seiji no kiseki* [The History of Postwar Conservative Politics]. Vols. 1 and 2. Tokyo: Iwanami Shoten, 1994.

Hara Yoshihisa. *Kishi Nobusuke: Kensei no seijika* [Kishi Nobusuke: A Politician of Influence]. Tokyo: Iwanami Shoten, 1995.

——. *Nichi-Bei kankei no kōzu: Anpo kaitei o kenshō suru* [The Mechanics of the Japanese-US Relationship: An Examination of the Revision of the Security Treaty]. Tokyo: NHK Books, 1991.

——. *Sengo Nihon to kokusai seiji: Anpo kaitei no seiji rikigaku* [Postwar Japan and International Relations: The Political Dynamics of the Security-Treaty Revision]. Tokyo: Chuokoronsha, 1988.

Hata Ikuhiko. *Shiroku: Nihon saigunbi* [The Historical Record: Japan's Rearmament]. Tokyo: Bungeishunjū, 1976.

Hatano Sumio. *Taiheiyō sensō to Ajia gaikō* [The Pacific War and Japan's Diplomacy in Asia]. Tokyo: University of Tokyo Press, 1996.

Hatoyama Ichirō. *Hatoyama Ichirō kaikoroku* [Hatoyama Ichirō Memoir]. Tokyo: Bungeishunjū Shinsha, 1957.

Hidaka Rokurō, ed. *1960, 5-gatsu 19-nichi* [May 19, 1960]. Tokyo: Iwanami Shoten, 1960.

Hiwatari Yumi. *Sengo seiji to Nichi-Bei kankei* [Postwar Politics and Japanese-US Relations]. Tokyo: University of Tokyo Press, 1990.

Hosoya Chihiro. *San Furanshisuko kōwa e no michi* [The Path to the San Francisco Peace Treaty]. Tokyo: Chuokoronsha, 1984.

Igarashi Takeshi. *Sengo Nichi-Bei kankei no keisei: Kōwa, Anpo to Reisengo no shiten ni tatte* [The Formation of Postwar Japanese-US Relations: From the Perspective of the Peace Treaty, the Security Treaty, and the Post–Cold War Era]. Tokyo: Kodansha, 1995.

Immerman, Richard H., ed. *John Foster Dulles and the Diplomacy of the Cold War.* Princeton: Princeton University Press, 1990.

Inoki Masamichi. *Hyōden Yoshida Shigeru* [A Critical Biography of Yoshida Shigeru]. Vols. 1–4. Tokyo: Chikuma Shobo, 1995.

Inoki Takenori. *Keizai seichō no kajitsu, 1955–1972* [The Fruits of Economic Growth: 1955-1972]. Vol. 7 of *Nihon no kindai* [Japan's Modern Age]. Tokyo: Chuokoron Shinsha, 2000.

Iokibe Makoto, ed. *Sengo Nihon gaikōshi* [A History of Postwar Japanese Diplomacy]. Tokyo: Yuhikaku, 1999.

——. *Senryōki: Shushō-tachi no shin-Nihon* [The Occupation Period: How the Prime Ministers Envisioned the New Japan]. Vol. 3 of *20-seiki no Nippon* [Japan in the 20th

Century]. Tokyo: Yomiuri Shimbunsha, 1997.

Ishii Osamu. *Reisen to Nichi-Bei kankei: Pātonāshippu no keisei* [The Cold War and Japanese-US Relations: The Formation of a Partnership]. Tokyo: Japan Times, 1989.

Ishikawa Masumi. *Sengo seiji-shi* [Postwar Political History]. Tokyo: Iwanami Shoten, 1995.

Itō Takashi, and Watanabe Yukio, eds. *Zoku Shigemitsu Mamoru shuki* [Shigemitsu Mamoru Diary, Sequel]. Tokyo: Chuokoronsha, 1988.

Iwami Takao. *Heika no goshitsumon: Shōwa Tennō to sengo seiji* [Imperial Questions: The Shōwa Emperor and Postwar Politics]. Tokyo: Mainichi Shimbunsha, 1992.

——. *Kishi Nobusuke: Shōwa no kakumeika* [Kishi Nobusuke: Shōwa Revolutionary]. Tokyo: Gakuyo Shobo, 1999.

Iwanaga Kenkichirō. *Sengo Nihon no seitō to gaikō* [Political Parties and Diplomacy in Postwar Japan]. Tokyo: University of Tokyo Press, 1985.

Kan Hideki. *Bei-So Reisen to Amerika no Ajia seisaku* [The US-Soviet Cold War and American Asia Policy]. Kyoto: Minerva Shobo, 1992.

Katsumoto Seiichirō, Nishida Taketoshi, Eguchi Bokurō, Yasugi Ryūichi, Yamamoto Jirō et al., eds. *Kindai Nihon sōgō nenpyō* [A Comprehensive Chronology of Modern Japan]. 3rd ed. Tokyo: Iwanami Shoten, 1991.

Kennan, George F. *Memoirs: 1925–1950.* Boston: Little, Brown, 1967.

Kinnard, Douglas. *President Eisenhower and Strategy Management: A Study in Defense Politics.* Lexington: University Press of Kentucky, 1977.

Kishi Nobusuke, Yatsugi Kazuo, and Itō Takashi. *Kishi Nobusuke no kaisō* [Kishi Nobusuke's Reminiscences]. Tokyo: Bungeishunjū, 1981.

Kishi Nobusuke. *Kishi Nobusuke kaikoroku: Hoshu gōdō to Anpo kaitei* [Kishi Nobusuke Memoir: The Conservative Coalition and the Revision of the Security Treaty]. Tokyo: Kōsaidō Shuppan, 1983.

Kitaoka Shinichi. *Jimintō: Seikentō no 38-nen* [The LDP: 38 Years in Power]. Vol. 1 of *20-seiki no Nippon* [Japan in the 20th Century]. Tokyo: Yomiuri Shimbunsha, 1995.

——. *Seitō seiji no saisei: Sengo seiji no keisei to hōkai* [The Rebirth of Party Politics: The Formation and Collapse of Postwar Politics]. Tokyo: Chuokoronsha, 1995.

Kōno Ichirō. *Ima dakara hanasō* [What I Can Now Say]. Tokyo: Shunyodo Shoten, 1958.

Kōno Yasuko. *Okinawa henkan o meguru seiji to gaikō: Nichi-Bei kankeishi no bunmyaku* [The Politics and Diplomacy of the Return of Okinawa: The Historical Context of Japanese-US Relations]. Tokyo: University of Tokyo Press, 1994.

Kōsaka Masataka. *Saishō Yoshida Shigeru* [Yoshida Shigeru as Prime Minister]. Tokyo: Chuokoronsha, 1968. In *Kōsaka Masataka chosakushū* [The Writings of Kōsaka Masataka], vol. 4, edited by Iokibe Makoto, Sakamoto Kazuya, Nakanishi Hiroshi, and Sako Susumu (Tokyo: Toshi Shuppan, 2000).

Kōsaka Masataka, Sako Susumu, and Abe Bunji, eds. *Sengo Nichi-Bei kankei nenpyō* [A Chronology of Postwar Japanese-US Relations]. Tokyo: PHP Institute, 1995.

Lee, Jong Won. *Higashi Ajia Reisen to Kan-Bei-Nichi kankei* [The Cold War in East Asia and Korean-US-Japanese Relations]. Tokyo: University of Tokyo Press, 1996.

Matsuoka Hiroshi. *Daresu gaikō to Indoshina* [Dulles Diplomacy and Indochina]. Tokyo: Dobunkan Shuppan, 1988.

Melanson, Richard A., and David Mayers, eds. *Reevaluating Eisenhower: American Foreign*

Policy in the 1950s. Champaign: University of Illinois Press, 1987.

Minka Hōritsu Bukai, ed. *Hōritsu Jihō rinji zōkan: Anpo jōyaku, sono hihanteki kentō* [Hōritsu Jihō Extra Edition: Security Treaty, a Critical Examination]. Tokyo: Nippon Hyōronsha, 1969.

Miscamble, Wilson D. *George F. Kennan and the Making of American Foreign Policy, 1947–1950.* Princeton: Princeton University Press, 1992.

Miura Yōichi. *Yoshida Shigeru to San Furanshisuko kōwa* [Yoshida Shigeru and the San Francisco Peace Treaty]. Vols. 1 and 2. Tokyo: Otsuki Shoten, 1996.

Miyazaki Yoshimasa. *Jitsuroku: Seikai 25-nen* [An Authentic Account: 25 Years in the Political Sphere]. Tokyo: Yomiuri Shimbunsha, 1970.

Miyazato Seigen. *Amerika no Okinawa tōchi* [US Rule of Okinawa]. Tokyo: Iwanami Shoten, 1966.

Miyazawa Kiichi. *Tōkyō-Washinton no mitsudan* [Secret Talks between Tokyo and Washington]. Tokyo: Chuokoron Shinsha, 1999.

Murakawa Ichirō, ed. *Daresu to Yoshida: Purinsuton daigaku shozō Daresu bunsho o chūshin toshite* [Dulles and Yoshida: As Seen Primarily through Materials in the Collection of Princeton University]. Tokyo: Kokusho Kankōkai, 1991.

Muroyama Yoshimasa. *Nichi-Bei Anpo taisei* [The Japanese-US Security Treaty Framework]. Vols. 1 and 2. Tokyo: Yuhikaku, 1992.

Nagai Yōnosuke. *Reisen no kigen: Sengo Ajia no kokusai kankyō* [The Origins of the Cold War: The International Environment of Postwar Asia]. Tokyo: Chuokoronsha, 1978.

Nakamura Akira. *Sengo seiji ni yureta kenpō 9-jō: Naikaku hōseikyoku no jishin to tsuyosa* [Postwar Political Threats to Article 9 of the Constitution: The Confidence and the Power of the Cabinet Legislation Bureau]. Tokyo: Chūōkeizai-sha, 1996.

Nakamura Takahide. *Shōwa-shi II: 1945–89* [The History of the Shōwa Period, Part 2: 1945–89]. Tokyo: Tōyō Keizai Shimpōsha, 1993.

NHK reporting teams. *NHK Supesharu, sengo 50-nen, sono toki Nihon wa* [NHK Special, 50 Years after the War, Japan Back Then]. Vol. 1. Tokyo: NHK, 1995.

Nishimura Kumao. *San Furanshisuko heiwa jōyaku* [The San Francisco Peace Treaty]. Vol. 27 of *Nihon gaikō-shi* [History of Japan's Foreign Relations], edited by Kajima Institute of International Peace. Tokyo: Kajima Institute, 1971.

———. *San Furanshisuko heiwa jōyaku: Nichi-Bei Anpo jōyaku* [The San Francisco Peace Treaty: The Japanese-US Security Treaty]. Tokyo: Chuokoronsha, 1999. Contains four works, including *Anzen hoshō jōyaku ron* [The Security Treaty Debate], originally published by Jiji Press, 1959, and "San Furanshisuko heiwa jōyaku ni tsuite" [On the San Francisco Peace Treaty].

Ōhinata Ichirō. *Kishi seiken: 1241-nichi* [The Kishi Government: 1,241 Days]. Tokyo: Gyōsei Mondai Kenkyūjo, 1985.

Ōmori Minoru. *Tokuhain 5-nen: Nichi-Bei gaikō no butaiura* [Five Years as a News Correspondent: Behind the Scenes of Japanese-US Diplomacy]. Tokyo: Mainichi Shimbunsha, 1959.

Ōtake Hideo. *Saigunbi to nashonarizumu: Hoshu, riberaru, shakai minshu shugisha no bōeikan* [Rearmament and Nationalism: Conservative, Liberal, and Social Democratic Perspectives on Defense]. Tokyo: Chuokoronsha, 1988.

Pach, Chester J., Jr., and Elmo Richardson. *The Presidency of Dwight D. Eisenhower.* Lawrence: The University Press of Kansas, 1991.

Packard III, George R. *Protest in Tokyo: The Security Treaty Crisis of 1960.* Westport: Greenwood Press, 1966.

Prussen, Ronald W. *John Foster Dulles: The Road to Power.* New York: Free Press, 1982.

Sasaki Takuya. *Fūjikome no keisei to hen'yō: Kenan, Achison, Nittse to Torūman Seiken no Reisen senryaku* [The Development and Shift of Containment: Kennan, Acheson, Nitze, and the Truman Administration's Cold War Strategy]. Tokyo: Mitsumine Shobo, 1993.

Schaller, Michael. *Altered States: The United States and Japan since the Occupation.* New York: Oxford University Press, 1997.

Shimoda Takesō and Nagano Nobutoshi, eds. *Sengo Nihon gaikō no shōgen: Nihon wa kō shite saisei shita* [Witness of Japan's Postwar Diplomacy: Japan's Revival]. Vols. 1 and 2. Tokyo: Gyōsei Mondai Kenkyūjo, 1984–85.

Shindō Eiichi and Shimokōbe Motoharu, eds. *Ashida Hitoshi nikki* [Ashida Hitoshi Diary]. Vols. 6 and 7. Tokyo: Iwanami Shoten, 1986.

Shiota Ushio. *Kishi Nobusuke.* Tokyo: Kodansha, 1996.

Sneider, Richard. *US-Japanese Security Relations: A Historical Perspective.* New York: Columbia University Press, 1982.

Sodei Rinjirō and Takemae Eiji, eds. *Sengo Nihon no genten: Senryōshi no genzai* [The Roots of Postwar Japan: The History of the Occupation Today]. Vols. 1 and 2. Tokyo: Yūshisha, 1992.

Soeya Yoshihide. *Nihon gaikō to Chūgoku: 1945–1972* [Japanese Diplomacy and China: 1945–1972]. Tokyo: Keio University Press, 1995.

Tanaka Akihiko. *Anzen hoshō: Sengo 50-nen no mosaku* [Military Security: Fifty Postwar Years of Searching]. Vol. 2 of *20-seiki no Nippon,* edited by Kitaoka Shinichi et al. Tokyo: Yomiuri Shimbunsha, 1997.

Tanaka Takahiko. *Nis-So kokkō kaifuku no shiteki kenkyū: Sengo Nis-So kankei no kiten, 1945–1956* [A Historical Study of the Restoration of Japanese-Soviet Relations: The Starting Point for Postwar Japanese-Soviet Ties, 1945–1956]. Tokyo: Yuhikaku, 1993.

Taoka Ryōichi. *Kokusaihōjō no jieiken* [The Right of Self-Defense in International Law]. Revised edition. Tokyo: Keiso Shobo, 1981.

Tōgō Fumihiko. *Nichi-Bei gaikō 30-nen: Anpo, Okinawa to sono go* [Thirty Years of Japanese-US Diplomacy: The Security Treaty, Okinawa, and Later]. Tokyo: Chuokoronsha, 1989.

Toyoda Jō. *Kokō no gaishō Shigemitsu Mamoru* [Shigemitsu Mamoru: The Solitary Foreign Minister]. Tokyo: Kodansha, 1990.

Toyoshita Narahiko, ed. *Anpo jōyaku no ronri: Sono seisei to tenkai* [The Logic of the Security Treaty: Its Formation and Application]. Tokyo: Kashiwa Shobo, 1999.

——. *Anpo jōyaku no seiritsu: Yoshida gaikō to tennō gaikō* [The Birth of the Security Treaty: Yoshida Diplomacy and Imperial Diplomacy]. Tokyo: Iwanami Shoten, 1996.

Uchino Tatsurō. *Japan's Postwar Economy: An Insider's View of Its History and Its Future.* Translated by Mark A. Harbison. New York: Kodansha International, 1983.

Uemura Hideki. *Saigunbi to 55-nen taisei* [Rearmament and the 1955 Framework]. Tokyo: Bokutakusha, 1995.

Watanabe Akio, ed. *Sengo Nihon no saishōtachi* [The Prime Ministers of Postwar Japan].

Tokyo: Chuokoronsha, 1995.
——, ed. *Sengo Nihon no taigai seisaku: Kokusai kankei no hen'yō to Nihon no yakuwari* [Japan's Postwar Foreign Policy: Shifts in International Relations and the Roles of Japan]. Tokyo: Yuhikaku, 1985.
Watanabe Akio and Miyazato Seigen, eds. *San Furanshisuko kōwa* [The San Francisco Peace Treaty]. Tokyo: University of Tokyo Press, 1986.
Watanabe Yukio. *Shigemitsu Mamoru: Shanhai jihen kara Kokuren kamei made* [Shigemitsu Mamoru: From the Shanghai Incident to UN Membership]. Tokyo: Chuokoronsha, 1996.
Weinstein, Martin E. *Japan's Postwar Defense Policy, 1947–1968*. New York: Columbia University Press, 1971.
Yasukawa Takeshi. *Wasureenu omoide to korekara no Nichi-Bei gaikō: Pāruhābā kara hanseiki* [Indelible Memories and the Future of Japanese-US Relations: A Half Century since Pearl Harbor]. Tokyo: Sekai-no-Ugoki-sha, 1991.
Yomiuri Shimbun Postwar History Group, ed. *"Saigunbi" no kiseki* [The Story of "Rearmament"]. Tokyo: Yomiuri Shimbunsha, 1981.
Yoshida Shigeru. *Kaisō jūnen* [A 10-Year Memoir]. Vols. 1–4. Tokyo: Chuokoronsha, 1998.
——. *Sekai to Nihon* [The World and Japan]. Tokyo: Chuokoronsha, 1992.
——. *Yoshida Shigeru shokan* [Yoshida Shigeru's Letters]. Tokyo: Chuokoronsha, 1994.
Yoshida Shigeru Memorial Foundation, ed. *Ningen Yoshida Shigeru* [Yoshida Shigeru the Man]. Tokyo: Chuokoronsha, 1991.
Yoshimoto Shigeyoshi. *Kishi Nobusuke den* [A Biography of Kishi Nobusuke]. Tokyo: Tōyō Shokan, 1957.
Yoshitsu, Michael M. *Japan and the San Francisco Peace Settlement*. New York: Columbia University Press, 1983.

Papers and book chapters, etc.

Aruga Tadashi. "Nichi-Bei anzen hoshō jōyaku no kaitei" [Revising the Japanese-US Security Treaty]. In *Kokusai kankyō no hen'yō to Nichi-Bei kankei* [Japanese-US Relations in a Changing International Environment], edited by Hosoya Chihiro and Aruga Tadashi. Tokyo: University of Tokyo Press, 1987.
Dickinson, Frederick. "Nichi-Bei Anpo taisei no hen'yō: MSA kyōtei ni okeru saigunbi ni kansuru ryōkai" [The Metamorphosis of the Japanese-US Security Arrangement: Acknowledgement of Rearmament under the Mutual Security Act Agreements]. Pts. 1 and 2. *Hōgaku ronsō* [Kyoto Law Review] 121, no. 4 (July 1987); 122, no. 3 (December 1987).
Eldridge, Robert D. "Jōji F Kenan, PPS to Okinawa: Beikoku no Okinawa seisaku kettei katei, 1947–1949" [George F. Kennan, the Policy Planning Staff, and Okinawa: The Process of US Policymaking toward Okinawa]. *Kokusai seiji* [International Relations] 120 (February 1999).
Eldridge, Robert D., and Kusunoki Ayako. "To Base or Not to Base? Yoshida Shigeru, the 1950 Ikeda Mission, and Post-Treaty Japanese Security Conceptions." *Kobe University Law Review* 33 (1999).
Hatakeyama Hirobumi. "Keishokuhō kaisei to seijiteki rīdāshippu" [The Revision of the

Police Duties Execution Act and Political Leadership]. In *Nihon seiji no sōten: Jirei kenkyū ni yoru seiji taisei no bunseki* [The Issues in Japanese Politics: Analyzing the Political System through Research on Concrete Examples], edited by Ōtake Hideo. Tokyo: San-Ichi Shobo, 1984.

Hatano Sumio. "'Saigunbi' o meguru seijirikigaku: Bōeiryoku 'zenzō' e no michinori" [The Political Dynamics of "Rearmament": Arriving at a 'Gradual Expansion' of Defense Capabilities]. In *Nenpō kindai Nihon kenkyū* [Journal of Modern Japanese Studies], vol. 11, *Kyōchō seisaku no genkai: Nichi-Bei kankeishi, 1905–1960* [The Limits of Collaboration-Oriented Policy: The History of Japanese-US Relations, 1905–1960], edited by Kindai Nihon Kenkyūkai [Society of Modern Japanese Studies]. Tokyo: Yamakawa Shuppansha, 1989.

——. "Yoshida Shigeru to 'saigunbi'" [Yoshida Shigeru and "Rearmament"]. In *Ningen Yoshida Shigeru* [Yoshida Shigeru the Man], edited by the Yoshida Shigeru Memorial Foundation. Tokyo: Chuokoronsha, 1991.

Hiwatari Yumi. "Kishi gaikō ni okeru Tōnan Ajia to Amerika" [Southeast Asia and the United States in Kishi Diplomacy]. In *Nenpō kindai Nihon kenkyū* [Journal of Modern Japanese Studies], vol. 11, *Kyōchō seisaku no genkai: Nichi-Bei kankeishi, 1905–1960* [The Limits of Collaboration-Oriented Policy: The History of Japanese-US Relations, 1905–1960], edited by Kindai Nihon Kenkyūkai [Society of Modern Japanese Studies]. Tokyo: Yamakawa Shuppansha, 1989.

Hosoya Yūichi. "Igirisu gaikō to Nichi-Bei dōmei no kigen, 1948–50: Sengo Ajia Taiheiyō no anzen hoshō wakugumi no keisei katei" [UK Diplomacy and the Origins of the Japanese-US Alliance, 1948–1950: The Process of the Formation of a Security Framework in Postwar Asia-Pacific]. *Kokusai seiji* [International Relations] 117 (March 1998).

Iguchi Haruo. "Jon Fosutā Daresu no gaikō shisō: Senzen-sengo no renzokusei" [John Foster Dulles's Diplomatic Philosophy: Prewar-Postwar Continuity]. *Doshisha Amerika kenkyū* [Doshisha US Studies] 34 (March 1998).

Ikeda Shintarō. "Chūritsu shugi to Yoshida no makki gaikō" [Neutralism and Yoshida's Late-Phase Diplomacy]. In *Anpo jōyaku no ronri: Sono seisei to tenkai* [The Logic of the Security Treaty: Its Formation and Application], edited by Toyoshita Narahiko. Tokyo: Kashiwa Shobo, 1999.

——. "Jon Arison to Nihon saigunbi: 1952–1953" [John Allison and Japanese Rearmament: 1952–1953]. *Gaikō jihō* [Diplomacy Journal], no. 1343 (November–December 1997).

Ishii Osamu. "Reisen no '55-nen taisei'" [The '1955 System' in the Cold War]. *Kokusai seiji* [International Politics] 100 (August 1992).

Kitaoka Shinichi. "Kishi Nobusuke: Yashin to zasetsu" [Kishi Nobusuke: Ambition and Foundering]. In *Sengo Nihon no saishōtachi* [The Prime Ministers of Postwar Japan], edited by Watanabe Akio. Tokyo: Chuokoronsha, 1995.

Kōsaka Masataka. "Kishi Nobusuke to sengo seiji" [Kishi Nobusuke and Postwar Politics]. *Voice* (November 1987). Also in *Kōsaka Masataka chosakushū* [The Writings of Kōsaka Masataka], vol. 4, edited by Iokibe Makoto, Sakamoto Kazuya, Nakanishi Hiroshi, and Sako Susumu (Tokyo: Toshi Shuppan, 2000).

Kusunoki Ayako. "Senryōka Nihon no anzen hoshō kōsō: Gaimushō ni okeru Yoshida Dokutorin no keisei katei: 1945–1949" [Occupied Japan's Approach to National Security: The Process of Developing the Yoshida Doctrine in the Foreign Ministry].

Rokkōdai ronshū hōgaku seijigaku-hen [The Rokkodai Ronshu, Law and Political Science] (Daigakuin Hōgaku Kenkyūkai, Kobe University) 45, no. 3 (March 1999).

Nakanishi Hiroshi. "Kōwa ni muketa Yoshida Shigeru no anzen hoshō kōsō" [Yoshida Shigeru's Security Concept in Approaching the Peace Treaty]. In *Kantaiheiyō no kokusai chitsujo no mosaku to Nihon: Daiichiji Sekai Taisengo kara 55-nen taisei seiritsu* [Japan and the Pursuit of International Order in the Pacific Basin: From the End of World War I to the Formation of the 1955 Framework], edited by Itō Yukio and Kawada Minoru. Tokyo: Yamakawa Shuppansha, 1999.

——. "Sengo Ajia, Taiheiyō no anzen hoshō wakugumi no mosaku to Nihon, 1949–51" [The Search for a Postwar Asian/Pacific Security Structure and Japan, 1949–51]. In *Nenpō kindai Nihon kenkyū* [Journal of Modern Japanese Studies], vol. 16, *Sengo gaikō no keisei* [Formation of Postwar Diplomacy], edited by Kindai Nihon Kenkyūkai [Society of Modern Japanese Studies]. Tokyo: Yamakawa Shuppansha, 1994.

——. "Yoshida-Daresu kaidan saikō: Mikan no anzen hoshō taiwa" [A Reappraisal of the Yoshida-Dulles Talks: An Unfinished Security Dialogue]. *Hōgaku ronsō* [Kyoto Law Review] 140, no. 1/2 (November 1996).

Nishi Haruhiko. "Nihon no gaikō o ureeru" [Worried about Japanese Diplomacy]. *Chūō Kōron* (February 1960).

Ōhira Zengo. "Shūdanteki jieiken no hōri" [The Legal Logic of the Right of Collective Self-Defense]. In *Anzen hoshō taisei no kenkyū* [A Study of the Security Framework], vol. 1, edited by Anzen Hoshō Kenkyūkai [Security Research Association]. Tokyo: Jiji Press, 1960.

Sakaguchi Kiyoshi. "Shūdanteki jieiken ni kansuru seifu kaishaku no keisei to tenkai" [The Development and Implementation of the Government's Interpretation of the Right of Collective Security]. Pts. 1 and 2. *Gaikō jihō* [Diplomacy Journal] 1330 (July/August 1996); 1331 (September 1996).

Sakai Tetsuya. "Gaikōkan no shōzō: Shigemitsu Mamoru" [Portrait of a Diplomat: Shigemitsu Mamoru]. Pts. 1 and 2. *Gaikō Forum* 10 (July 1989); 11 (August 1989).

Sakamoto Kazuya. "Aizenhauā no gaikō senryaku to Nihon 1953–1954 nen" [Eisenhower's Diplomatic Strategy and Japan 1953–1954]. Pts. 1 and 2. *Hōgaku ronsō* [Kyoto Law Review] 122, no. 3 (December 1987); 123, no. 3 (June 1988).

——. "Anpo kaitei ni okeru sōgosei no mosaku: Jōyakukuiki to jizenkyōgi o megutte" [The Striving for Mutuality in the Revision of the Security Treaty: The Treaty Area and Prior Consultation]. *Kokusai seiji* [International Relations] 115 (May 1997).

——. "Beikoku kokka anzen hoshō kaigi seisaku bunsho NSC 5516/1 ni tsuite" [National Security Council Report NSC 5516/1]. *Hōkei ronsō* [Journal of Law and Economics] (Mie University) 7, no. 2 (March 1990).

——. "Ikeda-Robātoson kaidan saikō" [Ikeda-Robertson Talks of 1953: A Reconsideration]. *Hōkei ronsō* [Journal of Law and Economics] (Mie University) 9, no. 1 (December 1991).

——. "Kakuheiki to Nichi-Bei kankei: Bikini jiken no gaikō shori" [Nuclear Weapons and Japanese-US Relations: The Diplomatic Handling of the Bikini Incident]. In *Nenpō kindai Nihon kenkyū* [Journal of Modern Japanese Studies], vol. 16, *Sengo gaikō no keisei* [Formation of Postwar Diplomacy], edited by Kindai Nihon Kenkyūkai [Society of Modern Japanese Studies]. Tokyo: Yamakawa Shuppansha, 1994.

——. "Kishi Shushō to Anpo kaitei no ketsudan" [Prime Minister Kishi and the Decision to Revise the Security Treaty]. *Handai hōgaku* [Osaka Law Review] 45, no. 1 (June 1995).

——. "Nichi-Bei Anpo jizenkyōgisei no seiritsu o meguru gimon: Chōsen hantō yūji no baai" [Doubts about the Origins of the Provisions for Prior Consultation in the Japanese-US Security Treaty: In the Event of an Emergency on the Korean Peninsula]. *Handai hōgaku* [Osaka Law Review] 46, no. 4 (October 1996).

——. "Nichi-Bei Anpo ni okeru sōgosei no katachi: Gaidorain minaoshi ni yosete" [Forms of Mutuality in Japanese-US security: Examining Revisions to the Guidelines]. *Gaikō Forum* 113 (December 1997).

——. "Nis-So kokkō kaifuku kōshō to Amerika: Daresu wa naze kainyū shita ka" [The Restoration of Japanese-Soviet Relations and the United States: Why Dulles Got Involved]. *Kokusai seiji* [International Politics] 105 (January 1994).

——. "San Furanshisuko Taisei no kakuritsu: Nichi-Bei Anpo jōyaku no kaitei" [The Establishment of the San Francisco System: Reworking the Japanese-US Security Treaty]. In *Sengo kaikaku to sono isan* [Postwar Reforms and Their Legacy], edited by Nakamura Masanori, Amakawa Akira, Yoon Keun Cha, and Igarashi Takeshi, vol. 6 of *Sengo Nihon senryō to sengo kaikaku* [The Postwar Occupation of Japan and Postwar Reforms]. Tokyo: Iwanami Shoten, 1995.

——. "Shigemitsu hōbei to Anpo kaitei kōsō no zasetsu" [Shigemitsu's US Visit and the Collapse of His Proposal for Revising the Security Treaty]. *Hōkei ronsō* [Journal of Law and Economics] (Mie University) 10, no. 2 (December 1992).

Shimada Yōichi. "Nichi-Bei-Kan kankei to Nihon no dōmei seisaku, 1945–51" [Japanese-US-Korean Relations and Japan's Alliance Policy: 1945–51]. Pts. 1 and 2. *Hōgaku ronsō* [Kyoto Law Review] 113, no. 2 (May 1983); 113, no. 5 (August 1983).

Tabata Shigejirō. "The New Treaty of Security and the Right of Self-Defence." *Journal of International Law and Diplomacy* 59, no. 1/2 (July 1960).

Takamatsu Motoyuki. "Gaikōkan no shōzō Jon F Daresu" [John F. Dulles: Portrait of a Diplomat]. Pts. 1 and 2. *Gaikō Forum* 2 (November 1988); 3 (December 1988).

Takeda Tomoki. "Shigemitsu Mamoru no 'kakushin' no ronri: Sono keisei katei to senchū, sengo no renzokusei o megutte" [The Logic behind Shigemitsu Mamoru's "Reforms": Its Formative Process and Continuity through the Wartime and Postwar Years]. *Tōkyō Toritsu Daigaku hōgakkai zasshi* [Tokyo Metropolitan University Journal of Law and Politics] 38, no. 2 (December 1997).

Uemura Hideki. "Anpo kaitei to Nihon no bōei seisaku" [The Security-Treaty Revision and Japan's Defense Policy]. *Kokusai seiji* [International Relations] 115 (May 1997).

Yasuhara Yōko. "Keizai enjo o meguru MSA kōshō: Sono kyozō to jitsuzō" [Negotiations for Economic Assistance under the Mutual Security Act: Their Virtual Image and Their Real Image]. *Japanese Journal of American Studies* 22 (1988).

Yoshitsugu Kōsuke. "Ikeda-Robātoson kaidan to dokuritsugo no Yoshida gaikō" [The Ikeda-Robertson Talks and Yoshida's Post-Independence Diplomacy]. *Nenpō Nihon gendaishi* [Journal of Contemporary Japanese History] 4 (1998).

——. "MSA kōshō to saigunbi mondai" [The Mutual Security Act and Rearmament Issues]. In *Anpo jōyaku no ronri: Sono seisei to tenkai* [The Logic of the Security Treaty: Its Formation and Application], edited by Toyoshita Narahiko. Tokyo:

Kashiwa Shobo, 1999.

Periodicals

Sankei Shimbun
Asahi Shimbun
Mainichi Shimbun
Yomiuri Shimbun
The New York Times

Index

Note: Page numbers in *italics* refer to photographs.
The abbreviation 'n' refers to an endnote; 't' refers to a table.

C

D

T

About the Author

Sakamoto Kazuya was born in Fukuoka Prefecture in 1956. He graduated from the Law Department of Kyoto University in 1979, receiving his master's degree from the same institution in 1981. From 1982 to 1985, he studied diplomatic history at Ohio University, after which he served as an assistant professor in the Law Department at Kyoto University and as an associate professor in the School of Humanities and Social Sciences at Mie University and the Law Department at Osaka University. He was awarded a doctoral degree from Kyoto University in 2002. Until 2021, he was a professor specializing in international politics and diplomatic history at the Graduate School of Law and Politics at Osaka University. Professor Sakamoto co-authored *Sengo Nihon gaikōshi* [Japan's Postwar Diplomatic History] (Tokyo: Yūhikaku, 1999), winner of the Yoshida Shigeru Prize in 1999, and is the author of *Nichi-Bei dōmei no kizuna* [The Bonds of the Japan-US Alliance] (Tokyo: Yūhikaku, 2000), winner of the Suntory Academic Prize in 2000. The latter was re-released as an expanded edition in April 2020, of which this book is a translation.

（英文版）日米同盟の絆：安保条約と相互性の模索 増補版
The Bonds of the Japan-US Alliance: The Japan-US Security Treaty and the Search for Mutuality

2022年３月27日　第１刷発行

著　者　　坂元一哉
英　訳　　公益財団法人日本国際問題研究所
発行所　　一般財団法人出版文化産業振興財団
〒101-0051 東京都千代田区神田神保町2-2-30
電話　03-5211-7283
ホームページ　https://www.jpic.or.jp/

印刷・製本所　大日本印刷株式会社

定価はカバーに表示してあります。

Printed in Japan
ISBN 978-4-86658-233-7